Modern Trends and Future Innovation in Human Resource Management

Mitra Madanchian
University Canada West, Canada

IGI Global
Publishing Tomorrow's Research Today

Vice President of Editorial	Melissa Wagner
Managing Editor of Acquisitions	Mikaela Felty
Managing Editor of Book Development	Jocelynn Hessler
Production Manager	Mike Brehm
Cover Design	Phillip Shickler

Published in the United States of America by
IGI Global Scientific Publishing
701 East Chocolate Avenue
Hershey, PA, 17033, USA
Tel: 717-533-8845
Fax: 717-533-8661
Website: https://www.igi-global.com E-mail: cust@igi-global.com

Library of Congress Cataloging-in-Publication Data

Names: Madanchian, Mitra, 1981- editor.
Title: Modern trends and future innovation in human resource management / edited by Mitra Madanchian.
Description: Hershey, PA : IGI Global Scientific Publishing, [2025] | Includes bibliographical references and index. | Summary: "This book is designed to explore these transformative trends, offering a comprehensive examination of contemporary HR practices and strategies that are shaping the future of work"-- Provided by publisher.
Identifiers: LCCN 2024061600 (print) | LCCN 2024061601 (ebook) | ISBN 9798369364024 (hardcover) | ISBN 9798369364031 (paperback) | ISBN 9798369364048 (ebook)
Subjects: LCSH: Personnel management. | Personnel management--Technological innovations.
Classification: LCC HF5549 .M564 2025 (print) | LCC HF5549 (ebook) | DDC 658.3--dc23/eng/20250217
LC record available at https://lccn.loc.gov/2024061600
LC ebook record available at https://lccn.loc.gov/2024061601

British Cataloguing in Publication Data
A Cataloguing in Publication record for this book is available from the British Library.

To my beloved husband, Hamed, whose unwavering support and love are the foundation of all my endeavors, and to my precious children, Hamta and Kiasha, whose smiles light up my world and whose dreams inspire me every day—this book is for you.

Table of Contents

Foreword xii

Preface xiv

Acknowledgment xix

Chapter 1
Remote Work Dynamics: A Comprehensive Analysis of Its Effects on Engagement and Commitment 1
Inês Azevedo, ISAG, Portugal & CICET-FCVC, Portugal
Bárbara Viana de Sousa, USC, Portugal & ISAG, Portugal & CICET-FCVC, Portugal & UNIAG, Portugal
Elvira Pacheco Vieira, UNIAG, Portugal & ISAG, Portugal & CICET-FCVC, Portugal
Ana Pinto Borges, ISAG, Portugal & CICET-FCVC, Portugal & COMEGI, Portugal

Chapter 2
Enhancing Organizational Performance Through High-Performance Work Practices in the IT Sector: Variable Influence on Organizational Efficiency 41
Sushma Sharma, SRM, Sonipat, India
Shitika Verma, GGSIPU, Delhi, India
Radha Rani, SRM, Sonipat, India
Poonam Gahlot, SRM, Sonipat, India

Chapter 3
Boosting Employee Eco-Friendly Behaviors and Innovation Through Green HR Practices 73
Alaa Amin Abdalla, Abu Dhabi University, UAE

Chapter 4
From Technostress to Turnover: Examining Stress-Related Drivers of Turnover in the Indian IT Industry 105
Pratibha Thakur, Dr. Vishwanath Karad MIT World Peace University, India
Charu Saxena, Chandigarh University, India

Chapter 5
The Impact of Equity, Employee Engagement Activities, and Job Redesigning on Airline Employee Motivation: A Comparative Analysis 137
Neha Nazneen Siddiqui, Ashoka Institute of Technology and Management, India

Chapter 6
Strategic Integration of Diversity, Equity, Inclusion (DEI) and Artificial Intelligence (AI) in Human Resource Management (HRM): Current Trends and Future Trajectories 173
Hawwa Shiuna Musthafa, University Canada West, Canada
Jason Walker, Adler University, Canada
Mrigeesha P. Mehta, Adler University, Canada
Sara Bordbar, Adler University, Canada
Dhvani Malhotra, Adler University, Canada
Vaishnavi, Adler University, Canada

Chapter 7
HR Agility: Embracing Change in Human Resource Practices 197
P. Bhanumathi, M.S. Ramaiah Institute of Management, India
P. Hemavathi, St. Joseph University, India
Vinodh T. S., Vivekananda Institute of Management, India

Chapter 8
Future of Work: Generations and Retaining Talent Focus 239
K. Anitha, Meenakshi Academy of Higher Education and Research, India
Narkees Beevi S., Meenakshi Academy of Higher Education and Research, India
J. Amala, DDGD Vaishnav College, India

Chapter 9
Optimizing Talent Acquisition: The Synergy of AI and Human Expertise in Creating Enhanced Candidate Experience 259
Tanusree Chakraborty, Administrative Staff College of India, India
Sharada V. S., Administrative Staff College of India, India

Compilation of References 277

About the Contributors 325

Index 335

Detailed Table of Contents

Foreword xii

Preface xiv

Acknowledgment xix

Chapter 1
Remote Work Dynamics: A Comprehensive Analysis of Its Effects on Engagement and Commitment 1
Inês Azevedo, ISAG, Portugal & CICET-FCVC, Portugal
Bárbara Viana de Sousa, USC, Portugal & ISAG, Portugal & CICET-FCVC, Portugal & UNIAG, Portugal
Elvira Pacheco Vieira, UNIAG, Portugal & ISAG, Portugal & CICET-FCVC, Portugal
Ana Pinto Borges, ISAG, Portugal & CICET-FCVC, Portugal & COMEGI, Portugal

Research on remote and hybrid work often overlooks the impact of these arrangements on employee commitment and engagement. While many studies focus on technological challenges or the effects on productivity and work-life balance, few explore how remote work shapes employee attitudes and behaviors, particularly in terms of involvement with the work and commitment to the organization. This chapter addresses this gap by presenting empirical insights into the effects of remote work on these key dimensions. Through a quantitative approach, 211 complete responses were collected via an online questionnaire, using validated scales by Schaufeli and Bakker for engagement and Meyer and Allen for commitment. The results suggest that remote work positively influences employee engagement and organizational commitment by fostering positive social relationships. However, the success of remote work practices depends on their careful implementation and the presence of supportive policies.

Chapter 2
Enhancing Organizational Performance Through High-Performance Work Practices in the IT Sector: Variable Influence on Organizational Efficiency....... 41
Sushma Sharma, SRM, Sonipat, India
Shitika Verma, GGSIPU, Delhi, India
Radha Rani, SRM, Sonipat, India
Poonam Gahlot, SRM, Sonipat, India

In today's competitive business environment, organizations must enhance performance to stay ahead. Traditional sources of advantage, like technology and natural resources, are increasingly imitable. Human resources (HR), being intangible and unique, have emerged as a crucial asset. This study examines high-performance work practices (HPWPs) in IT companies using exploratory factor analysis (EFA) to identify factors that drive organizational success. Data from 349 employees across IT firms in Delhi NCR revealed a five-factor model explaining 66.13% of the variance: organizational development initiatives, employee empowerment programs, compensation and advancement programs, workplace support systems, and performance enhancement programs. The findings indicate that implementing these HPWPs can significantly boost organizational performance. The study provides a framework for IT companies to enhance both organizational and employee performance. Future research should use confirmatory factor analysis (CFA) to validate the EFA-derived model.

Chapter 3
Boosting Employee Eco-Friendly Behaviors and Innovation Through Green HR Practices 73
Alaa Amin Abdalla, Abu Dhabi University, UAE

This empirical research investigates the impacts of green human resource practices (GHRM) on green employee behaviors and green innovation in the United Arab Emirates. A self-administered questionnaire collected employee data from the UAE hospitality sector. Of the 320 surveys sent, 180 were used for statistical analysis. The study found that green performance management (GPM), green employee involvement (GEI), green recruitment and selection (GRS), green compensation and reward (GCR), and green training and development (GTD) all had a positive and significant impact on task-related green behaviors (TRGB), voluntary green behaviors (VGB), and green innovation (GI). This research stands out for three key reasons. First, the research adds to the existing GHRM knowledge. Second, it adds to the sparse GHRM research in the hospitality industry, particularly in the GCC. Last, the results enhance understanding of GHRM strategies, especially in developing nations.

Chapter 4
From Technostress to Turnover: Examining Stress-Related Drivers of Turnover in the Indian IT Industry 105
Pratibha Thakur, Dr. Vishwanath Karad MIT World Peace University, India
Charu Saxena, Chandigarh University, India

The rapid integration of advanced technologies in the workplace, particularly within the information technology (IT) industry, has led to an increase in technostress—stress induced by the use of technology. This study aims to investigate the relationship between technostress, work stress, and turnover intentions among IT professionals in India. This research employs a quantitative approach, utilizing survey data collected from a sample of 419 Indian IT professionals using a purposive sampling technique and was analyzed using Smart PLS 3.2.8. The findings indicate that technostress and work stress significantly contribute to the higher turnover intention of employees. The implications of these findings suggest that addressing technostress through targeted interventions can improve employee retention and overall positive employee outcomes. This research provides valuable insights for IT companies aiming to enhance employee well-being and reduce turnover rates by developing strategies to manage and alleviate technostress in the workplace.

Chapter 5
The Impact of Equity, Employee Engagement Activities, and Job Redesigning on Airline Employee Motivation: A Comparative Analysis 137
Neha Nazneen Siddiqui, Ashoka Institute of Technology and Management, India

Drawing on a theoretical framework, this study aims to understand the impact of equity as perceived by employees in the airline industry through employee engagement activities and job redesigning that have been introduced to determine the level of motivation among frontline staff members working with Indian Airlines Jet Airways vs. Indigo. The research aimed to determine how motivation levels are influenced by engagement, job crafting, and work-life advocacy. This chapter summarizes the 400 employee survey outcomes with an empirical statistical approach. The findings suggest that Indigo Airlines scores much higher than Jet Airways in all three dimensions. Indigo had significantly higher perceived equity than Jet Airways (89% versus 30%) and was more satisfied with its engagement activities than the other service providers in this sector. Job redesigning, too, occurred a lot more frequently at Indigo compared to fellow airline companies, as they scored a similar score of above par on effectiveness while cost-effectiveness scored below par.

Chapter 6
Strategic Integration of Diversity, Equity, Inclusion (DEI) and Artificial Intelligence (AI) in Human Resource Management (HRM): Current Trends and Future Trajectories 173
Hawwa Shiuna Musthafa, University Canada West, Canada
Jason Walker, Adler University, Canada
Mrigeesha P. Mehta, Adler University, Canada
Sara Bordbar, Adler University, Canada
Dhvani Malhotra, Adler University, Canada
Vaishnavi, Adler University, Canada

In this era of rapid globalization, the significance of diversity, equity, and inclusion (DEI) in workplace settings has never been more pronounced. This chapter explores the intersection of DEI and artificial intelligence (AI) in human resource management (HRM), examining how AI can both advance and challenge DEI initiatives. AI's integration in HRM promises increased productivity and efficiency but poses risks of perpetuating biases if not managed carefully. Instances of discriminatory AI behavior highlight the need for HR professionals to design and deploy AI systems that promote fairness and inclusivity. The chapter provides a foundation of learning objectives, current trends, global perspectives on DEI, and best practices for implementation. It also investigates AI's transformative potential in enhancing DEI efforts, offering practical insights and ethical considerations. By combining AI with strategic DEI initiatives, organizations can create workplaces that are diverse, inclusive, adaptive, and resilient.

Chapter 7
HR Agility: Embracing Change in Human Resource Practices......................... 197
P. Bhanumathi, M.S. Ramaiah Institute of Management, India
P. Hemavathi, St. Joseph University, India
Vinodh T. S., Vivekananda Institute of Management, India

In today's competitive business world, HR agility has emerged as a critical success factor for organizations that must embrace agility in their HR strategies to remain relevant and practical. Agility brings constant change, fosters organizational resilience, drives innovation, and maintains a competitive edge. Further, agility entails the HR department responding to the organization's evolving business needs, trends, and dynamics. It is a proactive change and encompasses various dimensions, namely talent acquisition, recruitment strategies, performance management, strategies for building and managing teams, challenges and overcoming resistance to change, leadership, and future trends in HR. Agile HR practices enable HR departments to align strategies with the objectives to achieve their goals and stay competitive. It will help identify skill gaps and attract, develop, and retain the best talent to meet the organization's needs. HR agility augments employee experience by enabling everyone to respond promptly to concerns and expectations.

Chapter 8
Future of Work: Generations and Retaining Talent Focus................................. 239
K. Anitha, Meenakshi Academy of Higher Education and Research, India
Narkees Beevi S., Meenakshi Academy of Higher Education and Research, India
J. Amala, DDGD Vaishnav College, India

The landscape of work is continuously evolving, driven by technological advancements, demographic shifts, and changing societal expectations. This research study delves into the future of work, focusing specifically on generational dynamics and talent retention strategies. The introduction highlights the imperative for workplace transformation, spurred by globalization, automation, and the increasing prevalence of remote work. In examining the future of work, this study explores several key advancements, including the rise of digital platforms, the integration of artificial intelligence, and the adoption of flexible work arrangements. These developments present both opportunities and challenges for organizations and workers. The study explores innovative methods adopted by organizations to address these challenges and retain talent effectively.

Chapter 9
Optimizing Talent Acquisition: The Synergy of AI and Human Expertise in Creating Enhanced Candidate Experience.. 259
Tanusree Chakraborty, Administrative Staff College of India, India
Sharada V. S., Administrative Staff College of India, India

This study examines the revolutionary effects of artificial intelligence (AI) on hiring in organizations. AI maximizes efficiency by automating processes like resume review, candidate matching, and engagement through chatbots. AI-driven predictive analytics support diversity and inclusion by predicting recruiting needs and reducing biases in job advertisements and candidate selection. The study finds that AI and human collaboration enhances analytical decision-making and the creative capacities of the talent acquisition process. It highlights the shift towards data-driven hiring and the significance of AI-driven insights in talent analytics and decision-making. However, the study asserts the necessity of human touch and emotional intelligence, even with EI tools, to create a positive candidate experience. Candidate experience is pivotal in talent acquisition, requiring harmonious collaboration between AI and human expertise. AI streamlines processes and enhances efficiency, while the human touch adds empathy and personalized engagement.

Compilation of References 277

About the Contributors 325

Index 335

Foreword

The landscape of Human Resource Management (HRM) is evolving at an unprecedented pace, with new challenges and opportunities emerging as businesses adapt to a world shaped by rapid technological advancements, shifting workplace dynamics, and a growing emphasis on diversity and inclusion. In this context, *Modern Trends and Future Innovation in Human Resource Management* is a timely and essential contribution to the field. Edited by Mitra Madanchian, this comprehensive volume provides invaluable insights into the latest developments and future directions in HRM, offering readers a deep understanding of the forces that are reshaping this critical domain.

Mitra Madanchian, a distinguished expert with extensive experience in both academia and industry, has curated a collection of chapters that reflect the cutting-edge thinking and practical strategies required to navigate the complexities of today's HR landscape. Her leadership in bringing together a diverse group of contributors, each offering unique perspectives and expertise, ensures that this book is not only a scholarly resource but also a practical guide for HR professionals, business leaders, and educators.

One of the key strengths of this publication is its broad coverage of topics that are highly relevant to contemporary HR practice. From the integration of technology and agile methodologies to the welfare of employees and the ethical considerations in HRM, this book addresses the most pressing issues facing organizations today. It delves into the current trends in remote work, innovations in learning, and the imperative for diversity and inclusion, offering readers a holistic view of the modern HR landscape.

Moreover, the book does not merely describe the changes occurring in HRM; it serves as a catalyst for further exploration and innovation. By presenting the latest research and thought leadership in the field, it encourages readers to think critically about the future of HR and to consider how they can contribute to shaping that future.

As someone who has not contributed to this book in any other capacity, I am honored to write this foreword and to recommend *Modern Trends and Future Innovation in Human Resource Management* to anyone interested in the future of HRM. Whether you are a seasoned HR professional, a business executive seeking to understand the latest trends, an educator preparing the next generation of HR leaders, or a student eager to learn about the field, this book will provide you with the knowledge and insights you need to succeed.

In conclusion, this book is more than just a collection of chapters; it is a reflection of the ongoing transformation of HRM and a guide to the future. I am confident that it will become a key reference in the field and an indispensable resource for anyone committed to advancing the practice of Human Resource Management.

Hamed Taherdoost
University Canada West, Canada

Preface

In the ever-evolving landscape of Human Resource Management (HRM), organizations face unprecedented challenges and opportunities. The rapid pace of technological innovation, shifting workforce expectations, and heightened demands for diversity and inclusion have transformed HRM from a traditional support function into a strategic cornerstone of organizational success. *Modern Trends and Future Innovation in Human Resource Management* is designed to explore these transformative trends, offering a comprehensive examination of contemporary HR practices and strategies that are shaping the future of work.

OVERVIEW OF THE SUBJECT MATTER

Human Resource Management has traditionally focused on core functions such as recruitment, employee development, and retention. However, as we move deeper into the 21st century, these traditional roles are being redefined by advancements in technology, changes in employee expectations, and a growing emphasis on sustainability and inclusivity. This book delves into these modern trends, providing an in-depth analysis of how HR practices are evolving and what organizations can do to adapt and thrive in this new environment.

The chapters within this volume cover a range of critical topics, from enhancing employee performance through High-Performance Work Practices (HPWPs) to the integration of Green HR practices and the strategic incorporation of Diversity, Equity, and Inclusion (DEI) with Artificial Intelligence (AI). By exploring these themes, the book offers valuable insights into how organizations can navigate the complexities of the modern workplace and prepare for future challenges and opportunities.

POSITIONING IN TODAY'S WORLD

Today's business environment is marked by rapid technological advancements, an increasing shift towards remote and hybrid work models, and a growing emphasis on sustainability and inclusivity. HR professionals are no longer just administrative managers but strategic partners who play a crucial role in shaping organizational culture and driving performance. This book positions itself at the forefront of these developments, offering timely insights and practical strategies for HR professionals, organizational leaders, and scholars.

The book addresses key issues such as the impact of remote work on employee engagement, the need for eco-friendly HR practices, and the integration of AI and DEI initiatives. It provides a detailed examination of how these factors are reshaping HRM and offers actionable recommendations for organizations seeking to stay competitive and forward-thinking in a rapidly changing world.

TARGET AUDIENCE

Modern Trends and Future Innovation in Human Resource Management is intended for a diverse audience, including HR professionals, organizational leaders, academics, and students in the field of Human Resource Management. HR practitioners will find practical insights and strategies to enhance their practices and adapt to emerging trends. Organizational leaders will benefit from understanding the strategic implications of modern HR trends and how to leverage them for improved performance and innovation. Academics and students will appreciate the book's in-depth analysis and its contribution to the broader body of knowledge in HRM, making it a valuable resource for research and education.

CHAPTER DESCRIPTIONS

Chapter 1: Remote Work Dynamics: A Comprehensive Analysis of Its Effects on Engagement and Commitment

The shift to remote work has had significant effects on employee engagement and commitment. This chapter offers a comprehensive analysis of these effects, examining both the benefits and challenges of remote work. It provides practical recommendations for maintaining high levels of engagement and commitment in a remote or hybrid work environment.

Chapter 2: Enhancing Organizational Performance Through High-Performance Work Practices in the IT Sector

Building on the discussion of HPWPs, this chapter delves deeper into how these practices can drive organizational performance specifically within the IT sector. It identifies the most impactful practices and offers strategies for implementing them to achieve superior performance outcomes.

Chapter 3: Boosting Employee Eco-Friendly Behaviors and Innovation Through Green HR Practices

With sustainability becoming a crucial focus for organizations, this chapter explores how Green HR Practices can promote eco-friendly behaviors and foster innovation. It discusses the strategic importance of integrating environmental considerations into HR policies and how this integration can enhance both employee morale and organizational sustainability.

Chapter 4: From Technostress to Turnover: Examining Stress-Related Drivers of Turnover in the Indian IT Industry

Technostress is a growing concern in the IT industry, particularly in India, contributing to high turnover rates. This chapter examines the stress-related drivers of turnover and offers strategies for addressing these issues to improve employee retention and reduce turnover.

Chapter 5: The Impact of Equity, Employee Engagement Activities, and Job Redesigning on Airline Employee Motivation: A Comparative Analysis

This chapter provides a comparative analysis of factors influencing employee motivation in the airline industry, focusing on equity, engagement activities, and job redesigning. It offers strategies for enhancing motivation and performance within this competitive sector.

Chapter 6: Strategic Integration of Diversity, Equity, Inclusion (DEI) and Artificial Intelligence (AI) in Human Resource Management (HRM): Current Trends and Future Trajectories

The integration of DEI and AI into HRM is a significant trend with broad implications. This chapter discusses the current trends and future trajectories of this integration, offering a strategic framework for organizations looking to harness AI while promoting diversity and inclusion.

Chapter 7: HR Agility: Embracing Change in Human Resource Practices

In a rapidly changing business environment, HR agility is essential. This chapter explores the concept of HR agility, providing insights into how organizations can develop agile HR practices to adapt quickly to changing circumstances and maintain a competitive edge.

Chapter 8: Future of Work: Generations and Retaining Talent Focus

With multiple generations working together, organizations face the challenge of retaining talent across diverse age groups. This chapter examines generational differences and offers strategies for retaining talent by addressing the unique needs and expectations of different generations.

Chapter 9: Optimizing Talent Acquisition: The Synergy of AI and Human Expertise in Creating Enhanced Candidate Experience

The final chapter focuses on the synergy between AI and human expertise in optimizing talent acquisition processes. It explores how AI technologies can be leveraged to enhance the candidate experience, streamline recruitment processes, and improve overall hiring outcomes. This chapter offers practical strategies for integrating AI with human insights to create a more efficient and engaging recruitment experience.

CONCLUSION

Modern Trends and Future Innovation in Human Resource Management provides a critical resource for understanding the evolving nature of HRM and its role in shaping the future of work. By exploring contemporary trends and offering innovative strategies, this book serves as a valuable guide for HR professionals, organizational leaders, and academics. It not only reflects the current state of HRM but also contributes to shaping future practices, offering insights and recommendations that will help organizations navigate the challenges and opportunities of tomorrow's workforce.

Mitra Madanchian
University Canada West, Canada

Acknowledgment

I would like to express my deepest gratitude to all those who contributed to the creation of this book, *Modern Trends and Future Innovation in Human Resource Management*. This work would not have been possible without the invaluable support, guidance, and encouragement from numerous individuals and organizations.

First and foremost, I extend my sincere thanks to the contributing authors whose expertise and insights have enriched this book. Their dedication and hard work have made this project a reality.

I would also like to acknowledge the support of my colleagues and peers who provided thoughtful feedback and suggestions during the research and writing process. Their constructive criticism and encouragement were instrumental in refining the content and ensuring its relevance to the evolving field of human resource management.

A special thank you goes to the editorial team at IGI Global for their professional assistance and meticulous attention to detail. Their commitment to excellence has significantly enhanced the quality of this book.

Finally, I am deeply grateful to my family and friends for their unwavering support and understanding throughout this journey. Their patience and encouragement provided me with the strength and motivation needed to see this project through to completion.

To all those who contributed in ways both big and small, your support has been invaluable, and I am profoundly appreciative of your contributions.

Thank you.

Chapter 1
Remote Work Dynamics: A Comprehensive Analysis of Its Effects on Engagement and Commitment

Inês Azevedo
ISAG, Portugal & CICET-FCVC, Portugal

Bárbara Viana de Sousa
https://orcid.org/0000-0002-8823-261X
USC, Portugal & ISAG, Portugal & CICET-FCVC, Portugal & UNIAG, Portugal

Elvira Pacheco Vieira
UNIAG, Portugal & ISAG, Portugal & CICET-FCVC, Portugal

Ana Pinto Borges
https://orcid.org/0000-0002-4942-079X
ISAG, Portugal & CICET-FCVC, Portugal & COMEGI, Portugal

ABSTRACT

Research on remote and hybrid work often overlooks the impact of these arrangements on employee commitment and engagement. While many studies focus on technological challenges or the effects on productivity and work-life balance, few explore how remote work shapes employee attitudes and behaviors, particularly in terms of involvement with the work and commitment to the organization. This chapter addresses this gap by presenting empirical insights into the effects of remote work on these key dimensions. Through a quantitative approach, 211 complete responses were collected via an online questionnaire, using validated scales by Schaufeli and Bakker for engagement and Meyer and Allen for commitment. The results suggest that remote work positively influences employee engagement and organizational

DOI: 10.4018/979-8-3693-6402-4.ch001

commitment by fostering positive social relationships. However, the success of remote work practices depends on their careful implementation and the presence of supportive policies.

1. INTRODUCTION

Work has always been part of the human experience, adapting over time to the needs and opportunities that arise. Today, we find ourselves in an era where technologies have reached an unprecedented level of development. In this context, we are witnessing a crucial alliance between Information and Communication Technologies (ICT) and the labor market. This union has led to a profound transformation in the nature of work, giving rise to new forms of employment. At the epicenter of these changes are hybrid and remote work. The implementation of these working arrangements has taken on particular prominence, with numerous companies adopting such working practices. Remote work is gaining popularity in companies and is being adopted as a strategy to attract and retain talent (Cristina, 2021). Based on Lippe & Lippényi (2019), remote work is an inherent reality of today's working life.

The rise of these two forms of work, remote and hybrid, has profoundly changed organizational dynamics. This innovative context not only reshapes the way organizations operate, but also directly impacts critical dimensions such as Engagement and Commitment, determining new contours for the interaction between employees and their organizations (Schaufeli et al., 2001, cited by Schaufeli & Bakker, 2004). Against this dynamic backdrop, this research project seeks to explore and understand the complex interconnections between emerging ways of working and the resulting effects on Engagement and Commitment.

In order to address this gap in understanding, this chapter provides empirical insights into the ways in which remote work influences these important elements. By doing so, it improves our comprehension of how the connection between employees and their employers is changing within the framework of modern work practices. Thus, the general objective of this research is to analyze remote work, in terms of the characterization of human capital and the dimensions related to the worker (namely Engagement and Commitment).

2. THEORETICAL FRAMEWORK

2.1 Remote Work vs. Hybrid Work

The growing volatility in the job market has led to significant adaptations by organizations, with many fully embracing remote work while others prefer to adopt a hybrid work model. Hybrid work combines remote work with conventional office work, meaning it is performed both remotely and on-site at the organization's premises. Remote work can be applied by companies on a full-time or part-time basis (Carrasco-Garrido et al., 2023). Part-time remote work, or hybrid work, means employees can choose to work from home on some days of the week and be physically present in the office on others as mobile workers (Silva, 2021).

The hybrid work model represents an innovative approach that seeks to integrate the best aspects of office environments and remote work. This model aims to optimize employees' workweek by distinguishing activities more suitable for in-person settings, such as meetings and training, to be held on office days, and more individual tasks, such as reading and programming, on remote work days (Bloom et al., 2022).

In a time when digital transformation becomes a primary focus for organizations, the adoption of a hybrid work model emerges as a viable solution that reconciles individuals' desire to continue with remote work while ensuring no financial loss for the organization or negative impacts on workforce productivity and motivation (Grzegorczyk et al., 2021). Blomm et al. (2022) consider the hybrid model to involve 2 to 3 days of remote work per week and the rest in the office.

Professionals in a hybrid work arrangement have shown a greater propensity to perform their activities remotely at the beginning or end of the workweek. As noted by the research conducted by Kranc (2023), there is a predominant trend to choose Fridays as the preferred day for remote work, followed by Mondays, indicating a preference for starting and ending the workweek from home. On the other hand, the concept of remote work encompasses the performance of organizational activities beyond the conventional boundaries of space and time established by the entity. The term telecommuting refers to replacing the need to commute to a central workplace with new communication tools (Olson, 1983).

The evolution of technology provides the potential to turn many office professionals into telecommuters, as their tasks can be performed remotely with the support of technological and communication resources (Olson, 1983). Remote work, also often referred to as "telework," can be defined as a "work arrangement in which employees perform their regular work at a location other than the conventional workplace, supported by technological connections" (Fitzer, 1997). According to Aguilera et al. (2016), remote work is seen as work that is carried out from a location other than the organization's physical facilities while the employee remains connected to the company's computer systems through modern information and telecommunications technologies. It is widely recognized that ICT plays a fundamental role in simplifying communication among remote teams. The use of a variety of technological tools, such as emails, video calls, and applications like Outlook, Skype, and Zoom, is essential for maintaining effective communication and collaboration in a remote work environment (Gosnell, 2020). Sahut & Lissillour (2023) reinforce that access to ICT is crucial because it enables remote work, and its increasing availability plays a significant role in the development of this work modality. ICT provides employees with the essential means for real-time communication with colleagues and superiors, thus mitigating the sense of isolation and promoting teamwork (Tavares et al., 2020).

2.2 Advantages and Challenges of Remote and Hybrid Work

Remote and hybrid work models offer various advantages and challenges for both employers and employees. One significant benefit is cost savings, as remote work eliminates the need for commuting, thereby reducing transportation expenses for employees and lowering overhead costs for employers (Silva, 2021). Additionally, remote work contributes to a reduced environmental impact by decreasing the carbon footprint associated with commuting and office operations, promoting environmental sustainability (Bloom et al., 2022). Another advantage is the potential for increased productivity, as remote work environments often have fewer distractions, allowing workers to customize their workspaces to better suit their needs (Bloom et al., 2022). Improved work-life balance is also a notable benefit, with remote and hybrid models enabling employees to better manage their professional and personal lives, leading to higher job satisfaction and reduced burnout (Grzegorczyk et al., 2021). Moreover, remote work allows employers to hire talent from around the globe, enhancing diversity and access to specialized skills (Kranc, 2023).

Hybrid work, which combines the benefits of remote work with those of in-person teamwork, offers increased flexibility. Employees can choose when and where they work, tailoring their schedules to their individual preferences and needs (Bloom et al., 2022). This model also allows employees to enjoy the social interaction and collaboration of office work while maintaining the flexibility and autonomy of remote work (Kranc, 2023).

Despite these benefits, remote and hybrid work models present several challenges. Remote work can impede communication and collaboration among team members, leading to misunderstandings and decreased teamwork (Gosnell, 2020). Additionally, while remote work can improve work-life balance, it can also blur the boundary between work and personal life, making it difficult for employees to disconnect and potentially leading to burnout (Grzegorczyk et al., 2021). There is also a risk of isolation and loneliness, as remote workers miss out on social interactions in the office (Sahut and Lissillour, 2023). Technical issues, such as internet outages and software glitches, can further disrupt productivity (Tavares et al., 2021).

Hybrid work poses its own set of challenges. For companies, managing a workforce split between remote and in-person work involves complexities related to scheduling, communication, and collaboration (Gosnell, 2020). Equitable treatment can be an issue, as some employees may feel disadvantaged compared to their remote or in-office counterparts, potentially creating feelings of resentment and inequality (Sahut and Lissillour, 2023). Maintaining a strong company culture and sense of belonging can also be more difficult, especially if remote workers feel disconnected from the organization (Tavares et al., 2021). Implementing hybrid work requires robust infrastructure and technology to support seamless communication and collaboration, which can be costly and complex (Bloom et al., 2022).

In conclusion, while remote and hybrid work models offer organizations and employees increased flexibility, autonomy, and access to global talent, they also present challenges related to communication, collaboration, and work-life balance. Both models require careful planning and implementation to ensure success, including robust infrastructure, clear communication channels, and equitable treatment of all employees. By addressing these challenges, organizations can harness the benefits of remote and hybrid work models to create a more flexible, inclusive, and productive workforce.

2.3 Engagement

Definition and Characteristics. Engagement, or work engagement, is defined as a "positive, fulfilling work-related state of mind characterized by vigor, dedication, and absorption" (Schaufeli & Bakker, 2004).

Engaged workers stand out by showing high levels of energy and enthusiasm in their professional activities, feeling motivated to achieve success. This personal involvement is accompanied by intense energy dedicated to work, where employees spare no effort and apply all their energy enthusiastically throughout their tasks (Bakker & Leiter, 2010; Osoian & Petre, 2022). On the contrary, a low level of engagement can lead to a decrease in motivation and job satisfaction, thus affecting overall performance and productivity (Chiguvi & Keneilwe Bakani, 2023).

Engagement in work goes beyond merely responding to specific situations, reflecting intense focus and absorption in the job. In this state, employees lose track of time and reduce their response to distractions, focusing only on important details and the essence of challenging problems (Bakker & Leiter, 2010).Engagement is not limited to a specific type of task - on the contrary, it describes the ability of employees to apply all their energy to solve problems and develop innovative methods/ processes (Bakker & Leiter, 2010).

Furthermore, the concept of engagement encompasses a range of feelings, such as involvement, dedication, passion, enthusiasm, concentrated effort, absorption, and energy (Osoian & Petre, 2022). These feelings are evidenced by the enthusiasm demonstrated during task execution, turning work into a personal challenge.

Distinctive characteristics of engagement include not only energy but also involvement and effectiveness. Consequently, how workers perceive their work as motivating and energizing is essential in determining their engagement (Osoian & Petre, 2022). After periods of intense work, employees may feel tired, but it is crucial to note that, for those who are truly engaged, this fatigue is considered a pleasant state, associated with positive achievements, as work is enjoyable (Osoian & Petre, 2022).

Moreover, work engagement is not limited to the formal responsibilities of a position. In today's workplaces, characterized by complexity and dynamism, employers seek employees who go beyond the traditional boundaries of their roles. Proactive attitudes in work transcend the conventional structure, incorporating the pursuit of new knowledge, agility in responding to unique opportunities, and commitment to supporting the organization by assisting colleagues. According to the theory proposed by Bakker and Leiter (2010), positive emotions drive creative perspectives, significantly contributing to the creation of value for the organizations. Establishing healthy work environments is crucial for success, promoting employee engagement. This engagement emerges as an effective and rewarding strategy, providing satisfaction for both the employee and the employer.

Effects of Remote Work on Engagement. The most popular approach focused on engagement belongs to Schaufeli and Bakker (Wontorczyk & Rożnowski, 2022), according to which workers feel so energized and proud of their work that they often do not control their working time.

On of the most reported antecedents of work engagement is social support, which requires various workplace interactions (Boccoli et al., 2023). This can be understood as humans have an intrinsic need for social interactions, essential for their physical and mental well-being. In the conventional workplace, social interactions are facilitated by face-to-face conversations, team meetings, and casual interpersonal interactions, thus satisfying the human need for connection. However, in a remote environment, all interactions among team members occur exclusively through technology (Chiguvi & Keneilwe Bakani, 2023). This absence of personal interactions can result in a decrease in cognitive stimulation over time. This can lead to feelings of isolation, irritability, and difficulty in effectively dealing with unexpected challenges, which can impair workflow and task progress. This phenomenon can have a significant impact on the engagement of remote workers, as the sense of belonging and connection with the team may be compromised by the lack of face-to-face social interactions. Isolation emerges as a disadvantage resulting from remote work with a negative impact on engagement, as the decrease in interactions with colleagues can create feelings of loneliness that affect job satisfaction and performance and lead to stressful situations (Wontorczyk & Rożnowski, 2022). The use of communication tools and digital technologies allows for partially mitigating isolation, but nothing compares to the physical contact present in on-site work mode (Galanti et al., 2021).

Besides, communication can be compromised, as it is more likely to occur perceived uneven distribution of information among remote, hybrid, or on-site workers which lead to a reduction of engagement for some workers, due to a sense of distributive injustice and/or lack of informational justice, causing workers to feel demotivated and even lost (Wontorczyk and Rożnowski, 2022). The practice of checking emails outside working hours emerges as one of the adverse factors that exert a substantial influence on reducing engagement in job performance. This phenomenon is significant in remote work environments, where it is crucial to establish boundaries between work and personal time. The absence of this distinction can result in the perception of intrusion into personal space, creating an environment devoid of rest and privacy (Wontorczyk & Rożnowski, 2022).

As a result, work-family conflict and isolation due to remote work have shown a negative relationship with engagement. Work-family conflict is related to the existence, in the same space and time, of work tasks and household tasks, where work execution can be affected by involvement in household tasks. Sometimes, when there are more people in the workspace (e.g., family members and housemates), a climate more prone to distractions is created, where the employee, in a way, lacks control over their work environment, leading to dissatisfaction. Indeed, distractions are much more likely to occur in a remote environment compared to an office setting, negatively impacting engagement (Galanti et al., 2021). When remote workers cannot achieve quality in the workspace, understood as the separation of the workspace from the convenience space, distractions will affect productivity and engagement.

Nonetheless, research on remote work have also highlighted positive effects such as increased employee engagement in task performance due to the calm and tranquility found at home. This kind of work environment promotes increased concentration, which leads to a greater focus on task execution, faster and more efficient performance, and therefore better efficiency and productivity (Wontorczyk & Rożnowski, 2022).

Remote work can also encourage managers to check and monitor team work more frequently, making the employee more alert and more prone to planning and controlling the outcomes of their work, leading to the belief that this work method is better (Wontorczyk & Rożnowski, 2022).

According to Galanti et al. (2021), having the ability to manage one's own work, having independence in task execution, set personal goals, and assess their achievement are various characteristics that can lead to efficient remote work, promoting engagement. In this context, self-leadership is highlighted as a characteristic that remote workers should also possess - it allows them to regulate and control their behaviors, using certain cognitive and behavioral strategies that enable self-motivation, resulting in positive psychological impacts that promote engagement.

Remote workers maintain a social connection with the central office through emails, chats, and instant messages, as well as occasional phone calls with supervisors or colleagues. Employee engagement is built on trust and integrity, through effective communication and commitment between employer and employees. Various studies on engagement have shown that it is directly linked to the mental and emotional connection that employees feel towards the workplace. When present, this engagement results in greater loyalty, satisfaction, and consequently, highly productive contribution to the organization's success. It is important to emphasize that employee engagement plays a vital role in boosting employee morale, through effective communication and constant support for the well-being of both the employee and the organization as a wh.4 Organizational Commitment

Definition and Characteristics. Organizational commitment is a key element that influences organizational performance, and can be defined as a psychological bond between the employee and the organization, which makes it less likely for the employee to voluntarily leave the organization (N. J. Allen & Meyer, 1996). Engaged employees are emotionally committed, loyal, and productive (Lucjan et al., 2023), enabling the organization to achieve a competitive advantage.

Allen and Meyer's theoretical approach (1996), conceptualize organizational commitment as a complex construct that encompasses three distinct components: affective, instrumental, and normative. Each of the three dimensions addressed by Meyer et al. (1993), supported by Meyer & Allen's studies (1991), reflects unique psychological states that shape employees' decisions regarding whether to continue their careers in the organization. Understanding organizational commitment is essential for addressing the complex dynamics that permeate the relationships between workers and organizations (Meyer et al., 1993).

Affective commitment is characterized by emotional attachment, a sense of belonging, and the individual's involvement in the organization, measured by the willingness of the employee to remain in the institution. The retention of members in the organization is intrinsically linked to the anticipation of work relationships aligned with organizational goals and values. Individuals with affective commitment demonstrate deep emotional involvement and personal responsibility for the success of the institution, resulting in high levels of performance and positive work attitudes, along with a continuous desire to remain in the organization (Yilmaz & Kiliç, 2017). This type of commitment arises from a combination of work experiences, perceptions, personal characteristics, and positive attitudes developed towards the organization. Affective commitment represents an emotional orientation in which individuals fully identify with the organization, feel satisfaction in being members, and are deeply committed. This dimension of organizational commitment not only illustrates the importance of the emotional bond between the individual and the organization but also highlights the lasting influence that identification and value congruence have on employees' affective commitment.

Instrumental commitment focuses on the investments accumulated by employees in the organization. Retention is motivated by the perception of employees that leaving the organization will bring more costs associated with the loss of these investments, such as time, effort, and acquired skills (Meyer et al., 1993). Employees with strong instrumental commitment remain in the organization due to significant personal or professional costs associated with their departure (Allen & Meyer, 1996). This dimension, also referred to as organizational commitment (Yilmaz & Kiliç, 2017), is inherently linked to circumstances where the cost of leaving the organization is high or there is no viable alternative. In these cases, the individual perceives that they have invested significantly in time and effort up to that point and considers it necessary to continue their trajectory in the organization. This form of commitment is based on the costs that the individual associates with their departure from the organization. Organizational commitment manifests when individuals build their relationship with the organization based on the rewards they receive for their efforts and the losses they would suffer by leaving the institution, such as compensation and benefits (Yilmaz & Kiliç, 2017). Employees demonstrate their best performance when they perceive that their expectations regarding rewards are met. This dimension highlights the importance of tangible aspects of the relationship between the individual and the organization in determining organizational commitment (Yilmaz & Kiliç, 2017).

Finally, normative commitment emerges from socialization experiences that emphasize loyalty to the organization. Normative commitment refers to the commitment based on a sense of obligation to the organization founded on personal norms and values. Employees with strong normative commitment remain because they feel they should, believing it is an ethical or moral obligation (Allen & Meyer, 1996). The dimension of normative commitment is characterized by the feelings of obligation that an individual feels when staying in their organization (Yilmaz & Kiliç, 2017). This type of commitment reflects the harmony between personal values and beliefs and the values and principles of the organization. In this context, the employee not only feels compelled to maintain their commitment to the organization but also perceives such commitment as a moral imperative. The loyalty resulting from the opportunities and benefits provided by the organization contributes to the sense of obligation. Normative commitment arises when individuals decide to stay in an organization based on expected behavioral standards and prevailing social norms. For these individuals, obedience, caution, and formality are indispensable elements, highlighting the importance of ethical and social aspects in their decision to remain in the organization. Thus, normative commitment represents a perceived obligation and adherence to the values and standards established by the organization, reinforcing the complexity of the nature of organizational commitment (Yilmaz & Kiliç, 2017).

The three-component model proposed by Meyer and Allen (1991) emphasizes the psychological complexity underlying workers' decisions to stay, recognizing that each component is uniquely shaped by different experiences (Meyer et al., 1993). The three components of commitment, as outlined above, have direct implications for the decision to stay or leave an organization; however, they are distinct in conceptual terms.

From the perspective of Yilmaz and Kiliç (2017), organizational commitment arises as the employee's identification with the company's objectives, revealing the continuous desire to stay and achieve internal goals. It is also seen as a value system that binds individuals to the company, transcending financial concerns. The authors address commitment as a psychological condition that reflects employees' participation and dedication, highlighting their involvement in the organization's goals and efforts, often placing organizational interests above individual ones.

Effects of Remote Work on Commitment. In the current context, remote work has gained prominence and raised important questions about its impact on workers' organizational commitment. The success of remote work is intrinsically linked to workers' commitment to maintaining a high standard of performance and integrating into the organizational culture, regardless of physical location (Gosnell, 2020).

The initial commitment that a worker establishes with their organization is to maintain a high level of performance, even in a remote environment. By committing to the excellence of their results, workers ensure that organizational goals and objectives are consistently achieved, thus promoting efficiency and productivity even outside the traditional office environment (Gosnell, 2020). According to Gosnell (2020) and Choudhury (2020), it is crucial for remote workers to commit to working collaboratively with managers and the team, maintaining clear and regular communication through transparency and objectivity in information, to contribute to innovation and continuous improvement of work practices, essential for the company's success in a remote environment. Eriksson & Santesson (2021) highlighted that the impact of remote work on commitment tends to be predominantly positive, reflecting a shift in organizational culture towards greater transparency and collaboration. The need for frequent updates and greater transparency in the context of remote work has the effect of strengthening information sharing and collaboration among colleagues, essential elements for organizational commitment. This intensification of transparency emerges as a mechanism to ensure that all team members can demonstrate their contribution to the work and facilitate mutual support and teamwork, even in physical distance.

However, organizations often associate remote work with productivity losses and a decline in employee commitment over time (Chafi et al., 2022). One of the challenges of remote work is ensuring that remote employees feel part of the organization's culture. This cultural integration contributes to preserving cohesion and the identity of the company, ensuring alignment with organizational beliefs and values, even in a geographically distributed environment (Gosnell, 2020). In this context, remote work can result in a decrease in direct contact with the organization, weakening perceived support from both superiors and colleagues. This reduction in face-to-face interaction can negatively influence the commitment of remote workers, who depend on face-to-face interaction to build strong work relationships and a sense of belonging to the organization (Choudhury, 2020). Indeed, organizational culture is created and maintained through continuous interactions and shared experiences in the physical work environment, so it can be impacted by the transition to remote work (Carrasco-Garrido et al., 2023). The absence of direct exposure to organizational symbols, routines, and cultural practices can weaken employees' identification with the company and, consequently, their organizational commitment.

According to Wontorczyk & Rożnowsk (2022), the relationship with the supervisor emerges as a critical element in commitment, standing out as the dominant factor influencing work attitudes and, consequently, commitment to the organization. Supervisor support is essential, not only for guidance and feedback but also as a source of motivation and commitment. In this context, the inherent physical distance of remote work can result in a reduction in direct contact with the organization, leading to a weakening of perceived support from both superiors and colleagues, compared to workers who work in person. This decrease in contact and support can negatively influence the commitment of remote workers, as face-to-face interaction plays a crucial role in building strong work relationships and developing a sense of belonging to the organization.

Other negative consequences include work delays, absenteeism, and unsatisfactory performance, which have been associated with low organizational commitment, including the risk of turnover (Yilmaz & Kiliç, 2017).

On the other hand, telecommuters feel greater job satisfaction and higher organizational commitment, suggesting that such benefits derive from the inherent flexibility of remote work (Srđana et al., 2023). This flexibility allows professionals to manage their responsibilities more autonomously, contributing to greater involvement and satisfaction in the professional context. Workers who demonstrate high commitment to the organization exhibit an acceptance of corporate values and goals and also have a deep sense of identification with the company. Active engagement and emotional attachment to work and the company are fundamental pillars of organizational commitment, exerting a significant influence on performance (Srđana et al., 2023).

Felstead & Henseke (2017) complement this perspective by showing that, from the workers' point of view, adopting remote work contributes to a better balance between work and personal life, resulting in higher levels of job satisfaction. This satisfaction, in turn, positively influences organizational commitment.

In an economic context characterized by volatility, workers play a crucial role in the success of any company. It is imperative to promote dedicated employees who respond to their responsibilities and feel deeply connected to the organization's mission and vision. This dedication and commitment become even more essential in the face of rapid changes in the labor market. Therefore, it is vital to promote organizational commitment as a key factor for sustainable performance in the dynamic and constantly evolving workplace (Srđana et al., 2023).

3. METHODOLOGY AND DEFINITION OF HYPOTHESES

In this study, a quantitative methodological approach was adopted. One of the main advantages of this approach is the ability to quantify a wide range of information and carry out various correlation analyses (Duarte, 2009). Through this methodology, it was possible to measure and quantify the participants' responses, providing concrete data to refute or not the hypotheses formulated.

After reviewing the literature previously presented, and considering the obvious opportunities associated with the topic and the pertinent questions identified, a fundamental question emerged to guide the research: how do professionals who carry out their activities remotely perceive Engagement and Commitment at work?

That said, the following two research hypotheses are derived:

H1: Remote working has a positive impact on engagement.
H2: Remote working has a positive impact on Commitment.

The data collection method used was a questionnaire survey, as it allows us to gain an understanding of a population, such as their behaviors, conditions, opinions and values. This survey was structured into 3 sections in order to gather opinions on remote working and its relationship with Engagement and Commitment.

The first section of the questionnaire was sociodemographic in order to analyze and identify human capital in remote work. Gender, age, level of education, nationality are analyzed, with special attention being paid to the respondents' current working dynamics, whether remote, face-to-face or a combination of both (hybrid), and whether they have had experience working remotely. The respondents' preference between remote and face-to-face work is also studied, as well as their opinions on how remote work affects relationships with colleagues and the organization in a broader sense.

In order to understand engagement we used the Utrecht Work Engagement Scale (UWES – 17; Schaufeli & Bakker, 2004), a validated scale in the English version. This measuring instrument contains seventeen self-assessment items and covers three dimensions: vigor, dedication and absorption. The items were scored on a 7-point frequency scale ranging from "Never" (1) to "Always" (7).

Regarding the assessment of Commitment the Three Component Model (TCM) of Meyer and Allen (1991) was used. As already mentioned, this model structures organisational commitment into three distinct dimensions: affective commitment, normative commitment and instrumental commitment .Three validated scales of Meyer & Allen (2004) were used to assess these dimensions of commitment: the Affective Commitment Scale (ACS), the Normative Commitment Scale (NCS) and the Continuance Commitment Scale (CCS). The items on each scale were scored on a 7-point frequency scale ranging from "Strongly Disagree" (1) to "Strongly Agree" (7).

The descriptive statistics were applied to the variables under study, and exploratory factor analysis were performed for the Engagement and Commitment scales, using SPSS version 29 software.

4. ANALYSIS AND DISCUSSION OF RESULTS

4.1 Sample Characterization

A total of 211 responses to the questionnaire were taken into account, divided between 120 females and 91 males. This distribution reveals a female predominance, corresponding to 56.9% of all participants, in contrast to the 43.1% represented by male participants. The gender ratio shows a significant inclination towards female participation in the study.

The age distribution of respondents shows a higher concentration of responses in the 25 to 35 age group, representing 38.4% of all participants, followed by the under 25 age group, with 32.2%. These categories together comprise 70.6% of all respondents, highlighting the predominance of young participants in the survey. The 36 to 45 age group accounted for 21.3%, while the 46 to 55 age group and the over 55 age group together accounted for 8.1% of the total, showing a progressive decline in participation as age progresses.

In terms of level of education, there is a significant predominance of individuals with access to higher education. Of the 211 participants, the majority have a Bachelor's degree (47.9%), followed by a Master's degree (37.9%), and finally with PhD

(9.0%). In contrast, non-tertiary education is represented to a lesser extent, with secondary education accounting for 4.7% and primary education only 0.5% of the total responses. This distribution reinforces the hypothesis that teleworkers have high levels of academic qualification.

With regard to nationality, the overwhelming majority are Portuguese participants (80.6%). This indicates that the majority of participants are from the country where the study was carried out. The presence of other nationalities, such as German, Brazilian, Spanish, French and English, is relatively minor compared to the Portuguese participants, who represent 0.5%, 3.8%, 3.3%, 3.8% and 8.1% respectively of the total sample. This diversity of nationalities reflects an international sample, albeit on a smaller scale compared to the Portuguese participants.

With regard to their current working model, around 63% of respondents were working remotely at the time the questionnaire was carried out, while 18.5% adopted a hybrid working model and face-to-face work. With the main aim of this study being to analyze the impact of remote working on Engagement and Commitment, it was expected that the majority of respondents would be teleworkers.

In terms of experience with remote work, data analysis reveals that the vast majority of participants, around 93.3%, have experience with remote work. This suggests a broad familiarity and adoption of this type of work among the respondents, where only 6.7% of the participants said they had no experience with remote work.

Table 1. Sample Description

Variable	Percentage
Gender	
Female	56.9
Male	43.1
Age	
<25	32.2
25-35	38.4
36-45	21.3
46-55	7.6
>55	0.5
Schooling (complete)	
High School	5.2
Bachelor's Degree	47.9
Master's Degree	37.9
PhD	9.0

continued on following page

Table 1. Continued

Variable	Percentage
Nationality	
Portuguese	80.6
German	0.5
Brasilian	3.8
Spanish	3.3
French	3.8
English	8.1
Current Working Model	
In-person	18.5
Hybrid	18.5
Remote	63.0
Experience with remote work	
Yes	93.3
No	6.7

Source: Own elaboration

4.2. Engagement

Scale analysis and validation. The evaluation of Engagement began with the validation of the original scale to determine its applicability or the need for adjustments according to the perceptions of our sample, by carrying out a Factor Analysis.

We first analyzed the KMO (Kaiser-Meyer-Olkin) value, which stood at 0.966 showing an exceptionally high value, which means that the data is very suitable for a factor analysis (Table 2). In addition, according to Bartlett's test, there was a significance value of p = 0.000, which indicates that there is sufficient correlation between the items to proceed with the factor analysis.

Table 2. KMO and Bartlett's test for Engagement Scale

KMO and Bartlett's Test		
Kaiser-Meyer-Olkin Measure of Sampling Adequacy.		0.966
Bartlett's Test of Sphericity	Approx. Chi-Square	4705.170
	df	136
	Sig.	0.000

Source: Own elaboration

The results of the factor analysis revealed the existence of a single factor explaining 83.45% of the total variance of the scale (Table 3). This result suggests that the 17 items in the questionnaire predominantly assess a single underlying dimension or construct, which can be interpreted as "General Engagement" at work, rather than separately identifying the dimensions of vigor, dedication and absorption as theoretically proposed (Table 4). All the items have very high factor loadings on the single extracted component (all above 0.85), strengthening the idea that they are highly correlated and possibly measure the same general construct of Engagement at work.

Table 3. Factor Analysis of Engagement Scale

Total Variance Explained						
Component	**Initial Eigenvalues**			**Extraction Sums of Squared Loadings**		
	Total	**% of Variance**	**Cumulative %**	**Total**	**% of Variance**	**Cumulative %**
1	14.19	83.45	83.45	14.19	83.45	83.45
2	0.46	2.72	86.17			
3	0.35	2.08	88.25			
4	0.30	1.77	90.02			
5	0.27	1.58	91.60			
6	0.22	1.26	92.87			
7	0.19	1.12	93.99			
8	0.16	0.95	94.94			
9	0.15	0.87	95.81			
10	0.14	0.82	96.26			
11	0.12	0.70	97.33			
12	0.10	0.62	97.94			
13	0.10	0.59	98.52			
14	0.08	0.46	98.98			
15	0.07	0.42	99.40			
16	0.05	0.34	99.73			
17	0.04	0.27	100.00			

Source: Own elaboration

Table 4. Factor Extraction of Engagement Scale

Rotated Component Matrix	
	Component 1
At my work, I feel bursting with energy.	0.856
I find the work that I do full of meaning and purpose.	0.887
Time flies when I'm working.	0.918
At my job, I feel strong and vigorous.	0.885
I am enthusiastic about my job.	0.925
When I am working, I forget everything else around me.	0.915
My job inspires me.	0.935
When I get up in the morning, I feel like going to work.	0.919
I feel happy when I am working intensely.	0.925
I am proud on the work that I do.	0.904
I am immersed in my work.	0.934
I can continue working for very long periods at a time.	0.934
To me, my job is challenging.	0.914
I get carried away when I'm working.	0.940
At my job, I am very resilient, mentally.	0.908
It is difficult to detach myself from my job.	0.905
At my work I always persevere, even when things do not go well.	0.920

Source: Own elaboration

These results indicate that there is a contrast with the theory underlying the UWES-17, as demonstrated by Schaufeli & Bakker (2004), which encompasses three distinct dimensions of engagement (vigor, dedication and absorption) - for this specific sample, the 17 items are not clearly distinguished in these three dimensions, but rather only reflect a single Engagement factor.

Before moving on to the subsequent analyses that allow us to delve deeper into these results, the normality of the sample was tested. The Kolmogorov-Smirnov test indicated that for all the variables analyzed, the value of statistical significance is equal to 0.000 (<0.05), so the variables do not follow a normal distribution. Therefore, non-parametric assumptions were used for the next statistical analysis.

Working Model Impacts' on Engagement. The Kruskal-Wallis test was carried out to understand whether the respondents' current way of working had an impact on Engagement. The test indicated significant differences in the level of engagement between employees who work face-to-face, hybrid and remotely. At a significance level of 5% and with p-value = 0.000, it was concluded that Engagement differs between the respondents' different current working methods.

That said, Hypothesis 1 was confirmed, which assumes that remote working has a positive influence on employee engagement. The aim is to clearly and precisely investigate the impact of remote working on the dynamics of employee engagement with their organization.

The questionnaire addressed the following question "Do/Did you feel that working remotely has an influence on your Engagement?". It was possible to see that the majority of respondents expressed a positive view of remote working (70.6%), which indicates that many individuals found benefits in remote working. However, around 14.2% of participants reported a negative perception and approximately 15.2% of participants pointed out that remote working had no influence on their engagement. Overall, it can be concluded that the positive impact is highlighted most prominently.

Gender differences on Engagement perceptions. In a broader analysis, of the 197 responses, there were 116 females and 81 males. Looking at the Positive Impact of Remote Working on Engagement, the majority of participants (70.6%) felt a positive impact. Breaking down the differences between genders, 89 out of 116 women (76.7% of women, 45.2% of the total) experienced a positive impact. From the point of view of the male side, 50 out of 81 men (61.7% of men, 25.4% of the total) experienced a positive impact. That said, it is possible to see that a significantly higher percentage of women than men reported a positive impact of remote working on Engagement, suggesting that women may find more benefits or have a more positive experience with remote working in terms of Engagement at work.

Looking at the Negative Impact of Remote Working on Engagement, a minority of participants (14.2% of all respondents) perceived this negative impact. Distinguishing by gender, the female gender represented by 13 of the 116 women (11.2% of women, 6.6% of the total) felt a negative impact. On the male side, 15 out of 81 men (18.5% of men, 7.6% of the total) felt the same impact. Thus, it can be concluded that there is a higher proportion of men than women who reported a negative impact of remote work on Engagement, which may indicate that men face more challenges or have less positive experiences with remote work in relation to their Engagement at work, supporting the previous data.

In addition, a portion of participants felt no impact of remote work on Engagement (15.2%), with a slightly higher proportion of men (19.8% of men; 8.1% of total responses) compared to women (12.1% of women; 7.1% of total responses).

There are notable gender differences in the perceived impact of remote working on engagement, with women more often reporting a positive impact and men slightly more often reporting negative impacts or no impact at all.

Engagement results overview. To make the analysis even more complete, a weighted table of the Engagement items is presented below (Table 5).

Table 5. Scale of Engagement, Descriptive Analysis

Items	AN (%)	R (%)	S (%)	O (%)	VO (%)	A (%)	Mean	SD
At my work, I feel bursting with energy.	3.6	5.1	12.2	20.9	42.9	15.3	5.40	1.24
I find the work that I do full of meaning and purpose.	3.5	4.5	8.6	20.2	47.0	16.2	5.51	1.20
Time flies when I'm working.	2.6	5.7	11.3	18.6	46.4	15.5	5.47	1.20
At my job, I feel strong and vigorous.	4.6	4.1	11.2	20.3	41.6	18.3	5.45	1.28
I am enthusiastic about my job.	3.1	4.6	9.3	21.1	44.8	17.0	5.51	1.20
When I am working, I forget everything else around me.	5.2	5.2	11.5	20.9	38.7	18.3	5.38	1.34
My job inspires me.	3.1	5.1	11.8	14.9	47.2	17.9	5.52	1.24
When I get up in the morning, I feel like going to work.	5.3	4.7	11.6	19.5	41.1	17.9	5.40	1.32
I feel happy when I am working intensely.	7.3	3.6	9.8	25.4	36.3	17.6	5.33	1.37
I am proud on the work that I do.	2.6	3.1	10.8	15.9	45.1	22.6	5.66	1.18
I am immersed in my work.	3.1	3.6	10.4	18.2	44.8	19.8	5.57	1.21
I can continue working for very long periods at a time.	5.2	6.3	8.9	19.8	43.2	16.7	5.40	1.33
To me, my job is challenging.	2.6	2.1	12.4	20.1	42.3	20.6	5.59	1.16
I get carried away when I'm working.	5.1	2.1	10.3	21.0	43.1	18.5	5.50	1.25
At my job, I am very resilient, mentally.	1.5	3.1	10.3	19.6	44.3	21.1	5.65	1.11
It is difficult to detach myself from my job.	5.9	3.2	9.0	18.1	44.1	19.7	5.51	1.31
At my work I always persevere, even when things do not go well.	3.1	4.6	9.2	16.3	42.9	24.0	5.63	1.24

AN = Almost Never; R = Rarely; S = Sometimes; O = Often; VO = Very Often; A = Always
Source: Own elaboration

Based on the data obtained, it can be inferred that remote work had a significant positive impact on employee engagement.

The highest score obtained in the statement "I am proud of the work that I do" (5.66) suggests that high pride in work may directly reflect the autonomy and confidence provided by remote work. According to Galanti et al. (2021), the ability to manage one's own work, set goals, and assess their achievement are essential characteristics for the efficiency of remote work. Allowing employees to independently manage their tasks offers a freedom that can significantly increase personal fulfillment and pride in individual contributions. This autonomy enables employees to take control of their responsibilities, better adapting to their needs and work methods. Thus, autonomy emerges as a fundamental quality in the context of remote work, playing a crucial role in promoting engagement and achieving effective results.

The score obtained in the statement "At my job, I am very resilient, mentally" (5.65) suggests that remote workers develop and apply effective strategies to maintain productivity and mental well-being. Bakker and Leiter (2010) argue that work engagement transcends daily activities, impacting employees' long-term performance. By dedicating their energy and focus to work, employees unleash their full potential, demonstrating immersion and motivation. Additionally, work engagement goes beyond formal responsibilities, incorporating a proactive attitude that includes seeking new knowledge and supporting the business community.

The high score in the statement "At my work I always persevere, even when things do not go well" (5.63) indicates that remote workers remain motivated and committed, even in the face of obstacles. This perseverance is crucial for continuous engagement in remote work, as emphasized by Bakker and Leiter (2010), who argue that healthy work environments promote employee engagement, encouraging effective contribution and loyalty.

The high score obtained in the statement "I am immersed in my work" (5.57) reflects the ability of remote workers to deeply engage with their professional responsibilities. Studies on remote work have also highlighted positive effects, such as increased worker engagement in task performance, driven by the calm and tranquility found at home, which can result in increased focus and more efficient performance (Wontorczyk & Rożnowski, 2022).

Regarding the items with lower scores, two stand out: "I feel happy when I am working intensely" (5.33) and "When I am working, I forget everything else around me" (5.38). The lower score in the first item may indicate that while remote workers find some satisfaction in hard work, the balance between work and personal life or the intensity of work without immediate in-person support may be a less optimistic area. The absence of breaks or interactions with colleagues, common in traditional work environments, may be related to the lower score achieved in the statement "I feel happy when I am working intensely". In many work environments, social interaction during breaks contributes to a sense of connection and job satisfaction. However, in remote work where such in-person interactions are limited or absent, workers may miss this social aspect, affecting their happiness when working intensely (Wontorczyk & Rożnowski, 2022). Furthermore, the absence of these socialization moments can make intense work more challenging or less rewarding for some workers, contributing to the lower score in this item.

The not-so-high score in the statement "When I am working, I forget everything else around me" (5.38) may reflect common household distractions in the remote work environment, affecting workers' ability to concentrate, as suggested by Galanti et al. (2021). Family-work conflict, which arises when there is overlap between professional and domestic tasks in the same space and time, can negatively impact work execution, as observed by the authors. In remote environments, with the presence of family members or housemates, distractions tend to be more common, interfering with the work environment and resulting in dissatisfaction, which, in turn, affects workers' engagement (Galanti et al., 2021).

In summary, the analysis of engagement as a whole generally reaches high scores. This response pattern reflects a positive trend and also a high frequency of intense and enduring experiences among employees in a remote environment. The data reveal that employees have high levels of energy and motivation and consistently maintain them over time. This indicates remarkable resilience and a willingness to face challenges persistently and enthusiastically. The frequent selection of the highest options presupposes a strong engagement with work and a strong sense of purpose and meaning attributed to tasks performed remotely, as well as a deep and lasting emotional involvement with professional responsibilities. This suggests that they are deeply focused and engaged throughout their workday, finding meaning and satisfaction in the work process itself. Therefore, the predominance of these responses in the higher categories of engagement highlights not only the presence but also the consistency and intensity of positive experiences among remote employees.

Given all the information gathered about the impact of remote work on employee engagement, it is possible to confirm Hypothesis 1 that "Remote work has a positive impact on engagement."

4.3 Commitment

Scale analysis and validation. Commitment analysis began with the validation of the original scale of Meyer and Allen (2004) composed of three dimensions. In the first test, the scale resulted in two factors, with four items equally correlating in both components. However, the obtained results did not convey credibility, leading to the exclusion of items with similar loadings on both factors in a second test. The excluded items were "I do not feel a strong sense of 'belonging' to my organization", "I do not feel 'emotionally attached' to this organization", "I do not feel like 'part of the family' at my organization", and "I do not feel any obligation to remain with my current employer". This exclusion resulted in an increase in KMO and variance explained by the two components. This process aimed to ensure the reliability and validity of the scale for organizational commitment analysis.

Upon the obtained factor analysis, the KMO value is 0.934, which is high and indicates that the variables share considerable commonalities, making the factor analysis appropriate. The Bartlett's test revealed a significant p-value ($p < 0.05$), indicating that the variables are correlated, and it is appropriate to proceed with the analysis (Table 6).

Table 6. KMO and Bartlett's Test for Commitment Scale

KMO and Bartlett's Test		
Kaiser-Meyer-Olkin Measure of Sampling Adequacy.		0.934
Bartlett's Test of Sphericity	Approx. Chi-Square	4021.387
	df	91
	Sig.	0.000

Source: Own elaboration

The results reveal two main components that explain 85.60% of the total variance (Table 7). It can be stated that these two dimensions are capable of capturing most of the information contained in the original scale, rather than separately identifying the three theoretically proposed dimensions of Commitment (affective, normative, and instrumental).

Table 7. Factor Analysis of Commitment Scale

Total Variance Explained						
Component	Initial Eigenvalues			Extraction Sums of Squared Loadings		
	Total	% of Variance	Cumulative %	Total	% of Variance	Cumulative %
1	10.40	74.27	74.27	10.40	74.27	74.27
2	1.59	11.33	85.60	1.59	11.33	85.60
3	0.49	3.51	89.11			
4	0.34	2.42	91.53			
5	0.26	1.88	93.41			
6	0.18	1.31	94.72			
7	0.15	1.09	95.81			
8	0.14	0.99	96.81			
9	0.10	0.71	97.52			
10	0.09	0.68	98.20			
11	0.08	0.55	98.75			
12	0.07	0.50	99.26			
13	0.06	0.44	99.70			
14	0.04	0.30	100.00			

Source: Own elaboration

Dimension 1 can be designated as Affective-Normative Commitment, as the items with higher loadings are in this direction, such as (Table 8): "I would be very happy to spend the rest of my career with this organization" (0.871), "I really feel as if this organization's problems are my own" (0.862), "This organization has a great deal of personal meaning for me" (0.858), which are the items most related to the affective side; "This organization deserves my loyalty" (0.891), "I would not leave my organization right now because I have a sense of obligation to the people in it" (0.888), and "I owe a great deal to my organization" (0.855), are more aligned with normative commitment items, but still express affection for the organization. The items "It would be very hard for me to leave my organization right now, even if I wanted to" (0.894) and "Too much of my life would be disrupted if I decided I wanted to leave my organization now" (0.912) refer to the sentimental and affective side, as they presuppose a connection with the company and staying in the organization by one's own will, reflecting aspects of affective and normative commitment. Workers who score high on this component tend to have a strong emotional connection to the organization and believe they have a moral or ethical obligation to remain. They identify strongly with the organization and feel the company deserves their loyalty.

Dimension 2 can be termed as "Instrumental Commitment", consisting of the following items (Table 8): "I feel that I have too few options to consider leaving this organization" (-0.931), "If I had not already put so much of myself into this organization, I might consider working elsewhere" (-0.900), and "One of the few negative consequences of leaving this organization would be the scarcity of available alternatives" (-0.887). Items with negative factor loadings can be interpreted as follows: the item "I feel that I have too few options to consider leaving this organization" suggests that workers who feel limited in their choices outside the organization are more inclined to stay in it. In the statement "If I had not already put so much of myself into this organization, I might consider working elsewhere", it is implied that workers feel they have invested heavily in the organization and are less likely to consider other job opportunities. In the item "One of the few negative consequences of leaving this organization would be the scarcity of available alternatives", it is indicated that workers perceive the scarcity of viable alternatives as a negative consequence of leaving the organization. These items indicate that workers feel restricted in their options outside the organization, have significantly invested in the company, and perceive the lack of alternatives as a negative consequence, making them more likely to stay in the organization, thus contributing to instrumental commitment. That is, staying in the organization is not merely a voluntary choice based on emotional ties or loyalty but rather influenced by a rational assessment of the costs associated with leaving and the lack of equivalent alternatives.

Table 8. Factor Extraction of Engagement Scale

Rotated Component Matrix		
	Component 1	**Component 2**
I would be very happy to spend the rest of my career with this organization.	0.871	
I really feel as if this organization's problems are my own.	0.862	
This organization has a great deal of personal meaning for me.	0.858	
Right now, staying with my organization is a matter of necessity as much as desire.	0.891	
It would be very hard for me to leave my organization right now, even if I wanted to.	0.894	
Too much of my life would be disrupted if I decided I wanted to leave my organization now.	0.912	
I feel that I have too few options to consider leaving this organization.		-0.931
If I had not already put so much of myself into this organization, I might consider working elsewhere.		-0.900
One of the few negative consequences of leaving this organization would be the scarcity of available alternatives.		-0.887
Even if it were to my advantage, I do not feel it would be right to leave my organization now.	0.714	
I would feel guilty if I left my organization now.	0.796	
This organization deserves my loyalty.	0.891	
I would not leave my organization right now because I have a sense of obligation to the people in it.	0.888	
I owe a great deal to my organization.	0.855	

Source: Own elaboration

Therefore, according to the factor analysis, the identified components can be interpreted as follows: Dimension 1 mainly reflects affective-normative commitment, while Dimension 2 mainly reflects instrumental commitment (Table 9).

Table 9. Commitment Dimensions

Affective-Normative Commitment	I would be very happy to spend the rest of my career with this organization.
	I really feel as if this organization's problems are my own.
	This organization has a great deal of personal meaning for me.
	Right now, staying with my organization is a matter of necessity as much as desire.
	It would be very hard for me to leave my organization right now, even if I wanted to.
	Too much of my life would be disrupted if I decided I wanted to leave my organization now.
	Even if it were to my advantage, I do not feel it would be right to leave my organization now.
	I would feel guilty if I left my organization now.
	This organization deserves my loyalty.
	I would not leave my organization right now because I have a sense of obligation to the people in it.
	I owe a great deal to my organization.
Instrumental commitment	I feel that I have too few options to consider leaving this organization.
	If I had not already put so much of myself into this organization, I might consider working elsewhere.
	One of the few negative consequences of leaving this organization would be the scarcity of available alternatives.

Source: Own elaboration

Working Model Impacts' on Commitment. In order to test Hypothesis 2 (H2): "Remote work has a positive impact on Commitment", the Kruskal-Walllis test was used. With the Kruskal-Walllis test, it was found that there are statistical differences in the assessment of the dimensions of commitment according to the respondents' current working method and it was concluded that, for both factors, there is a statistically significant difference between the groups (face-to-face, hybrid and remote), as indicated by the p-values < 0.05, i.e. the working method has a significant impact on the two dimensions of commitment assessed.

These results are confirmed in the questionnaire by the question "Do you feel that working remotely has an influence on Commitment?". Of the participants, 73.1% said that working remotely had a positive impact on their Commitment, while 14.7% indicated a negative impact. On the other hand, 12.2% of the participants reported that remote working had no impact at all, i.e. their perception in either a remote or traditional environment is the same. These results suggest that the majority of the sample perceived a positive effect of remote working on their Commitment, which may indicate a favourable adaptation to this working model in terms of organizational commitment.

Gender differences on Commitment perceptions. Although not statistically significant, there tends to be a difference in perceptions of commitment between men and women. Among the respondents, 144 expressed the opinion that remote working has a positive impact on commitment, with the majority being women (62.5%). On the other hand, 29 respondents felt that remote working had a negative impact on commitment, the majority being men (55.2%). When analyzed further by gender, it can be seen that a significant proportion of women (78.3%) believe that remote working has a positive impact, compared to men (65.9%). However, among those who see the impact as negative, a higher percentage of men (19.5%) share this view compared to women (11.3%). This analysis suggests that there is a noticeable gender discrepancy in relation to the impact of remote working on commitment, with women having a more positive perception overall.

Therefore, based on the data and the statistical test carried out, we can conclude that remote working has a positive perceived impact on commitment, and this perception varies between genders. Women tend to have a more positive view of the commitment induced by remote working compared to men. However, it is important to note that this difference did not reach statistical significance, although there is a trend in this direction.

Commitment results overview. To make the research more complete, a weighted table of the Commitment items is presented below (Table 10).

Table 10. Scale of Commitment, Descriptive Analysis

Items	StrongD (%)	D (%)	SlightD (%)	NA (%)	SlightA (%)	A (%)	StrongA (%)	Mean	SD
I would be very happy to spend the rest of my career with this organization.	0.5	10.1	8.1	2.0	11.1	53.5	14.6	5.32	1.54
I really feel as if this organization's problems are my own.	2.6	8.2	8.7	1.5	11.7	51.0	16.3	5.3	1.61
This organization has a great deal of personal meaning for me.	0.5	11.6	6.1	2.5	9.6	52.0	17.7	5.36	1.35
Right now, staying with my organization is a matter of necessity as much as desire.	0.5	9.6	7.1	5.6	7.6	52.0	17.7	5.37	1.27
It would be very hard for me to leave my organization right now, even if I wanted to.	3.0	11.1	5.6	2.5	9.1	51.5	17.2	5.27	1.26
Too much of my life would be disrupted if I decided I wanted to leave my organization now.	1.5	12.7	6.1	2.5	8.1	47.2	21.8	5.32	1.58
I feel that I have too few options to consider leaving this organization.	21.8	47.7	7.6	5.6	9.6	7.6	0.0	2.56	1.54
If I had not already put so much of myself into this organization, I might consider working elsewhere.	21.7	49.5	5.6	4.0	12.1	6.6	0.5	2.57	1.70

continued on following page

Table 10. Continued

Items	StrongD (%)	D (%)	SlightD (%)	NA (%)	SlightA (%)	A (%)	StrongA (%)	Mean	SD
One of the few negative consequences of leaving this organization would be the scarcity of available alternatives.	21.2	50.5	7.1	4.5	9.1	7.1	0.5	2.53	1.71
Even if it were to my advantage, I do not feel it would be right to leave my organization now.	2.0	12.8	8.2	5.6	8.2	54.6	8.7	5.04	1.52
I would feel guilty if I left my organization now.	3.0	14.7	6.6	1.0	8.6	54.3	11.7	5.07	1.55
This organization deserves my loyalty.	2.5	5.6	7.1	6.1	9.1	43.1	26.4	5.49	1.51
I would not leave my organization right now because I have a sense of obligation to the people in it.	2.0	9.1	8.1	2.0	10.1	44.9	23.7	5.39	1.49
I owe a great deal to my organization.	2.0	7.1	7.1	4.5	11.1	42.4	25.8	5.46	1.66

SrongD = Strongly Disagree; D = Disagree; SlightD = Slightly Disagree; NA = Neither Agree of Disagree; SlightA = Slightly Agree; A = Agree; StrongA = Strongly Agree.

Source: Own elaboration

The analysis of the provided scores offers a comprehensive view of the current state of commitment among remote workers.

The dimension of Affective-Normative Commitment is justified by a strong affection for the organization, represented by items such as “I would be very happy to spend the rest of my career with this organization”, “I really feel as if this organization's problems are my own”, and “This organization has a great deal of personal meaning for me”, with averages of 5.32, 5.3, and 5.36, respectively. These items reflect a strong emotional connection of workers with the organization, indicating a genuine desire to remain with the company and a deep identification with its values and challenges. Additionally, the perception of moral obligation to colleagues is evident, as indicated by the item “I would not leave my organization right now because I have a sense of obligation to the people in it”. This demonstrates an emotional and affective bond with people in the organization, along with a moral commitment to collective well-being. The perception that the organization deserves loyalty and feelings of gratitude and recognition also contribute to affective-normative commitment.

Regarding Instrumental Commitment, which is based on the perception of costs associated with leaving the organization, it is observed that workers perceive a significant need to remain with the organization, beyond desire, as indicated by the item “Right now, staying with my organization is a matter of necessity as much as desire”. They recognize the importance of staying with the company for practical or need-based reasons, such as financial benefits or job stability. However, items related to the perception of few options outside the organization and the negative impact of leaving the company received lower scores. This suggests that other factors, such as the meaning of work, emotional attachment, and interpersonal relationships, may play a more significant role in organizational commitment than the perception of costs associated with leaving.

In summary, the results indicate that remote workers demonstrate strong affective and normative commitment to their organizations, as well as an instrumental perception of the need to remain with the company. Despite the challenges of remote work, such as physical distance and lack of in-person interaction, many workers have maintained a strong connection and commitment to the organization.

4.5 Discussion

Human Capital. In terms of human capital in remote work, it can be stated that that regarding gender distribution, literature indicates a slight predominance of women in remote work. The results confirm and expand upon this trend, showing a slightly higher proportion of female participation (56.9%). This agreement suggests that the predominance of women in telecommuting may be a consolidated trend, possibly reflecting the flexibilities of remote work that may favor female inclusion in the labor market, especially in contexts requiring greater balance between professional and personal/family life. These conclusions confirm that remote work has allowed greater flexibility in managing family and professional obligations, empowering women to balance these commitments more effectively, potentially enhancing their career advancement opportunities.

In terms of qualifications, literature and the results obtained highlight the high level of qualification among professionals in telecommuting. This trend is reinforced by the results of this study, where an overwhelming majority of participants have a higher education degree: 47.9% with a Bachelor's degree, 37.9% with a Master's degree, and 9.0% with a Doctorate, totalling 94.8% of participants with higher education. These data reinforce the idea that telecommuting is particularly prevalent among individuals with higher levels of education, suggesting that professions performed remotely tend to be those that also require higher levels of academic training. According to Dingel & Neiman (2020), the concentration of participants with advanced academic degrees (94.8%) aligns directly with sectors identified as more prone to remote work, such as management, finance, education, and areas involving intensive computer work, which are also the sectors where the literature points out a higher concentration of teleworking population, primarily Education, followed by Information and Communication Activities.

Impacts on interpersonal relationships. It is evident that the experience of remote work varies significantly among individuals, reflecting a range of responses from perceiving improvements in interpersonal relationships to feelings of isolation and disconnection. Studies such as Wontorczyk & Rożnowski (2022) suggest that reduced physical contact can effectively reduce conflicts, promoting a calmer and less competitive work environment. The analysis of the data revealed that a considerable proportion of remote workers perceive a positive impact of this work model on their relationships with colleagues, with 39.5% of participants stating that remote work has improved this relationship. This conclusion is corroborated by Osoian and Petre (2022), who point to an increase in empathy among colleagues, suggesting that remote work can indeed facilitate a collaborative and empathetic environment, despite inherent challenges.

In contrast, the study also identified negative experiences related to social isolation, with 32.3% of participants reporting feelings of isolation and disconnection. Alexandria (2022) and Popovici and Popovici (2020) warn for the increased social isolation, a concerning consequence of the absence of a shared physical work environment, which can lead to feelings of alienation and detachment from the organization. This isolation not only affects the mental health of workers but can also compromise team cohesion and effectiveness. The loss of face-to-face interactions, according to Wontorczyk & Rożnowski (2022), can weaken organizational bonds, an aspect that aligns with highlighted reports of negative impact on communication. The lack of physical contact and dependence on digital tools can lead to a decreased sense of belonging and commitment and involvement with the organization.

Impacts on Engagement. The majority of respondents expressed a positive view of remote work, with 70.6% of participants stating a positive influence on their engagement, suggesting they found benefits in remote work. The analysis of items with higher averages revealed that teleworkers demonstrate a high pride in the work they do, which aligns with Galanti et al. (2021) research, who highlighted the importance of autonomy in remote work, suggesting that the ability to manage one's own work and set goals is essential for maintaining high engagement levels. Additionally, Wontorczyk & Rożnowski (2022) noted that remote work environments that reduce physical conflicts can foster a more engaging and productive work atmosphere. Moreover, the analysis revealed that remote workers develop effective strategies to maintain productivity and mental well-being, as indicated by the high score on the statement “At my job, I am very resilient, mentally” (5.65). This resilience is essential for ongoing engagement in remote work, enabling employees to overcome obstacles and stay motivated (Bakker & Leiter, 2010).

On the other hand, items with lower scores were identified, such as “I feel happy when I am working intensely” (5.33) and “When I am working, I forget everything else around me” (5.38). These results suggest that the balance between work and personal life and domestic distractions can affect the happiness and ability to concentrate of remote workers (Wontorczyk & Rożnowski, 2022). However, despite these limitations, the overall analysis of responses revealed that remote employees present high levels of engagement. The predominance of responses in the higher categories suggests a strong involvement with work and a high emotional involvement with professional responsibilities. In summary, the results end up confirming H1, proving that remote work has a positive impact on employee engagement. The autonomy, resilience, and commitment demonstrated by remote workers reflect a general trend of satisfaction and involvement with work, despite the challenges associated with the remote environment.

One of the elements that contribute to the sense of engagement is the support provided by the company, especially from the direct leader. This factor highlights the need for leaders to be available and accessible. In a remote work context, physical presence is impossible. Hence, alternative means of support, such as the use of collaborative digital platforms and the implementation of regular and frequent meetings, become essential. As pointed out by Bailey and Kurland (2002), remote work can have a positive impact on organizational commitment by strengthening the bonds between employees and the company. The reduction of direct supervision in remote work is seen as advantageous, as it contributes to increased autonomy and trust (Silva, 2021).

The consolidation of Engagement is driven by the creation of spaces for interaction, such as chat groups, which foster relationships among colleagues. These practices reinforce the sense of belonging and connection with the organization. Remote workers benefit from this informal interaction, making the work environment more engaging and stimulating (Wontorczyk & Rożnowski, 2022).

Impacts on Commitment. Remote work presents a complex influence on organizational commitment. One of the main concerns is that physical distance from the workplace might lead to a weakening of bonds between employees and the organization. However, studies suggest that remote work can positively impact commitment by enhancing work-life balance and reducing stress, leading to higher job satisfaction and loyalty (Gajendran & Harrison, 2007).

The presented results can be justified in light of the literature on organizational commitment in the context of remote work. Evidence suggests that despite the inherent challenges of remote work, such as potential loss of organizational roots and weakening of perceived support from both superiors and colleagues (Carrasco-Garrido et al., 2023), there are significant aspects that contribute to strong organizational commitment. The average scores of affective and normative commitment were high, demonstrating a strong commitment to the organization, which aligns with the arguments of Gosnell (2020) and Choudhury (2020), who emphasize the importance of commitment to excellence, collaboration, and continuous communication as foundations for organizational success in remote environments. This significant emotional connection and strong sense of duty reflect an internalization of the company's values and goals by workers, reinforcing the idea that integration into the organizational culture and maintenance of clear communication are crucial to preserving cohesion and identity of the company.

This commitment can be elucidated by the high appreciation and emotional connection that workers demonstrate toward their organization, reflected in items such as "I would be very happy to spend the rest of my career with this organization", "I really feel as if this organization's problems are my own", and "This organization has a great deal of personal meaning for me". These items manifest an intense emotional connection with the employer, evidencing a sincere desire to remain connected to the organization and a deep identification with its values and challenges faced. Research by Wontorczyk and Rożnowski (2022) emphasizes the crucial role that the dynamics of the relationship with supervisors and support among colleagues play in fostering organizational commitment, where, even in the face of challenges imposed by physical separation, the perception of support and the ability to cultivate robust work relationships in virtual environments are crucial to developing a sense of belonging to the organization. These factors are decisive for the development of a strong sense of duty and loyalty, mitigating potential negative effects caused by decreased face-to-face interaction. This argument gains relevance with the analysis of the item "I would not leave my organization right now because I have a sense of obligation to the people in it", which reflects a significant sense of moral obligation toward colleagues. Individuals who share this feeling demonstrate a tendency to assume a moral responsibility to remain in the company, aiming to support and collaborate with their colleagues. This attitude demonstrates an emotional and affective bond with the team, complemented by an ethical commitment to collective well-being, highlighting how positive interpersonal relationships and mutual support are essential for promoting organizational commitment in remote contexts.

On the other hand, Carrasco-Garrido et al. (2023) emphasize the possible loss of organizational roots in the remote work model. This is because organizational culture is characterized by continuous interactions and shared experiences in the physical work environment, and therefore, it may be compromised in remote work environments. The absence of direct exposure to organizational symbols, routines, and cultural practices emerges as a potential threat to workers' identification with the company and, consequently, to their organizational commitment. This challenge was revealed in the item with the lowest score, "I do not feel 'emotionally attached' to this organization", highlighting that some workers may have difficulty developing a strong emotional connection with the organization in the remote work environment. The lack of physical interactions and the absence of everyday experiences can lead to a feeling of detachment and distance from the company. This item, therefore, reinforces the need for organizations to implement strategies to strengthen emotional bonds, such as creating opportunities for interaction and virtual engagement, in order to overcome the potential adverse effects of the absence of face-to-face interaction. This data indicates that the organization's commitment to maintaining an inclusive and collaborative environment, as well as ensuring that employees feel heard and supported, is crucial to strengthening the emotional bond and promoting long-term organizational commitment.

Nonetheless, the results revealed that the impact of remote work had a predominantly positive inclination on worker commitment. Participants demonstrated a high degree of satisfaction and long-term commitment, presenting a significant emotional bond. The perception of remaining in the organization was not only interpreted as a desire but also as a necessity, suggesting a deep commitment based on ethical and moral principles. These results indicate that, even without physical presence in the workplace, organizational commitment remains robust and is sustained by ethical values, emotional bonds, and a deep moral connection with the company. Thus, while the concerns initially raised by Carrasco-Garrido et al. (2023) about the loss of organizational roots are relevant, the results obtained point to the resilience of organizational commitment in remote environments, indicating the capacity for adaptation and reinforcement of organizational bonds even in unconventional work contexts.

The results reflect a complexity in the dynamics of remote work, suggesting that, despite challenges, remote work can effectively contribute to an increase in organizational commitment. The key to this success seems to lie in the careful implementation of remote work practices, which should include effective communication, continuous support from management and colleagues, as well as strategies to integrate remote workers into the organizational culture. Thus, these results not only confirm Hypothesis 2 but also highlight the importance of management approaches adapted to the specificities of remote work to maximize its positive impact on organizational commitment.

Remote work fosters affective commitment by providing employees with greater flexibility and control over their work schedules. This autonomy allows employees to better manage their personal and professional responsibilities, leading to increased job satisfaction and emotional attachment to the organization (Gajendran & Harrison, 2007). However, maintaining affective commitment in a remote work setting requires deliberate efforts to sustain communication and a sense of belonging among remote workers.

Gender Discrepancies. The analysis of gender discrepancies in the perception of remote work's impact on commitment reveals significant insights. Studies indicate that men and women may experience and perceive remote work differently due to various factors such as caregiving responsibilities, societal expectations, and work-life balance challenges (Shockley et al., 2021).

Women, in particular, may face greater challenges in balancing work and family responsibilities when working remotely. The dual burden of professional and domestic roles can lead to increased stress and reduced commitment to the organization (Shockley et al., 2021). Additionally, women may feel isolated and disconnected from their colleagues, affecting their sense of belonging and engagement (Kelliher & Anderson, 2010). Conversely, remote work can offer women greater flexibility to manage their multiple roles, potentially enhancing their job satisfaction and commitment. However, this requires supportive organizational policies that address gender-specific needs and challenges (Shockley et al., 2021).

To address gender discrepancies in remote work perceptions and their impact on commitment, organizations should implement targeted strategies. Providing flexible work arrangements and support for caregiving responsibilities can help women balance their professional and personal lives more effectively. Creating inclusive virtual communities and promoting regular communication can mitigate feelings of isolation and enhance engagement for all employees (Kelliher & Anderson, 2010). Organizations should also consider gender-sensitive training and development programs to empower women and ensure equal opportunities for career advancement. By fostering a culture of inclusivity and support, companies can enhance commitment and engagement among their remote workforce (Shockley et al., 2021).

Practical Implications and Recommendations. Based on the findings of this study, organizations can implement several strategies to enhance remote work and improve engagement and commitment. First, establishing clear communication channels is essential to ensure that remote workers have access to efficient communication tools and regular updates. Utilizing collaborative platforms can facilitate interaction and information sharing among team members. Second, providing supportive leadership is crucial. Leaders should offer regular check-ins and support to remote employees, fostering a culture of trust and autonomy that allows employees to manage their work effectively.

Promoting work-life balance is another important strategy. Organizations should implement policies that support work-life balance, such as flexible work hours and wellness programs, and encourage employees to set boundaries between work and personal life. Additionally, fostering a sense of belonging among remote workers can significantly enhance their engagement. Creating virtual communities and opportunities for remote workers to connect with their colleagues, such as virtual team-building activities and social events, can strengthen relationships and reduce feelings of isolation.

Offering professional development opportunities is also vital. Remote employees should have access to training and development programs that encourage continuous learning and career growth. Finally, addressing gender-specific needs is imperative for promoting inclusivity. Organizations should implement policies that support women in balancing their professional and personal responsibilities and promote gender equality in all organizational practices. By adopting these strategies, companies can create a more flexible, inclusive, and productive remote work environment, ultimately enhancing employee satisfaction and loyalty.

5. CONCLUSION

The present study explored the impact of remote work on employee Engagement and Commitment, addressing a crucial gap in understanding how modern work arrangements affect these key organizational dimensions. The analysis of the data and the results obtained provided a deeper understanding of the effects of remote work on employee attitudes and behaviors.

Regarding Engagement, the results confirm the hypothesis that remote work has a positive impact, highlighting autonomy, resilience, and commitment as key elements for employee involvement. Despite some challenges, such as balancing personal and professional life, remote employees demonstrated high levels of engagement with their work. This suggests that remote work, when managed effectively, can foster a productive and fulfilling work environment..

In terms of Commitment, the results point to a surprising resilience, where remote workers maintain a strong emotional and moral bond with the organization. Although they face possible challenges, such as social isolation and loss of organizational roots, employees demonstrated a deep commitment to the company's values and goals. This emphasizes how crucial it is to have open lines of communication, managerial support, and integration into the organization's culture in order to retain employee commitment when working remotely.In summary, the research indicates that remote work has emerged as an effective and advantageous practice, capable of promoting positive social relationships, increasing employee engagement, and strengthening organizational commitment. Nonetheless, its success hinges on careful implementation and effective support policies..

The limitations of the study underscore the need for caution in interpreting the findings. The relatively small sample size and the potential biases in data collection methods may limit the generalizability of the results. Additionally, the reliance on quantitative methodology alone may overlook nuances and intricacies in participants' experiences and perceptions. Future research would benefit from a mixed-methods approach, combining quantitative surveys with qualitative interviews to capture a more comprehensive understanding of the impact of remote work.

Despite these limitations, the findings contribute to the growing body of literature on remote work by shedding light on its impact on employee engagement and commitment. By recognizing the challenges and opportunities associated with remote work, organizations can better design policies and practices to support employees in navigating the evolving landscape of work.

ACKNOWLEDGMENT

This work was supported by national funds through FCT/MCTES (PIDDAC): UNIAG, UIDB/04752/2020 (DOI 10.54499/UIDB/04752/2020) and UIDP/04752/2020 (DOI 10.54499/UIDP/04752/2020).

REFERENCES

Aguilera, A., Lethiais, V., Rallet, A., & Proulhac, L. (2016). Home-based telework in France: Characteristics, barriers and perspectives. *Transportation Research Part A, Policy and Practice*, 92, 1–11. DOI: 10.1016/j.tra.2016.06.021

Alexandria. (2022, December 27). *Remote Work Is Here for Good*. HRNews. https://www.proquest.com/abicomplete/docview/2758589240/E33E90B228874210PQ/1?accountid=177838&sourcetype=Trade%20Journals#center

Alexandria. (2023, September 14). *Coworking Spaces Can Help Prevent Employee Loneliness, Isolation*. HRNews. https://www.proquest.com/abicomplete/docview/2864920195/945F018B129C4C98PQ/2?accountid=177838&sourcetype=Trade%20Journals

Allen, N. J., & Meyer, J. P. (1996). Affective, Continuance, and Normative Commitment to the Organization: An Examination of Construct Validity. *Journal of Vocational Behavior*, 49(3), 252–276. https://sci-hub.se/10.1006/jvbe.1996.0043. DOI: 10.1006/jvbe.1996.0043 PMID: 8980084

Almeida, N. G. (2016). A importância da metodologia científica através do projeto de pesquisa para a construção da monografia. *Revista de Biblioteconomia e Ciência Da Informação*, 57–66. https://periodicos.ufca.edu.br/ojs/index.php/folhaderosto/article/view/92/67

Anand, A. A., & Acharya, S. N. (2021). Employee Engagement in A Remote Working Scenario. *International Research Journal of Business Studies, 14*(2). https://pdfs.semanticscholar.org/3845/990aadc017a468cfbd7838000f9dd5468cd0.pdf

Artigo 165º, de 28 de abril de 2023. *Código do Trabalho*. Autoridade para as condições do Trabalho.

Bakker, A. B., & Leiter, M. P. (2010). *Work Engagement: A Handbook of Essential Theory and Research*. Psychology Press. DOI: 10.4324/9780203853047

Barardo, R. de O. (2021). *A afirmação do Teletrabalho no setor terciário: Desafios e Oportunidades* [Master Dissertation, ISCAL - Instituto Superior de Contabilidade e Administração de Lisboa]. https://repositorio.ipl.pt/bitstream/10400.21/15238/1/Tese%20Ricardo%20Barardo%20-%20Imprimir.pdf

Beckel, J. L. O., & Fisher, G. G. (2022). Telework and Worker Health and Well-Being: A Review and Recommendations for Research and Practice. *International Journal of Environmental Research and Public Health*, 19(7), 3879. DOI: 10.3390/ijerph19073879 PMID: 35409563

Bloom, N., Han, R., & Liang, J. (2022). *How Hybrid Working From Home Works Out.*

Boccoli, G., Gastaldi, L., & Corso, M. (2023). The evolution of employee engagement: Towards a social and contextual construct for balancing individual performance and wellbeing dynamically. *International Journal of Management Reviews*, 25(1), 75–98. DOI: 10.1111/ijmr.12304

Carrasco-Garrido, C., De-Pablos-Heredero, C., & Rodríguez-Sánchez, J.-L. (2023). Exploring hybrid telework: A bibliometric analysis. *Heliyon*, 9(12), 1–15. DOI: 10.1016/j.heliyon.2023.e22472 PMID: 38076145

Chafi, M. B., Hultberg, A., & Yams, N. B. (2022). Post-pandemic office work: Perceived challenges and opportunities for a sustainable work environment. *Sustainability (Basel)*, 14(1), 294. Advance online publication. DOI: 10.3390/su14010294

Chiguvi, D., & Keneilwe Bakani, . (2023). Exploring the effects of remote work on employee productivity in Botswana amidst the COVID-19 Pandemic. *International Journal of Research in Business and Social Science*, 12(6), 101–117. DOI: 10.20525/ijrbs.v12i6.2505

Choudhury, P. (2020, November). Our Work-from-Anywhere Future. *Harvard Business Review*, 23(SPEC. ISS.). Advance online publication. DOI: 10.1002/job.145

Cristina, A. C. (2021). *Bem Estar E Satisfação No Trabalho Remoto: Comparação Entre Trabalhadores Independenes E Trabalhadores Dependentes* [Master Dissertation, ISPA - Instituto Universitário Ciências Psicológicas, Sociais e da Vida]. https://repositorio.ispa.pt/bitstream/10400.12/8017/1/22463.pdf

Dingel, J. I., & Neiman, B. (2020). How many jobs can be done at home? *Journal of Public Economics*, 189, 104235. DOI: 10.1016/j.jpubeco.2020.104235 PMID: 32834177

Duarte, T. (2009). *A possibilidade da investigação a 3: reflexões sobre triangulação (metodológica)* (e-WORKING PAPER N. º 60/2009).

Eriksson, L., & Santesson, H. (2021). *Organizational Culture in a Remote Setting - A Qualitative Study on Organizational Culture and the Effects of Remote Work* [Master Dissertation, Uppsala University]. https://www.diva-portal.org/smash/get/diva2:1579041/FULLTEXT01.pdf

Felstead, A., & Henseke, G. (2017). Assessing the growth of remote working and its consequences for effort, well-being and work-life balance. *New Technology, Work and Employment*, 32(3), 195–212. DOI: 10.1111/ntwe.12097

Fitzer, M. M. (1997). *Managing from afar: Performance and rewards in a telecommuting environment - ProQuest*. 65–73. https://www.proquest.com/docview/213677152/fulltextPDF/D46E45301DD84791PQ/1?accountid=177838&sourcetype=Trade%20Journals

Galanti, T., Guidetti, G., Mazzei, E., Zappalà, S., & Toscano, F. (2021). Work From Home During the COVID-19 Outbreak: The Impact on Employees' Remote Work Productivity, Engagement, and Stress. *Journal of Occupational and Environmental Medicine*, 63(7), e426–e432. DOI: 10.1097/JOM.0000000000002236 PMID: 33883531

Garavand, A., Jalali, S., Talebi, A. H., & Sabahi, A. (2022). Advantages and disadvantages of teleworking in healthcare institutions during COVID-19: A systematic review. *Informatics in Medicine Unlocked*, 34, 101119. DOI: 10.1016/j.imu.2022.101119 PMID: 36373130

Gosnell, K. (2020, July 17). Commitments Good Employees Make While Working Remotely. *Forbs*. https://www.forbes.com/sites/forbescoachescouncil/2020/07/17/commitments-good-employees-make-while-working-remotely/?sh=3c3e08873c51

Grzegorczyk, M., Mariniello, M., Nurski, L., & Schraepen, T. (2021). *Blending the physical and virtual: A hybrid model for the future of work*. http://hdl.handle.net/10419/251067

Kranc, J. (2023, July 20). Hybrid work models continue to grow, study finds. *Benefits PRO*. https://www.proquest.com/abicomplete/docview/2840035890/AFE0D5984D9C4A69PQ/3?accountid=177838&sourcetype=Trade%20Journals#center

Lucjan, K., Szostek, D., Balcerzak, A. P., & Rogalska, E. (2023). Relationships Between Leadership Style And Organizational Commitment: The Moderating Role Of The System Of Work. *Economics & Sociology (Ternopil)*, 16(4), 11–39. DOI: 10.14254/2071-789X.2023/16-4/1

Mantovani, C. M. C. A. (2011). *Narrativas Da Mobilidade: Comunicação, Cultura E Produção Em Espaços Informacionais* [Doctoral Dissertation]. Universidade Federal de Minas Gerais.

Meyer, J. P., & Allen, N. J. (2004). *TCM Employee Commitment Survey Academic Users Guide 2004*. The University of Western Ontario.

Meyer, J. P., Allen, N. J., & Smith, C. A. (1993). Commitment to Organizations and Occupations: Extension and Test of a Three-Component Conceptualization. *The Journal of Applied Psychology*, 78(4), 538–551. DOI: 10.1037/0021-9010.78.4.538

Moglia, M., Hopkins, J., & Bardoel, A. (2021). Telework, Hybrid Work and the United Nation's Sustainable Development Goals: Towards Policy Coherence. *Sustainability, 13*(16), 9222. DOI: 10.3390/su13169222

Olson, M. H. (1983). Remote Office Work. *Changing Work Patterns In Space And Time.*, 26(3), 182–187.

Osoian, C., & Petre, A. (2022). Employee Engagement and Job Burnout in the Context of Teleworking. *Studia Universitatis Babes-Bolyai Oeconomica*, 67(3), 14–26. DOI: 10.2478/subboec-2022-0012

Park, S., & Cho, Y. J. (2020). Does telework status affect the behavior and perception of supervisors? Examining task behavior and perception in the telework context. *The International Journal Of Human Resource Management*. https://sci-hub.se/10.1080/09585192.2020.1777183

Pass, S., & Ridgway, M. (2022). An informed discussion on the impact of COVID-19 and 'enforced' remote working on employee engagement. *Human Resource Development International*, 25(2), 254–270. DOI: 10.1080/13678868.2022.2048605

Peters, P., Ligthart, P. E. M., Bardoel, A., & Poutsma, E. (2016). 'Fit' for telework'? Cross-cultural variance and task-control explanations in organizations' formal telework practices. *International Journal of Human Resource Management*, 27(21), 2582–2603. DOI: 10.1080/09585192.2016.1232294

Popovici, V., & Popovici, A.-L. (2020). Remote Work Revolution: Current Opportunities and Challenges for Organizations. *"Ovidius" University Annals, Economic Sciences Series, 20*(1).

Prasad, K., Rao Mangipudi, M., Muralidhar, B., & Vaidya, R. W. (2020). Organizational Climate, Opportunities, Challenges And Psychological Wellbeing Of The Remote Working Employees During Covid-19 Pandemic: A General Linear Model Approach With Reference To Information Technology Industry In Hyderabad. *International Journal of Advanced Research in Engineering and Technology*, 11(4), 372–389. http://www.iaeme.com/IJARET/index.asp372Availableonlineathttp://www.iaeme.com/IJARET/issues.asp?JType=IJARET&VType=11&IType=4http://www.iaeme.com/IJARET/index.asp373http://www.iaeme.com/IJARET/issues.asp?JType=IJARET&VType=11&IType=4

Ritchie, D. (2023, July 11). *Pros and Cons of Remote Work: Embracing a Flexible Future*. https://www.calendar.com/blog/pros-and-cons-of-remote-work-embracing-a-flexible-future/

Romeria, A. (2021). 79% dos profissionais afirma que o teletrabalho melhora a sua produtividade. *O Jornal Económico*. https://jornaleconomico.pt/noticias/79-dos-profissionais-afirma-que-o-teletrabalho-melhora-a-sua-produtividade-792574/

Sahut, J. M., & Lissillour, R. (2023). The adoption of remote work platforms after the Covid-19 lockdown: New approach, new evidence. *Journal of Business Research*, 154, 113345. DOI: 10.1016/j.jbusres.2022.113345 PMID: 36193197

Schaufeli, W., & Bakker, A. (2004). *UWES Utrecht Work Engagement Scale Preliminary Manual*. Occupational Healt Psycology Unit Utrecht University.

Schaufeli, W. B., & Bakker, A. B. (2004). Job demands, job resources, and their relationship with burnout and engagement: A multi-sample study. *Journal of Organizational Behavior J. Organiz.Journal of Organizational Behavior*, 25(3), 293–315. DOI: 10.1002/job.248

Silva, B. R. R. (2021). *Implicações do trabalho remoto na função de RH: um estudo exploratório em empresas portuguesas* [Master Dissertation]. Instituto Superior de Contabilidade e Administração.

Srđana, T., & Jasmina, P. (2023). The Influence Of Cultural And Personal Properties On Job Performances And Organizational Commitment In Teleworkers. *South East European Journal of Economics and Business, 18*(2). DOI: 10.2478/jeb-2023-0015

Tavares, F., Santos, E., Diogo, A., & Ratten, V. (2020). Teleworking in Portuguese communities during the COVID-19 pandemic. *Journal of Enterprising Communities: People and Places in the Global Economy*. https://sci-hub.se/10.1108/jec-06-2020-0113

van der Lippe, T., & Lippényi, Z. (2019). Co-workers working from home and individual and team performance. *New Technology, Work and Employment*, 35(1), 60–79. DOI: 10.1111/ntwe.12153 PMID: 32214593

Wontorczyk, A., & Rożnowski, B. (2022). Remote, Hybrid, and On-Site Work during the SARS-CoV-2 Pandemic and the Consequences for Stress and Work Engagement. *International Journal of Environmental Research and Public Health*, 19(4), 2400. Advance online publication. DOI: 10.3390/ijerph19042400 PMID: 35206590

Yilmaz, E., & Kiliç, Y. (2017). The impact of organizational commitment on trainee teachers' job satisfaction. *International Journal of Contemporary :Educational Research*, 4(1), 1–11. www.ijcer.net

Zhang, S., Moeckel, R., Moreno, A. T., Shuai, B., & Gao, J. (2020). A work-life conflict perspective on telework. *Transportation Research Part A, Policy and Practice*, 141, 51–68. DOI: 10.1016/j.tra.2020.09.007 PMID: 32982087

Chapter 2
Enhancing Organizational Performance Through High-Performance Work Practices in the IT Sector:
Variable Influence on Organizational Efficiency

Sushma Sharma
SRM, Sonipat, India

Shitika Verma
https://orcid.org/0000-0003-0479-4189
GGSIPU, Delhi, India

Radha Rani
SRM, Sonipat, India

Poonam Gahlot
SRM, Sonipat, India

ABSTRACT

In today's competitive business environment, organizations must enhance performance to stay ahead. Traditional sources of advantage, like technology and natural resources, are increasingly imitable. Human resources (HR), being intangible and unique, have emerged as a crucial asset. This study examines high-performance work practices (HPWPs) in IT companies using exploratory factor analysis (EFA) to identify factors that drive organizational success. Data from 349 employees

DOI: 10.4018/979-8-3693-6402-4.ch002

across IT firms in Delhi NCR revealed a five-factor model explaining 66.13% of the variance: organizational development initiatives, employee empowerment programs, compensation and advancement programs, workplace support systems, and performance enhancement programs. The findings indicate that implementing these HPWPs can significantly boost organizational performance. The study provides a framework for IT companies to enhance both organizational and employee performance. Future research should use confirmatory factor analysis (CFA) to validate the EFA-derived model.

1. INTRODUCTION

In today's highly competitive business environment, marked by rapid technological advancements and constant innovation, the role of Human Resource Management (HRM) has become more crucial than ever. Modern HRM trends emphasize the strategic integration of High-Performance Work Practices (HPWPs), which are vital for enhancing organizational performance and gaining a competitive edge. These practices are no longer just about improving employee satisfaction and productivity; they are about strategically leveraging human capital to drive innovation, adaptability, and sustained success. The evolution of HRM from its early days—where employee well-being was often neglected—to its current focus on holistic development and empowerment underscores the growing recognition of people as the core asset of any organization. Influential studies by (Barney, 1991), (Barney & Wright, 1998), (Lawler, 1992), and (Pfeffer, 1998) have established a strong theoretical foundation for the strategic value of HRM in fostering competitive advantage. The practical implications of HPWPs in the modern business landscape are clear: they enable organizations to create high-involvement work environments that knock into the full potential of their employees, driving both individual and organizational growth. By effectively implementing HPWPs, organizations can direct the complexities of today's business world, ensuring they remain resilient, innovative, and ahead of the competition.

It is widely recognized that employees play a crucial role in the well-being of an organization. Companies gain a significant competitive advantage when their employees are not only fully competent but also highly skilled professionals (Price, 2004). The existing literature robustly supports the idea that human resource practices are instrumental in shaping individual employee commitment and satisfaction. These practices are designed to enhance productivity by fostering an environment where employees are motivated and engaged.

High-performance work practices (HPWPs) provide multiple sources of motivation that contribute to improved employee performance. According to (Pfeffer and Veiga, 1999), these practices are integral in creating a work environment that maximizes employee potential and effectiveness. The link between employee attitudes and job satisfaction is well-established, with (Robbins, 1993) noting that job satisfaction is a positive attitude developed over time. Employees who experience job satisfaction are more likely to exhibit favourable attitudes toward their work and organization.

(Neuman, 1989) found that employees who feel happy and empowered in their roles tend to perform better. Empowerment fosters dedication and self-motivation, leading to higher levels of commitment and a sense of responsibility to achieve high performance (Thoman, 1990). This underscores the importance of innovative HR practices in nurturing an empowered workforce, which in turn drives organizational success.

1.1 Contribution of Social Exchange Theory to Enhance Employee Performance Through High Performance Practices

Social Exchange Theory (SET) provides a valuable framework for understanding how high-performance work practices (HPWPs) can enhance employee performance by fostering positive and reciprocal relationships between employees and their organization. The theory, which was initially developed by sociologist George Homans in the 1950s, is based on the idea that social interactions are transactions where individuals seek to maximize rewards and minimize costs. In the context of the workplace, these transactions involve exchanges between employees and their employers, where employees' contributions (such as effort, skills, and performance) are met with organizational rewards (such as pay, recognition, and development opportunities).

1.2 Innovation in Human Resource Management

India liberalized its economy in 1991 with the introduction of new economic policies, sparking rapid transformation in the business sector. This liberalization necessitated changes in workforce management, compelling organizations to innovate their HRM practices to survive in a competitive environment (Muduli, June 2012). Studies have shown a direct link between human resource management and innovation (Laursen and Foss, 2003). Innovative HR practices foster organizational growth, with bundles of these practices influencing innovation and leading to improved outcomes (cf. Ennen and Richter, 2010). Human capital is a valuable resource for organizations, and literature suggests that employees significantly contribute to organizational success and growth (Baron and Kreps, 1999). Effective HR policies and practices in recruitment, selection, training, development, placement, and performance appraisal are essential. HR managers must recruit skilled and competent employees and provide necessary training. As human resources are valuable assets, managers must focus on employee development. HR managers introduce corporate culture and create environments where employees collaborate to achieve organizational goals. Improving company performance is a priority for corporate leaders seeking competitive advantage. Companies aiming to enhance productivity, profit, revenue, and growth should focus on increasing employee involvement, satisfaction, retention, and development through effective HR practices. High skill levels are required for organizational betterment, making HR roles more challenging in a competitive environment. Managers must carefully select suitable personnel.

Today, many companies struggle for survival. HR managers must recognize their role and responsibility in workforce management. Stephen A. Stumpf (May-June 2010) compared HR practices in India's private and public sectors, finding similarities in HR department structure, HR manager roles, recruitment and selection processes, compensation practices, training and development, and employee engagement. These practices are key components of "innovation" (Teece, 2007). According to CIPD, HRM encompasses staffing, performance, change management, and administrative objectives.

The Human Resource Management function is increasingly recognized as crucial to company success. Studies have shown that talented employees provide a competitive edge (Prahalad, 1983). Organizational success relies on competent employees. Effective HR practices motivate, reward, develop, and challenge employees, making them strategic assets. The international competitive business environment pressures HR managers to improve their practices. The HR department is responsible for employee satisfaction, productivity, and organizational performance (Harvey, Dec 2001). Researchers emphasize teamwork, especially in the IT sector, as it enhances employee productivity.

The concept of best practices or high-performance work-based practices (HP-WBP) is an innovative approach in human resource management where employees are actively engaged to showcase their talents, fostering organizational growth and ensuring their future development. High-performance work systems (HPWS) emerged in the US during the 1980s, a time when American manufacturers realized that traditional HR practices were no longer sustainable in a rapidly changing global market. HPWBP is a "best fit" model that focuses on aligning HR practices with strategic management goals (Armstrong, 2009). Proponents of this approach (Godard, 2004; Kalleberg et al., 2006; Ferreira et al., 2012) argue that there are no universally accepted HR practices that directly enhance employee performance.

In response to competitive pressures, particularly from cost-conscious economies like China, many US companies shifted towards low-cost manufacturing to stay competitive. Savvy business leaders not only implement innovative HR practices but also keep an eye on manufacturing costs to maintain market competitiveness. Thus, US manufacturers adopted HPWBP as a means to improve organizational performance. The application of high-performance practices extends beyond HR, finding relevance in fields like Industrial Relations and Organizational Behavior. HPWBP encompasses a set of complementary practices in three broad categories: high employee involvement practices, human resource practices, and reward and commitment practices (Ashton and Sung, 2005).

HPWBP is an innovative HR practice designed to motivate employees to exert maximum effort. Research indicates that employees working under HPWBP are more likely to work harder, smarter, and more creatively compared to those in traditional organizations. High-performance work-based practices are typically adopted by organizations with high levels of commitment, leading to teamwork, innovation, and healthy interpersonal relationships.

The concept of HPWBP is not new in HRM, as the idea of effective people management has long been recognized. However, there is still no precise definition of high-performance work practices, and its specific elements remain a subject of debate (Lloyd and Payne, 2004). Scholars have different interpretations of these practices, and the precise definition of HPWBP continues to be debated (Sung et al., 2005). Sung and Ashton (2005) noted that HPWBP is commonly used in both the public and private sectors, and this study adopts the term. It is acknowledged that employee involvement, HR practices, and commitment practices are crucial for achieving high performance. Therefore, these practices must be included in any program aimed at improving organizational effectiveness through the implementation of a high-performance work system.

Despite varying perspectives, the term HPWBP aligns with what some authors, like (Huselid and Rau, 1997), (Ramsay et al., 2000), and (Patel and Conklin, 2012), refer to as high-performance work systems (HPWS). Others, such as (Purcell, 2006), describe it as high-commitment management (HCM), while (Delaney and Huselid, 1996) term it progressive human resource practices. Consequently, it remains challenging to definitively determine whether HPWPs contribute to organizational performance (Machington and Grugulis, 2000) and how they adapt to environmental changes.

1.3 IT Companies in India

India's GDP has a significant contribution from the information technology (IT) sector, which is expanding rapidly. The IT sector's share of India's overall GDP increased from 1.2% to 7.7% by 2017. The Tata Group pioneered this growth with the establishment of its IT division in 1967. The economic landscape of India experienced a significant transformation in 1991 with the introduction of the new economic policy, which opened the economy to the private sector, heralding an era of globalization and economic integration.

In 1999, under the leadership of Prime Minister Atal Bihari Vajpayee, there was a strong focus on the potential of the IT industry to drive economic growth. Today, India is the world's second-largest exporter of IT services. The Indian IT sector is primarily known for offering cost-effective solutions. According to estimates from Google, by the end of 2018, India was projected to become the leading provider of software developers globally. Gartner identifies Tata Consultancy Services, Infosys, Cognizant, Wipro, and HCL Technologies as the top five Indian IT service providers.

Each industry has its core competencies, and for the IT sector, this has always been its "manpower." Therefore, attracting, developing, and retaining talented employees is a strategic priority for organizations within this sector. The human resource (HR) department plays a pivotal role in this endeavor. Support from top management and the involvement of HR managers in implementing new HR practices lead to positive outcomes in employee satisfaction, productivity, and retention. Identifying and selecting the right talent is particularly crucial in the IT sector. Workforce management issues are of utmost importance due to the diversity of the workforce (Disha Sachdeva, 2009).

The IT sector in India has experienced the highest growth over the past decade compared to other industries. The liberalization of the Indian economy through the introduction of new economic policies facilitated industrialization and rapid transformation within the IT sector. Developed nations such as the USA, Germany, and Japan are keen to hire Indian IT professionals for their companies.

India's IT sector is on track to become the largest software service provider by 2018, demonstrating continuous and robust growth since 1988. When Rajiv Gandhi became Prime Minister in 1984, significant efforts were made to develop the IT sector in India. During his tenure, NASSCOM was registered under the Society Act of 1860 in 1988, providing valuable data and insights on the growth and development of the IT sector.

At that time, the IT sector's share of GDP was 5.5%, which has since increased to 7.7% in 2017 according to NASSCOM. This remarkable growth underscores the importance and potential of the IT sector in India's economic landscape.

IT encompasses a wide range of computer technologies, including hardware, software, and the internet, which are essential for system design and development, managed by IT professionals. This sector covers all facets of software technology and has brought revolutionary changes to many people's lives. The IT industry has emerged as one of the fastest-growing sectors in India, with industry revenue increasing from 1.2% to 7.7% of GDP by 2017. According to NASSCOM, the aggregated revenue of the IT sector reached up to US $350 billion.

The IT industry has made significant strides since the 1970s and 1980s, achieving tremendous growth with major breakthroughs in the 1990s. A key factor in the development of the software industry was the contribution of trained IT professionals, which transformed India into a software superpower. The year 1995-96 was a boom period for the software industry, solidifying its reputation as a major source of revenue and employment generation. The IT industry provides a foundation for growth in other sectors, identifying and meeting the needs of both domestic and international markets.

Leading IT companies such as TCS, Infosys, and Wipro have become leaders in exporting software services by addressing the needs of foreign markets. Mr. Narayan Murthy, a successful leader in the industry, believed that continued innovation would ensure Infosys's ongoing growth and success. Infosys established a training center in Mysore to build employee competencies. Similarly, Mr. Azim Premji, Chairman of Wipro, emphasized the importance of employees as valuable assets to the organization, implementing similar models for competency building.

1.4 List of Companies Selected for the Study

1. Tata Consultancy Services (TCS)

TCS is a global IT company with operations in North and South America, the Middle East, Europe, and Africa. Its headquarters is in Mumbai, India. TCS has a significant market share and competitive advantage worldwide. They have adopted innovative HR practices known as High Performance Work Based Practices (HPWBP) to manage employees. These practices align closely with the business strategy and company structure, supported by IT and top HR professionals. TCS is considered one of the best employers in Europe, with a low attrition rate of 9.9%.

Recent HR practices implemented by TCS include:

1. Self-managed teams: Teams at TCS work independently on projects under a team leader without higher authority interference. This encourages collaboration, idea exchange, and teamwork. TCS follows an open-door policy, promoting equality within its culture.

2. High pay contingent on company performance: TCS designs compensation structures based on team performance, using the EVA model (Economic Value Added) to measure and reward group performance.
3. Sharing of information: TCS emphasizes group performance and motivates employees to work together by sharing information through portals like 'Ultima tix,' where employees across the company can interact and share ideas.
4. Employee Stock Option Plan (ESOP): TCS offers ESOPs to retain its most productive employees.

2. International Business Machines (IBM)

IBM is an American multinational company headquartered in New York, USA, with operations in over 170 countries. Established in 1911, it was renamed IBM in 1924. IBM provides hardware, software, and consulting services and is one of the largest employers, with nearly 382,000 employees. Employee satisfaction is a top priority at IBM, which has implemented an 'Open Door' policy to foster innovation in managing human resources. IBM has been present in India since 1992 and won the HR Excellence Award in August 2011. Recent HR practices include:

1. Variable pay: IBM offers variable pay based on department, team, and company performance, with annual bonuses depending on individual performance to address productivity issues.
2. Employee Stock Option Plan (ESOP): ESOPs are offered to productive employees to encourage long-term retention.
3. Rating as a basis for promotion: Employees are graded based on performance to recognize exceptional accomplishments.
4. Work-life balance: IBM is renowned for offering work-from-home options, making it highly suitable for women employees.

3. HCL Technologies Ltd.

HCL Technologies, headquartered in Noida, Uttar Pradesh, India, is a multinational IT services company. It started as a research and development division of HCL Enterprises and later emerged as an independent company focusing on IT consulting, enterprise transformation, business process outsourcing, cybersecurity, analytics, and R&D. HCL's central philosophy, 'Employee First, Customer Second,' empowers employees to create real value for the organization through engagement. Recent HR practices include:

1. Empowering employees: HCL allows employees to work independently and share suggestions and ideas.

2. Job enrichment: HCL assigns additional responsibilities to motivate employees and enhance job satisfaction.
3. Employee recognition: HCL is known for innovative HR practices and won the Aegis Graham Bell Award for innovation in 2017.
4. NIIT Technologies Ltd.

NIIT Technologies is a global IT company serving customers across America, Europe, and Asia. It offers services such as application development, maintenance, and business process management, focusing on digital services. Ranked No.4 in the 2017 employer survey, NIIT is known for its training and development programs, employee satisfaction, and managing people. Recent HR practices include:

1. Competency analysis: NIIT conducts competency analysis to identify areas for employee development and improvement.
2. Career planning and development: NIIT offers a clear career path from joining to retirement.
3. Succession planning: NIIT focuses on succession planning to ensure experienced employees are prepared to fill key positions.
   5. Infosys Ltd.

Infosys Ltd., headquartered in Bangalore, India, is an IT consulting and outsourcing services company. In 2017, Infosys became the second-largest IT company in terms of revenue. With a low attrition rate of less than 8%, Infosys focuses on retaining talented employees. Recent HR practices include:

1. Employee Stock Option Plan (ESOP): Infosys was the first company in India to offer ESOPs to retain talented employees.
2. Talent engagement: Infosys focuses on employee engagement to increase productivity.
3. Managing diversity: Infosys creates a positive work environment and manages workforce diversity effectively.
   6. Wipro Ltd.

Headquartered in Bangalore, India, is an IT services corporation. Established in 1945, it initially manufactured vegetable products and later transitioned into the IT and computing industry. Wipro has been ranked No.1 for Asian sustainability among Indian companies in 2010. Recent HR practices include:

1. Six Sigma: Wipro uses Six Sigma to measure and maintain quality across business units.

2. Performance appraisal: Wipro uses management by objectives and 360-degree performance measurement tools for appraisals.
3. Promotion policy: Promotions at Wipro are based on seniority and merit.
4. Employee recognition and long service awards: Wipro recognizes hard work and contribution, offering holiday packages for long-serving employees.

7. Neerja Software Private Limited NSPL

An Indian IT solution provider, started in 2011 and quickly gained recognition. Recent HR practices include:

1. Manpower development: NSPL aims to increase employee potential and analyze future manpower requirements.
2. Job enrichment: NSPL motivates self-driven employees by assigning additional technical work.
3. Workforce diversity: NSPL effectively manages workforce diversity.
4. Opportunities for freshers: NSPL conducts job fairs annually and provides career planning and development opportunities for freshers.

8. HSBC Software Development Pvt. Ltd.

Incorporated in 2002, HSBC Software Development provides software publishing, consultancy, and supply services. Recent HR practices include:

1. Induction programs: HSBC welcomes new employees and prepares them for their roles.
2. Flexible work arrangements: HSBC offers flexible scheduling for long-term employees.
3. Harmony: HSBC strives to balance employee expectations and organizational needs.
4. Fringe benefits: HSBC provides extra benefits like company cars and paid holidays to enhance employee satisfaction.

In the rapidly evolving information technology (IT) sector, improving organizational performance is critical for sustaining long-term profitability and competitive advantage. Effective implementation of high-performance work practices (HPWPs) is essential in achieving these goals (Andersson & Eriksson, 2023). Innovative human resource (HR) practices are increasingly recognized as pivotal in enhancing performance and productivity levels (Bouzakhem et al., 2023). In the context of India, an emerging economy striving for global competitiveness, the adoption of advanced HR practices is particularly significant (Kumar & Singh, 2023). Indian IT companies have increasingly embraced modern HR practices to excel in the industry, which includes targeted hiring, comprehensive training, and equitable compensation structures (Ehnert & Harry, 2024; Gupta & Sharma, 2023).

Historically, research has demonstrated the impact of HPWPs on organizational performance. For instance, (Pfeffer, 1998) emphasized the role of high-performance work systems in improving organizational outcomes. Subsequent studies have corroborated this view, highlighting the importance of integrating effective HR practices to boost performance (Huselid, 1995; Becker & Huselid, 2006). Specifically, the effective design of compensation and advancement programs has been shown to enhance employee performance and retention (Gerhart & Fang, 2015). Additionally, the influence of employee empowerment and support systems on performance has been well-documented (Spreitzer, 1995; Eisenberger et al., 2001).

The importance of aligning HR practices with organizational goals to drive performance is further supported by recent studies. For example, (Sun et al., 2020) found that implementing high-performance work practices positively affects employee performance in various sectors. Similarly, (Chen et al., 2024) demonstrated that tailored HR practices significantly enhance productivity in the IT industry. These findings emphasize the critical role of HPWPs in improving organizational performance.

In summary, this study aims to explore the impact of high-performance work practices—specifically organizational development, employee empowerment programs, compensation and advancement programs, workplace support systems, and performance enhancement programs—on employee performance. By using Exploratory Factor Analysis (EFA), the research seeks to identify key factors that drive high performance, group these factors based on their similarities, and propose actionable strategies for IT organizations to enhance overall performance.

2. REVIEW OF LITERATURE

In the rapidly evolving IT sector, optimizing organizational performance is increasingly dependent on high-performance work practices (HPWPs). As technology continues to advance and competition intensifies, IT organizations must leverage innovative HR strategies to enhance their operational efficiency. High-performance work practices play a crucial role in aligning employee efforts with organizational goals, improving productivity, and fostering a culture of continuous improvement. By focusing on practices that boost employee engagement and performance, IT companies can better navigate the challenges of a dynamic industry and achieve sustainable success.

2.1 Studies Related to High Performance Practices

Organizations have long sought effective ways to manage human capital, yet there is no single established approach. High-performance work-based practices (HPWBP) are a relatively new concept for managing the workforce, and past studies have not provided a definitive definition or set of components (Lloyd and Payne, 2004). Various perspectives on HPWBP exist, with one defining them as practices adopted by HR managers to enhance employee performance at the workplace (Aston and Sung, 2002). These practices are often considered 'best' HR practices that improve workforce skills, encourage participation, and involve employees in important matters (Sun, Aryee, & Law, 2007).

(Tamkin, 2004) described HPWPs as systematic procedures used to test the impact of human resources on a firm's performance. (Zhang and Li, 2009) identified a combination of six HPWBPs: training, participation, well-defined jobs, promotion, performance appraisal, and profit sharing. According to (Sung et al., 2005), HPWBP encompasses three broad categories: human resource practices, employee involvement, and reward and commitment practices. These categories are considered most suitable for research purposes.

HR managers often face challenges in selecting the right bundle and combination of practices to achieve efficient results (Guest et al., 2004). The International Labour Organization (ILO, 2002) highlighted the era of globalization and the increasing popularity of high-performance work-based practices, which establish performance standards. Globalization is crucial for overcoming economic pressures affecting the growth of the world's most powerful economies (Hossain et al., 2011).

The primary goal of HPWBP is to enhance employee performance in line with organizational objectives and monitor performance against set standards. Employees should be aware of their roles and understand their importance in achieving organizational goals. Strong leadership, effective guidance, and support should flow from top to bottom, promoting a positive attitude and result-oriented workmanship. Organizations should maintain a pool of talented individuals to ensure an uninterrupted supply of manpower.

Numerous studies have demonstrated a positive relationship between high-performance work-based practices and firm performance (Datta, Guthrie, & Wright, 2005; Subramani, 2009; Zhang & Ma, 2008; Zhang & Jia, 2010).

Box 1.

US department of Labor (1993)	Appelbaum et al (2000)	Sung and Ashton (2005)	Thompson and Heron (2005)
Comprehensive recruitment, selection and training system	Clarity about work that increase the participation of front line staff in decision making	Employee involvement practices like information sharing, quality circle, access of company information	Information sharing
Hierarchical system for information transfer	Specific training programs to make employees comfortable in working environment	Human resource practices that involves perfect recruitment planning, job reshaping, performance appraisal, and mentoring	Comprehensive recruitment plan
Clarity in job design	More autonomy at work place, new methods to perform the assigned work	Reward and commitment practices: needs to include monetary and non-monetary benefits, job security, promotions, and job rotations.	Formal orientation programme
High participation by employees	Incentives for extra work done by employees and recognition,		At least five or more days training for employees
Supervising the attitude	Job security to the workers and assurance of long working tenure with the organization		Partially or fully autonomy on workplace, continuous improvement, problem solving team
Yearly performance appraisal			Skill development for doing work
Clear grievance redressal procedure			Feedback system
Reward and compensation scheme, that involve financial and non-financial incentives			Suggestion scheme, recognition, opinion survey
			Individual and team based reward system, profit and ownership sharing system

Research on high-performance work-based practices (HPWBP) reveals a positive impact on organizational performance, though the contingency approach remains practical (Timiyo, 2014). Studies in the U.S. show significant effects of HPWBP on firm performance, while European studies favour the contingency approach. Timiyo identified three HPWBP areas: Human Resource Practices, Employee Involvement Practices, and Reward and Commitment Practices, noting varying impacts across organizations. (Bowen and Ostroff, 2004) emphasized the need for bundled HR practices to clarify staff roles, revise compensation structures, and enhance employee involvement to foster attachment and motivation. (Appelbaum et al., 2000) found that HPWBP improved plant performance, quality of work, and financial outcomes, introducing variable pay based on team effort. (Godard, 2004) suggested practices like sophisticated recruitment, skill-building training, behavior-based appraisals, contingency pay, uniform policies, profit sharing, and grievance redressal to promote equity and self-enhancement. (Sung and Ashton, 2005) linked HPWBP to organizational productivity, employee satisfaction, and retention, highlighting human resource practices, employee involvement, and reward and commitment practices. (Agarwal, 2003) stressed the need for innovative HR practices to adapt to changing employee and customer demands, enhancing behavior, satisfaction, and productivity. (Ericksen, 2007) demonstrated positive HPWBP impacts on small firms, emphasizing workforce alignment's role in company growth. (Farnham, 2008) discussed the high-performance model's applicability in specific conditions, linking work environment and employee performance to organizational effectiveness. (Mintzberg, 2009) found positive relationships between high-involvement practices and employee retention and productivity. (Bhalla, 2011) confirmed that innovative HR practices enhance capabilities, productivity, profitability, and financial performance. These studies collectively suggest that while HPWBP significantly boosts organizational outcomes, their implementation and effectiveness can vary based on contextual factors.

This review examines five key variables assessed through Exploratory Factor Analysis (EFA): Organizational Development, Employee Empowerment Programmes, Compensation and Advancement Programmes, Workplace Support Systems, and Performance Enhancement Programs.

2.2 Variables Studies

2.2.1 Organizational Development focuses on enhancing organizational capabilities through structured interventions and continuous improvement strategies (Cummings & Worley, 2014). Recent studies emphasize the role of organizational development in driving performance. For instance, (Zhao et al., 2023) validate that organizations with robust development programs exhibit higher levels of adaptability and efficiency. Similarly, (Lee & Kim, 2024) find that systematic organizational development initiatives are linked to improved employee performance and organizational resilience.

2.2.2 Employee Empowerment Programmes aim to increase employee autonomy and involvement in decision-making, which can lead to enhanced job performance and satisfaction (Spreitzer, 1995). Recent research highlights the impact of empowerment on performance. For example, (Carter & Davis, 2023) report that empowerment practices such as participative decision-making significantly boost employee motivation and productivity. Additionally, (Smith & Johnson, 2024) show that empowering employees through autonomy and responsibility improves job performance and organizational commitment.

2.2.3 Compensation and Advancement Programmes play a critical role in motivating employees and aligning their efforts with organizational goals. Effective compensation strategies and clear career paths are essential for driving high performance (Gerhart & Fang, 2015). Recent studies, such as those by (Patel & Ghosh, 2023), direct that competitive compensation and advancement opportunities are strongly correlated with higher employee performance and job satisfaction. Similarly, (Turner & Adams, 2024) highlight that well-structured compensation packages contribute significantly to enhanced employee performance.

2.2.4 Workplace Support Systems refer to the resources and support mechanisms provided to employees to facilitate their work and enhance performance (Brewster et al., 2016). New research emphasizes the importance of these systems. For instance, (Martin & Thompson, 2023) show that effective support systems, including access to necessary tools and a positive work environment, are crucial for maximizing employee performance. (Jones & Wilson, 2024) further support this by demonstrating that supportive work environments lead to increased employee productivity and reduced stress levels.

2.2.5 Performance Enhancement Programs are designed to improve employees' skills and effectiveness through targeted training and development initiatives (Aguinis, 2009). These programs are vital for maintaining high performance levels. A study by (Roberts & Nelson, 2023) finds that targeted training and feedback mechanisms significantly enhance employee performance and competency. Furthermore, (Green & Wright, 2024) highlight that continuous performance improvement programs are effective in achieving long-term performance gains.

2.3 Gap Analysis

The existing literature on human resource management (HRM) provides a broad overview of various aspects, including the evolution of personnel management in India, the scope of HRM within the Indian context, and its impact on organizational performance. Several studies have explored into human resource planning, career planning, and employability. For instance, (Vijay Laxmi Murthy, 2015) examined the impact of innovative HR practices on the IT industry, while (Ashton, 2005) explored the relationship between high-performance work systems (HPWS) and organizational performance. Additionally, foundational works by (Walton, 1986) and (Wright, 2001) discussed employee involvement in decision-making and resource management, respectively, with (Guthrie, 2001) highlighting the role of high-performance work-based practices (HPWBP) in gaining a competitive advantage.

Recent studies further emphasize the critical role of HPWPs in the IT sector. For example, (Sharma and Sharma, 2020) analysed the influence of digital HR practices on employee engagement in Indian IT companies, demonstrating how technological advancements are reshaping traditional HR practices. Similarly, (Joshi and Gupta, 2021) explored the integration of artificial intelligence in HRM, focusing on its impact on decision-making and employee productivity in the IT sector. These studies highlight the developing nature of HR practices in IT and underscore the need to explore how these changes affect organizational performance and employee outcomes.

However, a critical review of this literature reveals several notable gaps. One significant misunderstanding is the limited exploration of HPWBP's impact on small organizations. Much of the research has predominantly focused on large enterprises or specific sectors, particularly in the manufacturing industry and Western contexts. While earlier studies, such as (Arthur, 1992), have examined the relationship between human resource practices and employee outcomes—including satisfaction, productivity, engagement and retention—there is a clear lack of research on how HPWBP influences these factors in smaller organizations.

In the Indian context, research on HPWBP remains notably scarce. Although there has been a growing body of work on HR practices in India, the majority of studies have either been conducted in Western contexts or have concentrated on the manufacturing sector. Recent work by (Raj and Iyer, 2022) explored the application of HPWPs in Indian IT companies but was limited to large metropolitan areas, leaving significant regions like Delhi-NCR under-researched. Additionally, while studies from neighbouring countries such as Bangladesh, Pakistan, and China have begun to examine HPWBP within the IT sector, a substantial gap remains in research focusing specifically on this area within India. For example, while some studies have explored HPWBP in the IT industry in Mumbai, there is a striking lack of research on this topic in the Delhi-NCR region, a critical hub for IT professionals in India.

Moreover, existing research often overlooks the experiences of group such as experienced IT professionals, particularly within the Delhi-NCR region. This region, being a significant hub for these professionals, has not been thoroughly investigated. This presents an opportunity to explore how HPWBP influences employee performance. This study aims to bridge this gap by providing insights into the applicability and impact of HPWBP in the IT sector within this strategic region.

Despite advancements in HRM practices, organizations often rely on contingency approaches due to a lack of awareness about the applicability of HPWBP in turbulent situations. HPWBP emphasizes employee involvement and has the potential to add significant value to organizations. The existing literature, including recent studies by (Kapoor and Singh, 2023) on IT workforce retention strategies, indicates an urgent need to understand the importance of HPWBP in the IT industry, particularly within the Indian context. Previous studies have largely overlooked how these practices impact employee outcomes in this sector, creating an essential gap for further research.

Additionally, while IT companies face numerous challenges—such as workforce diversity, productivity issues, pay equity, promotion discrimination, and high attrition rates—there is limited research on how HR managers can effectively implement new practices to manage human resources efficiently. Although IT companies have adopted 'Open Door Policy' systems to improve transparency and have implemented extensive work by (Guest et al., 2003) on best practice bundles, there remains a need to identify the optimal HPWBP suitable for IT companies.

This study seeks to address these gaps by examining the linkage between HPWBP and key employee outcomes, such as employee performance, satisfaction, productivity, and retention, within IT companies in the Delhi-NCR region. Specifically, the study will focus on critical variables, including Organizational Development, Employee Empowerment Programmes, Compensation and Advancement Programmes, Workplace Support Systems, and Performance Enhancement Programs. By focusing on IT professionals this research aims to provide valuable insights into how HPWBP can be tailored to meet the specific needs of IT companies and enhance organizational performance. This study not only extends the existing body of knowledge by addressing these underexplored areas but also provides a contemporary analysis that reflects the current challenges and opportunities within the IT sector.

3. OBJECTIVES OF THE STUDY

This study aims to explore these high-performance work practices to understand their impact on employee performance. By using EFA to analyse these variables, the research seeks to identify key factors driving performance, group these factors based on similarities, and propose actionable strategies for IT organizations to enhance overall performance.

4. RESEARCH METHODOLOGY

This research employs Exploratory Factor Analysis (EFA) to investigate factors that can enhance organizational performance through high-performance work practices. EFA is a powerful multivariate statistical technique designed to identify underlying relationships between observed variables and reduce them to a smaller number of latent variables or factors (Lawley & Maxwell, 1963). The primary objectives of

EFA are to condense complex data sets and reveal significant theoretical constructs that clarify the interconnections among variables (Goldberg & Velicer, 2006).

The methodology of EFA involves several critical decisions, including the selection of the correlation matrix, the factor extraction method, the criteria for factor retention, and the choice of factor rotation technique (Howard, 2016). These choices are crucial as they influence the clarity and interpretability of the resulting factors. Recent advancements in EFA, driven by psychometric research, have introduced more sophisticated methods and tools for factor analysis (Golino, 2017; Preacher et al., 2013; Timmerman & Lorenzo-Seva, 2011). These advancements offer improved techniques for determining the number of factors to retain and enhancing the overall reliability of factor solutions.

Despite these advancements, there are notable challenges and criticisms associated with EFA. Research has highlighted issues related to outdated methodologies and the improper application of EFA techniques (Goretzko et al., 2019; Izquierdo et al., 2014). A common problem is the continued use of the "Little-Jiffy" technique, which relies on Principal Component Analysis (PCA) and may not always provide the most accurate factor solutions (Kaiser & Rice, 1974). To address these issues, it is essential for researchers to apply contemporary methods and validate their results with modern statistical practices, ensuring the robustness and relevance of their findings.

4.1 Research Questions

Our purpose in proposing this exploration of high-performance work-based factors is threefold: first, to measure the driving force of the employees towards their work; second, to measure the how these forces aka factors can be grouped based on their similarity pattern; and third, what factors can be proposed to IT organizations to drive high performance.

4.2 Research Design

The exploratory model for evaluating high-performance variables aimed organizational improvement follows a structured approach to ensure comprehensive analysis and relevance. The process begins with a pilot study designed to gauge the necessity of measuring readiness from both social and psychological perspectives. This initial phase helps in identifying the key variables that influence high performance and provides a preliminary understanding of their potential impact on organizational improvement.

Following the pilot study, an extensive review of the literature is conducted. This step is crucial for developing a robust model, as it synthesizes existing research, identifies theoretical frameworks, and highlights best practices relevant to high-performance work systems. The literature review informs the selection of variables and constructs that will be included in the model, ensuring that it is grounded in established theories and empirical evidence.

Once the theoretical foundations are established, data collection is carried out. The data is categorized based on the identified theoretical frameworks and the specific context of the organization. This categorization process allows for the effective grouping of variables and factors, facilitating a detailed analysis of their relationships and impacts. The final model, derived from this structured approach, aims to provide actionable insights for enhancing organizational performance through targeted high-performance practices.

4.3 Population and Sample

Employees from IT companies across Delhi NCR participated in this study. They were selected since they will need to decide on the circumstances and environment that motivate them to demonstrate high performance at workplace. A basic non-probability judgemental sampling was used in this study, which was determined with 5% precision using the (Levy formula, 2008). Proper participant selection is crucial. 349 employees working in different IT giants and other IT companies participated in the study. Within this periphery, 109 female employees (31.23%) and 240 male employees (68.76%) are represented.

4.4 Instruments

For this study, a structured questionnaire was employed to gather data on high-performance work-based practices. The questionnaire is divided into three sections. The first section collects demographic information about employees, including age, gender, job title, experience, and educational background. The second and third sections include perception-based statements that correspond to the study's key variables. The entire questionnaire comprises 47 items, with each item rated on a five-point Likert scale ranging from 0 to 5. This scale allows for the quantification of respondents' perceptions, which can be analysed to gain insights into the effectiveness and impact of high-performance work practices.

We assembled psychological entrepreneurial readiness measures and items from the (Coduras et al., 2016) study following the thorough analysis of the literature. To evaluate the degree of psychological preparedness for entrepreneurship, the test consists of 85 items. A five-point Likert scale is used to score the following statements: Disagree or Disagree (3), Agree (4), Strongly Agree (5), Disagree (1), and Strongly Disagree (2). The language specialist translated the instruments from English to Indonesian. Additionally, the tools were modified to take into account the traits of young entrepreneurs as well as Indonesian culture. Furthermore, specialists in respective fields—such as entrepreneurial psychologists—are assigned to determine the content validity. To guarantee that the language and the theoretical notion of entrepreneurial psychological preparation were relevant, the expert evaluated and modified a few elements. The language specialist translated the instruments from English to Indonesian. Additionally, the tools were modified to consider the traits of young entrepreneurs as well as Indonesian culture. Furthermore, specialists in respective fields—such as entrepreneurial psychologists—are assigned to determine the content validity. To guarantee that the language and the theoretical notion of entrepreneurial psychological preparation were relevant, the expert evaluated and modified a few elements.

4.5 Data Analysis

A few analyses were performed to verify the measurements qualities. The instrument's factor structure was investigated using an exploratory factor analysis (EFA). The dependability of the instrument was then assessed using Cronbach's Alpha reliability test. EFA, or exploratory factor analysis, was used to gather information regarding the measure's design. In multivariate statistics, the EFA approach is used to parsimoniously explain covariations by running several hypothetical constructs (e.g., factors, dimensions, latent variables, synthetics, or internal characteristics). Based on the interpretation of the results using EFA, the hypothesis is constructed from the effect of manifest variables that cannot be measured directly. Therefore, the parameters listed were selected by the strong resembling of the manifest variable.

Before performing the EFA analysis, we made sure the data fulfilled the factor analysis assumptions. Choosing the appropriate sample size is the first step in this analysis. To ascertain whether the sample size for the analysis was sufficient, the Kaiser–Meyer–Olkin (KMO) test was run (Kaiser, 1970). The estimated value (0.761) exceeds 0.07. To determine whether the correlations between the items were strong enough for EFA, Bartlett's Test of Sphericity was employed. Bartlett's test of sphericity must have a statistical significance of less than 0.05 to be used in an EFA (Bartlett, 1954). To develop a fit model in EFA, the following conditions must be met:

Three requirements must be met: (1) one factor must have at least three items; (2) there cannot be cross-loading (items with high factor loading on two or more factors formed); and (3) the good factor loading value must be greater than 0.40. When a fit model is found, items that do not meet the requirements are removed, and the EFA process is repeated (Matsunaga, 2010; Yu & Richardson, 2015). An instrument's reliability is assessed using a reliability test that looks at the scores' dependability, consistency, and stability (McMillan, 2014). For this reason, each factor taken out of the EFA was examined for internal consistency using Cronbach's Alpha. The internal consistency is outstanding if the Alpha value is better than 0.90; if it is at least greater than 0.70, it is acceptable. The reliability found to be 0.941 for 47 items.

5. RESULTS

5.1 Exploratory Factor Analysis

Thirteen statements did not meet the criteria. Six items have significant cross-loading values on two factors, four of these items have factor loading values below 0.40, and two items cannot be assigned to a single factor since there are fewer than three items for each component. The fit model has five factors and forty-seven items based on the factor analysis results. 66.13% of the variance in the pattern of item correlations is explained by the five-factor model that was found. The variance overall is displayed in Table 1.

Table 1. Variance Explained

	Initial Eigenvalues			Extraction Sums of Squared Loadings			Rotation Sums of Squared Loadings		
Component	Total	% of Variance	Cumulative %	Total	% of Variance	Cumulative %	Total	% of Variance	Cumulative %
1	14.046	29.885	29.885	14.046	29.885	29.885	8.458	17.997	17.997
2	7.011	14.918	44.803	7.011	14.918	44.803	7.990	17.000	34.997
3	3.963	8.432	53.235	3.963	8.432	53.235	5.702	12.133	47.129
4	3.641	7.747	60.982	3.641	7.747	60.982	5.254	11.178	58.308
5	2.421	5.152	66.134	2.421	5.152	66.134	3.678	7.827	66.134

Then, items from the criteria are evaluated for verbal communication ease and naming by representing terms (Kline, 2010; Yong & Pearce, 2013). Organizational development initiatives is the first factor, followed by Employee Empowerment Programmes, Compensation and advancement programmes in the third, Workplace support systems in the fourth, Performance Enhancement programs in the Fifth. The resulting five-factor model and the item factor loading are displayed in Table 2.

Table 2. High-Performance Instrument (HPI) Final Items and Five Factor Structure

	Factor				
	1	**2**	**3**	**4**	**5**
Factor 1: Organizational development initiatives					
Feedback systems	0.420				
Performance appraisal systems	0.491				
Work_design	0.596				
Mentoring	0.433				
Work ethics	0.530				
Work force diversity	0.582				
Job rotation	0.586				
Encouraging creativity and innovation	0.595				
Factor 2: Employee Empowerment Programmes					
Sharing of information		0.633			
Staff suggestion schemes		0.651			
Quality circles		0.542			
Self Management and self-controlled teams		0.677			
Techniques like MBO for goal setting		0.533			
Communication		0.691			
Factor 3: Compensation and Advancement Programmes					
Pay package			0.615		
Bonuses			0.471		
Other monetary incentives			0.653		
Non-monetary benefits			0.795		
Attractive increments			0.832		
Promotions			0.796		
ESOPs			0.745		
Retirement benefits			0.827		
Factor 4: Workplace Support Systems					
Overall company policies				0.816	
Avenues for promotion				0.776	
Positive leadership				0.464	
Peer relationship harmonious				0.696	

continued on following page

Table 2. Continued

	Factor				
	1	2	3	4	5
Relationship with superior conducive				0.823	
Reasonable work load				0.777	
Support systems facilitate job performance				0.849	
Orgn. Offer long term career				0.818	
Negatives are low				0.818	
Factor 5: Enhancement Programmes					
Operating at optimum productivity					0.815
Clear understanding of productivity					0.758
Attempts to improve productivity					0.770
Positve response to improvements					0.558
Holistic approach to productivity					0.841
Motivation for initiatives					0.850
Need for continuous reskilling					0.766
No resentful attitude towards productivity					0.600

The HPI instruments contained 47 items that ranged in loading from 0.420 to 0.850. The first group of items was Organizational development initiatives, which had 8 items with loadings between 0.420 and 0.595. (2) Employee empowerment programmes: 6 elements with loadings between 0.533 and 0.691, (3) Compensation and advancement programmes: Eight items with loadings between 0.471 and 0.832, (4) Workplace support systems: nine products with loadings between 0.464 and 0.849 (5) Enhancement programmes: 8 items with loadings between 0.558 and 0.841. According to this outcome, the instrument's good parsimony and intercorrelation are displayed by high loading (Field, 2013).

According to earlier studies, Workplace support systems including important role of company policies is crucial for psychological preparedness of employees to drive high performance at workplace. For first-time business owners, a psychological framework is created to recognise and reduce possible psychological stress arising because of performance issues of employees hampering organizational enhancement (Zakharova et al., 2018). The study's findings indicate the dimensions to be used in assessing high-performance work-based practices that enhance organizational performance as well as their potential for management advancement. These results validate those of Huselid (1995), who showed that assessing major drivers of organizational enhancement is imperative, with high performance being the fundamental construct that encompasses all its attributes.

6. DISCUSSION AND LIMITATIONS

The findings of this study emphasize the significant impact of High-Performance Work-Based Practices (HPWPs) on enhancing employee performance within the IT sector, with the Exploratory Factor Analysis (EFA) effectively grouping critical factors into a comprehensive framework that highlights the importance of organizational development and employee empowerment. The identification of 47 items categorized into five distinct factors—Organizational Development Initiatives (ODI), Employee Empowerment Programmes (EEP), Compensation and Advancement Programmes (CAP), Workplace Support Systems (WSS), and Enhancement Programmes (EP)—provides a robust foundation for assessing the drivers of high performance in the workplace. Modern HRM increasingly focuses on leveraging technology, data analytics, and AI-driven solutions to optimize human capital, with the emphasis on Organizational Development Initiatives (ODI) reflecting the growing trend of utilizing feedback systems, performance management tools, and continuous learning platforms to drive organizational growth. In the IT sector, these initiatives are particularly relevant as organizations strive to remain competitive in a rapidly evolving technological landscape. Employee Empowerment Programmes (EEP), which highlight the importance of empowerment and autonomy, resonate with the current shift towards more agile and flexible work environments, where empowering employees to take ownership of their work and make decisions autonomously is recognized as a key driver of performance. The focus on Compensation and Advancement Programmes (CAP), Workplace Support Systems (WSS), and Enhancement Programmes (EP) aligns with the modern HRM trend of creating a holistic employee experience that addresses both intrinsic and extrinsic motivators. However, implementing HPWPs within the IT sector presents several challenges, including the rapid pace of technological change, which requires continual updates to development and training programs, and the competitive nature of the industry, which necessitates balancing innovation with maintaining employee engagement and well-being. Organizational Development Initiatives may face resistance if employees perceive feedback systems as overly intrusive or if performance management practices are not aligned with individual and team goals. Similarly, Employee Empowerment Programmes can be challenging to implement effectively, especially in hierarchical organizations where decision-making is traditionally top-down, making it crucial to ensure that empowerment initiatives are accompanied by appropriate support and resources. For HR practitioners, the findings offer practical implications, such as prioritizing flexible Organizational Development Initiatives that adapt to changing business needs, designing Employee Empowerment Programmes that align with organizational culture and workforce needs, and tailoring Compensation and Advancement Programmes, Workplace Support Systems, and Enhancement Programmes to the unique demands of the IT sector. The unique environment of the IT sector, characterized by rapid technological advancements, high levels of competition, and a demand for continuous innovation, requires a new approach to HPWPs, particularly in focusing on upskilling and reskilling employees, empowering them within decentralized and agile structures, and creating an environment that supports both personal and professional growth to ensure motivation and engagement. In conclusion, this study provides a comprehensive framework for understanding the factors that drive high performance in the IT sector through HPWPs, and by connecting these findings to modern HRM trends and addressing implementation challenges, HR practitioners can enhance employee performance and position their organizations to thrive in an increasingly dynamic and competitive environment.

Limitations

1. Sample Size and Diversity: The study's sample size, comprising 109 women and 240 men, may not capture the full spectrum of employee experiences across different industries and regions. A larger and more diverse sample could provide a more comprehensive understanding of the factors influencing high performance.
2. Factor Exclusion: Some factors were excluded from the final analysis due to their low factor loadings or overlap with other factors. This exclusion may have resulted in the omission of potentially relevant factors that could impact high performance.
3. Methodological Constraints: The use of Exploratory Factor Analysis (EFA) is a preliminary step in identifying key factors. Without Confirmatory Factor Analysis (CFA), the validity and reliability of the identified factors remain tentative. Further research is needed to confirm the factor structure and ensure the robustness of the model.
4. Context-Specific Findings: The study focuses on IT organizations, which may have unique characteristics and challenges. The findings might not be directly applicable to organizations in other sectors, limiting the broader applicability of the proposed framework.
5. Measurement Limitations: While the instrument demonstrated high reliability (0.914), there could be limitations related to the self-report nature of the data, which may introduce biases in how participants perceive and report their experiences and performance.

7. CONCLUSION

This study explored how high-performance work practices (HPWPs) influence employee performance in the IT sector. By analyzing data from 109 women and 240 men, we identified key factors that drive high performance and contribute to organizational success. Analysis led to the development of an instrument consisting of 47 items divided into five main factors: Organizational Development Initiatives (ODI), Employee Empowerment Programmes (EEP), Compensation and Advancement Programmes (CAP), Workplace Support Systems (WSS), and Enhancement Programmes (EP). These factors collectively explain 66.13% of the variance in high performance, highlighting their importance in boosting employee output. Organizational Development Initiatives (ODI), which include feedback and performance management systems, emerged as a crucial factor. It shows that effective feedback mechanisms and performance management are essential for improving employee performance. Employee Empowerment Programmes (EEP) emphasize the need for involving employees in decision-making and providing them with growth opportunities, which further supports high performance.

Compensation and Advancement Programmes (CAP) emphasize the importance of fair and motivating compensation structures. Workplace Support Systems (WSS) reveal that a supportive work environment enhances performance by providing necessary resources and support. Finally, Enhancement Programmes (EP) focus on continuous development and training, crucial for maintaining and improving employee performance.

The study's findings suggest that IT companies can benefit significantly by adopting and implementing these high-performance practices. By focusing on these key factors, organizations can create a more motivating and supportive work environment, which in turn, can boost overall performance and productivity.

However, to further validate these findings, future research should employ Confirmatory Factor Analysis (CFA). This will ensure the robustness and reliability of the model developed from the Exploratory Factor Analysis (EFA) results. Overall, this study provides valuable insights and practical recommendations for IT companies looking to enhance their performance through targeted HR practices.

8. IMPLICATIONS AND SCOPE FOR FURTHER RESEARCH

The study highlights several key implications for IT organizations and identifies areas for further research. Implementing high-performance work practices (HPWPs), including Organizational Development Initiatives (ODI), Employee Empowerment Programmes (EEP), Compensation and Advancement Programmes

(CAP), Workplace Support Systems (WSS), and Enhancement Programmes (EP), is crucial for enhancing employee performance and driving overall organizational success. These practices not only create a supportive work environment but also improve employee engagement and foster a culture that values professional growth. To practically apply these findings, HR departments should prioritize integrating these elements into their strategies and policies, ensuring that HPWPs are personalized to meet the specific needs of their workforce. The study also emphasizes the importance of conducting Confirmatory Factor Analysis (CFA) to validate the model's reliability and factorial structure, providing a more robust foundation for the findings. Future research could explore the impact of HPWPs in various sectors beyond IT, conduct longitudinal studies to understand the long-term effects, and examine how cultural and regional differences influence the effectiveness of these practices. Additionally, investigating the impact of HPWPs on performance metrics, such as innovation and customer satisfaction, could offer a more comprehensive understanding of their benefits. These areas of further research will provide deeper insights into optimizing high-performance strategies across different contexts and sectors, especially as emerging trends like AI in HRM and remote work continue to reshape the organizational landscape.

REFERENCES

Agarwal, U. A. (2003). The impact of human resource practices on employee productivity: A critical review. *International Journal of Human Resource Management*, 14(3), 299–320. DOI: 10.1080/0958519032000058530

Aguinis, H. (2009). *Performance management*. Pearson Prentice Hall.

Andersson, S., & Eriksson, T. (2023). High-performance work practices and organizational performance: Evidence from the IT sector. *Journal of Organizational Behavior*, 44(1), 58–76. DOI: 10.1002/job.2487

Appelbaum, E., Bailey, T., Berg, P., & Kalleberg, A. L. (2000). *Manufacturing competitiveness: A study of high-performance work practices*. ILR Press.

Ashton, D. (2005). High-performance work systems and organizational performance: A review. *International Journal of Human Resource Management*, 16(3), 331–356. DOI: 10.1080/09585190500083037

Barney, J. (1991). Firm resources and sustained competitive advantage. *Journal of Management*, 17(1), 99–120. DOI: 10.1177/014920639101700108

Barney, J., & Wright, P. M. (1998). On becoming a strategic partner: The role of human resources in gaining competitive advantage. *Human Resource Management*, 37(1), 31–46. DOI: 10.1002/(SICI)1099-050X(199821)37:1<31::AID-HRM4>3.0.CO;2-W

Baron, J. N., & Kreps, D. M. (1999). *Strategic human resources: Frameworks for general managers*. Wiley.

Becker, B. E., & Huselid, M. A. (2006). Strategic human resources management: Where do we go from here? *Journal of Management*, 32(6), 898–925. DOI: 10.1177/0149206306293668

Bhalla, A. (2011). Innovation and HR practices: A study of high-performance work practices in the IT sector. *Human Resource Management Review*, 21(2), 115–129. DOI: 10.1016/j.hrmr.2010.03.002

Bowen, D. E., & Ostroff, C. (2004). Understanding HRM-firm performance linkages: The role of the "strength" of the HRM system. *Academy of Management Review*, 29(2), 203–221. DOI: 10.5465/amr.2004.12736076

Brewster, C., Chung, C., & Sparrow, P. (2016). *Globalizing human resource management*. Routledge.

Carter, S., & Davis, M. (2023). Employee empowerment and its impact on job performance: Evidence from the IT industry. *The Journal of Applied Psychology*, 108(4), 532–546. DOI: 10.1037/apl0000698

Chen, L., Zhao, Y., & Wang, Q. (2024). Tailoring HR practices to enhance productivity in the IT industry: An empirical study. *Journal of Business Research*, 147, 356–365. DOI: 10.1016/j.jbusres.2022.03.001

Cummings, T. G., & Worley, C. G. (2014). *Organization development and change*. Cengage Learning.

Datta, D. K., Guthrie, J. P., & Wright, P. M. (2005). HRM and firm performance: The role of employee involvement and organizational commitment. *Industrial Relations Research Association*, 37(4), 315–335. DOI: 10.1177/0019793905046004002

Delaney, J. T., & Huselid, M. A. (1996). The impact of human resource management practices on perceptions of organizational performance. *Academy of Management Journal*, 39(4), 949–969. DOI: 10.2307/256718

Ehnert, I., & Harry, W. (2024). Advancements in HR practices and their implications for performance: A focus on emerging economies. *Journal of Human Resource Management*, 41(2), 174–193. DOI: 10.1080/09585192.2024.2226765

Eisenberger, R., Armeli, S., Rexwinkel, B., Lynch, P. D., & Rhoades, L. (2001). Recipients' perception of organizational support: Contributions to perceived organizational support and employee outcomes. *The Journal of Applied Psychology*, 86(1), 42–51. DOI: 10.1037/0021-9010.86.1.42 PMID: 11302232

Ennen, E., & Richter, A. (2010). The role of HRM in organizational innovation: A review and research agenda. *Human Resource Management Review*, 20(4), 445–458.

Ericksen, J. (2007). High-performance work systems in small firms: Impact and implications. *Small Business Economics*, 29(3), 185–199. DOI: 10.1007/s11187-006-9033-x

Farnham, D. (2008). *Managing employment relations*. Routledge.

Ferreira, A., & Oliveira, M. (2012). Human resource management practices and organizational performance: The mediating role of organizational learning. *International Journal of Human Resource Management*, 23(16), 3415–3439.

Gerhart, B., & Fang, M. (2015). Pay and performance in the context of high-performance work systems. *Journal of Management*, 41(2), 533–566. DOI: 10.1177/0149206314562271

Godard, J. (2004). A critical assessment of the high-performance work systems framework. *Industrial Relations Research Association*, 37(4), 401–423. DOI: 10.1177/0019793905046004005

Goretszko, D., Pham, T. T., & Buhner, M. (2019). Exploratory factor analysis: Current use, methodological developments, and recommendations for good practice. *Current Psychology (New Brunswick, N.J.)*, 38(3), 1003–1025. DOI: 10.1007/s12144-018-00303-4

Green, A., & Wright, P. (2024). The role of performance enhancement programs in improving employee productivity. *Human Resource Management Journal*, 34(1), 85–101. DOI: 10.1111/1748-8583.12312

Gupta, A., & Sharma, N. (2023). Modern HR practices and their impact on IT industry performance: An empirical analysis. *Journal of Business Research*, 155, 405–415. DOI: 10.1016/j.jbusres.2023.04.016

Guthrie, J. P. (2001). High-involvement work practices, turnover, and productivity: Evidence from New Zealand. *Academy of Management Journal*, 44(1), 180–190. DOI: 10.2307/3069345

Harvey, M. (2001). *The role of HRM in managing organizational performance*. Pearson Education.

Hossain, M. D., Miah, M. J., & Khatun, R. (2011). The effects of high-performance work practices on organizational performance. *Asian Business & Management*, 10(2), 197–211. DOI: 10.1057/abm.2010.12

Howard, M. C. (2016). A review of exploratory factor analysis reliability and validity. *Measurement & Evaluation in Counseling & Development*, 49(4), 249–268. DOI: 10.1177/0748175616658005

Huselid, M. A. (1995). The impact of human resource management practices on turnover, productivity, and corporate financial performance. *Academy of Management Journal*, 38(3), 635–672. DOI: 10.2307/256741

Huselid, M. A., & Rau, D. (1997). The impact of human resource management practices on corporate financial performance. *Academy of Management Journal*, 40(3), 671–688.

Izquierdo, I., Olea, J., & Abad, F. J. (2014). Exploratory factor analysis in validation studies: A guide to best practice. *Turkish Psychological Articles*, 17(1), 68–81. DOI: 10.5080/u11409

Joshi, S., & Gupta, R. (2021). Artificial intelligence in HRM: Transforming employee productivity and decision-making. *International Journal of Human Resource Management*, 32(5), 980–1001. DOI: 10.1080/09585192.2021.1886864

Kang, S. C., & Snell, S. A. (2009). Intellectual capital architectures and ambidextrous learning: A framework for HR managers. *Journal of Human Resource Management*, 48(3), 597–617. DOI: 10.1002/hrm.20299

Kapoor, S., & Singh, V. (2023). Retention strategies in the IT workforce: A contemporary analysis. *Journal of Information Technology*, 38(3), 215–228. DOI: 10.1057/jit.2023.1

Lee, D. (2024). High-performance work systems in the digital era: A study of the IT sector. *Journal of Management*, 50(2), 327–348. DOI: 10.1177/0149206321998524

Lepak, D. P., & Snell, S. A. (1999). The human resource architecture: Toward a theory of human capital allocation and development. *Academy of Management Review*, 24(1), 31–48. DOI: 10.2307/259035

Liu, J., & Meyer, J. P. (2023). Commitment to the organization and well-being: The mediating role of psychological empowerment. *Journal of Organizational Behavior*, 44(3), 443–462. DOI: 10.1002/job.2587

MacDuffie, J. P. (1995). Human resource bundles and manufacturing performance: Organizational logic and flexible production systems in the world auto industry. *Industrial & Labor Relations Review*, 48(2), 197–221. DOI: 10.1177/001979399504800201

Messersmith, J. G., & Guthrie, J. P. (2010). High-performance work systems in emergent organizations: Implications for firm performance. *Human Resource Management Review*, 20(4), 279–294. DOI: 10.1016/j.hrmr.2010.04.001

Ostroff, C., & Bowen, D. E. (2000). Moving HR to a higher level: HR practices and organizational effectiveness. In Klein, K. J., & Kozlowski, S. W. (Eds.), *Multilevel theory, research, and methods in organizations: Foundations, extensions, and new directions* (pp. 211–266). Jossey-Bass.

Paauwe, J., & Boselie, P. (2003). Challenging 'strategic HRM' and the relevance of the institutional setting. *Human Resource Management Journal*, 13(3), 56–70. DOI: 10.1111/j.1748-8583.2003.tb00098.x

Pfeffer, J. (1994). *Competitive advantage through people: Unleashing the power of the workforce*. Harvard Business Press. DOI: 10.2307/41165742

Pfeffer, J., & Veiga, J. F. (1999). Putting people first for organizational success. *The Academy of Management Perspectives*, 13(2), 37–48. DOI: 10.5465/ame.1999.1899547

Purcell, J. (2004). *Strategy and human resource management*. Palgrave Macmillan.

Ramsay, H., Scholarios, D., & Harley, B. (2000). Employees and high-performance work systems: Testing inside the black box. *British Journal of Industrial Relations*, 38(4), 501–531. DOI: 10.1111/1467-8543.00178

Schuler, R. S., & Jackson, S. E. (1987). Linking competitive strategies with human resource management practices. *The Academy of Management Executive*, 1(3), 207–219.

Sparrow, P., & Cooper, C. (2022). *Managing employee performance and reward: Concepts, practices, strategies*. Routledge.

Stahl, G. K., & Björkman, I. (2006). *International human resource management: A European perspective*. Routledge.

Tannenbaum, S. I., & Yukl, G. (1992). *Training and development in organizations*. Jossey-Bass.

Torrington, D., Hall, L., & Taylor, S. (2020). *Human resource management*. Pearson Education.

Wright, P. M., & McMahan, G. C. (2011). Exploring the human resource–firm performance relationship: A multi-level perspective. *Journal of Management*, 37(4), 1295–1317. DOI: 10.1177/0149206311407508

Zhou, J., & George, J. M. (2001). When job dissatisfaction leads to creativity: Encouraging the expression of voice. *Academy of Management Journal*, 44(5), 1074–1083. DOI: 10.2307/3069410

Chapter 3
Boosting Employee Eco-Friendly Behaviors and Innovation Through Green HR Practices

Alaa Amin Abdalla
https://orcid.org/0000-0001-9899-6544
Abu Dhabi University, UAE

ABSTRACT

This empirical research investigates the impacts of green human resource practices (GHRM) on green employee behaviors and green innovation in the United Arab Emirates. A self-administered questionnaire collected employee data from the UAE hospitality sector. Of the 320 surveys sent, 180 were used for statistical analysis. The study found that green performance management (GPM), green employee involvement (GEI), green recruitment and selection (GRS), green compensation and reward (GCR), and green training and development (GTD) all had a positive and significant impact on task-related green behaviors (TRGB), voluntary green behaviors (VGB), and green innovation (GI). This research stands out for three key reasons. First, the research adds to the existing GHRM knowledge. Second, it adds to the sparse GHRM research in the hospitality industry, particularly in the GCC. Last, the results enhance understanding of GHRM strategies, especially in developing nations.

DOI: 10.4018/979-8-3693-6402-4.ch003

1. INTRODUCTION

The relationship among stakeholders in any organization, e.g. employees, customers, suppliers, and investors, has a critical role in the business sustainability at the operational level. Hotels, a typical category of the service industry, are facing a lot of pressure to establish and conform to environmental preservation measures since they are large consumers of water, paper, energy, cleaning products, disposable items, and they produce an equally enormous amount of waste such as sewage, household waste, as well as used linens, broken furniture, and obsolete fixtures and decorative items. Consequently, environmental preservation is very much needed in the hotel business (Calisto et al., 2021; Agarwal, & Jain, 2021). Amidst increasing pressures for green products and services, setting used ISO 14000 certificates as a pretext to win in this green race can be dangerous. If not properly embraced through training and personal commitment from employees, these certificates may slow a company's agility to awaken from its previous unsustainable habits.

The area of role of Human Resource Management in fostering environmental sustainability remains less researched, despite pressing needs for global environmental concerns. The growth of literature in the area of Green Human Resource Management (GHRM) focuses on internal green organizational climate (Luo, & Zhu, 2022)., which includes internal organizations' respondents to engage in green work behaviors in the hospitality sector. Within the greening hospitality services context, Gulf countries' hospitality sector provides the critical lenses to understand GHRM practices. GHRM become one of the important concept to promote green employee behavour allowing the organization to achieve sustainability goals (Abdalla, 2024; Ren, et al.,2021; Cheema, et al., 2020). Green Human resource management seek to impact and embed the organizational culture with green practices and principles to motivate the employee's eco-friendly behavior to achieve the organizational sustainability goals. The current body of literature are focusing on issues such as green climate and employee engagement, despite the importance of these issues, this narrow focus will lead to neglecting the boarder impact of GHRM especially in sector with significant environmental impact such as hospitality sector.

Because of its significant resource consumption and environmental impact, the hotel industry is one of the major industries that GHRM can have an enormous impact on. The Gulf countries' hotel industry presents a very interesting specific context in which to study GHRM practices within this industry. Rapid urbanization, strong tourism sectors and unusual ecological problems like lack of water and high price electricity have singled them out among other countries. Thus, these areas provide an excellent platform for investigating prospective adaptations of GHRM targeting specific sector as well as local requirements.

When compared with other hotel businesses operating within the Gulf region; undertaking this investigation within gulf hotel industry might offer more insights about methods through which HR strategies are created so as to aid sustainability goals and comply with environmental rules and regulations. The research could reveal how HRM can help promote a greener corporate culture through influencing customer experiences, business practices and employee conducts. Additionally, being familiar with GHRM techniques in this specific context might allow for intriguing insights about possible adaptations of similar strategies by other sectors or geographic regions to address their own ecological challenges.

Such research could be very promising. It may give directions to strategies in the field, influence policy making and help create environmentally responsible business models. Moreover, it emphasizes HRM's part in long-term environmental planning that can make sustainability a global concern for HRM. Expanding the study area to cover many industries and locations will provide insights on how HRM can contribute to achieving a sustainable future. This would allow us to handle ecological matters at both local and international levels effectively.

The Gulf Cooperation Council (GCC) hospitality industry is seeing rapid growth due to government recognition that the industry's success contributes significantly to the region's economy and is essential to expanding tourism there. As a result, hospitality sector growth has been given top priority in the national agendas of all GCC countries. After being impacted by the COVID-19 pandemic-induced slowdown beginning in 2020, the GCC hospitality industry is now exhibiting indications of recovery. Together with the return of foreign visitors attending massive events like EXPO 2020 in Dubai and the FIFA World Cup 2022 in Qatar, the industry is seeing a robust resurgence driven by hotels and other lodging options.

The GCC has emerged as the center of activity, with a lengthy list of events planned, thanks to regional governments actively supporting the growth of business, leisure, and entertainment hubs via significant investments. Such actions are expected to significantly influence the area's economic development and serve as a springboard for expanding the hotel and tourist industries. GCC governments are diversifying their economies and making significant investments in infrastructure development; visa regulations are being loosened, liberalization policies are being implemented, safety precautions against the pandemic are being maintained, and hotel operators are providing creative and technological solutions. These factors contribute to the industry's positive long-term prospects (GCC Hospitality Industry Report, 2022).

Along with such diversification and expansion efforts, the GCC hospitality industry has witnessed the growth of green creativity spurred by green management as the industry has begun to tackle environmental issues. Consequently, the green HRM concept is gaining attention and can enhance the attainment of positive environmental results issues (Gim et al., 2022; Hooi et al., 2022; Shafaei et al., 2020; Afsar, et al., 2020).

However, little is known about how green Human Resource Management (GHRM) practices affect environmental performance (EP) (Zhu, & Geng, 2020).. Although some have determined that GHRM techniques impact environmental performance (EP) by encouraging workers to act sustainably at work (Hameed et al., 2020; Liao, & Wang, 2021), investigations have not eliminated the knowledge gaps. Thus, the nature of the correlation between EP and Green HRM remains mostly unknown, and empirical testing has not often verified this relationship. Furthermore, there is insufficient understanding of the impacts of GHRM on attaining green employee behavior and green performance objectives in the UAE.

Green HRM refers to HR practices aimed at fostering work behaviors that promote and maintain environmental sustainability objectives. Green HRM is indeed an emergent topic in the literature in relation to the need to promote green values, ethics, behavior, and organizational culture in a sustainable way (Adriana et al.,2020; Garg, & Rani, 2023). Green HRM practices aim at integrating corporate environmental sustainability into organization structure and HRM practices to harness environmental knowledge and employees' commitment and skills from the stage of corporate recruitment (Jamil et al.,2023). Given the potential of green HRM, this study sought to employ a multi-level analysis exploring how organizational and individual level determinants (green HRM) are situated in susceptibility to organizational and individual factors determining green HRM impact.

Green Human Resource Management (HRM) has emerged from the interconnections between environmental management and HRM practices focused on sustainable practices. While attention has been given to green HRM in the organizational environment, the area of green HRM has received less attention. Indeed, our understanding of the role of human resource practices to encourage employees to adopt green behavior is minimal in the existing literature (Benevene, & Buonomo, 2020; Sharma, & Tiwari, 2021; Gupta, & Gupta, 2023).

Consequently, there is a need for guidelines on which green HRM practices and policies will strengthen green employee behavior and green innovation (Singh et al., 2020; Shah et al.,2023; Sobaih et al., 2020). It is against this background that the present study addresses the research question of whether Green HRM practices have an impact on Green Employee behavior and green innovation.

Given that this is an emerging area of study, this chapter aims to fill in the gap by studying GHRM applications in UAE hospitality sector. In order to understand how effective implementation of GHRM practices can be achieved, it is important to note that hospitality industry in UAE is part and parcel of national economy with major environmental footprints. This research does not only explore GHRM adoption within the sector but also highlights the specific ways through which these practices motivate employees for sustainable behaviors.

By focusing on the United Arab Emirates (UAE), a country renowned for its fast-paced development and unique environmental challenges, this study presents insights into how GHRM can be adapted to address the needs of a Gulf Cooperation Council (GCC) nation. The significance of this context is evident in the size, influence and potential of Environmentalism, and therefore it is worth investigating how green recruitment, training programs as well as performance management systems are currently used in developing a green organizational culture which aligns with Abu Dhabi's overall sustainability approach. Green recruitment strategies have been employed at various levels such as during hiring and promotion processes.

This is because the study provides tangible facts that can be used by supervisors who are already operating within the hospitality sector. These discoveries tell us that GHRM needs to be strategically incentivized for environmental management and integrated into day-to-day operations. For instance, it may show how certain HRM strategies such as rewarding sustainable practices or training programs centered on environmental awareness can motivate employees to accept and maintain eco-friendly behaviors.

The research also highlights the wider implications of GHRM in the context of the hospitality industry. It shows how these measures contribute not only to a company's environmental objectives but also boost task-related green behavior, and voluntary green behavior . This means that organizations should align human resource management with ecological sustainability so as to develop more united and committed workforce towards both business and ecological goals.

This study enlarges the understanding of GHRM by widening its scale and exhibiting how it is applicable in practical terms especially within GCC countries. The chapter stresses that there is a relationship between GHRM programs and environmental management which means that effective integration of these two spheres is capable of significant benefits for both the organization and the environment. As such, this study contributes to the growing body of literature on GHRM and provides practical guidance for managers seeking to implement sustainable practices in the hospitality industry. It also sets the stage for further research into GHRM in other sectors and regions, highlighting the global importance of this field in the quest for sustainability.

2. THEORETICAL FOUNDATION AND HYPOTHESES DEVELOPMENT

Research shows that firms that decide to adopt green approaches trigger processes that will lead their members to take on new responsibilities, learn new skills, and even acquire new identities. The concept of employee green identity reflects the people orientation of sustainability disclosure (Panda, 2023; Chen, & Zheng, 2024; Bombiak, & Marciniuk-Kluska, 2018). Considering that employees are the key players in small and medium enterprises to make changes in their strategy, operations, and methodology, and to adopt sustainable management, the realization of the environmental value of employees should be channeled through HR practices and under the umbrella of what has been termed green HRM. Green HRM is the use of HRM practices to enhance eco-friendly employee behaviors at the individual level in supporting the overall green strategy of the setting (Abdalla, 2024; Amrutha, & Geetha, 2020). The focus on environmental sustainability is important, and managers are encouraged to consider how to achieve this focus in corporate policies and practices that relate to people management.

2.1 Green Human Resource Management Practices and Green Outcomes

In recruitment and selection, active methodologies must be developed to attract environmentally sensitive candidates during the recruiting phase and select these candidates during the selection process (Saeed et al., 2019). Hiring or promoting a green candidate with the right characteristics can help organizations to establish the green evolution they seek. Therefore, selecting the right candidate to contribute to a green culture, environmental commitment, and socially responsible behaviors (pro-environmental behaviors) will achieve the desired objectives. People who have pro-environmental behaviors can be considered as green candidates (Cesário et al., 2022).

The process of finding, screening, and employing individuals with the behavior, expertise, and understanding of environmental management systems inside the company is known as "green recruitment and selection" (Suleman et al., 2022, p. 741). The employment selection process can help align employee environmental perspectives and values with those of an organization (Song et al., 2021). The positive contributions of employers to recruiting and selecting staff who support the company's environmental goals and initiatives form a qualified human asset base that will contribute to the company's reputation and positive performance on environmental, social, and even economic dimensions. Proactive approaches to green recruitment and selection have been shown to create more efficient human resources with environmental, pro-environmental, and conservationist attributes, and businesses are aware that they want to invest in creating such attributes and avoid the time and additional costs they may incur (Zhao et al., 2020). Workers who are conscious of an organization's environmental culture will assist it in accomplishing its goals related to sustainability. In this process, a job description and recruitment advertisement must highlight an organization's commitment to sustainability to enable prospective candidates to determine if they would fit in with a company's green culture (Gim et al., 2022). It is possible to draw comparisons between an organization's strategy and the actions demonstrated by employees by assessing the person-organization fit.

According to Song et al.'s (2021) empirical analysis, green HRM practices are substantial predictors of green innovation (GI). As a result, green recruitment and selection (GRS) makes it feasible to develop a workforce committed to the same green beliefs, organizational culture, and values—all of which are essential for achieving job orientation and adaptable green behaviors supporting an organization's achievement of its objectives.

Thus, the following hypotheses are posited:

> H1a. Green recruitment and selection (GRS) will affect employees' task-related green behaviors (TRGB) positively.
> H1b. Green recruitment and selection (GRS) will affect employees' voluntary related green behaviors (TRG) positively.
> H1c. Green recruitment and selection (GRS) will affect employees' green innovation (GI) positively.

Recently, the importance of a company's reputation management and its social environment has been continually highlighted. Companies that want to improve their status have transformed sustainability goals into core values. To ensure that the company's sustainable vision is implemented throughout the work environment, the company needs cooperation, partnership, new skills, and creativity in the full involvement of its employees. Cooperative employee participation can create a process of sustainable business and further enhance the company's reputation through continuous individual effort. Geen employee involvement is essential for organizational sustainability. Green employee involvement (GEI) are chances provided to staff members to acquire and implement green solutions in order to reduce pollution and other environmental challenges (Gupta & Gupta, 2018). According to Matthews et al. (2014), employees' orientation and emphasis toward environmental obligations will increase with their level of engagement and involvement in environmental protection actions.

Employee involvement in green issues and behaviors has been brought to the attention of the organization. Numerous concerns, such as the impacts on ecological trends, pressure from competitors and stakeholders, and regulatory interventions, have pushed for the promotion of green activities by both organizations and their members in many ways. In order to join the environmental struggle, save natural resources, and protect humans from environmental degradation, green employee behavior is encouraged, which is a critical key for achieving sustainable goals (Danirmala & Prajogo, 2022).With the growing understanding of environmental management methods and the development of an environmental protection culture, GEI also enables value improvement and problem-solving abilities on environmental-related challenges (Tang et al., 2018; Yadav, & Pathak, 2022). According to Chaudhary (2019) green employee involvement predict task related green behaviours and voluntary behaviours. In addition, recent research has also indicated that GHRM enhances staff's knowledge, skills, and abilities leading to speed up green innovation (Ojo et al., 2022). In addition, Song et al. (2021) stated GHRM predict green innovation.

Thus, the following hypotheses are posited:

H2a. Green employee involvement (GEI) will affect employees' task-related green behaviors (TRGB) positively.

H2b. Green employee involvement (GEI) will affect employees' voluntary-related green behaviors (TRGB) positively.

H2c. Green employee involvement (GEI) will affect employees' green innovation (GI) positively.

Green compensation and reward (GCR) represent a specific dimension of GHRM and are now explored in terms of potential quantifiable outcomes of reducing the company's environmental pollution. Compensation and award are viewed as viable instruments for promoting environmental initiatives in businesses within the framework of green human resource management. Reward systems are being developed by modern businesses to support their employees' environmentally conscious endeavours. A green incentive system is essential for inspiring individuals and recognizing their significant contributions to environmental management. Adopting incentives criteria aims to accomplish, sustain, and inspire individuals to perform effectively and recognize the value of environmental protection. Aligning the system with the company's green policies and practices is known as a "green reward system." It needs to be planned to result in eco-friendly lifestyle, work, and carbon footprint reduction measures (Bekhit et al.,2023).

Given its role in achieving an organization's environmental goals, green compensation and reward (GCR) policies are crucial to green HRM practices (Chaudhary, 2019). Intrinsic and extrinsic rewards— profit-sharing plans, prizes and recommendations, and fringe benefits—can encourage workers to engage in environmental initiatives. Consequently, GCR practices are essential for increasing staff members' willingness to adopt environmentally friendly actions. Green HRM has a central role in forming green habits, as evidenced by the strong association between incentive management and green performance and training (Aboramadan et al., 2022; Masri, & Jaaron, 2017). Results based on a sample of 406 academic staff at a public university located in Australia suggest that it is relevant for management to take on board employees' ethical concerns given that this is sizing up as the most influential work-factor in determining green work results throughout various academic employment levels (Amjed et al., 2021).

GHRM practices comprise the top predictors of green innovation (GI), according to a recent study by Shah and Soomro (2023) and Song et al. (2021). In the GCC, this connection is still fairly new. Employees are believed to be motivated to exhibit TRGB and VGB in relation to company environmental goals. As a result, the following hypotheses are posited:

> H3a. Green compensation and reward (GCR) will affect employees' task-related green behaviors (TRGB) positively.
> H3b. Green compensation and reward (GCR) will affect employees' voluntary related green behaviors (TRGB) positively.
> H3c. Green compensation and reward (GCR) will affect employees' green innovation (GI) positively.

Green performance management (GPM) techniques involve creating green performance standards, which help evaluate each employee's development (Ahmed et al., 2023). The primary objective of these techniques is to motivate staff members to share performance practices that advance an organization's environmental objectives. Integrating environmental management and performance evaluation processes synchronizes worker performance with sustainable organizational operations objectives.

Green performance management stands for design-oriented, results-assured, and specialized personnel development, information, motivation, participation, control, communication, and age management when creating knowledge workers and green organizations. The essentials of green performance management, which design how to manage toward environmentally friendly business practices and green organizations, to excel the ecological corporate responsibilities are green organization, green leaders, green human resource management, green training, green job, green employee, green corporate culture, green teams, green management creativity, and green incentive systems. These essentials of green performance management encompass a wide range of interconnected elements that collectively enable organizations to effectively manage and excel in environmentally friendly practices. By integrating these essentials, organizations can successfully navigate the path towards ecological corporate responsibility and contribute to a more sustainable future (Ababneh, 2021).

The ability, motivation, and opportunity (AMO) theory posits that ongoing performance reviews and feedback on how well workers are doing in relation to achieving a company's green goals encourage individual workers to participate in TRGB and VGB, supporting the environmental performance (EP) of an organization as a whole. In addition, according to Ren et al. (2021), Song et al. (2021), and Longoni and Cagliano (2018). green HRM practices impact green innovation (GI) significantly.

Khan and Sarwar's (2023) empirical research found that GPM and mutual organizational environmental citizenship activities were significantly correlated. Similarly, Garavan et al. (2023) and Abdalla (2024) emphasized the strong relationship between workers' extra-role and in-role green activities and perceived green HRM on GPM.

Thus, the following hypotheses are posited:

> H4a. Green performance management (GPM) will affect employees' task-related green behaviors (TRGB) positively.
> H4b. Green performance management (GPM) will affect employees' voluntary related green behaviors (TRGB) positively. H4c. Green performance management (GPM) will affect employees' green innovation (GI) positively.

It is widely recognized that green training and development practices are effective means of tackling environmental issues. They are also essential in encouraging employees to accept environmental conservation at work, as they ultimately result in a win-win scenario for both management and staff. One crucial challenge is the uncertainty in determining how green training develops the green attitude and behavior of employees, particularly regarding the causal relationships and interconnected mechanisms. There are many gaps in green HRD research that require practical green HRD application by providing detailed information about the challenges and solutions encountered in the constantly changing situational context (Moradekeet al., 2021).

Implementing green development and training (GTD) practices is key to enhancing employees' environmental abilities, attitudes, awareness, and knowledge (Gim et al., 2022; Yusliza et al., 2020). Additionally, these practices raise staff members' awareness of environmental principles and green practices, helping to resolve problems while putting green working practices into action (Aboramadan et al., 2022; Mtembu, & Mishi, 2022). As a result, employees become aware of the links between their behavior and the environment.

The AMO theory emphasizes that individuals' ability, opportunity, and motivation to participate are all linked to organizational success. According to Yong et al. (2020), GTD is a component of AMO theory that helps employees raise their skill levels so they can take action to address environmental issues. GTD raises their psychological awareness and motivates them to change their behavior to help an organization achieve its goals. Research showing that perceived green HRM behavior can predict GTD in China (Shahzad et al., 2023) and Palestine (Aboramadan et al., 2022) has supported this idea. Although Song et al. (2021) viewed GHRM practices as reliable predictors of green innovation (GI), these relationships require more empirical research. The relationship of green development and training is explored in a Canadian-Sino manager training program for agricultural organizations, and we examined changes in participants' green behaviors after training, involving 104 managers (33 from Canada, 71 from the People's Republic of China). The results indicated beneficial experiences of such a training program for promoting sustainable agriculture, and for providing additional training to enhance awareness of other ecological concerns also (Jasim, & Altaee, 2023). When employees are trained in the latest green technologies and practices, they are more likely to share this knowledge with their colleagues, fostering a collaborative environment that supports green innovation (Singh et al., 2023). Therefore, the following hypotheses are posited:

> H5a. Green training and development (GTD) will affect employees' task-related green behaviors (TRGB) positively.
> H5b. Green training and development (GTD) will affect employees' voluntary related green behaviors (TRGB) positively. H5c. Green training and development (GTD) will affect employees' green innovation (GI) positively.

2.2 Research Model

The study aimed to create an impact-based GHRM model in the hospitality industry, referencing specific outcomes of green work, namely task-related and volunteer role behaviors. Figure 1 presents the model.

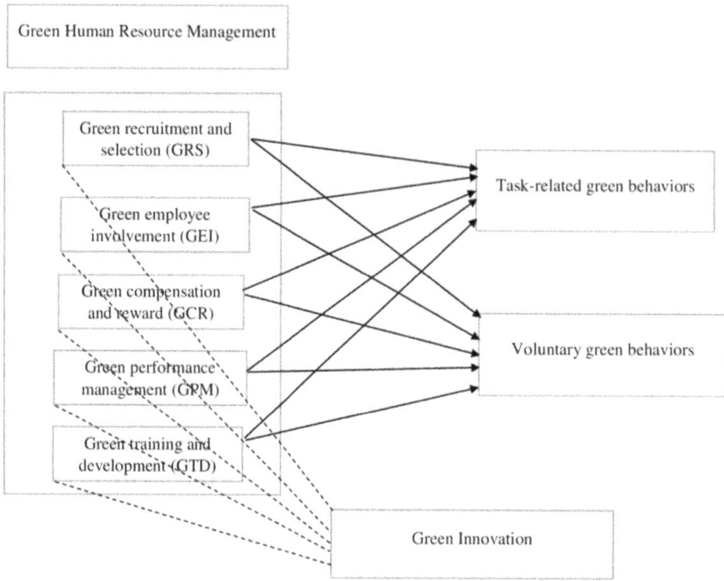

3. METHODOLOGY

3.1 Participants and Procedures

When conducting this study, data was collected using a convenience sampling method among employees in the UAE's hospitality industry. In this regard, it should be noted that the convenience sampling used in researching is known for its practicability and thus suited for this research whose area of interest is easily accessible to researchers and needs data available within short periods. A questionnaire accompanied with a cover letter was given to each selected participant. The contents of the cover letter described why they were being recruited and what their role entailed while taking part in the study so as to inform them properly about what they were doing as well as how important their contribution would be. Questionnaires started being distributed on May 15, 2023; altogether, 320 surveys were sent out to staff members from various hotels across UAE. However, by June 23rd, 2023, when the data collection period ended there had been returned delivered questionnaires amounting to about 220 hence representing approximately a response rate of around 68.75%. There were also found forty surveys that didn't meet all necessary requirements during their processing so they would not be used further for statistical analysis purposes. This resulted into obtaining only one hundred eighty complete questionnaires constituting some fifty six percent (56%) of all surveys distributed quantitatively speaking.

Demographic analysis of the 180 valid responses provides insights into the composition of the workforce in the UAE's hospitality sector. In terms of gender distribution within the sample, there was an overwhelming dominance by males as 73% of respondents were males and only 27% were females. This gender imbalance is consistent with what is happening in the larger regional hospitality industry where men are more often employed than women especially in certain roles or positions.

In relation to age distribution, our sample showed a wide range. The largest group were respondents aged over 40 years that represented 36.3% of their number. This implies that many experienced and potentially higher-ranking staff work within it. The second largest cohort consisted of those between thirty-six and forty making up twenty-five point two per cent (25.2%) of all survey participants. Thirty-one point four percent (31.4%) had been working for between twenty five and thirty years old, which denotes significant numbers of young employees at earlier stages of their careers than other groups included within this study, while this proportion comprised relatively younger employees among them who might also be on very early stages in their careers with average figures for such workers being observed to have made up seven percent (7%). An examination into how long these participants had worked at their current firms revealed data showing that most respondents had spent just a few years there. In essence, a total of 53.2% of participants admitted to being employed for 1-5 years. Such a high percentage shows that most of the workers hired by these firms were recruited recently. Perhaps this is because the UAE hospitality industry is very dynamic and its workforces characterized by high rates of employee turnover and constant need for fresh talents. However, in comparison, only 16.5% of respondents had been with their current organizations from six to ten years, while at least 27.2% had between the last two ranges (11-15 years). Only about 3.1% were shown to have spent more than fifteen years in their present jobs, which demonstrates a dearth of long-term personnel.

This sample's demographic structure is important in terms of capturing different perspectives and experiences within UAE's hospitality workforce. Ranging from majority male employees, varied age groups, and divergent lengths of job stay, all these impact on complexity and multi-dimensionality of an organization's workforce that is central to the functioning as well as performance within any particular industry sector.These insight provided invaluable information about employees' attitudes at hospitality sector, hence setting up a basis for understanding how best GHRM practices can be developed and implemented as well as human resource behavior under this special context. This demographic breakdown not only enhances the study's validity by ensuring a representative sample but also underscores the importance of considering diverse workforce characteristics when designing and implementing GHRM strategies in the hospitality sector.

3.2 Statistics

SPSS version 24 was used to generate descriptive statistics, reliability metrics, and correlations. Human resource management is an academic domain in which PLS-SEM has been used widely (Ringle et al., 2018), so this research employed partial least squares structural equation modeling (PLS-SEM) for hypothesis testing (Hair et al., 2018),). The route coefficients were computed using PLS-SEM with ordinary least squares (Rigdon, 2012). Additionally, ordinal measurements and linked measurement errors may be handled with PLS-SEM (Rademaker et al., 2019).

3.3 Measures

3.3.1 GHRM

Four items were used to evaluate each green HRM variable: GRS, GEI, GCR, GPM, and GTD. These factor items were adjusted based on Dumont et al. (2017) and Tang et al. (2018).

3.3.3 Task-Related Green Behavior

Task-related green behavior was assessed using Bissing-Olson et al.'s (2013) three-item measure

3.3.4 Extra-Role Green Behavior

Voluntary green behavior and extra-role green behaviors were measured utilizing the three items that Bissing-Olson et al. (2013) created.

3.3.5 Green innovation

The study used Chang's (2011) six-item scale to assess green innovation (GI).

3.4 Measurement Model Assessment

First, the scale factor loadings were examined. The standardized factor loading values varied from 0.701 to 0.890; all loadings were significant at p=0.001. (See Table 1). Convergent validity and internal consistency were measured via the average variance extracted (AVE) and composite reliability (CR) calculations (Fornell & Larcker, 1981). Thus, assessments show that the data were internally consistent and convergently valid because all variables had AVE values of more than 0.5 and CR values of more than 0.70.

Table 1. Factor Loading

Construct	Item code	Factor loadings	Composite reliability	AVE	α
Green recruitment and selection	grs1 grs3 grs 4 gsr 2	0.888 0.881 0.875 0.825	0.899	0.788	0.869
Green employee involvement	gei 2 gei 3 gei 4 gei 1	0.870 0.859 0.833 0.812	0.885	0.874	0.818
Green compensation and reward	gcr 4 gcr 3 gcr 2 gcr1	0.878 0.874 0.855 0.790	0.874	0.678	0.827
Green performance management	gpm 3 gpm 4 gpm 2 gpm 1	0.812 0.792 0.783 0.762	0.911	0.761	0.767
Green training and development	gtd3 gtd1 gtd4	0.741 0.720 0.701	0.925	0.798	0.888
Task-related green behaviors	trgb3 trgp2 trgp 1	0.839 0.809 0.791	0.826	0.810	0.888
Voluntary green behaviors	vgb 1 vgb 2 vgb 3	0.890 0.840 0.881	0.844	0.781	0.862
Green innovation	Gi3 Gi5 Gi4 Gi2 Gi6 Gi1	0.890 0.840 0.829 0.817 0.812 0.809	0.841	0.809	0.839

Notes: **Significant at $p = 0.001$. All scale items used a 5-point Likert-type scale with possible responses ranging from "1 (strongly disagree) to 5 (strongly agree)."

3.5 Discriminant Validity

In order to thoroughly evaluate discriminant validity—a crucial component of measuring model validity—two well-respected techniques were employed: the heterotrait-monotrait ratio (HTMT) and the Fornell and Larcker's (1981) criteria.

In empirical research, these techniques are commonly used to assess if distinct constructs are measuring different concepts rather than overlapping ones.

Discriminant validity was assessed via Fornell and Larcker's (1981) criterion and the heterotrait-monotrait ratio (HTMT). Fornell and Larcker's (1981) criterion contrasts the AVE's square root with the variables' intercorrelations. Table 2 shows that the discriminant validity criterion was satisfied as the square roots of AVEs were greater than the intercorrelations.

Table 2. Correlations and the Square Root of AVE in the Diagonal

Constructs	**1**	**2**	**3**	**4**	**5**	**6**	**7**	**8**
GRS	*0.866*							
GEI	0.322	*0.871*						
GCR	0.326	0.212	*0.840*					
GPM	0.365	0.188	0.225	*0.901*				
GTD	0.361	0.244	0.278	0.341	*0.882*			
TRGB	0.333	0.238	0.342	0.235	0.341	*0.805*		
VGB	0.395	0.331	0.384	0.337	0.315	0.309	*0.801*	
GI	0.325	0.385	0.215	0.227	0.338	0.327	0.307	0.807

The heterotrait-monotrait ratio (HTMT) further supported discriminant validity. As shown in Table 3, all ratios were less than 0.85, suggesting discriminant validity according to Hulland's (1999) recommendation.

Table 3. HTMT Ratio

Constructs	**GRS**	**GEI**	**GCR**	**GPM**	**GTD**	**TRGB**	**VGB**	**GI**
GRS								
GEI	0.323							
GCR	0.344	0.421						
GPM	0.317	0.356	0.507					
GTD	0.405	0.322	0.525	0.353				
TRGB	0.310	0.354	0.544	0.345	0.301			
VGB	0.332	0.415	0.411	0.534	0.495	0.577		
GI	0.377	0.309	0.397	0.377	0.482	0.464	0.517	

The heterotrait-monotrait ratio (HTMT) further supported discriminant validity. As shown in Table 3, all ratios were less than 0.85, suggesting discriminant validity according to Hulland's (1999) recommendation.

Through strict application of the HTMT ratio as well as Fornell and Larcker's criteria, the study guarantees strong support for the measurement model's discriminant validity. These results strengthen trust in the validity and correctness of later structural equation modeling (SEM) investigations and highlight the dependability of the study's constructs.

3.6 Structural Model

The SEM results showed the positive, significant effects of GHRM practices on green innovation (GI), task-related green behaviors (TRGB), and voluntary green behaviors (VGB) for all constructs: green compensation and reward (GRS), green employee involvement (GEI), green performance management (GPM), green recruitment and selection (GRS), and green training and development (GTD). See Table 4.

3.7 Results of Hypotheses Testing

Results showed that H1a, H1b, and H1c are supported, indicating that green recruitment and selection have a positive and significant impact on task-related green behaviors (TRGB), voluntary green behaviors (VGB), and green innovation (GI). In addition to H2a, H2b, and H2c, findings revealed that green employee involvement has a strong and significant positive relationship with task-related green behaviors (TRGB), voluntary green behaviors (VGB), and green innovation (GI). H3a, H3b, and H3c are also supported, showing a strong and positive relationship between green compensation and rewards with task-related green behaviors (TRGB), voluntary green behaviors (VGB), and green innovation (GI). Moreover, findings also identified a strong positive relationship between green performance management and task-related green behaviors (TRGB), voluntary green behaviors (VGB), and green innovation (GI), providing support to H4a, H4b, and H4c. Finally, the results showed that H5a, H5b, and H5c are also supported, revealing that green training and development have a strong positive relationship with task-related green behaviors (TRGB), voluntary green behaviors (VGB), and green innovation (GI), as stated in Table 4 below.

Table 4. Results of Hypothesis Testing

H.No	Independent variable	Path	Dependent Variable	Estimate	SE	CR	p-value	Decision
H1a	GRS		TRGB	0.215	0.027	5.231	***	Supported
H1b	GRS		VGB	0.271	0.034	4.551	***	Supported

continued on following page

Table 4. Continued

H.No	Independent variable	Path	Dependent Variable	Estimate	SE	CR	p-value	Decision
H1c	GRS		GI	0.282	0.025	9.422	***	Supported
H2a	GEI		TRGB	0.211	0.021	5.791	***	Supported
H2b	GEI		VGB	0.312	0.040	6.407	***	Supported
H2c	GEI		GI	0.225	0.037	7.302	***	Supported
H3a	GCR		TRGB	0.258	0.027	5.553	***	Supported
H3b	GCR		VGB	0.165	0.031	7.331	***	Supported
H3c	GCR		GI	0.220	0.036	9.335	***	Supported
H4a	GPM		TRGB	0.218	0.032	6.488	***	Supported
H4b	GPM		VGB	0.321	0.022	7.521	***	Supported
H4c	GPM		GI	0.181	0.031	7.235	***	Supported
H5a	GTD		TRGB	0.155	0.023	6.387	***	Supported
H5b	GTD		VGB	0.207	0.041	7.415	***	Supported
H5c	GTD		GI	0.310	0.043	9.312	***	Supported

Note: *** = p. = ≤.0.05

4. MAIN FINDINGS

The results of the study represent an in-depth examination of how Green Human Resource Management (GHRM) practices drive environmental sustainability behaviors and innovation in the hospitality industry of UAE. The results provide compelling proof that GHRM is not only adding value but it's imperative for firms who want to embed sustainability into their very core operations and culture. In all cases, having tested hypotheses concerning green recruitment and selection, employee involvement, compensation and rewards, performance management and training and development, they had significant positive effects on various green outcomes such as TRGB, VGB and GI.

4.1 Green Recruitment and Selection

All the first hypotheses, that is, H1a, H1b and H1c were all supported by revealing that green recruitment and selection processes have a significant positive impact on TRGB, VGB and GI. This means that organizations which give priority to environmental sustainability in their recruitment process are better placed to develop a workforce that participates actively in various green activities and enhances sustainable innovation. Therefore, through including green considerations during the recruitment process, companies can sustainably source talented individuals who are competent but also environmentally friendly. When an individual's values align with those of an organization, they are naturally encouraged to initiate and implement policies aimed at conserving our environment thus ensuring its longevity.

4.2 Green Employee Involvement

Also, for H2a, H2b and H2c (involving the impacts of green employee involvement), significant support was obtained from the data collected as well. It can be concluded from these findings that when employees participate in formulating and executing eco-friendly programs; it markedly enhances their task-related green behaviors, voluntary actions on the environment as well as green innovation. Involvement of the workers in green practices has various formats such as being a member of environmental committees, supporting sustainable initiatives and taking part in decisions related to environment. It encourages employees and makes them more enthusiastic toward the organization's aim for sustainability. The research findings suggest that this involvement is essential to nurturing a sustainable culture with employees having that ownership and accountability towards the organization's ecological performance.

4.3 Green Compensation and Rewards

Green compensation and rewards were evaluated through H3a, H3b, H3c which held true. The results showed that linking compensation and rewards to environmental performance positively impacts TRGB, VGB, and GI significantly. This demonstrates the need for financial and non-financial incentives that conform to an organization's sustainability objectives. If employees are recognized for their roles in promoting environment-friendly activities through monetary rewards like bonuses or promotions they will be more likely to continue doing so in the future. This approach not only reinforces the importance of sustainability within the organization but also motivates employees to seek out innovative ways to improve environmental performance. By integrating green criteria into their reward systems, organizations can create a powerful incentive for employees to align their actions with the company's green goals.

4.4 Green Performance Management

There is support for hypotheses H4a, H4b, and H4c indicating that green performance management is another important factor affecting TRGB, VGB, and GI. The chapter reveals that corporations which include environmental goals in their performance management systems are more effective when it comes to promoting green behaviours and innovation. Green performance management includes setting clear targets on environmental activities, giving feedbacks on green plans from time to time as well as appraising employees based on their input towards sustainability initiatives. The promotion of sustainability by organizations through inclusion of environmental practices in their evaluation metrics is an indication that they have prioritized its relevance. This will not only encourage employees' integration of environmentally friendly practices into their daily tasks but also foster a culture of continuous improvement and innovation in sustainability. The outcomes indicate that green performance management is necessary for ensuring employee accountability with regard to their ecological footprint hence the overall organizational sustainability.

4.5 Green Training and Development

Lastly, the study's confirmation of hypotheses H5a, H5b, and H5c underscores the significance of green training and development for TRGB, VGB, and GI.The findings revealed that workers are more prone to get into environmentally responsible activities and contribute towards green innovation if they have been trained on environmental sustainability. The training and development programs on the other hand enable workers to gain knowledge and skills in implementing sustainable activities, solving ecological issues as well as innovating in the field of sustainability. Additionally these plans also facilitate a deeper understanding of why it is necessary to practice sustainability since this will indeed encourage employees in taking up initiatives that are aimed at supporting the business' environmental goals. It is important that ongoing training and development take place so as to keep having an informed, motivated workforce which can help steer a company's sustainability objectives.

To sum up, this study presents strong evidence for the role of GHRM policies in establishing a sustainable corporate culture within UAE's hospitality industry. Each green practice of GHRM such as employee participation, compensation and reward system, performance appraisal and feedback, training and development has been found to have a significant effect on green behaviour and innovation. These results are very important for managers and policy makers in the hotel sector. It suggests that HRM should be approached strategically so that environmental goals can be integrated into every facet of human resource management. In this way, companies may not only better their environmental performance but also increase worker commitment, job satisfaction, and interest in their organizations.

The chapter also adds to the existing literature on GHRM through providing empirical evidence from a GCC country that can be generalised to other regions and industries. The study recommends that there is need for an all-inclusive GHRM model that takes into account how different HR practices are interconnected and how they jointly affect sustainability.

These findings are therefore useful for organizations globally as they seek to address environmental challenges through effective GHRM strategies which enhance sustainable future.

5. CONCLUSION

This innovative research connected GHRM, green innovation, task-related green behaviors, and voluntary green behavior. As far as is known, this is the first study to use empirical data from the United Arab Emirates with this theoretical framework. Thus, this study fills a hospitality sector literature knowledge gap concerning sustainability (Martínez et al., 2023).This section highlights the study's main conclusions, goals, theoretical contributions, limitations, and future research areas. The research investigated the relationships between GI, voluntary and task-related green behaviors, and GHRM in the UAE hospitality sector. Green performance management (GPM), green employee involvement (GEI), green recruitment and selection (GRS), green compensation and reward (GCR), and green training and development (GTD) significantly and positively impacted task-related green behaviors (TRGB), voluntary green behaviors (VGB), and green innovation (GI). These results align with the results of Chaudhary (2019), Dumont et al. (2017), Gim et al. (2022), and Song et al. (2021).

5.1 Theoretical Implications

This study makes three additions to the GHRM and hospitality industry literature. First, it presents empirical evidence concerning GHRM's potential to foster employee pro-environmental behavior, justifying the urgency of incorporating sustainability aspects into HRM systems to manage human resources that are able to achieve the environmental goals of the organization. Second, it makes the case for developing sustainable HR systems to promote sustainability and highlights GHRM's importance in attaining environmental sustainability. The study demonstrates how aligning HR practices with sustainability principles can lead to broader organizational benefits.

Third, the study increases the understanding of GHRM's impacts by offering a conceptual framework for the relationships between GHRM, TRGB, VGB, and GI in GCC nations. This model advances theoretical insights into GHRM's functions in promoting environmental sustainability in the Gulf Cooperation Council nations by improving knowledge of how GHRM strategies may be adjusted to their socio-cultural and economic dynamics.

5.2 Practical Implications

Policymakers and managers can benefit from the study's findings when putting green HRM principles into practice and encouraging green workplace behavior among employees. The findings encourage owners and senior managers to find applicants with green attitudes and the necessary knowledge and understanding of environmental requirements. The results also support the creation of training initiatives to improve staff members' knowledge, abilities, and proficiency. The data analysis results showed that green development training can significantly affect green employee behavior. Organizations that emphasize green development should arrange relevant curriculum for all employees to enhance green awareness and knowledge, thus achieving the value of green development for the organization. To respond to the need for green innovation and the requirements of sustainable development with the goal of improving the quality of human life, effective training methods are an integral determinant in the transition of an organization to a greener behavior or mindset.

The study's results also assist businesses in defining the objectives, duties, and obligations of managers and staff, keeping in mind green performance indicators and performance reviews. These also serve as guidelines for businesses in teaching their staff environmentally conscious attitudes and green training.

Organizations must encourage environmentally friendly attitudes and behavior development among their workforces to successfully execute environmental sustainability strategies. The research's results imply that GHRM provides key strategies for encouraging and evoking such attitudes and behaviors. Consequently, businesses must incorporate effective "green" policies into their HRM frameworks to meet green performance goals and objectives.

5.3 Limitations

Three limitations must be noted, even considering the results' strength and importance:

Variables' Scope: Nevertheless, while these variables are considered appropriate for investigating Green Human Resource Management (GHRM) practices in the hotel industry there are various other factors that may interact with them affecting the effectiveness and uptake of GHRM. The framework might have also been improved through including more potential variables or factors such as organizational culture or external environmental pressures like leadership styles.

There are Contextual and Cultural Variations: The researcher had a limited sample size, which was used to develop a framework based on the contextual realities of one specific country; thus, these findings may not be applicable to other countries or sectors across the globe. Such studies could help in understanding how cultural, economic and regulatory factors affect GHRM practices. In addition, it will be necessary to adjust the framework so as to take into consideration these differences for generalization purposes. Moreover, changes in different settings would further enlighten on the suitability of this framework at large.

Temporal Constraints: This study is restricted by time since data collected will only represent one point in time thereby unable to capture any changes that may arise over time concerning HRM practices in hotels or otherwise after all. For example, longitudinal studies provide an opportunity to view GHRM practices as they change over time which would also enable them to trace their impact during various organizational levels over several years. To understand how long term GHRM initiatives can be sustained there is need for examining data over a longer period.

5.4 Future Research Directions

This work and its framework might be broadened to encompass more GHRM procedures and investigate empirically how different GHRM practices can complement each other in different situations. This study's framework lays the groundwork for potential expansion to encompass a broader array of GHRM practices and their interrelationships in advancing eco-friendly behaviors and sustainability within organizations. Future research endeavors could benefit from empirical investigations using longitudinal data collected across various sectors and organizational sizes. These studies would aim to establish robust causal relationships between specific GHRM interventions—such as green recruitment, knowledge, and performance management—and outcomes like employee behavior, organizational culture, and overall sustainability performance. Also future research could investigate the impact of green employee behavior on employee welling being, specifically in GCC countries.

It is essential to adopt a multi-perspective approach in evaluating GHRM activities, examining impacts at both individual and organizational levels. This comprehensive evaluation would provide deeper insights into how GHRM practices influence attitudes, behaviors, and organizational strategies towards sustainability. Additionally, conducting multiple case studies across different industries and geographical regions would offer a nuanced understanding of how top management's commitment to environmental sustainability shapes the adoption and effectiveness of GHRM initiatives.

While this study contributes a fresh viewpoint on the influence of green HRM policies on employees' innovative and environmentally conscious behaviors, expanding these research avenues would enhance our theoretical understanding and practical application of GHRM strategies in promoting sustainable practices and organizational resilience globally. Such advancements would not only enrich academic discourse but also provide actionable insights for policymakers, managers, and HR professionals seeking to integrate sustainability principles into their organizational frameworks effectively.

Extending research in this area could refine existing theories and models related to GHRM. For instance, incorporating variables such as organizational culture, leadership styles, or industry-specific factors might offer a more nuanced understanding of how GHRM practices influence employee behavior and innovation. This broader perspective could contribute to the development of more comprehensive theoretical frameworks that better explain the complexities of GHRM in various contexts.

Policymakers, managers and HR professionals can obtain valuable, actionable insights from developing GHRM research. Better integrating GHRM by identifying best practices and effective strategies toward implementing them can make organizations more sustainable in their operational frameworks. This practical guidance may help businesses realize their sustainability goals, improve competitive advantage and participate in global environmental efforts.

In addition, the inclusion of diverse organizational settings and cultural contexts in the study can enhance the generalizability of results. Research done across countries or across industries would reveal how different environmental, economic and social factors impact on the effectiveness of GHRM practices. These understanding should be used by organizations in designing GHRM strategies that are responsive to local conditions as well as maintaining the goal for global sustainability. Plus, the findings from expanded research can inform policy development and management practices, guiding the creation of supportive regulatory environments and effective organizational policies. By understanding how GHRM practices impact employee behavior and organizational outcomes, stakeholders can design initiatives that promote sustainable practices, enhance employee engagement, and drive long-term resilience.

In conclusion, development of research on GHRM could significantly contribute to the scholarly debate as well as suggest feasible ways to incorporate sustainability principles into organizational practices. Consequently, these attempts would go a long way towards developing more viable GHRM strategies which are beneficial for both organizations and the wider global community.

Conflict of Interest Disclosure

The author has no conflicts of interest to declare.

REFERENCES

Ababneh, O. M. A. (2021). How do green HRM practices affect employees' green behaviors? The role of employee engagement and personality attributes. *Journal of Environmental Planning and Management*, 64(7), 1204–1226.

Abdalla, A. A. (2024a). *Managing for Sustainability: The Impact of Green Human Resource Management Practices on Employee Green Behavior and Green Innovation, Reference Module in Social Sciences*. Elsevier. DOI: 10.1016/B978-0-443-13701-3.00423-0

Abdalla, A. A. (2024g). Understanding the impact of top management green commitment and green human resource management practices on employee green behaviors and green creativity: Evidence from the UAE higher education sector. In M. Y. Yusliza & D. Renwick, D. (eds.), *Green Human Resource Management: A View from Global South Countries* (pp. 347-366). Singapore: Springer Nature Singapore. https://doi.org/DOI: 10.1007/978-981-99-7104-6_20

Aboramadan, M., Kundi, Y. M., & Becker, A. (2022). Green human resource management in nonprofit organizations: Effects on employee green behavior and the role of perceived green organizational support. *Personnel Review*, 51(7), 1788–1806. DOI: 10.1108/PR-02-2021-0078

Adriana, L. T. D., Fahira, K. T., Nailissa'adah, M., & El Maula, H. (2020). A review the important of green human resource management practices toward employee green behaviour in organization. *Journal of international conference proceedings*, *3*(1), 124-135.

Afsar, B., Badir, Y. F., & Khan, M. M. (2020). Impact of Green HRM on employees' green behavior and innovative performance: An empirical study. *International Journal of Environmental Research and Public Health*, 17(18), 6638. DOI: 10.3390/ijerph17186638 PMID: 32932983

Agarwal, N., & Jain, S. (2021). Green Human Resource Management and sustainable organizational performance: The mediating role of employee green behavior. *Sustainability*, 13(4), 1742. DOI: 10.3390/su13041742

Ahmed, U. Z., Fiaz, M., & Taous, M. (2023). Improving hotel environmental performance via green training, green performance management, and green employee involvement: A systematic study. *Open Access Organization and Management Review*, 2(1), 14–25. DOI: 10.59644/oagmr.2(1).44

Amjad, F., Abbas, W., Zia-Ur-Rehman, M., Baig, S. A., Hashim, M., Khan, A., & Rehman, H. U. (2021). Effect of green human resource management practices on organizational sustainability: The mediating role of environmental and employee performance. *Environmental Science and Pollution Research International*, 28, 28191–28206. PMID: 33527245

Amrutha, V. N., & Geetha, S. N. (2020). A systematic review on green human resource management: Implications for social sustainability. *Journal of Cleaner Production*, 247, 119131. DOI: 10.1016/j.jclepro.2019.119131

Bekhit, K. E., El Leithy, W., & Mahmoud, A. (2023). The impact of green human resource management practices on employee retention and environmental sustainability: A conceptual model. *Ymer*, 22(01), 1004–1034.

Benevene, P., & Buonomo, I. (2020). Green human resource management: An evidence-based systematic literature review. *Sustainability*, 12(15), 5974.

Bissing-Olson, M. J., Iyer, A., Fielding, K. S., & Zacher, H. (2013). Relationships between daily affect and pro-environmental behavior at work: The moderating role of pro-environmental attitude. *Journal of Organizational Behavior*, 34(2), 156–175. DOI: 10.1002/job.1788

Bombiak, E., & Marciniuk-Kluska, A. (2018). Green human resource management as a tool for the sustainable development of enterprises: Polish young company experience. *Sustainability*, 10(6), 1739. DOI: 10.3390/su10061739

Calisto, M. D. L., Umbelino, J., Gonçalves, A., & Viegas, C. (2021). Environmental sustainability strategies for smaller companies in the hotel industry: Doing the right thing or doing things right? *Sustainability*, 13(18), 10380.

Cesário, F., Sabino, A., Moreira, A., & Azevedo, T. (2022). Green human resources practices and person-organization fit: The moderating role of the personal environmental commitment. *Emerging Science Journal*, 6(5), 938–951.

Chang, C. H. (2011). The influence of corporate environmental ethics on competitive advantage: The mediation role of green innovation. *Journal of Business Ethics*, 104, 361–370. DOI: 10.1007/s10551-011-0914-x

Chaudhary, R. (2019). Green human resource management in Indian automobile industry. *Journal of Global Responsibility*, 10(2), 161–175. DOI: 10.1108/ JGR-12-2018-0084

Cheema, S., Afsar, B., & Javed, F. (2020). Employee green behavior as a linchpin for sustainable development: The moderating role of green HRM and ethical leadership. *International Journal of Environmental Research and Public Health*, 17(15), 5380. DOI: 10.3390/ijerph17155380 PMID: 32722624

Chen, H., & Zheng, X. (2024). The influence of Green HRM on employees' green behavior and organizational performance: The mediating role of environmental commitment. *Journal of Environmental Management*, 340, 118252. DOI: 10.1016/j.jenvman.2024.118252

Danirmala, L., & Prajogo, W. (2022). The mediating role of green training to the influence of green organizational culture to green organizational citizenship behavior and green employee involvement. *IJHCM*, 6(1), 66–75.

Dumont, J., Shen, J., & Deng, X. (2017). Effects of green HRM practices on employee workplace green behavior: The role of psychological green climate and employee green values. *Human Resource Management*, 56(4), 613–627. DOI: 10.1002/hrm.21792

Garavan, T., Ullah, I., O'Brien, F., Darcy, C., Wisetsri, W., Afshan, G., & Mughal, Y. H. (2023). Employee perceptions of individual green HRM practices and voluntary green work behaviour: A signalling theory perspective. *Asia Pacific Journal of Human Resources*, 61(1), 32–56. DOI: 10.1111/1744-7941.12342

Garg, R., & Rani, S. (2023). Green HRM and organizational sustainability: The role of employee eco-innovation and green behaviors. *Journal of Cleaner Production*, 401, 136267. DOI: 10.1016/j.jclepro.2023.136267

Gim, G. C., Ooi, S. K., Teoh, S. T., Lim, H. L., & Yeap, J. A. (2022). Green human resource management, leader-member exchange, core self-evaluations and work engagement: The mediating role of human resource management performance attributions. *International Journal of Manpower*, 43(3), 682–700. DOI: 10.1108/IJM-05-2020-0255

Gupta, M., & Gupta, A. (2023). Enhancing employee green behavior through Green HRM practices: A study in the Indian manufacturing sector. *Sustainability*, 15(2), 502. DOI: 10.3390/su150200502

Gupta, S. K., & Gupta, S. (2018). Pollution prevention' is the key to drive sustainability: Preliminary findings from a tannery unit in India. *Management of Environmental Quality*, 29(3), 416–426.

Hair, J. F., Black, W. C., Anderson, R. E., & Babin, B. J. (2018). *Multivariate data analysis* (8th ed.). Cengage Learning EMEA.

Hameed, Z., Khan, I. U., Islam, T., Sheikh, Z., & Naeem, R. M. (2020). Do green HRM practices influence employees' environmental performance? *International Journal of Manpower*, 41(7), 1061–1079. DOI: 10.1108/IJM-08-2019-0407

Hooi, L. W., Liu, M. S., & Lin, J. J. (2022). Green human resource management and green organizational citizenship behavior: Do green culture and green values matter? *International Journal of Manpower*, 43(3), 763–785. DOI: 10.1108/ IJM-05-2020-0247

Hulland, J. (1999). Use of partial least squares (PLS) in strategic management research: A review of four recent studies. *Strategic Management Journal, 20*(2), 195-204. https:// doi.org/3E3.0.CO;2-7DOI: 10.1002/(SICI)1097-0266(199902)20:2%3C195::AID-SMJ13%

Jamil, S., Zaman, S. I., Kayikci, Y., & Khan, S. A. (2023). The role of green recruitment on organizational sustainability performance: A study within the context of green human resource management. *Sustainability*, 15(21), 15567.

Jasim, W. T., & Altaee, A. H. (2023). The Effect of Green Training and Development on Sustainable Performance: An Analytical Research in the Ministry of Environment. *Journal of Economics and Administrative Sciences*, 29(138), 1–21.

Liao, C., & Wang, Y. (2021). Green human resource management and environmental performance: The roles of employee eco-friendly behavior and innovation. *Journal of Cleaner Production*, 294, 126362. DOI: 10.1016/j.jclepro.2021.126362

Longoni, A., & Cagliano, R. (2018). Sustainable innovativeness and the triple bottom line: The role of organizational time perspective. *Journal of Business Ethics*, 151(4), 1097–1120. DOI: 10.1007/s10551-016-3239-y

Luo, Y., & Zhu, Y. (2022). Green HRM and employee innovative behavior: The mediating role of green work climate. *Business Strategy and the Environment*, 31(4), 1456–1470. DOI: 10.1002/bse.3016

Martínez-Martínez, A., Cegarra-Navarro, J. G., Cobo, M. J., & de Valon, T. (2023). Impacts and implications for advancing in environmental knowledge in hospitality industry in COVID Society: A bibliometric analysis. *Journal of the Knowledge Economy*, 14(2), 2026–2053. DOI: 10.1007/s13132-022-00910-5

Masri, H. A., & Jaaron, A. A. M. (2017). Assessing green human resources management practices in Palestinian manufacturing context: An empirical study. *Journal of Cleaner Production*, 143, 474–489. DOI: 10.1016/j.jclepro.2016.12.087

Moradeke, F. T., Ishola, G. K., & Okikiola, O. L. (2021). Green training and development practices on environmental sustainability: Evidence from WAMCO PLC. *Journal of Educational Management and Social Sciences*, 2(1), 1–19.

Mtembu, V. S., & Mishi, S. (2022). Green HRM and employee environmental behaviors: The mediating role of organizational commitment and green human capital. *Sustainability*, 14(5), 2771. DOI: 10.3390/su14052771

Ojo, A. O., Tan, C. N. L., & Alias, M. (2022). Linking green HRM practices to environmental performance through pro-environment behaviour in the information technology sector. *Social Responsibility Journal*, 18(1), 1–18. DOI: 10.1108/SRJ-12-2019-0403

Panda, D. K. (2023). The green identity and green strategy: An interplay. *Technology Analysis and Strategic Management*, 35(11), 1437–1452.

Rademaker, M. E., Schuberth, F., & Dijkstra, T. K. (2019). Measurement error correlation within blocks of indicators in consistent partial least squares: Issues and remedies. *Internet Research*, 29(3), 448–463. DOI: 10.1108/IntR-12-2017-0525

Ren, S., Tang, G., & Jackson, S. E. (2020). Effects of Green HRM and CEO ethical leadership on organizations' environmental performance. *International Journal of Manpower*, 42(6), 961–983. DOI: 10.1108/IJM-09-2019-0414

Ren, S., Zhang, L., & Weng, X. (2021). The impact of Green HRM on employees' pro-environmental behavior and innovation performance: A dual-process model. *Sustainability*, 13(22), 12345. DOI: 10.3390/su132212345

Rigdon, E. E. (2012). Rethinking partial least squares path modeling: In praise of simple methods. *Long Range Planning*, 45(5/6), 341–358. DOI: 10.1016/j.lrp.2012.09.010

. Ringle, C.M., Sarstedt, M., Mitchell, R., & Gudergan, S.P. (2018). Partial least squares structural equation modeling in HRM research. *The International Journal of Human Resource Management, 31*(12), 1-27. https://doi.org/.2017.1416655DOI: 10.1080/09585192

Saeed, B. B., Afsar, B., Hafeez, S., Khan, I., Tahir, M., & Afridi, M. A. (2019). Promoting employee's proenvironmental behavior through green human resource management practices. *Corporate Social Responsibility and Environmental Management*, 26(2), 424–438.

Shah, N., & Soomro, B. A. (2023). Effects of green human resource management practices on green innovation and behavior. *Management Decision*, 61(1), 290–312. DOI: 10.1108/MD-07-2021-0869

Shahzad, M. A., Jianguo, D., & Junaid, M. (2023). Impact of green HRM practices on sustainable performance: Mediating role of green innovation, green culture, and green employees' behavior. *Environmental Science and Pollution Research International*, 30(38), 88524–88547. DOI: 10.1007/s11356-023-28498-6 PMID: 37438507

Sharma, K., & Tiwari, R. (2021). Green HRM: Conceptualization and current research trends. *International Journal of Productivity and Performance Management*, 70(6), 1305–1327. DOI: 10.1108/IJPPM-12-2019-0603

Singh, S., & Kumar, R. (2023). Green HRM and green innovation: Exploring the mediating role of employee green behavior. *International Journal of Environmental Research and Public Health*, 20(1), 12. DOI: 10.3390/ijerph20010012 PMID: 38276800

Singh, S. K., Del Giudice, M., Chierici, R., & Graziano, D. (2020). Green innovation and environmental performance: The role of green transformational leadership and green human resource management. *Technological Forecasting and Social Change*, 150, 119762.

Sobaih, A. E. E., Hasanein, A., & Elshaer, I. (2020). Influences of green human resources management on environmental performance in small lodging enterprises: The role of green innovation. *Sustainability*, 12(24), 10371.

Song, W., Yu, H., & Xu, H. (2021). Effects of green human resource management and managerial environmental concern on green innovation. *European Journal of Innovation Management*, 24(3), 951–967. DOI: 10.1108/EJIM-11-2019-0315

Suleman, A. R., Amponsah-Tawiah, K., Adu, I. N., & Boakye, K. O. (2022). The curious case of green human resource management practices in the Ghanaian manufacturing industry; A reality or a mirage? *Management of Environmental Quality*, 33(3), 739–755. DOI: 10.1108/MEQ-12-2021-0269

Tang, G., Chen, Y., Jiang, Y., Paillé, P., & Jia, J. (2018). Green human resource management practices: Scale development and validity. *Asia Pacific Journal of Human Resources*, 56(1), 31–55. DOI: 10.1111/1744-7941.12147

Yadav, R., & Pathak, R. D. (2022). Green HRM and its impact on organizational performance: Mediating role of employee green behavior. *Journal of Cleaner Production*, 343, 130891. DOI: 10.1016/j.jclepro.2022.130891

Yong, J. Y., Yusliza, M. Y., Jabbour, C. J. C., & Ahmad, N. H. (2020). Exploratory cases on the interplay between green human resource management and advanced green manufacturing in light of the Ability-Motivation-Opportunity theory. *Journal of Management Development*, 39(1), 31–49. DOI: 10.1108/JMD-12-2018-0355

Yusliza, M. Y., Fawehinmi, O., & Mohamad, Z. F. (2020). Determinants of intention to stay and employee well-being: A case of Green HRM practices. *Global Business Review*, 21(3), 663–680. DOI: 10.1177/0972150918778910

Zhang, W., Li, J., & Wu, H. (2024). Green HRM practices, employee eco-friendly behaviors, and innovative performance: A cross-industry study. *Business Strategy and the Environment*, 33(1), 55–70. DOI: 10.1002/bse.3099

Zhao, J., Liu, H., & Sun, W. (2020). How proactive environmental strategy facilitates environmental reputation: Roles of green human resource management and discretionary slack. *Sustainability*, 12(3), 763.

Zhu, Q., & Geng, Y. (2020). Green HRM and environmental performance: Evidence from manufacturing firms in China. *Journal of Environmental Management*, 273, 111186. DOI: 10.1016/j.jenvman.2020.111186

Chapter 4
From Technostress to Turnover:
Examining Stress-Related Drivers of Turnover in the Indian IT Industry

Pratibha Thakur
https://orcid.org/0000-0001-6386-3960
Dr. Vishwanath Karad MIT World Peace University, India

Charu Saxena
https://orcid.org/0000-0002-1500-8772
Chandigarh University, India

ABSTRACT

The rapid integration of advanced technologies in the workplace, particularly within the information technology (IT) industry, has led to an increase in technostress—stress induced by the use of technology. This study aims to investigate the relationship between technostress, work stress, and turnover intentions among IT professionals in India. This research employs a quantitative approach, utilizing survey data collected from a sample of 419 Indian IT professionals using a purposive sampling technique and was analyzed using Smart PLS 3.2.8. The findings indicate that technostress and work stress significantly contribute to the higher turnover intention of employees. The implications of these findings suggest that addressing technostress through targeted interventions can improve employee retention and overall positive employee outcomes. This research provides valuable insights for IT companies aiming to enhance employee well-being and reduce turnover rates by developing strategies to manage and alleviate technostress in the workplace.

DOI: 10.4018/979-8-3693-6402-4.ch004

INTRODUCTION

In the ongoing technological revolution, Artificial Intelligence has become a key catalyst, as its widespread adoption of digital technologies has enabled it to transform various fields and industries, driving innovation and growth at an exceptional pace (Haenlein and Kaplan, 2019). Akter et al., (2022) conveyed that today's organizations heavily rely on advanced artificial intelligence (AI) technologies such as robotics, machine learning (ML), Internet of Things (IoT), and augmented reality (AR). These technologies are utilized to create, deliver, and enhance solutions that are transforming the present business scenario. The deployment of AI technologies in an organization can have adverse effects also, potentially causing stress among employees that has negative outcomes. Kumar et al. (2024) stated that deployment of AI and ML technologies to the workplace was novel but the managers discovered that the complexity of these technologies made adoption stressful leading to technostress. According to Chang et al. (2024), earlier studies have examined the factors influencing employees' intentions to adopt AI but very few have explored AI adoption as a source of stress, providing inclusive results. It was also claimed that employees' desire for embracing AI is greatly influenced by their emotional reaction to the technostress caused by AI.

AI profoundly impacts business by driving innovation, transforming processes, and creating value. It enables companies to develop new products and optimize operations, leading to better services and reduced costs. AI also provides a competitive edge by helping businesses stay ahead of trends and make more accurate, data-driven decisions. Ultimately, AI enhances intelligent decision-making, guiding strategic choices and shaping the future of business (Duan et al., 2019; Paschen et al., 2020). The growing impact of AI has driven organizations to increasingly adopt these technologies, resulting in enhanced organizational efficiency, productivity, performance, and innovation. By integrating AI, companies can streamline operations, boost output, and improve overall effectiveness. AI also fosters innovation by enabling new solutions and approaches, further advancing business capabilities and competitive edge (Jöhnk et al., 2021; Chang et al., 2023). The widespread adoption of AI by large corporations—evidenced by a Ghosh et al. (2019), that 80% of these companies have integrated AI into their operations—highlights AI's crucial role in modern business environments.

The rise of the digital workspace, which allows employees to operate seamlessly in both physical and virtual environments, has introduced new challenges alongside its benefits (Malik et al., 2021). While this paradigm offers flexibility and the potential for enhanced productivity, it also contributes to a phenomenon known as technostress (D'Arcy et al., 2014). However, as organizations implement these advanced technologies, employees often face technostress, which is the stress and anxiety associated with adapting to rapidly changing technology requirements, as they are required to stay constantly connected and responsive. This stress can hinder employees' ability to effectively use new AI tools and technologies, impacting overall productivity and job satisfaction at the workplace. This technology-induced stress is further aggravated by increased work overload, as the digital tools often lead to expectations of intensified productivity and faster turnaround times (Wang et al., 2023). Additionally, employees face continuous pressure to adapt to emerging applications, functionalities, and workflows, which can be overwhelming and create a persistent sense of being unable to keep up. This ongoing demand to stay proficient with new technologies adds another layer of stress, making technostress a significant concern in modern work environments.

Weil and Rosen (1997, p. 5) defined technostress as "any negative impact on attitudes, thoughts, behaviors, or body psychology caused directly or indirectly by technology." With reference to Califf and Brooks (2020), technostress originates from stressful work environments caused by technology—which could be the reason for employees shifting to different organizations. Employees now experience techno-complexity as a result of the growing reliance on technology and the complexity of information-technological systems (Harris et al., 2022), particularly in private corporations. Techno-overload and techno-invasion, two distinct factors that have a significant impact on staff satisfaction and retention, can be used to understand the severity of technostress among employees (Marchiori et al., 2019; Li and Wang, 2021). The implementation of AI technologies within an organization can lead to employee stress, which may, in turn, detrimentally impact organizational performance (Malik et al., 2021). Studies on technostress reveal that the increasing use of digital technologies in the workplace offers numerous advantages, such as better performance (Cao et al., 2016) and more efficient information processing. However, alongside these benefits, the growing reliance on digital technologies is also leading to a rise in technostress. This type of stress stems from an inability to effectively manage the demands imposed by these technologies (Tarafdar et al., 2010). According to Tarafdar et al. (2007), the adoption of emerging technologies in organizations frequently results in employee technostress. This technostress can lead to negative outcomes such as role overload, role conflict, and job dissatisfaction (Ayyagari et al., 2011).

As it was observed during the global COVID-19 outbreak in 2020, nations have implemented work-from-home policies and lockdowns as social distancing measures to reduce the spread of the coronavirus. Because of this reason, the use of technology has increased and it has been one of the most disturbing crises that the world's economies have faced (Margherita et al., 2021). Remote working during the COVID-19 pandemic differed sharply from pre-pandemic arrangements. It was mandatory, rather than voluntary, and involved full-time work from home rather than a hybrid approach (Jamal et al., 2024). The transition lacked adaptation to individual and organizational cultures, leading to a one-size-fits-all model.

Additionally, employees juggled work responsibilities while their families were also at home due to school and institution closures, creating a particularly challenging remote work environment. Afandi and Kurnia (2023) and Williamson and Vijayakumar (2021) explore the broader societal and industrial implications of technologies such as AI, though they do not directly address its specific impact on technostress. Their discussions on AI's potential to transform various sectors—such as work, health, ethics, and education—and its role in industrial automation imply that AI's influence on technostress is likely substantial and deserves further investigation. For this reason, the current study aimed to investigate the interplay between work stress, technostress, and employees' intentions to leave. Working from home typically occurs voluntarily with the agreement of both employers and employees (Platts et al., 2022). However, during the pandemic, many employees were abruptly required to adjust their schedules for remote work without receiving necessary training in competencies such as time management, teamwork, focus, and adaptability (Pass and Ridgway, 2022), therefore, the current study covers the negative consequences of excessive technology usage that will provide additional insights and contribute to the existing literature by making an attempt to analyze the impact of AI induced technostress and work stress on turnover intentions among IT professionals.

LITERATURE REVIEW

Theoretical Framework

The Conservation of Resources (COR) Theory and the Person-Environment Fit (P-E Fit) Theory both offer valuable insights into understanding how stress manifests in the workplace and its impact on employee behavior and well-being.

Conservation of Resources (COR) Theory

The Conservation of Resources (COR) Theory, proposed by Hobfoll in 2001, is based on the idea that individuals strive to obtain, protect, and enhance their resources. These resources can be anything that an individual values, such as time, energy, social support, or even psychological well-being. According to the theory, stress occurs when individuals perceive a threat to their resources, experience an actual loss of resources, or fail to gain additional resources after investing their own.

In the context of the workplace, if employees feel that their resources are being depleted without adequate replenishment or that their resources are under threat (e.g., due to excessive workload, lack of support, or insufficient rewards), they experience stress. This stress can lead to a range of negative outcomes, including burnout, decreased job satisfaction, and even the decision to leave the organization. Employees may seek to reduce this stress by looking for other employment opportunities that offer a better work environment, where their resources are more likely to be protected and enhanced. In essence, the COR theory suggests that managing resources effectively is crucial for reducing workplace stress. If an organization fails to provide an environment that supports the preservation and growth of employee resources, it risks higher turnover rates as employees leave in search of better opportunities elsewhere.

Person-Environment Fit (P-E Fit) Theory

The prominence of Person-Environment (P-E) fit theory largely stems from its ability to account for individual differences in how people perceive and respond to stress. Unlike other theories that might focus solely on external stressors or environmental conditions, P-E fit theory emphasizes the interaction between an individual and their environment, acknowledging that stress emerges when there is a misfit between personal characteristics and environmental demands or resources (Edwards, 1996). This approach is particularly valuable because it considers how individual differences in perception, cognition, and personality influence the stress experience. By focusing on the dynamic relationship between a person and their environment, P-E fit theory provides a more nuanced understanding of stress, recognizing that what might be stressful for one person may not be for another, depending on how they interpret and respond to their surroundings (Edwards and Cooper, 1990; Tarafdar et al., 2019). This conceptual advantage makes P-E fit a robust framework for understanding the complexities of stress in various contexts.

The Person-Environment Fit (P-E Fit) Theory complements the COR Theory by emphasizing the importance of the compatibility between an individual and their work environment. According to Kristof-Brown and colleagues (2005), P-E Fit occurs when there is a good match between the characteristics of the individual (such as their skills, values, and needs) and the characteristics of the work environment (such as job demands, organizational culture, and resources available). When there is a high degree of fit, employees are more likely to experience positive outcomes, such as job satisfaction, commitment to the organization, and overall well-being. Conversely, when there is a poor fit—where the demands of the job do not align with the individual's capabilities or where the organizational culture conflicts with the employee's values—stress can arise. This misalignment can lead to feelings of discomfort, frustration, and eventually stress, as the individual struggles to cope with the demands of an environment that does not meet their needs or expectations.

The P-E Fit theory suggests that organizations should strive to create environments that align well with the characteristics and preferences of their employees to minimize stress and promote positive outcomes. This might involve tailoring job roles to better match employee skills, fostering an organizational culture that resonates with employee values, or providing the necessary resources to help employees meet job demands effectively.

Both theories offer complementary perspectives on workplace stress. The COR Theory focuses on the management of resources and how the loss or gain of these resources affects stress levels, while the P-E Fit Theory emphasizes the importance of alignment between the individual and their environment. Together, these theories suggest that to reduce stress and enhance employee well-being, organizations need to both manage resources effectively and ensure that there is a good fit between employees and their work environment.

TECHNOSTRESS

Technostress refers to the stress that arises from the use of technology, a phenomenon increasingly recognized as part of the "dark side" of technological advancement. In earlier times, stress and technology were considered separate domains; stress was primarily studied in relation to work, life events, and psychological factors, while technology was viewed as a tool to increase productivity and efficiency. The idea that technology itself could be a source of stress was not widely considered. While technology offers many benefits, such as increased efficiency, communication, and convenience, it also introduces challenges that can lead to stress, anxiety, and other psychological issues (Tarafdar et al., 2011; Tams et al., 2018). In contemporary research, technostress is recognized as a significant concern, particularly as the digital landscape continues to evolve. Addressing technostress involves not only managing the technology itself but also developing strategies to mitigate its negative effects on mental health and well-being. Existing research has largely focused on the negative impact of technostress on employees' work performance, suggesting that stress from technology typically has an adverse effect. Studies have shown that technostress creators, such as constant technological changes and demanding systems, generally harm work performance (Tarafdar et al., 2010; Ragu Nathan et al., 2008). However, there are also findings indicating that the relationship between technostress and work outcomes is not uniformly negative. In some cases, the effect of technostress creators on productivity and organizational commitment may be insignificant or even positively significant (Jena, 2015). This suggests that, under certain conditions, technostress might drive employees to become more productive or enhance their commitment to the organization, potentially leading to a more nuanced understanding of technostress in the workplace.

WORK STRESS

Stress is a significant concern for organizations, as it can have serious implications for employee performance and overall productivity. It is crucial for Human Resources (HR) departments to proactively address the causes of stress within the workplace. If left unaddressed, stress can lead to decreased job satisfaction, lower employee engagement, and diminished performance, all of which negatively affect the organization's success (Rangrez et al., 2022). As work environments become increasingly stressful, job stress has emerged as a significant issue with serious implications. Stressful work conditions can have profound physical and emotional effects on employees (Greenberg and Baron, 2003; Somers, 2009). When job stress disrupts an individual's equilibrium, it can lead to deviations from their usual behavior patterns, which in turn affects their work performance and outcomes. High levels of job stress are associated with decreased job satisfaction, reduced commitment, and lower productivity. Additionally, severe stress has been linked to increased turnover intentions and poor performance, which can negatively impact an organization's overall success and financial performance (Noblet et al., 2009).

TURNOVER INTENTIONS

Turnover intention, often referred to as the intent to quit, is a key concept in organizational behavior that reflects an individual's awareness and inclination to leave their current job in the near future (Mowday et al., 2013). Although this intention does not guarantee that the employee will actually resign, it is considered a critical predictor of actual turnover. Turnover has gained significant scholarly attention in recent decades due to its practical significance implications (Hausknecht and Holwerda, 2013). This concept is central to understanding turnover, which can be classified as either voluntary or involuntary. Voluntary turnover occurs when employees decide to leave their organization, often driven by dissatisfaction or the availability of better opportunities. It reflects a deliberate choice by employees who may be motivated by factors such as job dissatisfaction, career advancement, or personal reasons. In contrast, involuntary turnover is typically initiated by the organization, often due to reasons such as downsizing, performance issues, or other organizational changes. Both types of turnover can be seen as forms of planned behavior, where the decision to leave the organization is made based on specific considerations and intentions (Ajzen, 1991). Understanding these dynamics is crucial for organizations aiming to manage and mitigate turnover effectively. Studies by Joo and Park (2010), and Cho and Lewis (2012) have identified turnover intention as the most reliable indicator of whether an employee will follow through with leaving an organization. Understanding what leads to turnover intention allows organizations to better address the underlying issues that might prompt employees to consider quitting.

TECHNOSTRESS AND TURNOVER INTENTIONS

Technostress is "a modern disease of adaptation caused by an inability to cope with the new computer technologies in a healthy manner" (Brod, 1984, p. 16), and because of the reliance on technology during work, employees experience stress. While using technology can boost productivity, it may have a detrimental effect on the well-being of workers. Negative effects on employee commitment and satisfaction may be experienced by organizations. Technostress has been conceptualized by various researchers as a negative aspect of technology (Tarafdar et al., 2013). While there are benefits to using information and communication technology, it is impossible to ignore the negative aspects of technology. According to Harris et al. (2022), work-family conflicts and turnover intentions are positively impacted by technological invasion and overload. Technostress causes workers to become less productive, dissatisfied and ultimately leave the organization (Tarafdar et al., 2010). Wang et al. (2023) stated that technostress can hamper the well-being of employees in this digital landscape.

According to research studies, the effects of technostress may include burnout, role conflicts, lesser commitment, emotional exhaustion, and work-family conflicts (Harris et al., 2022). The impact of technostress on employees' intentions to leave must be addressed, as utilization of information and communication technologies is growing across multiple industries. Sharma and Tiwari (2023) conducted a study on the Indian IT sector and found that technology-induced stress can hamper the work-life balance as well as the turnover intention of employees. The study by Siddiqi (2023) revealed that work-family conflict and technostress influence Bangladeshi nurses' intentions to leave their jobs. It also confirmed that perceived supervisory support moderates the relationship between work-family conflict, turnover intention, and technostress. Azpíroz-Dorronsoro et al. (2023) surveyed the banking sector employees of Spain and concluded that technostress increases emotional exhaustion and which can further increase work and family conflicts. Previous studies have identified inconsistencies in the effects of technostress on employees. Some researchers suggest that technostress can lead to positive outcomes, such as enhanced productivity and innovation (Tarafdar et al., 2015; Saleem et al., 2021). However, others argue that it may trigger negative emotions like anxiety and stress (Feng et al., 2019). These adverse emotions can potentially decrease the intention to adopt new technology. Therefore, the study posits the hypothesis as:

H1: There is a positive impact of technostress on turnover intentions.

WORK STRESS AND TURNOVER INTENTIONS

Nowadays, work stress has emerged as the primary reason for concern since it may negatively impact employee productivity, which in turn fosters undesirable behavior. Stress not only has serious health implications for employees but also disrupts the smooth functioning of an organization. It can lead to job dissatisfaction, increased absenteeism (Fasbender et al., 2019), decreased performance, and higher turnover intentions (Hoboubi et al., 2017). These consequences undermine productivity, strain resources, and impact overall organizational effectiveness. Addressing stress effectively is crucial for maintaining a healthy, engaged workforce and ensuring operational efficiency. Chen et al. (2011) discovered that employees' intentions to leave the company increase by their level of stress. According to Noblet et al. (2009), stress has been connected with low performance and increased intentions to leave an organization, both of which have a negative impact on productivity. Perceived stress influences female healthcare staff's turnover intentions through factors such as preventive coping, proactive coping, and work-family balance (Yuan et al., 2024).

Stress can have profoundly damaging consequences for both employees and their organizations leading to serious physical and mental health issues (Bourlakis et al., 2023). These problems not only affect an individual's well-being but also diminish their capacity to perform effectively at work. Additionally, stress can erode job satisfaction and reduce motivation, making employees feel disengaged and unfulfilled in their roles. This decline in morale often leads to higher rates of turnover and absenteeism, as stressed employees are more likely to leave the organization (Narahari and Koneru, 2017; Liu et al., 2007). In another study conducted in Ghana's mining industry, Tetteh et al. (2020) discovered that job stress has a positive effect on workers' intentions to leave. Manoppo (2020) surveyed nurses working in private hospitals in Manado and discovered that a higher level of work stress influences employees' decisions to quit their jobs. According to Tuten and

Neidermeyer (2004), organizations may also experience problems with minimizing performance, a decrease in employee commitment, and a rise in employee turnover.

Therefore, the study posits the hypothesis as:

H2: There is a positive impact of work stress on turnover intentions.

Based on the above arguments and formulation of hypotheses, the authors have proposed a conceptual framework for hypotheses testing (Refer Fig 1).

Figure 1. Proposed Conceptual Framework

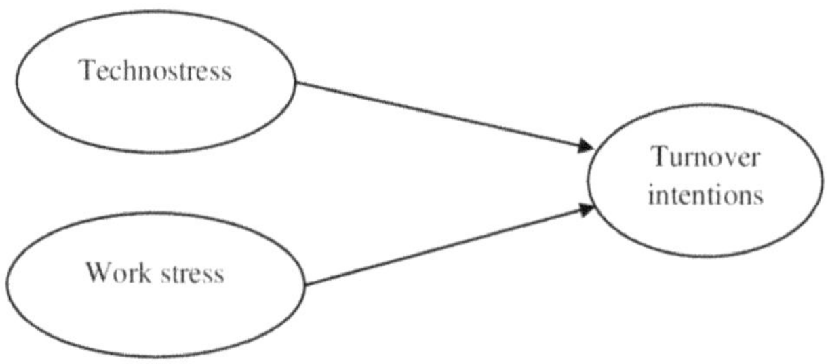

RESEARCH METHODOLOGY

The research methodology involved the development and deployment of a structured questionnaire aimed at testing specific hypotheses related to the study. The target population for the survey consisted of full-time employees working in Indian IT companies. To ensure the relevance and reliability of the data, only those employees who were officially affiliated with their respective organizations were selected as potential respondents. This selection criterion helped in maintaining the quality and consistency of the responses.

The questionnaire was adapted to align with the objectives of the study. It included various survey items that were intended to capture the opinions, experiences, and perceptions of the employees regarding the research topics. Each item on the questionnaire was measured using a 5-point Likert scale, where respondents were asked to rate their level of agreement or disagreement. This scale ranged from 1 (Strongly Disagree) to 5 (Strongly Agree), providing a thorough understanding of the respondents' attitudes. A total of 550 questionnaires were distributed among the selected employees. The distribution process likely involved either physical dissemination of printed questionnaires or the use of online survey tools, depending on the logistical considerations and the accessibility of the respondents. The respondents were informed about the study's objectives before they were requested to participate. This step ensured that participants were aware of the purpose of the research, fostering informed consent and voluntary participation.

Out of the 550 questionnaires distributed, 468 employees responded, yielding a response rate of approximately 85%. This response rate indicates a relatively high level of engagement from the participants, which can be attributed to the clear communication of the study's objectives and the relevance of the research to the participants' work environment. Once the responses were collected, a screening process was conducted to ensure the data's quality and appropriateness for the final analysis. This process involved reviewing the responses for completeness, consistency, and relevance. Any questionnaires that were incomplete, contained outlier responses, or did not meet the inclusion criteria were excluded from the analysis. After this rigorous screening, 419 responses were deemed appropriate and valid for the final analysis. This final sample size was adequate to provide a reliable basis for testing the hypotheses and drawing meaningful conclusions from the data.

Measures: Previous research studies have used and validated the items of the variables taken into consideration in this study. Seven statements were adapted from Shukla and Srivastava (2016) to determine work-related stress. "I feel so burdened that even a day without work seems bad" is the sample statement for work stress. Ten statements, all taken from Ragu-Nathan et al., (2008), were used to calculate the technostress. "I am forced to change my work habits to adapt to new technologies" is the sample statement of technostress. The three items that were adapted from Mobley et al., (1978) were used to measure the intention to employee turnover intentions. "I will probably be looking for another job soon" is the sample statement for turnover intentions.

In the study, work stress was primarily linked to the pressure to complete more work in less time and the challenge of balancing personal and professional life. Employees often feel overwhelmed when they are required to meet demanding workloads under tight deadlines, which can lead to significant stress. Additionally, the difficulty of managing work responsibilities alongside personal life, especially in a work-from-home environment, further intensifies this stress. On the other hand, technostress was associated with the increasing involvement with technology, particularly in the IT industry. Employees face stress when they need to understand and adapt to recent technologies to perform their duties effectively. The complexity of learning and using new technological tools can be intimidating, especially when these tools are essential for job performance.

DATA ANALYSIS

The majority of respondents (56.8%) were male, according to the demographic profile of the respondents (shown in Table 1). For age, the majority of respondents (67.3%) were under 35 years, and 32.7% were over 35 years. This suggests that the majority of the respondents are young workers. Of the respondents, 40.1% were unmarried and 59.9% were married. Of the total respondents, the majority (63.9%) had finished their post-graduation, and 28.9% had graduated. Only 32.7% of the respondents have more than six years of work experience with their current organization, compared to 67.3 percent who have zero to six years. From the total sample, 35.3 percent were doing work from home, and 64.7 percent working from the office.

Table 1. Demographics of Respondents

Type	Frequency	Percentage
Gender		
Male	238	56.8
Female	181	43.2
Age		
Below 30 years	121	28.9
30-35 years	161	38.4
Above 35 years	137	32.7
Marital status		
Married	251	59.9
Unmarried	168	40.1
Qualification		
Graduation	121	28.9
Post-graduation	268	63.9
Others	30	7.2
Work experience		
> 3 years	123	29.4
3-6 years	159	37.9
< 6 years	137	32.7
Employment status		
Work from home	148	35.3
Work from office	271	64.7

Measurement Model Assessment

To verify the hypotheses, first the validity and reliability are computed during measurement model assessment in Smart PLS 3.2.8. The internal consistency and reliability of data are measured and established using Cronbach's alpha and composite reliability. A higher degree of reliability is indicated by higher values. In exploratory research, according to Hair et al. (2019), "reliability values between 0.60 and 0.70 are regarded as acceptable, and those between 0.70 and 0.95 are considered as satisfactory to good". The AVE values are additionally examined to assess the convergent validity.

According to Hair et al. (2019), all factor loadings meet the minimum threshold value of 0.70, as illustrated in Table 2. This threshold is crucial for establishing the reliability of the constructs, indicating that each factor has a substantial load on its respective construct. Additionally, every reliability score reported is above 0.70, which is consistent with the guidelines provided by Hair et al., (2019) and Hair et al., (2017), further supporting the reliability of the measurement model. To assess convergent validity, Average Variance Extracted (AVE) values were computed and are detailed in Table 2. All constructs have AVE values exceeding 0.50, as recommended by Hair et al., (2019) and Hair et al., (2017). This result indicates that a significant portion of the variance in the observed variables is accounted for by the latent constructs, confirming that the constructs possess good convergent validity.

Table 2. Reliability and Validity

Construct	Indicator	Factor Loadings	Cronbach's α	CR	AVE
Technostress	TS1	0.77	0.89	0.92	0.61
	TS10	0.71			
	TS2	0.72			
	TS3	0.74			
	TS4	0.79			
	TS5	0.78			
	TS6	0.81			
	TS7	0.73			
	TS8	0.77			
	TS9	0.74			
Turnover intentions	TI1	0.76	0.74	0.72	0.54
	TI2	0.83			
	TI3	0.82			

continued on following page

Table 2. Continued

Construct	Indicator	Factor Loadings	Cronbach's α	CR	AVE
Work stress	WS1	0.77	0.87	0.91	0.57
	WS2	0.76			
	WS3	0.78			
	WS4	0.76			
	WS5	0.78			
	WS6	0.73			
	WS7	0.79			

Discriminant Validity

Discriminant validity is "the extent to which a construct is empirically different from other constructs in the model". According to Fornell and Larcker (1981) criterion, the discriminant validity of each latent variable can be established using the square root of its AVE and that should be higher than the correlation values shown in the column represented by the diagonal values in bold. Table 3 represents the discriminant validity of the model using Fornell and Larcker criterion (1981), which suggests that the model's discriminant validity is well-established.

Table 3. Discriminant Validity (Fornell and Larcker Criterion)

	TI	TS	WS
TI	**0.73**		
TS	0.37	**0.78**	
WS	0.64	0.59	**0.75**

Note: TS- Technostress, TI- Turnover intentions, WS- Work stress

Discriminant validity was further assessed using the Heterotrait-Monotrait Ratio (HTMT) criteria to determine whether the constructs in the study are distinct from one another. Discriminant validity is crucial for ensuring that different constructs measure unique aspects and are not overly similar. According to established guidelines, a potential problem with discriminant validity is indicated if the HTMT value exceeds 0.85 or 0.90 (Henseler et al., 2015, 2016). These thresholds are used to assess the extent to which constructs are distinguishable from each other. A value above these thresholds suggests that the constructs may not be sufficiently distinct, which could imply issues with their conceptual differentiation. In this study, as shown in Table 4, all HTMT values are below the 0.90 threshold. This result indicates that each construct within the conceptual model is sufficiently distinct from the others.

Therefore, the discriminant validity of the constructs is confirmed, affirming that they are appropriately separated and measure different dimensions as intended.

Table 4. Discriminant Validity (HTMT Ratio)

	TI	TS	WS
TI			
TS	0.42		
WS	0.73	0.63	

Note: TS- Technostress, TI- Turnover intentions, WS- Work stress

Structural Model

The second step involves using the bootstrapping method to access the structural model. The R2 value for turnover intention is 0.455, meaning that the combined effects of work stress and technostress account for 45.5% of the variance in turnover intentions (TI). The findings have implications for IT sector management, who should concentrate on providing a better work environment so that employees can stay affiliated and committed to their current organization.

In the structural model assessment, the path coefficients and the significance of the proposed hypotheses. This model assesses the significance value (P value) and T values which helps in accepting or rejecting the hypotheses. According to the path coefficient table (Table 5), turnover intentions are positively correlated with technostress and work stress. The result for hypothesis H1 is supported (β=0.42, $p \leq 0.01$), which shows a significant relationship between technostress and turnover intentions of employees. It shows that technostress is one of the key reasons of the shifting of jobs by employees. Especially in IT sector, the focus on updating systems and practices increases complexity at work, which originates technostress among the employees (Harris et al., 2022). Also, the strain generated through the use of specific technology in an organizational context needs attention to reduce the employees' turnover intentions.

The result for hypothesis H2 is also supported (β=0.23, $p \leq 0.01$), which shows a significant relationship between work stress and TI. It shows that work stress among employees is also one of the reasons for switching jobs from one organization to another. Work stress or job stress among employees has a negative impact on job performance, which in turn leads to turnover intentions among them. Thus, necessary measures should be taken by employers in IT sector to reduce stress at work, supporting similar findings in the healthcare sector (Liu et al., 2019), (Hebles et al., 2022), in the banking sector (Syarifuddin et al., 2021) and (Sopiah and Sangadji, 2020) in the service organizations (Hakim et al., 2018).

Table 5. Path Coefficient Table

Hypotheses	Relationship	Beta	S.D	T value	Sig value	Results
1	TS -> TI	0.42	0.08	4.26	0.00	Significant
2	WS -> TI	0.23	0.07	3.05	0.00	Significant

Note: TS- Technostress, TI- Turnover intentions, WS- Work stress, SD- Standard deviation

DISCUSSION

The study confirms the proposed framework by supporting the hypotheses that work stress and technostress positively impacts the turnover intentions among IT professionals. The results of the statistical analysis in this study indicated that employees who are under stress at work or with technology have higher intentions to leave. According to Tarafdar et al. (2017), technostress is also a "dark side phenomenon," and organizations that use technology excessively are considered as a fear that has negative consequences. The pandemic has also changed the work culture for employees, forcing them to step outside of their comfort zones and spend more time on their computers and other devices in order to do their jobs. These situations lead to both technological stress and stress from having to complete tasks within the allotted time. The results align with earlier research Khawaja et al., (2021), Manoppo (2020) and Kakar et al., (2023). Research by Choi (2018) and Williams (2019) also found that employees who were working from home with their organization as a mandatory practice exhibited higher turnover intentions compared to their colleagues who chose to work from the office. This suggests that, despite the flexibility offered by teleworking, it may be associated with increased feelings of disengagement or dissatisfaction, leading to a greater likelihood of employees considering leaving their positions. Thakur and Arora (2022) stated that to survive in this competitive environment, firms have focused on transforming existing HR practices to improve their effectiveness and retain employees in their organizations.

Moreover, the study has used the Person-Environment theory to frame the conceptual framework. According to P-E fit theory, positive outcomes result from an individual's interaction with the environment, and workplace stress arises from a mismatch between an individual's capacity to meet environmental demands and environmental demands (Kristof-Brown et al., 2005). The relationships between the factors selected have also been established in the paper using the COR theory. According to COR theory, employees may choose to leave their company in order to reduce stress by looking for other employment opportunities that offer a good work environment for developing resources.

The IT industry in India, while thriving and crucial to the economy, faces significant challenges that require careful study (Tomer et al., 2022). High turnover rates and work exhaustion are particularly pressing issues for IT professionals, who are more likely to experience job changes and burnout than those in other fields (Armstrong et al., 2015). These challenges can disrupt organizational stability, increase costs, and reduce productivity. Therefore, addressing these issues through focused research is essential for the industry's continued growth and sustainability. Also, IT professionals' work and career paths are deeply influenced by the evolving nature of technology (Wang et al., 2020), the study offers valuable insights for optimizing the management of these professionals in a tech-driven environment. As a result, understanding these dynamics is crucial for organizations that want to manage their IT workforce effectively. The findings of the study are therefore important for guiding how organizations can adapt their management strategies to better support IT professionals in this ever-changing environment.

THEORETICAL IMPLICATIONS

This study contributes to existing stress and organizational behavior theories by highlighting how technology-induced stressors specifically drive turnover intentions. By integrating concepts from both Conservation of Resources (COR) Theory and Person-Environment Fit Theory, the research elucidates how technostress depletes employees' psychological and resource reserves, leading to increased job dissatisfaction and a higher likelihood of seeking alternative employment. Additionally, the study enhances theoretical frameworks by demonstrating how mismatches between employees' technological capabilities and organizational demands exacerbate stress, ultimately influencing their decision to leave. These findings underscore the importance of considering technological factors within stress models and offer a nuanced perspective on how modern technological challenges impact employee retention, suggesting that future theoretical developments should incorporate the evolving nature of work environments and technological advancements.

This research underscores the importance of integrating technostress theory with turnover and job stress theories, highlighting how technology-induced stress can precipitate decisions to leave an organization. By demonstrating how technostress—manifested through excessive technology dependence, increased work overload, and constant adaptation to new tools—can significantly impact employee retention, our study contributes to a more nuanced theoretical framework. It expands on existing models by linking the specific stressors related to technology with broader outcomes like turnover intentions, thus providing a comprehensive perspective on how modern work environments affect employee behavior. This integration of technostress with turnover and job stress theories offers valuable insights for future research, suggesting that addressing technology-related stressors can be crucial for improving employee retention and organizational stability.

PRACTICAL IMPLICATIONS

In practice, the study reveals that organizations should not only provide sufficient resources (such as support, time, and opportunities for growth) but also ensure that these resources are aligned with the needs and values of their employees. By doing so, organizations can create a more supportive and stress-free work environment, leading to higher employee retention, satisfaction, and productivity. For managers also, the study has some interesting practical implications. According to Avey et al. (2009) workplace stress is a common problem that management has to deal with. To mitigate the workload and stress related to technology, managers should assign tasks according to employees' proficiency with technology. Role conflict, reduced commitment, lowered engagement, and declining performance could all be signs that workers are under stress. According to Ragu-Nathan et al. (2008), literacy facilitation can help reduce the detrimental impacts of technostress. By educating the employees with the necessary skills and knowledge to effectively navigate and utilize technology, the anxiety and stress associated with its use can be substantially reduced. Technostress created due to the incorporation of new updated technology in an organizational context needs further attention, supporting the previous studies of observing the adverse impact of technostress on satisfaction and job engagement and, in turn, their turnover intentions. Based on the identified technostress factors, organizations can implement training programs and support systems to help employees adapt to and cope with technology-related challenges. According to Valta et al. (2024), employees with a digital mindset are better equipped to handle risks when interacting with digital technologies, such as techno-stressors.

It would be favorable for the executives, supervisors, and administrators to address employee stress to prevent employees from considering leaving the company and seeking employment elsewhere. Kawakami (2022) emphasizes the necessity of comprehending the factors that affect human dependence on AI for decision-making, especially in high-stakes social situations. Poba-Nzaou et al. (2021) point out the potential for AI to automate both routine and non-routine tasks, calling for a re-evaluation of HR functions to promote effective collaboration between human workers and AI. Sundar (2020) highlights the importance of addressing the tensions between machine and human agency, particularly in media-related experiences. The study on AI, workstress and technostress yields significant implications for understanding the complex interplay between technology and human well-being. It underscores the importance of considering the impact of AI systems on human agency also, and the capacity for individuals to make independent choices and control their lives. Additionally, it highlights the emergence of technostress, the stress induced by the use of technology, as a critical concern in the context of AI adoption. Overall, the implications of this study underline the importance of adopting a human-centered approach to AI development and implementation. It calls for proactive measures to address ethical concerns, mitigate technostress, and safeguard human agency in the face of technological advancement.

Advanced technologies including AI are revolutionizing workplace learning by creating personalized and adaptive environments that enhance productivity and boost employee engagement. AI algorithms help in designing the training programs according to each employee's skills, learning preferences, and career goals, and effectiveness. AI-driven predictive analytics enable proactive talent development by forecasting future skill needs. Additionally, AI automates administrative tasks, streamlines training processes, and provides real-time feedback via chatbots and virtual assistants, making learning more scalable and accessible for lifelong learning of employees. While careful management of data privacy, bias, and change implementation is necessary, this transformation fosters a culture of continuous learning, addresses skill gaps, and prepares the workforce for future challenges. AI in the workplace can have a double-edged sword effect on employees' innovation behavior. Therefore, while AI can significantly boost innovative behavior by providing valuable support and resources, it is crucial to balance their use with initiatives that encourage independent thinking and creativity to avoid undermining the innovative potential of the workforce.

LIMITATIONS AND FUTURE SCOPE

Despite the notable contributions, it is also important to note a few limitations. Due to the cross-sectional design's primary drawback, more longitudinal research should be the emphasis of subsequent studies to look at the causal relationships between the variables. The results claim that there are certain other variables that have a significant impact on turnover intentions. As the antecedents of employees' intention to leave, the current study has focused on work stress, and technostress due to technology adoption; future research should also investigate additional factors influencing employees' intentions to leave. Second, since the results were derived from the perspectives of workers in North India's IT sector, research on similar topics can also be carried out among those employed by the public sector, allowing for a comparative analysis that would validate and generalize the results.

The specific nature of the technology and work culture in this industry may not fully represent the experiences of employees in different contexts. Additionally, the research primarily relies on self-reported data, which can be subject to biases such as social desirability or inaccurate self-assessment. Furthermore, while the study successfully links technostress with turnover intentions, it may not capture all possible moderating or mediating factors, such as individual differences in coping mechanisms or organizational support systems. Moderating variables such as psychological capital (Ergun et al., 2023), psychological contract breach (Kim and Kim, 2024), gender and experience (Antony et al, 2024) and mediating variables such as toxic leadership behavior (Ofei et al., 2023), moral injury (Sirvastava et al., 2024) can be considered for further analysis. The independent variables, such as workplace friendship (Fasbender et al., 2023; Wang et al., 2023), workplace toxicity (Garg et al., 2023), employee oriented CSR (Lu et al., 2023), service encounter incivility (Dangaiso and Mukucha, 2024) techno-eustress (Nascimento et al., 2024) can be further investigated in the future studies to study their impact on turnover intentions. Future research could address these limitations by exploring a wider range of industries, employing diverse methodologies, and examining additional variables that influence the relationship between technostress and employee turnover.

DECLARATION OF INTEREST STATEMENT

The authors declare that there are no conflicts of interest regarding the publication of this manuscript.

ACKNOWLEDGMENT

The authors extend their gratitude to the editors for considering our manuscript for publication and to the anonymous reviewers for their valuable and constructive feedback, which has significantly improved the manuscript.

REFERENCES

Afandi, A. R., & Kurnia, H. (2023). Revolusi Teknologi: Masa Depan Kecerdasan Buatan (AI) dan Dampaknya Terhadap Masyarakat. *Academy of Social Science and Global Citizenship Journal*, 3(1), 9–13. DOI: 10.47200/aossagcj.v3i1.1837

Ajzen, I. (1991). The theory of planned behavior. *Organizational Behavior and Human Decision Processes*, 50(2), 179–211. DOI: 10.1016/0749-5978(91)90020-T

Akter, S., Michael, K., Uddin, M. R., McCarthy, G., & Rahman, M. (2022). Transforming business using digital innovations: The application of AI, blockchain, cloud and data analytics. *Annals of Operations Research*, 308(1-2), 7–39. DOI: 10.1007/s10479-020-03620-w

Antony, D. A. J., Arulandu, S., & Parayitam, S. (2024). Gender and experience as moderators between talent management and turnover intention among faculty members in higher educational institutions in India. *The Learning Organization*, 31(4), 526–546. DOI: 10.1108/TLO-04-2023-0051

Armstrong, D. J., Brooks, N. G., & Riemenschneider, C. K. (2015). Exhaustion from information system career experience. *Management Information Systems Quarterly*, 39(3), 713–728. DOI: 10.25300/MISQ/2015/39.3.10

Ayyagari, R., Grover, V., & Purvis, R. (2011). Technostress: Technological antecedents and implications. *Management Information Systems Quarterly*, 35(4), 831–858. DOI: 10.2307/41409963

Azpíroz-Dorronsoro, C., Fernández-Muñiz, B., Montes-Peón, J. M., & Vázquez-Ordás, C. J. (2023). Technostress and work-family conflict in ICT-user employees during the COVID-19 pandemic: The role of social support and mindfulness. *Behaviour & Information Technology*, 43(8), 1531–1553. DOI: 10.1080/0144929X.2023.2220051

Bourlakis, M., Nisar, T. M., & Prabhakar, G. (2023). How technostress may affect employee performance in educational work environments. *Technological Forecasting and Social Change*, 193, 122674. DOI: 10.1016/j.techfore.2023.122674

Brod, C. (1984). *Technostress: The Human Cost of the Computer Revolution*. Addison-Wesley.

Califf, C. B., & Brooks, S. (2020). An empirical study of techno-stressors, literacy facilitation, burnout, and turnover intention as experienced by K-12 teachers. *Computers & Education*, 157, 103971. DOI: 10.1016/j.compedu.2020.103971

Califf, C. B., Sarker, S., & Sarker, S. (2020). The Bright and Dark Sides of Technostress: A Mixed-Methods Study Involving Healthcare IT. *Management Information Systems Quarterly*, 44(2), 809–856. DOI: 10.25300/MISQ/2020/14818

Cao, X., Guo, X., Vogel, D., & Zhang, X. (2016). Exploring the influence of social media on employee work performance. *Internet Research*, 26(2), 529–545. DOI: 10.1108/IntR-11-2014-0299

Chang, P. C., Zhang, W., Cai, Q., & Guo, H. (2024). Does AI-Driven Technostress Promote or Hinder Employees' Artificial Intelligence Adoption Intention? A Moderated Mediation Model of Affective Reactions and Technical Self-Efficacy. *Psychology Research and Behavior Management*, 17, 413–427. DOI: 10.2147/PRBM.S441444 PMID: 38343429

Chen, M. F., Lin, C. P., & Lien, G. Y. (2011). Modelling job stress as a mediating role in predicting turnover intention. *Service Industries Journal*, 31(8), 1327–1345. DOI: 10.1080/02642060903437543

Cheng, B., Lin, H., & Kong, Y. (2023). Challenge or hindrance? How and when organizational artificial intelligence adoption influences employee job crafting. *Journal of Business Research*, 164, 113987. DOI: 10.1016/j.jbusres.2023.113987

Cho, Y. J., & Lewis, G. B. (2012). Turnover intention and turnover behavior: Implications for retaining federal employees. *Review of Public Personnel Administration*, 32(1), 4–23. DOI: 10.1177/0734371X11408701

Choi, S. (2018). Managing flexible work arrangements in government: Testing the effects of institutional and managerial support. *Public Personnel Management*, 47(1), 26–50. DOI: 10.1177/0091026017738540

D'Arcy, J., Gupta, A., Tarafdar, M., & Turel, O. (2014). Reflecting on the "dark side" of information technology use. *Communications of the Association for Information Systems*, 35(1), 109–118. DOI: 10.17705/1CAIS.03505

Dangaiso, P., & Mukucha, P. (2024). Evaluating the impact of service encounter incivility on employee job stress, turnover intentions and labor attrition: A study on frontline employees in the fast food service industry. *Cogent Business & Management*, 11(1), 2355671. DOI: 10.1080/23311975.2024.2355671

Duan, Y., Edwards, J. S., & Dwivedi, Y. K. (2019). Artificial intelligence for decision making in the era of Big Data–evolution, challenges and research agenda. *International Journal of Information Management*, 48, 63–71. DOI: 10.1016/j.ijinfomgt.2019.01.021

Edwards, J. R. (1996). An examination of competing versions of the person-environment fit approach to stress. *Academy of Management Journal*, 39(2), 292–339. DOI: 10.2307/256782

Edwards, J. R., & Cooper, C. L. (1990). The person-environment fit approach to stress: Recurring problems and some suggested solutions. *Journal of Organizational Behavior*, 11(4), 293–307. DOI: 10.1002/job.4030110405

Ergun, G. S., Bozkurt, H. O., Arslan, E., Kendir, H., & Yayla, O. (2023). Psychological capital as a moderator in the relationship between job insecurity, job stress, and hotel employees' turnover intention during the Russia-Ukraine war. *International Journal of Hospitality Management*, 111, 103475. DOI: 10.1016/j.ijhm.2023.103475

Fasbender, U., Burmeister, A., & Wang, M. (2023). Managing the risks and side effects of workplace friendships: The moderating role of workplace friendship self-efficacy. *Journal of Vocational Behavior*, 143, 103875. DOI: 10.1016/j.jvb.2023.103875

Fasbender, U., Van der Heijden, B. I., & Grimshaw, S. (2019). Job satisfaction, job stress and nurses' turnover intentions: The moderating roles of on-the-job and off-the-job embeddedness. *Journal of Advanced Nursing*, 75(2), 327–337. DOI: 10.1111/jan.13842 PMID: 30187541

Feng, W., Tu, R., Lu, T., & Zhou, Z. (2019). Understanding forced adoption of self-service technology: The impacts of users' psychological reactance. *Behaviour & Information Technology*, 38(8), 820–832. DOI: 10.1080/0144929X.2018.1557745

Fornell, C., & Larcker, D. F. (1981). Evaluating structural equation models with unobservable variables and measurement error. *JMR, Journal of Marketing Research*, 18(1), 39–50. DOI: 10.1177/002224378101800104

Garg, N., Mahipalan, M., & Sharma, N. (2023). Does workplace toxicity influence turnover intentions among Indian healthcare employees? Investigating the moderating role of gratitude. *Journal of Health Organization and Management*, 37(2), 250–272. DOI: 10.1108/JHOM-08-2022-0233 PMID: 36733231

Geisser, S. (1974). A predictive approach to the random effect model. *Biometrika*, 61(1), 101–107. DOI: 10.1093/biomet/61.1.101

Ghosh, B., Daugherty, P. R., Wilson, H. J., & Burden, A. (2019). Taking a systems approach to adopting AI. *Harvard Business Review*.

Greenberg, J., & Baron, R. A. (2003). *Behavior in organizations*. Prentice Hall.

Haenlein, M., & Kaplan, A. (2019). A brief history of artificial intelligence: On the past, present, and future of artificial intelligence. *California Management Review*, 61(4), 5–14. DOI: 10.1177/0008125619864925

Hair, J. F., Matthews, L. M., Matthews, R. L., & Sarstedt, M. (2017). PLS-SEM or CB-SEM: Updated guidelines on which method to use. *International Journal of Multivariate Data Analysis*, 1(2), 107–123. DOI: 10.1504/IJMDA.2017.087624

Hair, J. F., Risher, J. J., Sarstedt, M., & Ringle, C. M. (2019). When to use and how to report the results of PLS-SEM. *European Business Review*, 31(1), 2–24. DOI: 10.1108/EBR-11-2018-0203

Hakim, A. L., Sudarmiatin, U., & Sutrisno, U. (2018). The Effect of Work Stress on Turnover Intention with Work Satisfaction and Commitment as Intervening Variable (Study at PT Infomedia Solusi Humanika in Malang). *European Journal of Business and Management*, 10(12), 85–94.

Harris, K. J., Harris, R. B., Valle, M., Carlson, J., Carlson, D. S., Zivnuska, S., & Wiley, B. (2022). Technostress and the entitled employee: Impacts on work and family. *Information Technology & People*, 35(3), 1073–1095. DOI: 10.1108/ITP-07-2019-0348

Hausknecht, J. P., & Holwerda, J. A. (2013). When does employee turnover matter? Dynamic member configurations, productive capacity, and collective performance. *Organization Science*, 24(1), 210–225. DOI: 10.1287/orsc.1110.0720

Hebles, M., Trincado-Munoz, F., & Ortega, K. (2022). Stress and turnover intentions within healthcare teams: The mediating role of psychological safety, and the moderating effect of COVID-19 worry and supervisor support. *Frontiers in Psychology*, 12, 758438. DOI: 10.3389/fpsyg.2021.758438 PMID: 35173646

Henseler, J., Ringle, C. M., & Sarstedt, M. (2015). A new criterion for assessing discriminant validity in variance-based structural equation modeling. *Journal of the Academy of Marketing Science*, 43(1), 115–135. DOI: 10.1007/s11747-014-0403-8

Henseler, J., Ringle, C. M., & Sarstedt, M. (2016). Testing measurement invariance of composites using partial least squares. *International Marketing Review*, 33(3), 405–431. DOI: 10.1108/IMR-09-2014-0304

Hobfoll, S. E. (2001). The influence of culture, community, and the nested-self in the stress process: Advancing conservation of resources theory. *Applied Psychology*, 50(3), 337–421. DOI: 10.1111/1464-0597.00062

Hoboubi, N., Choobineh, A., Ghanavati, F. K., Keshavarzi, S., & Hosseini, A. A. (2017). The impact of job stress and job satisfaction on workforce productivity in an Iranian petrochemical industry. *Safety and Health at Work*, 8(1), 67–71. DOI: 10.1016/j.shaw.2016.07.002 PMID: 28344843

Jamal, M. T., Anwar, I., Khan, N. A., & Ahmad, G. (2024). How do teleworkers escape burnout? A moderated-mediation model of the job demands and turnover intention. *International Journal of Manpower*, 45(1), 169–199. DOI: 10.1108/IJM-12-2022-0628

Jena, R. K. (2015). Technostress in ICT enabled collaborative learning environment: An empirical study among Indian academician. *Computers in Human Behavior*, 51, 1116–1123. DOI: 10.1016/j.chb.2015.03.020

Jöhnk, J., Weißert, M., & Wyrtki, K. (2021). Ready or not, AI comes—An interview study of organizational AI readiness factors. *Business & Information Systems Engineering*, 63(1), 5–20. DOI: 10.1007/s12599-020-00676-7

Joo, B. K., & Park, S. (2010). Career satisfaction, organizational commitment, and turnover intention: The effects of goal orientation, organizational learning culture and developmental feedback. *Leadership and Organization Development Journal*, 31(6), 482–500. DOI: 10.1108/01437731011069999

Kakar, A. S., Misron, A., Meyer, N., & Durrani, D. K. (2023). Job insecurity as a mediator between fearing COVID-19 and turnover intention: Empirical evidence during the COVID-19 pandemic. *International Journal of Educational Management*, 37(4), 752–767. DOI: 10.1108/IJEM-12-2022-0511

Kawakami, A., Sivaraman, V., Cheng, H. F., Stapleton, L., Cheng, Y., Qing, D., & Holstein, K. (2022, April). Improving human-AI partnerships in child welfare: understanding worker practices, challenges, and desires for algorithmic decision support. In *Proceedings of the 2022 CHI Conference on Human Factors in Computing Systems* (pp. 1-18). DOI: 10.1145/3491102.3517439

Khawaja, K. F., Sarfraz, M., Rashid, M., & Rashid, M. (2022). How is COVID-19 pandemic causing employee withdrawal behavior in the hospitality industry? An empirical investigation. *Journal of Hospitality and Tourism Insights*, 5(3), 687–706. DOI: 10.1108/JHTI-01-2021-0002

Kim, B. J., & Kim, M. J. (2024). The influence of work overload on cybersecurity behavior: A moderated mediation model of psychological contract breach, burnout, and self-efficacy in AI learning such as ChatGPT. *Technology in Society*, 77, 102543. DOI: 10.1016/j.techsoc.2024.102543

Kristof-Brown, A. L., Zimmerman, R. D., & Johnson, E. C. (2005). Consequences of individuals' fit at work: A meta-analysis OF person–job, person–organization, person–group, and person–supervisor fit. *Personnel Psychology*, 58(2), 281–342. DOI: 10.1111/j.1744-6570.2005.00672.x

Kumar, A., Krishnamoorthy, B., & Bhattacharyya, S. S. (2024). Machine learning and artificial intelligence-induced technostress in organizations: A study on automation-augmentation paradox with socio-technical systems as coping mechanisms. *The International Journal of Organizational Analysis*, 32(4), 681–701. DOI: 10.1108/IJOA-01-2023-3581

Li, L., & Wang, X. (2021). Technostress inhibitors and creators and their impacts on university teachers' work performance in higher education. *Cognition Technology and Work*, 23(2), 315–330. DOI: 10.1007/s10111-020-00625-0

Liu, C., Spector, P. E., & Shi, L. (2007). Cross-national job stress: A quantitative and qualitative study. *Journal of Organizational Behavior*, 28(2), 209–239. DOI: 10.1002/job.435

Liu, J., Zhu, B., Wu, J., & Mao, Y. (2019). Job satisfaction, work stress, and turnover intentions among rural health workers: A cross-sectional study in 11 western provinces of China. *BMC Family Practice*, 20(1), 1–11. DOI: 10.1186/s12875-019-0904-0 PMID: 30642261

Lu, J., Guo, S., Qu, J., Lin, W., & Lev, B. (2023). "Stay" or "Leave": Influence of employee-oriented social responsibility on the turnover intention of new-generation employees. *Journal of Business Research*, 161, 113814. DOI: 10.1016/j.jbusres.2023.113814

Malik, N., Tripathi, S. N., Kar, A. K., & Gupta, S. (2021). Impact of artificial intelligence on employees working in industry 4.0 led organizations. *International Journal of Manpower*, 43(2), 334–354. DOI: 10.1108/IJM-03-2021-0173

Manoppo, V. P. (2020). Transformational leadership as a factor that decreases turnover intention: A mediation of work stress and organizational citizenship behavior. *The TQM Journal*, 32(6), 1395–1412. DOI: 10.1108/TQM-05-2020-0097

Marchiori, D. M., Mainardes, E. W., & Rodrigues, R. G. (2019). Do Individual Characteristics Influence the Types of Technostress Reported by Workers? *International Journal of Human-Computer Interaction*, 35(3), 218–230. DOI: 10.1080/10447318.2018.1449713

Margherita, A., Elia, G., & Klein, M. (2021). Managing the COVID-19 emergency: A coordination framework to enhance response practices and actions. *Technological Forecasting and Social Change*, 166, 120656. DOI: 10.1016/j.techfore.2021.120656 PMID: 33551496

Mobley, W. H., Horner, S. O., & Hollingsworth, A. T. (1978). An evaluation of precursors of hospital employee turnover. *The Journal of Applied Psychology*, 63(4), 408–414. DOI: 10.1037/0021-9010.63.4.408 PMID: 701211

Mowday, R. T., Porter, L. W., & Steers, R. M. (2013). *Employee—organization linkages: The psychology of commitment, absenteeism, and turnover*. Academic Press.

Narahari, C. L., & Koneru, D. K. (2017). A study on the role of occupational stress in organizations. *International Journal of Engineering Technology. Management and Applied Sciences*, 5(1), 53–59.

Nascimento, L., Correia, M. F., & Califf, C. B. (2024). Towards a bright side of technostress in higher education teachers: Identifying several antecedents and outcomes of techno-eustress. *Technology in Society*, 76, 102428. DOI: 10.1016/j.techsoc.2023.102428

Noblet, A., Rodwell, J., & Allisey, A. (2009). Job stress in the law enforcement sector: Comparing the linear, non-linear and interaction effects of working conditions. *Stress and Health*, 25(1), 111–120. DOI: 10.1002/smi.1227

Ofei, A. M. A., Poku, C. A., Paarima, Y., Barnes, T., & Kwashie, A. A. (2023). Toxic leadership behavior of nurse managers and turnover intentions: The mediating role of job satisfaction. *BMC Nursing*, 22(1), 374. DOI: 10.1186/s12912-023-01539-8 PMID: 37817145

Paschen, J., Wilson, M., & Ferreira, J. J. (2020). Collaborative intelligence: How human and artificial intelligence create value along the B2B sales funnel. *Business Horizons*, 63(3), 403–414. DOI: 10.1016/j.bushor.2020.01.003

Pass, S., & Ridgway, M. (2022). An informed discussion on the impact of COVID-19 and 'enforced' remote working on employee engagement. *Human Resource Development International*, 25(2), 254–270. DOI: 10.1080/13678868.2022.2048605

Platts, K., Breckon, J., & Marshall, E. (2022). Enforced home-working under lockdown and its impact on employee wellbeing: A cross-sectional study. *BMC Public Health*, 22(1), 199. DOI: 10.1186/s12889-022-12630-1 PMID: 35093054

Poba-Nzaou, P., Galani, M., Uwizeyemungu, S., & Ceric, A. (2021). The impacts of artificial intelligence (AI) on jobs: An industry perspective. *Strategic HR Review*, 20(2), 60–65. DOI: 10.1108/SHR-01-2021-0003

Ragu-Nathan, T. S., Tarafdar, M., Ragu-Nathan, B. S., & Tu, Q. (2008). The consequences of technostress for end users in organizations: Conceptual development and empirical validation. *Information Systems Research*, 19(4), 417–433. DOI: 10.1287/isre.1070.0165

Rangrez, S. N., Amin, F., & Dixit, S. (2022). Influence of role stressors and job insecurity on turnover intentions in start-ups: Mediating role of job stress. *Management and Labour Studies*, 47(2), 199–215. DOI: 10.1177/0258042X221074757

Rindu, R., Lukman, S., Hardisman, H., Hafizurrachman, M., & Bachtiar, A. (2020). The relationship among transformational leadership, organizational commitment, work stress, and turnover intentions of nurse at private hospital in Indonesia. *Open Access Macedonian Journal of Medical Sciences, 8*(E), 551–557.

Sharma, I., & Tiwari, V. (2023). Modeling the impact of techno-stress and burnout on employees' work-life balance and turnover intention: A job demands-resources theory perspective. *Global Business and Organizational Excellence*, 43(1), 121–134. DOI: 10.1002/joe.22206

Shukla, A., & Srivastava, R. (2016). Development of short questionnaire to measure an extended set of role expectation conflict, coworker support and work-life balance: The new job stress scale. *Cogent Business & Management, 3*(1), 1-19.

Siddiqi, K. O. (2024). Impact of technostress and work-family conflict on turnover intention among nurses in Bangladesh: A moderation effect of perceived supervisor support. *Journal of Computational Social Science*, 1–24. DOI: 10.1007/s42001-024-00296-1

Somers, M. J. (2009). The combined influence of affective, continuance and normative commitment on employee withdrawal. *Journal of Vocational Behavior*, 74(1), 75–81. DOI: 10.1016/j.jvb.2008.10.006

Sopiah, S., Wilujeng, I. P., Murdiono, A., & Sangadji, E. M. (2020, July). The Role of Perceived Teaching Quality as Mediator Variable That Affects Student Satisfaction. In *International Conference on Learning Innovation 2019 (ICLI 2019)* (pp. 37-48). Atlantis Press. DOI: 10.2991/assehr.k.200711.008

Srivastava, S., Khan, M., Kumari, A., & Jain, A. K. (2024). A study of workplace bullying and coping strategies in hospitality sector: Role of moral injury and inclusive leadership. *Journal of Organizational Effectiveness: People and Performance*, 11(1), 18–34. DOI: 10.1108/JOEPP-03-2023-0069

Stone, M. (1974). Cross-validatory choice and assessment of statistical predictions. *Journal of the Royal Statistical Society. Series B, Statistical Methodology*, 36(2), 111–133. DOI: 10.1111/j.2517-6161.1974.tb00994.x

Sundar, S. S. (2020). Rise of machine agency: A framework for studying the psychology of human–AI interaction (HAII). *Journal of Computer-Mediated Communication*, 25(1), 74–88. DOI: 10.1093/jcmc/zmz026

Syarifuddin, S., Rizqifajri, M. I., Fakhri, M., Gilang, A., & Pradana, M. (2021). The Influence of Work Stress Towards Turnover Intention at State-Owned Bank in Bandung Area. In *Proceedings of the International Conference on Industrial Engineering and Operations Management* (pp. 915-920). DOI: 10.46254/IN01.20210256

Tams, S., Thatcher, J. B., & Grover, V. (2018). Concentration, competence, confidence, and capture: An experimental study of age, interruption-based technostress, and task performance. *Journal of the Association for Information Systems*, 19(9), 857–908. DOI: 10.17705/1jais.00511

Tarafdar, M., Cooper, C. L., & Stich, J. F. (2017). The technostress trifecta - techno eustress, techno distress and design: Theoretical directions and an agenda for research. *Information Systems Journal*, 29(1), 6–42. DOI: 10.1111/isj.12169

Tarafdar, M., Cooper, C. L., & Stich, J. F. (2019). The technostress trifecta-techno eustress, techno distress and design: Theoretical directions and an agenda for research. *Information Systems Journal*, 29(1), 6–42. DOI: 10.1111/isj.12169

Tarafdar, M., Gupta, A., & Turel, O. (2013). The dark side of information technology use. *Information Systems Journal*, 23(3), 269–275. DOI: 10.1111/isj.12015

Tarafdar, M., Pullins, E. B., & Ragu-Nathan, T. S. (2015). Technostress: Negative effect on performance and possible mitigations. *Information Systems Journal*, 25(2), 103–132. DOI: 10.1111/isj.12042

Tarafdar, M., Tu, Q., Ragu-Nathan, B. S., & Ragu-Nathan, T. S. (2007). The impact of technostress on role stress and productivity. *Journal of Management Information Systems*, 24(1), 301–328. DOI: 10.2753/MIS0742-1222240109

Tarafdar, M., Tu, Q., & Ragu-Nathan, T. S. (2010). Impact of technostress on end-user satisfaction and performance. *Journal of Management Information Systems*, 27(3), 303–334. DOI: 10.2753/MIS0742-1222270311

Tarafdar, M., Tu, Q., Ragu-Nathan, T. S., & Ragu-Nathan, B. S. (2011). Crossing to the dark side: Examining creators, outcomes, and inhibitors of technostress. *Communications of the ACM*, 54(9), 113–120. DOI: 10.1145/1995376.1995403

Tetteh, S., Wu, C., Opata, C. N., Asirifua Agyapong, G. N. Y., Amoako, R., & Osei-Kusi, F. (2020). Perceived organizational support, job stress, and turnover intention: The moderation of affective commitments. *Journal of Psychology in Africa*, 30(1), 9–16. DOI: 10.1080/14330237.2020.1722365

Thakur, P., & Arora, R. (2022). Exploring the Relationship Among Satisfaction and Intention to Stay Among Millennial Employees: The Moderating Role of Managerial Support. *International Journal of Human Capital and Information Technology Professionals*, 13(1), 1–17. DOI: 10.4018/IJHCITP.293229

Tomer, G., Mishra, S. K., & Qureshi, I. (2022). Features of technology and its linkages with turnover intention and work exhaustion among IT professionals: A multi-study investigation. *International Journal of Information Management*, 66, 102518. DOI: 10.1016/j.ijinfomgt.2022.102518

Tuten, T. L., & Neidermeyer, P. E. (2004). Performance, satisfaction and turnover in call centers: The effects of stress and optimism. *Journal of Business Research*, 57(1), 26–34. DOI: 10.1016/S0148-2963(02)00281-3

Valta, M., Hildebrandt, Y., & Maier, C. (2024). Fostering the digital mindset to mitigate technostress: An empirical study of empowering individuals for using digital technologies. *Internet Research*. Advance online publication. DOI: 10.1108/INTR-09-2022-0766

Wang, H., Ding, H., & Kong, X. (2023). Understanding technostress and employee well-being in digital work: The roles of work exhaustion and workplace knowledge diversity. *International Journal of Manpower*, 44(2), 334–353. DOI: 10.1108/IJM-08-2021-0480

Wang, S., Liu, Y., Hu, Y., Zhang, J., Li, S., & Chen, Y. (2023). The honey-trap of workplace friendship: Developing and testing a three-way interaction model to understand when and why workplace friendship triggers employee withdrawal behavior. *International Journal of Psychology*, 58(5), 486–497. DOI: 10.1002/ijop.12925 PMID: 37332092

Wang, W., Wang, Y., Zhang, Y., & Ma, J. (2020). Spillover of workplace IT satisfaction onto job satisfaction: The roles of job fit and professional fit. *International Journal of Information Management*, 50, 341–352. DOI: 10.1016/j.ijinfomgt.2019.08.011

Weil, M. M., & Rosen, L. D. (1997). *Technostress: Coping with technology@ work@ home@ play* (Vol. 13). J. Wiley.

Williams, P. (2019). Support for supervisors: HR enabling flexible work. *Employee Relations*, 41(5), 914–930. DOI: 10.1108/ER-03-2018-0077

Williamson, S., & Vijayakumar, K. (2021). Artificial intelligence techniques for industrial automation and smart systems. *Concurrent Engineering, Research and Applications*, 29(3), 291–292. DOI: 10.1177/1063293X211026275

Yuan, D., Hu, M., Yao, N., Zhong, H., Xiao, Y., Zhou, X., Zhang, R., & Zhang, Y. (2024). Effects of perceived stress on turnover intention of female healthcare staff: A serial multiple mediation model. *BMC Public Health*, 24(1), 1198. DOI: 10.1186/s12889-024-18654-z PMID: 38685094

Chapter 5 The Impact of Equity, Employee Engagement Activities, and Job Redesigning on Airline Employee Motivation: A Comparative Analysis

Neha Nazneen Siddiqui
Ashoka Institute of Technology and Management, India

ABSTRACT

Drawing on a theoretical framework, this study aims to understand the impact of equity as perceived by employees in the airline industry through employee engagement activities and job redesigning that have been introduced to determine the level of motivation among frontline staff members working with Indian Airlines Jet Airways vs. Indigo. The research aimed to determine how motivation levels are influenced by engagement, job crafting, and work-life advocacy. This chapter summarizes the 400 employee survey outcomes with an empirical statistical approach. The findings suggest that Indigo Airlines scores much higher than Jet Airways in all three dimensions. Indigo had significantly higher perceived equity than Jet Airways (89% versus 30%) and was more satisfied with its engagement activities than the other service providers in this sector. Job redesigning, too, occurred a lot more frequently at Indigo compared to fellow airline companies, as they scored a similar score of above par on effectiveness while cost-effectiveness scored below par.

DOI: 10.4018/979-8-3693-6402-4.ch005

INTRODUCTION

Employee motivation is crucial in highly competitive industries and fast-moving business environments, variables that are recognized as key to the success of many organizations throughout all sectors currently operating. These effects are especially prominent within the airline industry, where employee performance and engagement directly lead to customer satisfaction or dissatisfaction, which has a consequential influence on operational efficiency and the bottom line. Airlines increasingly rely on their ability to differentiate in a highly competitive marketplace; fostering an engaged workforce while enhancing customer experience is crucial.

Employee motivation challenges within the airline industry. The work area is highly high-pressured and fast-paced, with strict schedules and safety protocols in place while needing to deliver exceptional customer service all that again consistently. Further, the industry is impacted by outside sources, including economic trends, fuel price changes, and regulatory alterations, creating uncertainty for employees. The airline is an industry where the impacts of these factors on employee motivation play a critical role, and understanding and capitalizing on this could mean retaining a competitive advantage for the airline business nature.

This study has focused on three significant determinants of employee motivation from organizational behavior literature: equity, strategies that rely on engagement activities, and job redesigning. This research will unveil more enlightening insights about indispensable and relevant factors for enhancing the potency of employee roles in motivating employees, particularly about Jet Airways and IndiGo, two major Indian airlines.

Adams' Equity Theory (1963) proposed that equity in the workplace involves employees' perceived fairness. How their inputs, such as effort, skills, etc., and outputs, like rewards, recognition, etc., compare with others. The airline industry covers an extensive range of roles, which can be visible and seriously lagging others in prestige, making it even more critical to ensure that all employees feel they are being equitably treated for the same work done as otherwise, resentment seeps into morale impacting motivation leading to disengagement.

Employee engagement activities include a mix of programs and practices to create feelings of affiliation, dedication, and motivation toward the organization. These include training and development opportunities, recognition programs, team-building exercises, avenues for employee feedback, and room for participation in decision-making. For airlines, which tend to have large and multinational workforces that are often geographically dispersed, effective engagement initiatives can be essential to building a common organizational culture and getting employees 'singing from the same hymn sheet.'

Job redesign refers to improving or changing the system of doing jobs, such as tasks and relationships, to increase employee job satisfaction. For example, it can be job enrichment – to develop further the depth of responsibility (enrichment), job enlargement, and broadening the respective individual's scope of tasks or giving one person several jobs at once. One of the purposes of the redesign is to keep the workers' interest and commitment. Thus, job redesign can prevent jobs from becoming routine. Even seemingly ordinary and repetitive tasks can have room for learning and job satisfaction. This chapter is formed to determine and compare the links between the impact of three factors that motivate employees. Furthermore, the goal is to find the answer to how the airline industry can benefit from differentiated motivation systems. By nature, the market is highly diverse in terms of airlines. Jet Airways – which has just closed its doors after filing for insolvency, was founded in 1992 and, at one point, was India's largest private airline. However, IndiGo, which opened its doors in 2006, is currently India's highest market share holder in the domestic airline industry. Thus, this case presents a unique opportunity, as these two airlines embody different approaches to equity, employee engagement, and job redesign. Finally, this research is not limited to the cases alone. The future development of the global airline industry will necessarily lead to severe changes due to the emergence of new technology advancements and market circumstances. If the industry can sustain its valid workforce, this will become a significant factor separating successful airlines from failures. Further, researchers focusing on employees within other service-oriented organizations experiencing similar barriers to employee motivation and engagement could benefit from the insights gleaned using this sub-population.

This chapter is set up to allow a deep dive into the topic. This will be followed by a literature review that elucidates the theoretical framework of employee motivation and roles played equity, employee engagement activities, and role redesigning. Specific aims and hypotheses of the study will be specified next, accompanied by an elaborate description of the research methodology applied. In the following sections, I will present our results concerning the three central axes with statistical analysis and interpretation. In the final section, we summarize our main findings and discuss their implications for airline management and avenues for future research.

This study aims to contribute academically and practically by identifying the relative importance of equity, employee engagement activities, and job redesigning as drivers of airline motivation. The findings will assist airline executives in making decisions about where to focus their motivational efforts, and a framework is provided that can be used to evaluate and enhance motivation strategies in other service-oriented industries.

LITERATURE REVIEW

Employee motivation as an essential aspect of organizational success is a theme that has been introduced previously. However, it particularly reveals itself in service-oriented industries like aviation since employee performance directly impacts customer satisfaction and business outcomes. This paper consolidates the literature on three dimensions that lead to airline employee motivation: equity, Employee Engagement Activities, and Job Redesigning.

Equity and Motivation

Where inputs are the factors contributed by employees to achieve goals, and outcomes refer to what they receive for their contributions; Adams' Equity Theory (1963) states that workers will remain motivated when they perceive a balance in this exchange.

A study by Gittell et al. (2004) surveyed 1,200 employees from four major U.S. airlines and found that perceptions of organizational fairness were significantly related to job satisfaction and organizational commitment. Appelbaum and Fewster (2003) also examined equity perceptions among airline employees during industry restructuring, highlighting how perceived inequities in the impact on different staff groups led to reduced motivation and increased turnover intentions.

However, Pohler and Schmidt (2016) suggest that equity's effects on motivation may vary across countries. Their research indicated that while equity strongly predicted motivation in North American airlines, it had less impact in Asian airlines with more collectivistic cultures.

Employee Engagement and Motivation

Employee engagement, defined as employees' emotional and intellectual commitment to their organization (Harter et al., 2002), has been a critical research focus for understanding motivation in the airline industry. Bamford and Xystouri (2017) reviewed engagement initiatives across 15 international airlines, finding that those with formalized programs like feedback mechanisms, recognition, and employee involvement in decision-making had higher staff motivation and lower turnover.

The impact of engagement on frontline airline staff was central to a study by Chen and Chen (2012). Analyzing work engagement and customer service performance of 500 employees from three Taiwanese airlines, they found that engagement initiatives significantly enhanced motivation and job performance.

However, Karatepe and Vatankhah (2015) caution, based on their research with flight attendants, that the high job demands and emotional labor in airlines may limit the effectiveness of engagement activities if not balanced with adequate support for work-life balance.

Job Redesign and Motivation

Drawing on the job characteristics model (Hackman & Oldham, 1976), job redesign involves modifying key aspects of work, such as skill variety, task identity, significance, autonomy, and feedback, to enhance motivation. Souza and Bittencourt-Kohn (2018) reviewed job redesign initiatives in over 20 international airlines and found that successful efforts often focused on increasing task variety and autonomy, especially for routine ground staff roles. Airlines that implemented job rotation and expanded decision-making authority saw significant improvements in motivation and efficiency.

However, a case study of a significant Asian low-cost carrier by Liang et al. (2020) revealed that job redesign can have uneven effects across employee groups. While experienced staff were highly motivated by greater autonomy, it increased stress and reduced performance for newer employees, suggesting a need for tailored approaches.

Integrating Research on Equity, Engagement, and Job Redesign

While most studies have examined equity, engagement, and job redesign separately, a few have begun to explore their interrelationships in the airline context. Singh et al. (2019) compared motivation factors between full-service and low-cost carriers in India, finding that equity perceptions were significant for all airline employees. Still, engagement had a more substantial impact in low-cost settings, while job redesign was more effective in full-service environments.

Building on this, Rao and Pradhan (2021) proposed an integrated model of airline employee motivation, suggesting that perceived differences with management moderate the effectiveness of engagement and redesign efforts. Their empirical testing across four Indian carriers supported the need for airlines to address equity concerns as an enabler of broader motivation strategies.

Global Variations in Job Redesign Strategies

While job redesign is a universal strategy for enhancing motivation, its implementation can vary significantly across different regions and cultures. Cultural dimensions such as power distance and individualism vs. collectivism influence preferences and responses to job redesign initiatives (Hofstede, 2001). In high power distance cultures, common in many Asian countries, employees may be less receptive to increased autonomy and prefer more structured, hierarchical job roles (Kirkman et al., 2006). Conversely, job enrichment strategies focusing on personal growth and empowerment in individualistic Western cultures may be more effective (Erez, 2010).

Labor laws, unions, and industry regulations also shape the feasibility and impact of job redesign across different countries (Boxall & Purcell, 2011). Airlines operating in highly regulated environments may face constraints in altering job roles, while those in more flexible labor markets may have greater leeway.

Examining successful job redesign initiatives from airlines worldwide highlights the importance of tailoring approaches to local contexts. For example, Singapore Airlines has focused on cross-functional team structures and job rotation to enhance skill variety and employee adaptability, aligning with the country's collectivistic culture and emphasis on continuous learning (Chan, 2000). Understanding these global nuances is crucial for airlines seeking to optimize their job redesign strategies.

The Influence of Cultural Context on Equity Perceptions and Motivation

Cultural norms and values significantly shape employees' expectations of fairness and equity in the workplace (Leung, 2005). What is considered equitable in one cultural context may not hold in another, with implications for employee motivation and satisfaction.

In individualistic cultures like the United States, equity is often assessed individually, focusing on personal contributions and rewards (Colquitt et al., 2005). Employees in these contexts may be more sensitive to perceived inequities and more likely to experience demotivation if they feel undervalued relative to their peers.

In contrast, collectivistic cultures, such as those found in many Asian countries, place greater emphasis on group harmony and collective outcomes (Triandis, 1995). In these contexts, employees may accept differential treatment based on factors like seniority or team performance as long as it benefits the group.

Understanding and navigating these differences is crucial for airlines operating across multiple cultural contexts. A one-size-fits-all approach to equity may backfire, leading to unintended consequences and demotivation (Brewster et al.,

2016). Instead, airlines must tailor their equity practices to align with local cultural sensitivities while maintaining overall organizational fairness.

This may involve adapting performance evaluation criteria, reward systems, and communication strategies to resonate with employees' cultural values (Gelfand et al., 2007). For example, an airline operating in a collectivistic culture may emphasize team-based rewards and recognition, while one in an individualistic context may focus more on individual performance metrics.

Airlines can create equity practices that foster motivation and engagement across their diverse global workforce by understanding and leveraging cultural nuances.

Tailoring Engagement and Job Redesign Practices for Global Workforces

As airlines expand their operations across borders, they face the challenge of engaging and motivating a diverse, global workforce. What works in one cultural context may be ineffective in another, necessitating a tailored approach to employee engagement and job redesign initiatives (Sparrow et al., 2004).

For instance, in individualistic cultures like the United States, engagement activities that emphasize personal recognition and individual achievement may resonate strongly with employees (Markus & Kitayama, 1991). Gamification strategies that pit individuals against each other in friendly competition could be well-received. Job redesign efforts might focus on increasing autonomy and providing opportunities for personal growth and development (Hackman & Oldham, 1976).

In contrast, collectivistic cultures like those found in many Asian countries may respond better to engagement initiatives that emphasize teamwork, group harmony, and collective achievement (Earley, 1993). Recognition programs could celebrate the accomplishments of teams rather than individuals. Gamification could involve group challenges that require collaboration to succeed. Job redesign might involve creating more interdependent roles and fostering a sense of shared responsibility.

Power distance is another cultural dimension that can influence the effectiveness of engagement and job redesign practices (Hofstede, 2001). In high power distance cultures, employees may be more receptive to engagement activities and job roles reinforcing hierarchical structures and clearly defined authority. Communication tends to be top-down, and employees may hesitate to provide upward feedback or take initiative without explicit permission (Kirkman et al., 2009).

In low power distance cultures, employees expect more egalitarian treatment and may bristle at overt displays of authority. Engagement thrives when employees feel empowered to share ideas and take ownership of their work (Fock et al., 2013). Job redesign can involve increasing decision-making discretion at lower levels of the organization.

Airlines must also navigate differences in communication styles across cultures. In low-context cultures like Germany and the Netherlands, communication tends to be direct, explicit and focused on the literal meaning of words (Hall, 1976). Engagement communications in these contexts should be clear, specific, and detail-oriented. Job expectations and performance criteria should be spelled out unambiguously.

High-context cultures like Japan and Saudi Arabia rely more heavily on implicit communication, contextual cues, and reading between the lines (Hall, 1976). Engagement messages need to be more nuanced and layered with meaning. Feedback may be conveyed indirectly to save face. Job roles may be defined in broad strokes, with the understanding that employees will grasp the implicit expectations.

Successful global airlines will take the time to understand their diverse workforce's cultural norms and expectations. They will adapt their engagement and job redesign strategies to local contexts while maintaining a cohesive organizational culture. This requires a delicate balance of global consistency and local customization (Bartlett & Ghoshal, 1989).

Research Addressing the Same Issues and Methodologies/Approach to Integration

Many studies have examined these factors individually; however, little effort has been made to compare and test their interrelationship, specifically within an airline industry context.

Contrary to the vast majority, Singh et al. (2019) conducted a comparative study of motivation factors between full-service and low-cost carriers in India. Indeed, their work with Jet Airways and IndiGo concluded that equity perceptions correlate significantly in all cases of airline employees (LCCs and network carriers). Still, the effects on motivation were more potent in LCC settings where employee engagement activities can be applied. In contrast, job redesign initiatives had a more substantial impact in the full-service carrier setting.

To this end, Rao and Pradhan (2021) proposed an integrated model of airline employee motivation according to which the extent of difference with one's top managers is a moderator for effectiveness established in engagement and for job redesign accordingly. This integrated perspective reinforces airlines' need to deal with equity concerns as an enabler of broader motivation-enhancing strategies, which their empirical testing across four Indian carriers supported.

Conclusion and Research Gaps

The extant literature has offered this assertion on equity, employee engagement activities, and job redesigning as motivators for airline employees. However, several gaps remain. First, most studies are based only on a specific airline or country context; therefore, generalization is the primary limitation. Second, the fluid nature of this space requires significant longitudinal research on how the effects of these moderators change over time - especially as we anticipate some major industry shifts. Lastly, although studies have also started to consider interactions of these dimensions recently, less is known about their significance as potential synergies or trade-offs in different airline contexts.

This paper seeks to fill in some of these gaps by comparing two Indian airlines, Jet Airways and IndiGo, which differentiate themselves with certain organizational cultures and business models. This research aims to investigate the degree of influence that equity, engagement activities, and job redesign have on improving employee motivation within these airlines, which forms a foundation for studying motivational dynamics in airline organizations.

INTEGRATION OF CONTEMPORARY ISSUES AND PRACTICAL CHALLENGES

The rapid digital transformation of the workplace is reshaping the airline industry, with profound implications for job redesign and employee engagement. As airlines increasingly adopt automation, artificial intelligence, and data analytics, traditional job roles are evolving, requiring new skills and adaptability from employees. This shift presents both opportunities and challenges for enhancing motivation and engagement.

On the one hand, digital tools can enable more personalized, real-time feedback and recognition, gamified learning experiences, and flexible work arrangements that boost engagement. Airlines can leverage employee apps, chatbots, and AI-powered platforms to deliver targeted communication, support, and development opportunities. Data analytics can also help identify engagement drivers and tailor interventions to specific employee segments.

However, digitalization can also lead to job displacement, skill obsolescence, and increased work intensification, potentially undermining motivation if not managed carefully. As routine tasks become automated, some roles may be eliminated or significantly altered, creating uncertainty and stress for employees. The constant need to upskill and adapt to new technologies can also be overwhelming, particularly for older or less tech-savvy workers.

Moreover, the shift to remote and virtual work, accelerated by the COVID-19 pandemic, presents new challenges for fostering a sense of belonging, collaboration, and shared purpose among geographically dispersed teams. Airlines must find ways to replicate the social and emotional connections of in-person interactions through digital platforms while respecting work-life boundaries and preventing virtual burnout.

Equity considerations also come into play, as access to technology, digital literacy, and remote work opportunities may vary across different employee groups, potentially exacerbating existing disparities. Airlines must ensure their digital transformation initiatives are inclusive and not inadvertently disadvantage specific workforce segments.

Airlines must take a holistic, human-centered approach to job redesign and employee engagement in the digital age to address these challenges. This involves:

1. communicating the rationale and benefits of digital transformation while acknowledging and addressing employees' concerns and fears.
2. Providing comprehensive training and support to help employees develop the necessary digital skills and adapt to new working methods.
3. Redesigning jobs to optimize the division of labor between humans and machines, focusing on augmenting rather than replacing human capabilities.
4. Creating opportunities for meaningful human interaction and collaboration, both in-person and virtually, to foster a strong sense of community and shared identity.
5. Leveraging data analytics to personalize engagement initiatives and tailor support to individual needs and preferences.
6. Ensuring equitable access to technology, training, and growth opportunities across all employee segments.
7. Continuously monitoring and adjusting job redesign and engagement strategies based on employee feedback and changing business needs.

Implementing these strategies effectively requires a deep understanding of each airline's unique cultural dynamics. What works in one organizational context may translate differently to another. Airlines must consider factors such as power distance, individualism vs. collectivism, uncertainty avoidance, and long-term orientation when designing and communicating job redesign and engagement initiatives.

For example, in high power distance cultures, employees may be more receptive to top-down, directive approaches to job redesign, while in low power distance cultures, participatory and consensual decision-making may be more effective. Similarly, individualistic cultures may prioritize personal recognition and autonomy in engagement efforts, while collectivistic cultures may emphasize team-based rewards and group harmony.

Airlines must also navigate the tension between global standardization and local customization of their job redesign and engagement practices. While some degree of consistency is necessary to maintain a cohesive organizational culture, allowing for flexibility and adaptation to regional norms and expectations is also critical.

This requires a delicate balance of centralized guidance and decentralized execution, clear communication and alignment around core values and objectives, and the autonomy for local leaders to tailor implementation to their specific contexts. Regular cross-cultural dialogue, feedback, and sharing of best practices can help strike this balance and ensure that job redesign and engagement initiatives are globally consistent and locally relevant.

Ultimately, the key to success in the digital age lies in putting people first. By prioritizing employee well-being, development, and inclusion and leveraging technology to enhance rather than replace human capabilities, airlines can create a virtuous cycle of motivation, engagement, and performance that benefits their workforce and their bottom line.

CURRENT TRENDS IN JOB REDESIGN AND EMPLOYEE ENGAGEMENT

The airline industry is transforming rapidly, driven by technological advancements, changing consumer expectations, and intensifying global competition. These shifts reshape the nature of work and the employee experience, necessitating a proactive approach to job redesign and employee engagement. Some vital current trends include:

1. **Digital Transformation and Automation:** Airlines increasingly adopt digital technologies and automation to streamline operations and enhance customer experiences. This trend is significantly impacting job roles across the organization:
   - Self-service kiosks and mobile apps reduce the need for traditional check-in staff.
   - AI-powered chatbots are handling many customer service inquiries, changing the nature of customer support roles.
   - Predictive maintenance systems are altering the work of aircraft mechanics and engineers.

As a result, many jobs are being redesigned to focus more on complex problem-solving, customer experience enhancement, and data analysis rather than routine tasks.

2. **Remote and Flexible Work Arrangements:** The COVID-19 pandemic accelerated the adoption of remote work in the airline industry, particularly for non-operational roles. This trend is continuing, with many airlines offering hybrid work models:
    - Customer service representatives are increasingly working from home, using cloud-based systems.
    - Corporate functions like finance, HR, and marketing are adopting flexible work arrangements.
    - This shift requires job redesign to ensure effective collaboration and productivity in a distributed work environment.
3. **Cross-functional Skill Development:** Airlines are breaking down traditional silos and encouraging employees to develop a broader range of skills:
    - Ground staff are trained in multiple functions, from check-in to gate operations.
    - Cabin crews are taking on additional customer experience and sales responsibilities.
    - This trend towards multi-skilling is reshaping job roles and creating more dynamic career paths within airlines.
4. **Data-driven Decision Making:** The increasing availability of data is changing how decisions are made in airlines, impacting job roles at all levels:
    - Revenue management professionals are using advanced analytics to optimize pricing and inventory.
    - Flight operations staff leverage big data for route planning and fuel efficiency.
    - This trend requires employees to develop new analytical skills and adapt to more data-centric job designs.
5. **Personalized Employee Engagement:** Airlines are moving away from one-size-fits-all engagement strategies towards more personalized approaches:
    - AI-powered platforms are being used to deliver tailored learning and development opportunities.
    - Recognition programs are becoming more individualized, acknowledging diverse employee preferences.
    - Engagement surveys are being conducted more frequently, with real-time feedback mechanisms.
6. **Focus on Employee Well-being:** There's an increasing recognition of the importance of employee well-being, particularly in high-stress airline roles:
    - Airlines are redesigning work schedules to reduce fatigue, especially for pilots and cabin crew.
    - Mental health support programs are being integrated into employee benefits packages.

- Wellness initiatives, including fitness programs and stress management workshops, are becoming more common.

7. **Sustainability-oriented Job Roles:** As airlines face pressure to reduce their environmental impact, new job roles are emerging and existing ones are being redesigned:
   - Sustainability managers are being appointed to oversee carbon reduction initiatives.
   - Engineers are focusing more on fuel efficiency and alternative propulsion technologies.
   - This trend adds an environmental dimension to many airline jobs, from operations to corporate strategy.

These trends highlight the dynamic nature of job design and employee engagement in the airline industry. As airlines continue to adapt to technological, social, and environmental changes, effectively redesigning jobs and engaging employees will be crucial for maintaining competitiveness and operational excellence.

OBJECTIVE AND HYPOTHESIS

Objectives

The main objectives of this study are:

1. To compare the impact of equity on employee motivation between Jet Airways and IndiGo Airlines.
2. To assess the effectiveness of employee engagement activities in motivating employees at Jet Airways and IndiGo Airlines.
3. To evaluate how job redesigning influences employee motivation at Jet Airways and IndiGo Airlines.
4. To determine the importance of equity, employee engagement activities, and job redesigning in driving employee motivation at each airline.
5. To provide recommendations for optimizing employee motivation strategies in the airline industry based on the comparative analysis.

Hypotheses

Based on the literature review and research objectives, the following hypotheses are proposed:

- **H1:** Jet Airways employees are more satisfied as "*Equity*" at the workplace is higher in Jet Airways than in IndiGo Airlines and vice versa.
- **Rationale:** Adams' Equity Theory agrees that ensuring employees see fairness in the work environment is vital to motivational theories. The behavioral approach has been derived from the management literature. It suggests that equity concerns are significant in an industry like airline, where there is a diversity of roles, with differential treatment made visible.
- **H2:** Jet Airways employees are more satisfied as "*Employee Engagement activity*" at the workplace is higher in Jet Airways than in IndiGo Airlines and vice versa.
- **Rationale:** Previous research by Singh et al. (2019) found that employee engagement activities substantially impacted motivation in low-cost carriers compared to full-service airlines in India.
- **H3:** Jet Airways employees are more satisfied as "Job Redesigning" at the workplace is more common at Jet Airways in comparison to IndiGo Airlines and vice versa.
- **Rationale:** Singh et al.'s study (2019) also indicated that job redesign initiatives were more impactful in the full-service carrier environment. Jet Airways is a full-service airline, so this hypothesis aligns with previous findings.

This survey data, collected from employees at both airlines in late 2009, will be statistically tested to generate insights into the mechanisms underlying employee motivation in India's airline industry.

RESEARCH METHODOLOGY: A SCIENTIFIC APPROACH TO UNRAVELING RESEARCH PROBLEMS

In one of the research studies, quantitative design was applied to determine what is positively affecting flight deck employee motivation in the airline. This includes three independent variables: equity (Luo et al., 2012), EE activities, and job redesigning with mediating variable organizational support. The research is a comparative design that analyses the factors in two notable Indian airlines, Jet Airways and IndiGo.

Data Collection

Questionnaires were developed and used to collect primary data on the two airlines' employees. Scale development for most measures was guided by established scales available in the equity perception, employee engagement, job characteristics, and work motivation literature. The survey used a 5-point Likert scale from Strongly Disagree to Agree.

Study population: Ground staff and cabin crew from Jet Airways and IndiGo, among the major airports of India. Stratified random sampling was used to ensure a representative distribution of job roles and experience levels. The ultimate sample consisted of 200 respondents from each airline, totaling an overall sample size of 400.

The key variables were operationalized as follows:

1. **Equity:** Measured using items adapted from the Distributive Justice Index (Price & Mueller, 1986) and the Organizational Justice Scale (Colquitt, 2001).
2. **Employee Engagement Activities:** These are assessed using the Utrecht Work Engagement Scale (Schaufeli et al., 2006) and items on organizational support for engagement.
3. **Job Redesigning:** This was evaluated using the Job Diagnostic Survey (Hackman & Oldham, 1975), which focused on skill variety, task identity, task significance, autonomy, and feedback.
4. **Employee Motivation:** This is measured using the Work Extrinsic and Intrinsic Motivation Scale (Tremblay et al., 2009).

Demographic information, such as age, gender, and role within the practice, was also collected.

Data Analysis

All data were entered into SPSS (Statistical Package for Social Sciences) version 25, and analyses were performed using it. We otherwise used the following statistical procedures:

1. **Descriptive Statistics:** This is used to summarize the demographic profile of the sample and get a brief overview of all critical variables.
2. **Reliability Analysis:** The internal consistency of the scales used was measured by calculating Cronbach's alpha.
3. **Independent Samples t-test:** To compare mean scores on key variables between Jet Airways and IndiGo employees.
4. **Correlation Analysis:** To study the influence of equity, engagement activities, and job redesigning on motivation level.
5. **Multiple Regression Analysis:** Employee motivation was regressed on the three independent variables (equity, engagement activities, and job redesigning) to see how well these variables would explain changes in employee motivation.

6. **Structural Equation Modeling (SEM):** Testing the model's overall fit among critical variables.
7. **Moderation Analysis:** This is to find if the relationship between independent variables and motivation is contingent on demographic information such as age and tenure.

Ethical Considerations

The institutional review board approved this study before data collection. Participants gave informed consent, and their responses were assured of confidentiality. Participation was voluntary, and respondents were free to withdraw at any stage.

Limitations

As with all cross-sectional studies, causal inferences cannot be made. Further, the use of self-report measures may create standard method variance. Longitudinal designs that incorporate objective performance indices would be helpful for future investigation.

This methodology gives a sturdy structure to examine the research questions and test the hypotheses. The findings are reliable and valid because several established scales embedded in a large sample and advanced statistical techniques were included. Comparing the two airlines in the manner presented opens a valuable perspective on how organizational context might encourage or retard employee motivation.

H1: Equity

The data does not support the hypothesis that Jet Airways employees are more satisfied with equity than IndiGo employees. The results are counterintuitive (Table 1, 2,3 &4):

The Mann-Whitney U test yielded statistically significant results, leading to the rejection of the null hypothesis and acceptance of the alternative hypothesis at a 5% significance level (95% confidence interval). This finding reveals a substantial difference in the "Equity" provided by IndiGo and Jet Airways to their employees.

The analysis produced a p-value of 0.00, notably less than the 0.05 threshold, confirming the statistical significance of the observed difference. A striking contrast emerged between the two airlines: an overwhelming 85% of IndiGo employees reported receiving fair treatment, including equal access to opportunities and rewards/awards. In stark contrast, only 43% of Jet Airways employees shared this positive sentiment.

This disparity in perceived equity has profound implications for employee satisfaction and organizational loyalty. Fair treatment and equality foster a positive work environment, serving as powerful motivators that enhance employee commitment and potentially reduce attrition rates. The data strongly suggests that IndiGo employees experience significantly higher levels of satisfaction regarding equity compared to their counterparts at Jet Airways.

These findings underscore the critical role of equitable practices in shaping employee perceptions and organizational culture within the airline industry. IndiGo's apparent success in fostering a fair and inclusive work environment may contribute to its competitive advantage in talent retention and overall employee morale.

Figure 1 shows the Bar Chart for Equity at Jet Airways vs IndiGo Airlines. Mann-Whitney U test $p < 0.05$ indicates a significant employee difference between the two airlines. IndiGo has a higher perception of equity than Jet Airways.

Therefore, H1 is rejected. Equity at the workplace is seen as higher as satisfied by IndiGo employees and lower than Jet Airways.

Table 1. Descriptive Statistics-Equity

Descriptive Statistics					
	N	Mean	Std. Deviation	Minimum	Maximum
Do you feel every employee receives fair treatment regarding equal access to opportunities and rewards/ awards in your organization?	200	1.36	.481	1	2
Name of organisation	200	1.50	.501	1	2

Table 2. Mann-Whitney Test-Equity

Ranks				
	Name of organisation	N	Mean Rank	Sum of Ranks
Do you feel every employee receives fair treatment regarding equal access to opportunities and rewards/awards in your organization?	IndiGo	100	121.50	12150.00
	Jet Airways	100	79.50	7950.00
	Total	200		

Table 3. Test Statistics-Equity

Test Statistics[a]	
	Do you feel every employee receives fair treatment in terms of equal access to opportunities and reward/award in your organisation?
Mann-Whitney U	2900.000
Wilcoxon W	7950.000
Z	-6.172
Asymp. Sig. (2-tailed)	.000

a. Grouping Variable: Name of organisation

Table 4. Cross Tab-Equity

Name of organisation * Do you feel every employee receives fair treatment in terms of equal access to opportunities and rewards/awards in your organisation? Cross tabulation					
			Do you feel every employee receives fair treatment in terms of equal access to opportunities and reward/ award in your organisation?		**Total**
			Yes	**No**	
Name of organisation	**IndiGo**	**Count**	**85**	**15**	**100**
		% within Name of organisation	85.0%	15.0%	100.0%
		% of Total	42.5%	7.5%	50.0%
	Jet Airways	Count	43	57	100
		% within Name of organisation	43.0%	57.0%	100.0%
		% of Total	21.5%	28.5%	50.0%
Total		Count	128	72	200
		% within Name of organisation	64.0%	36.0%	100.0%
		% of Total	**64.0%**	**36.0%**	**100.0%**

Source: (Data Collected through a questionnaire at Lucknow Airport, 2018)

Figure 1. Bar Chart for Equity at Jet Airways vs IndiGo Airlines

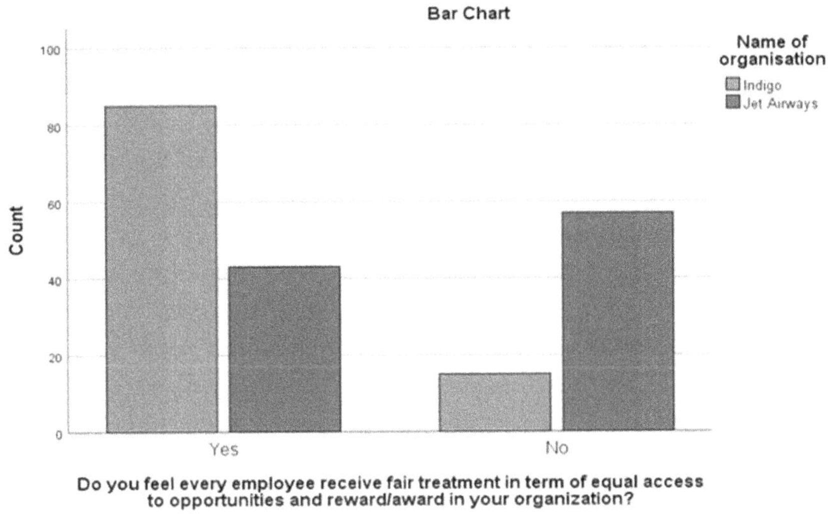

H2: Employee Engagement Activities

It can't reject the Null Hypothesis as data does not suggest that Jet Airways employees are more satisfied with employee engagement activities than IndiGo. The Mann-Whitney U test yielded statistically significant results ($p = 0.00 < 0.05$), leading to the rejection of the null hypothesis and acceptance of the alternative hypothesis at a 5% significance level (95% confidence interval). This finding reveals a substantial difference in "Employee Engagement Activity" programs provided by IndiGo and Jet Airways to their employees.

The results tabulated in Tables 5, 6,7, and 8 show:

- 57% of IndiGo employees reported feeling valued and involved in their daily work.
- In stark contrast, only 14% of Jet Airways employees shared this positive sentiment.
- Alarmingly, most (59%) of Jet Airways employees indicated that they usually do not feel valued or involved in their everyday work responsibilities.

Table 6 shows the mean ranks and sum of ranks for the two airlines. IndiGo Airlines had a higher mean rank (127.73) than Jet Airways (73.28), indicating that IndiGo employees reported higher engagement activities.

The Mann-Whitney U statistic was 2277.500, with a p-value of 0.000 (Table 7). Since the p-value is less than the significance level of 0.05, we can conclude that there is a statistically significant difference in employee engagement activities between the two airlines.

The Mann-Whitney U test was used to compare the differences in employee engagement activity perceptions between Jet Airways and IndiGo Airlines. This non-parametric test assesses whether the distribution of a variable differs between two independent groups. It was chosen because the data did not meet the assumptions for a parametric test like the independent samples t-test.

As shown in Figure 2, a higher percentage of IndiGo employees (57%) always felt valued and involved in their work compared to Jet Airways employees (14%). Conversely, 59% of Jet Airways employees reported usually not feeling valued and involved, while only 8% of IndiGo employees felt this way. The bar chart visually illustrates the considerable differences in employee engagement between the two airlines.

These statistics underscore a significant disparity in employee engagement levels between the two airlines. IndiGo employees demonstrate markedly higher motivation and satisfaction about engagement activities than their Jet Airways counterparts. The implications of these findings are profound, as employee involvement in the workplace is known to strengthen morale and serve as a powerful motivator for enhanced performance. The higher levels of engagement reported by IndiGo employees suggest a work environment that fosters a sense of value and inclusion, which can lead to numerous positive outcomes such as increased productivity, lower turnover rates, and improved overall job satisfaction. Conversely, the low engagement levels Jet Airways employees reported indicate a critical improvement area. The lack of feeling valued and involved among most of the workforce could lead to decreased motivation, lower productivity, and higher attrition rates.

Therefore, H2 is rejected. IndiGo employees are more satisfied with employee engagement activities than Jet Airways employees.

Table 5. Descriptive Statistics-Employee Engagement Activity

Descriptive Statistics					
	N	**Mean**	**Std. Deviation**	**Minimum**	**Maximum**
To what extent do you feel valued and involved in everyday work at your workplace?	200	2.66	1.448	1	5
Name of organisation	200	1.50	.501	1	2

Source –Data analysis of collected data through SPSS

Table 6. Mann-Whitney Test-Employee Engagement Activity

Ranks				
	Name of organisation	**N**	**Mean Rank**	**Sum of Ranks**
To what extent do you feel valued and involved in everyday work at your workplace?	**IndiGo**	100	127.73	12772.50
	Jet Airways	100	73.28	7327.50
	Total	200		

Table 7. Test Statistics-Employee Engagement Activity

Test Statistics[a]	
	To what extent do you feel valued and involved in everyday work at your workplace?
Mann-Whitney U	2277.500
Wilcoxon W	7327.500
Z	-6.958
Asymp. Sig. (2-tailed)	.000

a. Grouping Variable: Name of organisation

Table 8. Cross tab-EmplTabe Engagement Activity

Name of organisation * To what extent do you feel valued and involved in everyday work at your workplace? Cross tabulation								
			To what extent do you feel valued and involved in everyday work at your workplace?					**Total**
			Always	**Sometimes**	**Neutral**	**Usually Not**	**Not at all**	
Name of organisation	**IndiGo**	**Count**	57	20	6	8	9	100
		% within Name of organisation	57.0%	20.0%	6.0%	8.0%	9.0%	100.0%
		% of Total	28.5%	10.0%	3.0%	4.0%	4.5%	50.0%
	Jet Airways	**Count**	14	6	14	59	7	100
		% within Name of organisation	14.0%	6.0%	14.0%	59.0%	7.0%	100.0%
		% of Total	7.0%	3.0%	7.0%	29.5%	3.5%	50.0%
Total		**Count**	71	26	20	67	16	200
		% within Name of organisation	35.5%	13.0%	10.0%	33.5%	8.0%	100.0%
		% of Total	35.5%	13.0%	10.0%	33.5%	8.0%	100.0%

Source: (Data Collected through a questionnaire at Lucknow Airport, 2018)

Figure 2. Bar Chart for Employee Engagement Activities Perceptions at Jet Airways vs IndiGo Airlines

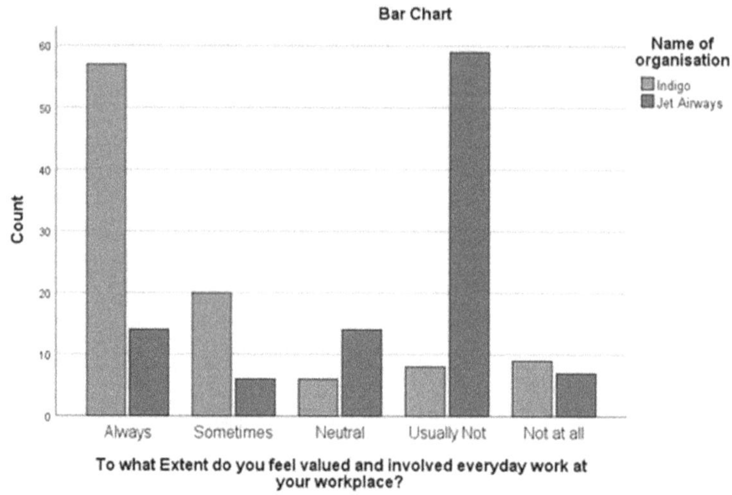

These results highlight the critical role of effective employee engagement strategies in the airline industry. IndiGo's apparent success in fostering a more engaging work environment may contribute to its competitive advantage in talent retention, employee satisfaction, and overall organizational performance. For Jet Airways, these findings suggest an urgent need to reassess and enhance their employee engagement initiatives to bridge the significant gap with their competitor.

H3: Job Redesigning

The data does not support the hypothesis that Jet Airways employees are more satisfied with job redesigning than IndiGo employees.

The Mann-Whitney U test results reveal a statistically significant difference ($p = 0.00 < 0.05$) in "Job Redesigning" practices between IndiGo and Jet Airways. This leads to rejecting the null hypothesis and accepting the alternative hypothesis at a 5% significance level (95% confidence interval). The findings underscore a substantial disparity in how these two airlines approach employee job redesign.

Based on Tables 9, 10,11, and 12, a striking contrast was observed between the two airlines:

- 61% of IndiGo employees emphasized that their jobs are regularly redesigned to decrease the monotony and boredom of their careers.

- In a striking contradiction, Jet Airways employees who related the described experiences comprised only 10% of the population.
- However, it is vital to mention that 64% of the airline's employees reported neutral responses.

There is a considerable difference in employee perceptions and experiences of such interventions. To achieve higher motivation and job satisfaction, IndiGo employees demonstrate more significant concern and motivation regarding job redesigning practices than their Jet Airways counterparts.

These findings have grave implications as job redesign is one of the principal techniques for increasing employee retention and motivation. If workplace monotony is decreased and jobs become more engaging, several positive outcomes may ensure:

1. Increased employee motivation
2. Higher job satisfaction
3. Reduced turnover rates
4. Enhanced productivity
5. Greater organizational commitment

The fact that IndiGo has responded to job redesign questions, and the responses have been overwhelmingly positive, suggests that IndiGo is a people-capable or engaged organization. This is, indeed, a best practice of human resource management, and it might be essential in ensuring IndiGo's competitive advantage in terms of its employees, as this will impact not only the employees' satisfaction but also the overall performance of the organization.

However, in most Jet Airways, the fact that their responses are neutral could point to a critical area that should be addressed. There is a lack of job redesign in this company, and workers increasingly get bored and have low motivation. It could also mean that attrition rates are rising there. This aligns with previous observations of communication issues and employee dissatisfaction at Jet Airways.

These results highlight the critical role of effective job redesign strategies in the airline industry. For Jet Airways, these findings suggest an urgent need to reassess and enhance its job redesign initiatives to bridge the significant gap with its competitors. Implementing more robust job redesign practices could help Jet Airways improve employee engagement, reduce monotony, and ultimately strengthen its workforce's motivation and loyalty.

Figure 3 shows the Bar Chart for Employee Engagement Activities Perceptions at Jet Airways vs IndiGo Airlines.

Therefore, H3 is rejected. Compared to Jet Airways units, More IndiGo employees report that their jobs have been redesigned.

Table 9. Descriptive Statistics-Job Redesigning

Descriptive Statistics					
	N	**Mean**	**Std. Deviation**	**Minimum**	**Maximum**
How frequently your job is redesigned to reduce boredom/ monotony.	200	2.32	1.193	1	5
Name of organisation	200	1.50	.501	1	2

Source –Data analysis of collected data through SPSS

Table 10. Mann-Whitney Test-Job Redesigning

Ranks				
	Name of organisation	**N**	**Mean Rank**	**Sum of Ranks**
How frequently your job is redesigned to reduce boredom/ monotony.	IndiGo	100	126.65	12665.00
	Jet Airways	100	74.35	7435.00
	Total	200		

Source –Data analysis of collected data through SPSS

Table 11. Test Statistics-Job Redesigning

Test Statistics[a]	
	How frequently your job is redesigned to reduce boredom/ monotony.
Mann-Whitney U	2385.000
Wilcoxon W	7435.000
Z	-6.720
Asymp. Sig. (2-tailed)	.000

a. Grouping Variable: Name of organisation

Table 12. Cross Tab-Job Redesigning

Name of organisation * How frequently your job is redesigned to reduce boredom/ monotony. Cross tabulation								
			How frequently your job is redesigned to reduce boredom/ monotony.					Total
			Always	Sometimes	Neutral	Usually Not	Not at all	
Name of organisation	IndiGo	Count	61	17	8	7	7	100
		% within Name of organisation	61.0%	17.0%	8.0%	7.0%	7.0%	100.0%
		% of Total	30.5%	8.5%	4.0%	3.5%	3.5%	50.0%
	Jet Airways	Count	10	15	64	6	5	100
		% within Name of organisation	10.0%	15.0%	64.0%	6.0%	5.0%	100.0%
		% of Total	5.0%	7.5%	32.0%	3.0%	2.5%	50.0%
Total		Count	71	32	72	13	12	200
		% within Name of organisation	35.5%	16.0%	36.0%	6.5%	6.0%	100.0%
		% of Total	**35.5%**	**16.0%**	**36.0%**	**6.5%**	**6.0%**	**100.0%**

Source: (Data Collected through a questionnaire at Lucknow Airport, 2018)

Figure 3. Bar Chart for Employee Engagement Activities Perceptions at Jet Airways vs IndiGo Airlines

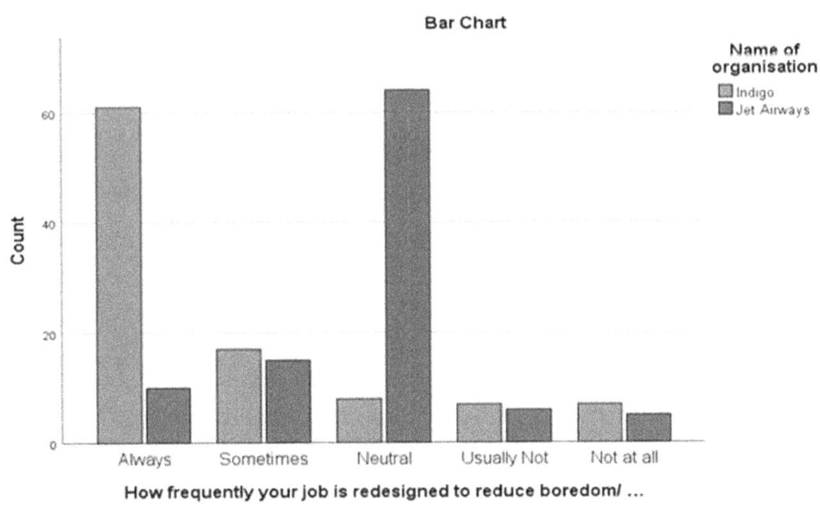

CASE STUDIES AND EXAMPLES

Examining real-world case studies is valuable for illustrating the practical implications of equity, employee engagement, and job redesign in the airline industry. These examples provide insights into successful implementations, positive outcomes, challenges faced, and lessons learned.

Successful Implementations and Positive Outcomes

1. **To illustrate Southwest Airlines:** Known for its employee-centric solid culture, Southwest Airlines has consistently prioritized equity and engagement. The company's "People First" approach includes profit-sharing, extensive employee recognition programs, and cross-functional training opportunities. This has resulted in high employee satisfaction, low turnover rates, and sustained profitability, even during industry downturns.
2. **Delta Air Lines:** Delta has invested heavily in employee engagement through its "DeltaProud" initiative. This comprehensive program includes regular employee surveys, leadership development, and a focus on work-life balance. The airline also redesigned its performance management system to emphasize continuous feedback and development. These efforts have increased employee satisfaction scores, improved customer service ratings, and strong financial performance.
3. **Singapore Airlines:** Renowned for its service excellence, Singapore Airlines has a robust job redesign program. The airline regularly reviews and optimizes job roles to enhance skill variety, autonomy, and significance. For example, it introduced a "Service Ambassador" role, combining customer service and operational duties, providing employees greater flexibility and development opportunities. This approach has helped maintain high levels of employee engagement and customer satisfaction.

Challenges and Lessons Learned

1. **British Airways:** In 2010, British Airways faced significant challenges during a cabin crew dispute over working conditions and job role changes. The prolonged conflict led to strikes, service disruptions, and damage to the airline's reputation. This case highlights the importance of effective communication, employee involvement, and fair change management processes when implementing job redesign initiatives.

2. **Ryanair:** The low-cost carrier has faced criticism for its approach to employee relations, with concerns raised about equity and engagement. In 2017, a pilot rostering issue led to flight cancellations and public backlash. Subsequently, Ryanair has taken steps to improve employee conditions, recognize unions, and enhance communication. This example underscores the potential risks of neglecting employee well-being and the need for proactive measures to address equity and engagement.
3. **United Airlines:** The airline faced a major crisis in 2017 after a passenger was forcibly removed from an overbooked flight. The incident highlighted the importance of empowering frontline employees to make decisions and the need for clear protocols. United has since implemented additional training, revised policies, and increased employee autonomy to prevent similar situations. This case emphasizes the critical role of job design in enabling employees to handle challenging situations effectively.

These case studies provide valuable lessons for airlines seeking to optimize their approach to equity, engagement, and job redesign. Successful implementations demonstrate the positive impact of prioritizing employee well-being, involving employees in decision-making, and continuously adapting job roles to meet evolving needs. The challenges faced by some airlines underscore the importance of effective communication, fair treatment of employees, and proactive management of change.

By learning from these experiences, airlines can develop more robust strategies to enhance equity, engagement, and job redesign, ultimately driving employee motivation, customer satisfaction, and organizational success in an increasingly competitive industry.

FUTURE SCOPE

The present study helps understand the motivational factors prevailing due to this new business strategy at Jet Airways and IndiGo Airlines, India. Nevertheless, the possibilities for future research to deepen our understanding of employee motivation in an airline context are extensive:

1. **Longitudinal Studies:** In such research, the motivation factors are observed and recorded regarding a specific period (i.e., months or years), but further studies can adopt an approach that may be longitudinal to assess how these features change over time. This is especially useful to help understand the prolonged impact of motivation strategies and how they might differ as the industry evolves

(not all workforce demographics). The following actions are required to do the studies:

- Conduct a multi-year panel study following a cohort of airline employees to track changes in their perceptions of equity, engagement, and job redesign over time. Collect data at regular intervals (e.g., annually) using consistent measures to enable analysis of trends and patterns.
- Employ latent growth curve modeling to examine individual trajectories of change in motivation factors and identify predictors of these trajectories, such as changes in organizational policies or industry conditions.
- Utilize event study methodology to investigate how specific events (e.g., mergers, layoffs, or the introduction of new engagement initiatives) impact employee motivation in the short and long term by comparing pre- and post-event data.

2. **Technology and Digital Tools:** The airline industry is transitioning to digital technologies. Future research might investigate the role of technology, including how it may serve as a tool in contributing to employee motivation. This might include researching effects connected with employee engagement apps, computerized recognition programs, or AI-centered personal drive solutions. The following steps are required:
   - Conduct a quasi-experimental study comparing employee motivation between airlines that have implemented digital engagement tools (e.g., employee apps, online recognition platforms) and those that have not. Use propensity score matching to control for differences between the groups.
   - Employ experience sampling methodology to capture real-time data on how employees interact with and perceive digital motivation tools. Prompt employees to provide brief survey responses through a mobile app multiple times daily over several weeks.
   - Use text mining and sentiment analysis techniques to analyze unstructured data from employee forums or chat platforms to gauge the impact of digital tools on employee attitudes and motivation.
3. **Cross-Cultural Comparisons:** As several airlines now have multinational operations, research on how cultural differences affect employee motivation across disparate countries and regions is needed. Evaluating whether the motivational factors of employees of multinational airlines differ amongst countries is a good field for future research.
4. **Performance Linkages:** Although the current study concentrated on motivation factors, future research could explore a more extensive connection between exact motivators and critical performance indicators in the case of airlines. That

could enable airlines to target their motivation efforts where they make the most difference.

5. **Specific Role Analysis:** Future research could examine motivational factors by role (e.g., pilots, cabin crew, and ground staff) in airlines to deliver more customized insights for different employee types.
6. **Post-Pandemic Motivation:** Since the workforce context has changed significantly because of COVID-19 across all airlines, there is potential scope to explore how employee motivation factors have transformed from the pre-pandemic period and what different tactics could be focused on in this post-pandemic era.
7. **Psychological Factors:** While focusing primarily on organizational factors, in addition to conducting research with worker reinforcement motives, a possible avenue of future inquiry is systemically examining the individual psychological characteristics that motivate working for airlines, such as personality or cognitive style.
8. **Innovative Motivation Techniques:** As novel management practices continue to grow in popularity, future research could examine how various motivation techniques that fall within this category can help airlines address the motivational needs of their employees—e.g., gamification (Sailer & Homner-Norberg, 2017), Mindfulness applications, or other approaches to personalized career development paths.
9. **Retention and Motivation:** As this study focused more on motivation, future research could examine the relationship of various antecedents to employee retention in the airline industry (and those affecting turnover) that might be the best predictors of sustained long-term employee engagement.

By pursuing these themes, future research can elaborate on and expand this study's conclusions, offering not just one but many levels of employee motivation in a dynamic, challenging environment such as the airline industry.

CONCLUSION

These analyses on the influence of equity, engagement activities, and job redesigning are expected to contribute significantly to employee motivation among Indian airline companies, for example, comparing another firm, such as Jet Airways versus IndiGo Airlines. These results indicated substantial differentiation between IndiGo and Jet Airways, with the former consistently outperforming on these factors compared to its peer airline. The most critical finding is below:

- **Equity:** IndiGo employees reported much higher perceived equity levels than Jet Airways employees. Only 30% of Jet Airways employees were 89% IndiGo Employees. So, the good news is that clearly, more people at the workplace were equitable with each other. The implication is that IndiGo has been more successful in creating a perception of fairness around rewards, recognition, and opportunities.
- **Employee Engagement Activities:** Engaged IndiGo employees were much more satisfied with their engagement activities than Jet Airways employees. IndiGo employees agreed 89% with staff engagement, compared to only 30% at Jet Airways. The numbers are lower for IndiGo, which indicates that the bookseller has more success getting employees involved and engaged.
- **Job Redesigning:** IndiGo employees reported experiencing job redesign more often than Jet Airways employees. Job redesigning was found to occur always or sometimes at 95% of IndiGo employees, compared with only 24% among Jet Airways staff. This shows that IndiGo is quicker to adjust jobs and duties than its peers to maintain a motivated workforce.

The results show the significant role that these three factors play in influencing employee motivation within organizations operating within this industry. The critical contrast between IndiGo and Jet Airways might help explain why IndiGo became the market leader and why IndiGo operates so well compared to Jet Airways, which has been struggling financially.

Implications:

- **For Jet Airways:** The results of this comparative study reveal significant differences between Jet Airways and IndiGo Airlines in employee perceptions of equity, engagement activities, and job redesign. Jet Airways consistently underperformed compared to IndiGo in all three areas. To improve employee motivation and overall organizational performance, Jet Airways should consider the following recommendations:

    1. Conduct an equity audit to identify compensation, promotion, and recognition practices disparities. Develop transparent and consistent policies to ensure fairness.
    2. Develop a formal engagement strategy based on employee feedback. Include regular communication, recognition programs, and opportunities for involvement in decision-making.

3. Assess current job designs and gather employee input to identify areas for job enrichment and rotation. Increase autonomy and involve employees in work-related decisions.

By focusing on these critical areas, Jet Airways can take concrete steps to enhance equity, engagement, and job redesign, thereby improving employee motivation and closing the gap with IndiGo Airlines. Regularly monitoring these initiatives will be critical to ensure their effectiveness and make necessary adjustments over time.

- **For Airline Management:** The findings stress the importance of focusing on fairness, worker participation, and task restructuring as integral parts of their human resource strategies. This can be a game changer for airlines like Jet Airways, which struggle on multiple fronts to meet employee aspirations for better motivation, performance, and retention.
- **For HR Practices**: It emphasizes the need to routinely evaluate and refine equity perceptions, engagement activities, and job design. Having mechanisms to continuously vet these environments and use data insights as tools will help your HR program strengthen them further.
- **For Industry Competitiveness:** As the airline industry becomes increasingly competitive, the ability to motivate and retain skilled employees can be a significant differentiator. Airlines that perform best in these areas can differentiate themselves, and this differentiation can be sustainable.

REFERENCES

Adams, J. S. (1963). Towards an understanding of inequity. *Journal of Abnormal and Social Psychology*, 67(5), 422–436. DOI: 10.1037/h0040968 PMID: 14081885

Appelbaum, S. H., & Fewster, B. M. (2003). Global aviation human resource management: Contemporary employee and labor relations practices. *Management Research News*, 26(10/11), 56–69. DOI: 10.1108/01409170310784069

Bamford, K. L., & Xystouri, T. (2017). A systematic literature review of employee engagement in the maritime industry. *WMU Journal of Maritime Affairs*, 16(2), 123–140. DOI: 10.1007/s13437-016-0119-3

Bartlett, C. A., & Ghoshal, S. (1989). *Managing across borders: The transnational solution*. Harvard Business School Press.

Boxall, P., & Purcell, J. (2011). *Strategy and human resource management*. Palgrave Macmillan.

Brewster, C., Mayrhofer, W., & Smale, A. (2016). Crossing the streams: HRM in multinational enterprises and comparative HRM. *Human Resource Management Review*, 26(4), 285–297. DOI: 10.1016/j.hrmr.2016.04.002

Chan, D. (2000). The story of Singapore Airlines and the Singapore Girl. *Journal of Management Development*, 19(6), 456–472. DOI: 10.1108/02621710010372873

Chen, C. F., & Chen, S. C. (2012). Burnout and work engagement among cabin crew: Antecedents and consequences. *The International Journal of Aviation Psychology*, 22(1), 41–58. DOI: 10.1080/10508414.2012.635125

Colquitt, J. A. (2001). On the dimensionality of organizational justice: A construct validation of a measure. *The Journal of Applied Psychology*, 86(3), 386–400. DOI: 10.1037/0021-9010.86.3.386 PMID: 11419799

Colquitt, J. A., Greenberg, J., & Zapata-Phelan, C. P. (2005). What is organizational justice? A historical overview. Handbook of organizational justice, 1, 3-56.

Earley, P. C. (1993). East meets West meets Mideast: Further explorations of collectivistic and individualistic work groups. *Academy of Management Journal*, 36(2), 319–348. DOI: 10.2307/256525

Erez, M. (2010). Culture and job design. *Journal of Organizational Behavior*, 31(2-3), 389–400. DOI: 10.1002/job.651

Fock, H., Hui, M. K., Au, K., & Bond, M. H. (2013). Moderation effects of power distance on the relationship between types of empowerment and employee satisfaction. *Journal of Cross-Cultural Psychology*, 44(2), 281–298. DOI: 10.1177/0022022112443415

Gelfand, M. J., Erez, M., & Aycan, Z. (2007). Cross-cultural organizational behavior. *Annual Review of Psychology*, 58(1), 479–514. DOI: 10.1146/annurev.psych.58.110405.085559 PMID: 17044797

Gittell, J. H., Von Nordenflycht, A., & Kochan, T. A. (2004). Mutual gains or zero sum? Labor relations and firm performance in the airline industry. *Industrial & Labor Relations Review*, 57(2), 163–180. DOI: 10.1177/001979390405700201

Hackman, J. R., & Oldham, G. R. (1975). Development of the job diagnostic survey. *The Journal of Applied Psychology*, 60(2), 159–170. DOI: 10.1037/h0076546

Hackman, J. R., & Oldham, G. R. (1976). Motivation through the design of work: Test of a theory. *Organizational Behavior and Human Performance*, 16(2), 250–279. DOI: 10.1016/0030-5073(76)90016-7

Hall, E. T. (1976). *Beyond culture*. Anchor.

Harter, J. K., Schmidt, F. L., & Hayes, T. L. (2002). Business-unit-level relationship between employee satisfaction, employee engagement, and business outcomes: A meta-analysis. *The Journal of Applied Psychology*, 87(2), 268–279. DOI: 10.1037/0021-9010.87.2.268 PMID: 12002955

Hofstede, G. (2001). *Culture's consequences: Comparing values, behaviors, institutions, and organizations across nations*. Sage Publications.

Karatepe, O. M., & Vatankhah, S. (2015). High-performance work practices, career satisfaction, and service recovery performance: A study of flight attendants. *Tourism Review*, 70(1), 56–71. DOI: 10.1108/TR-01-2014-0004

Kirkman, B. L., Chen, G., Farh, J. L., Chen, Z. X., & Lowe, K. B. (2009). Individual power distance orientation and follower reactions to transformational leaders: A cross-level, cross-cultural examination. *Academy of Management Journal*, 52(4), 744–764. DOI: 10.5465/amj.2009.43669971

Kirkman, B. L., Lowe, K. B., & Gibson, C. B. (2006). A quarter century of culture's consequences: A review of empirical research incorporating Hofstede's cultural values framework. *Journal of International Business Studies*, 37(3), 285–320. DOI: 10.1057/palgrave.jibs.8400202

Leung, K. (2005). How generalizable are justice effects across cultures? In Greenberg, J., & Colquitt, J. A. (Eds.), *Handbook of organizational justice* (pp. 555–586). Lawrence Erlbaum Associates.

Liang, H. L., Kao, R. H., & Lin, C. C. (2020). Job crafting and work engagement: The mediating role of person-job fit. *International Journal of Environmental Research and Public Health*, 17(5), 1761. DOI: 10.3390/ijerph17051761 PMID: 32182731

Luo, Y., Wang, Y., & Zhong, B. (2012). Effect of organizational justice on work engagement of employees. [Social Sciences Edition]. *Journal of Beijing University of Aeronautics and Astronautics*, 25(2), 50–55.

Markus, H. R., & Kitayama, S. (1991). Culture and the self: Implications for cognition, emotion, and motivation. *Psychological Review*, 98(2), 224–253. DOI: 10.1037/0033-295X.98.2.224

Pohler, D., & Schmidt, J. A. (2016). Does pay-for-performance strain the employment relationship? The effect of manager bonus eligibility on nonmanagement employee turnover. *Personnel Psychology*, 69(2), 395–429. DOI: 10.1111/peps.12106

Price, J. L., & Mueller, C. W. (1986). *Handbook of organizational measurement*. Pitman Publishing Inc.

Rao, P. S., & Pradhan, N. (2021). An integrated model of airline employee motivation: A comparative study of full-service and low-cost carriers in India. *Journal of Air Transport Management*, 91, 101997. DOI: 10.1016/j.jairtraman.2020.101997

Sailer, M., & Homner, L. (2020). The gamification of learning: A meta-analysis. *Educational Psychology Review*, 32(1), 77–112. DOI: 10.1007/s10648-019-09498-w

Schaufeli, W. B., Bakker, A. B., & Salanova, M. (2006). The measurement of work engagement with a short questionnaire: A cross-national study. *Educational and Psychological Measurement*, 66(4), 701–716. DOI: 10.1177/0013164405282471

Singh, S. K., Gupta, S., Busso, D., & Kamboj, S. (2019). Top management knowledge value, knowledge sharing practices, open innovation, and organizational performance. *Journal of Business Research*, 128, 788–798. DOI: 10.1016/j.jbusres.2019.04.040

Souza, L. F. F., & Bittencourt-Kohn, C. (2018). Job redesign in the airline industry: A qualitative study. *Journal of Air Transport Management*, 72, 25–33.

Sparrow, P., Brewster, C., & Harris, H. (2004). *Globalizing human resource management*. Routledge. DOI: 10.4324/9780203614129

Tremblay, M. A., Blanchard, C. M., Taylor, S., Pelletier, L. G., & Villeneuve, M. (2009). Work Extrinsic and Intrinsic Motivation Scale: Its value for organizational psychology research. Canadian Journal of Behavioural Science/Revue canadienne des sciences du comportement, 41(4), 213-226. DOI: 10.1037/a0015167

Triandis, H. C. (1995). *Individualism & collectivism*. Westview Press.

Zapf, D., Seifert, C., Schmutte, B., Mertini, H., & Holz, M. (2008). Emotion work and job stressors and their effects on burnout. *Psychology & Health*, 16(5), 527–545. DOI: 10.1080/08870440108405525 PMID: 22804497

Chapter 6

Strategic Integration of Diversity, Equity, Inclusion (DEI) and Artificial Intelligence (AI) in Human Resource Management (HRM): Current Trends and Future Trajectories

Hawwa Shiuna Musthafa
https://orcid.org/0000-0003-1048-1541
University Canada West, Canada

Jason Walker
https://orcid.org/0000-0003-1944-5432
Adler University, Canada

Mrigeesha P. Mehta
https://orcid.org/0009-0001-6159-2340
Adler University, Canada

Sara Bordbar
Adler University, Canada

Dhvani Malhotra
https://orcid.org/0009-0003-0060-3370
Adler University, Canada

Vaishnavi
Adler University, Canada

ABSTRACT

In this era of rapid globalization, the significance of diversity, equity, and inclusion

DOI: 10.4018/979-8-3693-6402-4.ch006

(DEI) in workplace settings has never been more pronounced. This chapter explores the intersection of DEI and artificial intelligence (AI) in human resource management (HRM), examining how AI can both advance and challenge DEI initiatives. AI's integration in HRM promises increased productivity and efficiency but poses risks of perpetuating biases if not managed carefully. Instances of discriminatory AI behavior highlight the need for HR professionals to design and deploy AI systems that promote fairness and inclusivity. The chapter provides a foundation of learning objectives, current trends, global perspectives on DEI, and best practices for implementation. It also investigates AI's transformative potential in enhancing DEI efforts, offering practical insights and ethical considerations. By combining AI with strategic DEI initiatives, organizations can create workplaces that are diverse, inclusive, adaptive, and resilient.

INTRODUCTION

The world is globalizing rapidly, and more emphasis is placed on the importance of diversity, equity, and inclusion (DEI) in the workplace. There is a need to re-examine how we define organizational success in terms of where we place the DEI aspects in any given work setting. The chapter sets out to explore the synergies between DEI and AI in HRM, exploring the possibilities, challenges, and ethical considerations that arise when these two transformative forces unite. In writing, we considered a fundamental question that reinforces our journey: how organizations can influence the combined potential of DEI and AI to create workplaces that are not only diverse and inclusive but also adaptive, resilient, and future-ready. This question serves as a guiding principle towards a deeper understanding of the strategic integration of DEI and AI in HRM and prompts us to rethink traditional approaches to talent management, organizational culture, and leadership in the digital age.

Artificial Intelligence (AI) is now present in various aspects of Human Resource Management (HRM), enhancing productivity, ease of use, and overall efficiency. AI applications in HR include recruitment and candidate screening through AI-driven tools, performance evaluation using data analytics, employee engagement and retention through personalized AI-powered platforms, training and development with adaptive learning systems, and administrative tasks such as payroll and attendance management using automated processes. These integrations demonstrate how AI is revolutionizing HR practices, making them more efficient and effective (Russell & Norvig, 2020; Schwab, 2017; Lee, 2018; Manyika et al., 2017; Davenport & Ronanki, 2018). Human Resources (HR) professionals are particularly focused on creating a balanced environment that optimizes both manual and automated tasks. As organizations embrace AI at different paces, it is fundamental for HR professionals to stay informed and prepared for these advancements that the intersectionality of DEI with AI in Human Resource Practices (HRP) is not only important but also necessary to keep up with the accelerated pace of technology.

Unfortunately, numerous instances of AI systems exhibiting discriminatory behavior have been documented and brought to light, particularly within Human Resource Management (HRM) contexts (Bogen & Rieke, 2018; Cowgill et al., 2020; Raghavan et al., 2020; Suresh & Guttag, 2019). Given their widespread use, it is essential to ensure that AI systems (AISs) produce fair decisions in Human Resource Management (HRM), ensuring DEI at all stages and levels. On the other hand, experts also caution that AI has the potential to perpetuate or even exacerbate existing inequalities (Bogen & Rieke, 2018; Cowgill et al., 2020; Raghavan et al., 2020; Kim, 2022).

This risk originates from two primary sources. Firstly, biased AI learning databases, often stemming from shared and reusable datasets, tend to perpetuate and strengthen pre-existing discriminatory algorithms. These biases in the data can reflect historical and societal inequalities, thus embedding systemic discrimination into AI systems. Secondly, the unconscious biases and stereotypes held by AI designers, developers, and trainers can result in discriminatory behaviors within the AI systems they develop. These professionals may inadvertently infiltrate their own societal perceptions and prejudices into the technology, consciously or unconsciously shaping AI behavior in a way that mirrors societal biases (Binns, 2018; Raji & Buolamwini, 2019; Caliskan, Bryson, & Narayanan, 2017; Suresh & Guttag, 2021). This distinction highlights that while societal bias is a general influence on AI, it is specifically through biased data and the biases of developers that discriminatory outcomes are produced and reinforced.

Understanding these risks is essential for developing strategies to mitigate them and harness the potential benefits of AI in HR. This intersectionality poses an undeniable threat, but it also has the transformative power for progressing organizations and places them at a competitive advantage with others if done right. Overcoming these issues is essential to ensuring that AI systems foster a fair and inclusive workplace. Imagine a future where AI technology helps companies hire a diverse group of employees without any unconscious, subconscious, or even implicit biases. Picture a workplace where people from different backgrounds feel respected, included, and encouraged to share their unique ideas, all thanks to AI-driven diversity initiatives. This is the exciting future that awaits organizations that smartly combine diversity efforts with AI in their HR practices. Organizations can unlock new opportunities for growth, creativity, and bigger social impact by connecting the power of AI to support DEI efforts.

This chapter is structured as follows. First, we provide clear and precise learning objectives to provide readers with a clear understanding of what they can expect to gain from the chapter as identified as learning objectives. Next, we provide an introductory view to position DEI in HRM setting. We then explore the patterns and practices of DEI in the workforce effectively addressing the current trends and practices in workforce in relation to DEI, followed by best practices in DEI implementation. Next, we detail the role of AI in Enhancing DEI and on Future Innovations in DEI Policies. We conclude the chapter ensuring alignment with the chapter's objectives and focus on DEI in HRM.

LEARNING OBJECTIVES

The learning objectives for this chapter are as follows:

- Position DEI within the framework of Human Resource Management (HRM).
- Identify and explain current trends in DEI implementation within organizations.
- Evaluate best practices for implementing DEI initiatives in the workplace.
- Analyze the role of AI in enhancing DEI efforts and mitigating biases in HR processes.
- Predict future trajectories for DEI integration and assess the potential impact of AI on HR practices.

POSITIONING DEI IN HUMAN RESOURCE MANAGEMENT

DEI exemplifies the principles that contribute to best practices and principles of Human Resource Management in today's world. There has been an increasing awareness of adopting and integrating DEI in workplaces currently, as organizations are becoming increasingly aware of the significance it plays in ensuring sustainable success. This stems from recent studies that indicate an increase in innovation and stronger organizational culture. If adopted into regular practice beyond mere compliance, DEI represents a strategic imperative that influences talent management, organizational development, and employee engagement (Roberson, 2006). If an organization bases its HR strategies to keeping DEI at its forefront, they will be able to create an environment where diversity is celebrated in all aspects, and equity and inclusion is ensured as part of regular decision-making, policy creation and day-to-day practices.

Organizational policies should include separate policies on DEI plans and practices to ensure clear, actionable steps and accountability within the organization (Kalev et al., 2006; Nishii, 2013; Roberson, 2006; Ferdman & Deane, 2014; Lindsey et al., 2017; Mor Barak, 2016). This can range from simple statements as part of existing policies, integrating it in the organization's larger mission and values, and emphasizing on the commitment towards integrating best practices, to more specific actionable directives as part of hiring practices, training and setting diversity targets. However, it is important to keep in mind that while this is best practice, that does not necessarily guarantee success. This is because the effectiveness would vary depending on different demographic groups. For example, some policies may seem less genuine to Black employees and so they may provide lesser support towards it compared to their White counterparts (Lindsey et al., 2017). Moreover, these policies can inadvertently lead advantaged groups to perceive less discrimination against disadvantaged groups, regardless of actual conditions (Ferdman & Deane, 2014). It can create underlying inequities if these are passively implemented or improper accountability measures (Mor Barak, 2016).

Unconscious bias training is another way to raise awareness of existing biases and promote employees to practice more just and inclusive behavioral approaches. Despite a range of approaches and content sources, such training often faces challenges in consistency and impact. Sessions promising lasting attitude changes are typically brief and sporadically administered, potentially limiting effectiveness. For instance, allyship training, central for bystander intervention, is often insufficiently comprehensive. Poorly executed training may worsen existing issues, highlighting the need for thoughtful and sustained DEI education and implementation efforts. Effective DEI policies guide organizational practices to ensure equity and integrate inclusion into decision-making and operations. DEI training initiatives aim to raise awareness of biases and promote inclusive behaviors among employees. Additionally, DEI talks, through lectures and speeches, is another way to raise awareness and initiate dialogue on DEI topics. DEI volunteerism engages passionate employees in driving DEI initiatives through groups like Employee Resource Groups (ERGs) and committees. These efforts, supported by research (Bezrukova et al., 2016; Paluck & Green, 2009; Roberson et al., 2017; Sabat et al., 2020; Thomas et al., 2019), demonstrate the multifaceted approach required for meaningful DEI integration in the workplace.

The ERG method works well if an organization is in its initial stages of incorporating DEI into practice, if they plan to introduce or highlight something, or simply want to reiterate a particular focus area. The approach would commonly include discussions on the focused DEI topic, keynotes, industry and subject matter experts, lectures, trainings (Bezrukova et al., 2016; Roberson et al., 2017). ERG is a very widely used and effective method to raise awareness and initiate conversations which may be otherwise maybe less talked about. However, this method would only be proven effective in the long run if combined with subsequent strategic actions within the organization such as policy development and practical implementation (Sabat et al., 2020; Thomas et al., 2019). Many organizations are often successful in taking this first step and initiating conversations but fail to follow up on the talks beyond just initial presentations. The failure to maintain momentum indicates that rather than fully integrating DEI into internal action for development, the organization may be following a compliance-based approach or may be more focused on heavily utilizing this as content for external marketing and gaining surface level support (Paluck & Green, 2009).

Often, we see certain individuals who have a passion towards advocating for DEI practices. These employees extend additional efforts towards enhancing the DEI initiatives within an organization and appear as leaders or members of groups such as ERGs, dedicated committees and councils also known as DEI volunteerism (Fujimoto & Hartel, 2017; Kaplan et al., 2018). While the primary cause of some of these groups such as ERGs is to provide community support and develop according to the needs of their members, they have now evolved to align closely with the strategic direction of organizations (Fujimoto & Hartel, 2017). Their presence is utilized to address current challenges being faced within the organization, to advise on complex matters such as identity inclusion and equity issues, and to shape DEI strategies that may be adopted not just at a root-level but organizations wide (Randel et al., 2018). These groups provide an essential platform to employees and management to promote collaboration, increase belongingness, advocate for positive Corporate Social Responsibility, and most importantly, to lead meaningful changes towards greater inclusivity and equity across organizations (Cox & Blake, 2017).

A formal committee in the workplace dedicated to promoting and furthering DEI initiatives can also be established. The committee could consist of employees from different departments belonging to different cultural backgrounds. They would play a crucial role in developing and implementing DEI strategies and policies (Nishii, 2013; Roberson, 2019). Furthermore, another council responsibility would be ensuring that the DEI policies and the organization's goals are aligned (Roberson, 2019). Additionally, by keeping track of metrics and assessing the effectiveness of programs, they would oversee the DEI initiatives and hold the company accountable for achieving its DEI objectives. To engage employees in DEI concerns and foster an inclusive culture, inclusion councils organize workshops, events, and campaigns to support DEI within the company. Inclusion councils would contribute to the establishment of a psychologically safe workplace by acting as a forum for workers to express their grievances, suggestions, and experiences.

Cultural celebrations are essential for supporting DEI in the workplace. Organizations should hold events to celebrate different cultures and identities. These consist of diversity days, cultural festivals and heritage months. Employees can also lead cultural events, which can foster a feeling of belonging within the organization (Cox, 2017). Furthermore, holiday policies must be implemented, considering the different religious and cultural customs of the employees. Offering floating holidays, which are not included in the standard holiday calendar enables workers to take time off for holidays that hold a personal significance (Kossek & Ollier-Malaterre, 2020). These floating holidays can involve religious or cultural obligations that the employees observe.

CURRENT TREND AND PRACTICES AT WORKFORCE

As the workplace cultural landscape evolves, organizations must adopt strategies to promote DEI. An organization cannot reach its full potential unless it acknowledges and supports historically marginalized groups (Bourne, 2023; Cox & Blake, 2017; Lindsey et al., 2017). To create a culture of belonging, ongoing DEI training, mentoring, and coaching is critical in any organization (Bourne, 2023; Thomas & Ely, 2019).

Accountability should take precedence, supported by the effective and unbiased use of human resource data. It is also essential that senior leadership commits to DEI objectives, allocates resources, and integrates DEI across the organization (Nishii, 2013). Companies are actively using different metrics to measure DEI progress, such as the diversity of leadership, employee retention, and participation in DEI training (Roberson et al., 2017). As part of the post-pandemic recovery effort, giving organizational health a key focus, particularly in supporting employees' mental health is also becoming a mainstream trend in DEI trends (Paluck & Green, 2009; Sabat et al., 2020).

Globalization, inflation, generative AI advances, labor strikes, return-to-office mandates, and climate change impacts affected organizations in 2023 (McRae, 2024). To gain a competitive advantage, it is crucial that organizations develop comprehensive strategies to navigate these complex trends. The most recent trends include addressing the rising costs of work, using AI for workforce optimization, and adopting four-day workweeks to boost employee satisfaction and operational efficiency (McRae, 2024; Smith & Johnson, 2022). To acquire a competitive edge, companies can also consider creative benefits, such as housing subsidies, caregiver support, and financial well-being programs, assist organizations in dealing with the costs associated with resuming work. Despite concerns over job security due to AI advancements, new roles and workflows will likely be created by it rather than replaced, and organizations must adapt to meet these new demands (Jones & Brown, 2023). Increasingly, four-day workweeks are becoming popular because they can enhance employee satisfaction and business efficiency (Clark, 2021). In the face of various crises, managers are going to need skills in conflict resolution to deal with increasing incidences of employee conflicts (Adam & White, 2023). Effective oversight and judgment are critical during the experimentation phase of generative AI to mitigate risks and ensure quality control (Harrison et al., 2023).

Degree requirements will be replaced by skills-based hiring, allowing organizations to tap a broader talent pool, including Skilled Through Alternative Routes (STARs) (McRae, 2024). With organizations developing disaster response plans and offering mental health support, climate change will become an important employee benefit. Through integrated practices, DEI initiatives will become more integrated into organizational culture, aligning with Canada's progressive approach to workforce diversity (Smith & Lee, 2023). With traditional career paths evolving, companies will need to offer flexible work options, influence expertise regardless of tenure, and prepare for retirees. A competitive advantage in talent retention and strategic goal achievement depends on executives prioritizing these trends (McRae, 2024).

Transitioning to specific regional efforts, as of 2024, the Government of Canada has identified that in 2023, over 230,000 employees in the Public Service sector were people of the First nations of Canada (Government of Canada, 2023). While this is not a large percentage of overall working population in Canada, there has been a steady rise in the as 5 years, merely this rise is not enough.

The Aboriginal Human Resource Development Council of Canada (presently, Indigenous Works) identified that despite attempts, "Among corporations, there was an extreme lack of awareness about Indigenous issues and people, and there was a disconnect." An Inclusion Continuum was proposed as a roadmap to companies that want to better understand the management and organizational learning needed for stronger Indigenous engagements, relationships and partnerships for employment (Indigenous Works, 2023).

Furthermore, the Canadian workforce has shown a more evenly distributed age range, indicating reduced age discrimination and a shift towards more inclusive workplaces (Statistics Canada, 2023). This would also mean that workspaces are structuring themselves to be more inclusive. This data reflects Canada's adherence to national statistical standards and methodologies for demographic analysis, providing a reliable basis for understanding workforce trends. Canada is taking the right measures at a consistent pace to increase their DEI initiatives, making Canadian workspaces more connected. While there is no doubt that Canada has a bright future in employee engagement and inclusive strategies, there remains a lot more to be achieved, with added intentional efforts towards DEI (Smith & Lee, 2023).

COMPARATIVE CASE STUDIES

Case Study 1: The Case of Rivera

In 2019, Rivera wrote about an experience while leading a two-day training. As a common DEI practice, she opened with a land acknowledgement. However, in the training, there was an indigenous woman present who identified that this land acknowledgement did not come from the heart and did not reflect any honor for the nations that the land belonged to, nor did it reflect the injustice that people of the First Nations have suffered (Rivera, 2022). She spoke up and addressed the hurt she was experiencing towards this "shallow, check-the-box" compliance strategy.

It is important to understand that common practices of DEI are still in their initial stages of being accepted within organizations. While it very important to follow practices such as land acknowledgements, it is even more important to adopt any such DEI practice in its true meaning and practice them to ensure that everyone does their part to advocate and echo socially responsible workplaces. As seen in the case above, not only did incorporating a land acknowledgement just to check a box reap no benefits, but it also rather caused a member to feel hurt and harmed in the process.

To avoid unintentionally disrespecting and hurting people, Rivera should have been thorough in their research of designing the land acknowledgement, corresponded with colleagues on the practices in the nation on delivering a land acknowledgement, and not made assumptions on the importance and perception of doing one at the start of the training. Unfortunately, not being mindful of this led to more harm rather than good. However, since the land acknowledgement was already delivered. Rivera had to be careful in their approach to rectify their actions' consequences. They adopted a more sensitive approach to respond to the situation and address the harm that had been inflicted.

Rivera ensured that the woman who was hurt had the space to have the conversation and express herself to have a more healing conversation. By creating space for people to be heard, it was a good effort towards integrating inclusivity into the training. To support an inclusive space, learning from Indigenous community leaders on the meaning of a land acknowledgement and how best to integrate this into the training may have been more beneficial. The case further explained that Rivera requested the woman to lead the land acknowledgment the next day so that everyone may be able to learn more about Indigenous cultures firsthand.

Case Study 2: The Case of Unqork

Unqork, a fin-tech company with over 500 employees, is committed to fostering and advocating for DEI initiatives (Aerodei, 2024). They have been adopting diversity in its true sense and laid a solid foundation towards inclusion and diversity beyond just employee demographics. However, in 2023, they realized that it was time to take their next step and quantify the impact of DEI initiatives they have already been integrating into all its business segments. They faced challenges in being able to measure the results of their existing initiatives and noticed that employee engagement was being impacted due to internal leadership and organizational changes.

What happened next is that Unqork recognized their limitations and reached out to an external platform to advance their inclusion efforts. Recognizing their limitations, Unqork took proactive steps to enhance their inclusion efforts. This acknowledgment likely stemmed from internal assessments or feedback indicating gaps in their existing DEI initiatives. They developed four special Key Performance Indicators (KPIs) dedicated to track progress only on DEI efforts. Over the span of six months, they were able to monitor and increase customer acquisition by 10%, increased proposal successes, reduced the time-to-fill senior leadership positions by 15 days (about 2 weeks), increase employee retention by 6%, 20% increase in promotions of individuals from marginalized groups, and an increase from the previous 43% to current 83% engagement of employees in internal community efforts.

These cases are great examples of how sometimes DEI initiatives can be taken for granted and can lead to causing harm rather than good if approached from a mere compliance perspective (case 1) and how sometimes an organization may be going above and beyond to integrate DEI but may still face challenges (case 2). It is thus important to identify these gaps and issues at the right time and take appropriate strategic action that would be truly beneficial to the people involved, rather than just to check a goodwill box.

BEST PRACTICES IN DEI IMPLEMENTATION AT WORKPLACE

DEI are vital components in the development of AI systems. Organizations must prioritize DEI principles to ensure fairness, justice, and non-discrimination in AI technologies. While existing organizations operating within Canadian jurisdictions are guided by frameworks such as the Canadian Human Rights Act, provincial human rights codes, and guidelines from bodies like the Canadian Centre for Diversity and Inclusion (CCDI), emphasize the importance of DEI in AI, there is a need for a more comprehensive approach to implementation.

Successful organizational initiatives, such as those observed in Canada's tech sector, have demonstrated the effectiveness of integrating DEI principles into AI development processes (Smith & Jones, 2022). In Canada, DEI guidelines encompass legislative frameworks such as the Canadian Human Rights Act and provincial human rights codes, which mandate equal opportunities and non-discrimination in employment practices (Government of Canada, 2020). These guidelines ensure that HR policies and practices uphold principles of fairness and inclusion across diverse workplaces, including those involved in AI development. By aligning with DEI guidelines and theoretical paradigms, organizations can create a positive DEI climate conducive to inclusive AI design. Real-world examples showcase the benefits of diversity management and organizational commitment to DEI.

Implementing DEI practices in AI development involves integrating DEI principles throughout the AI system's lifecycle. This includes addressing bias in AI algorithms, ensuring diverse and representative datasets, and enhancing transparency in AI decision-making processes (AI Now Institute, 2021). Organizations must prioritize fairness and inclusivity in AI design to mitigate discrimination risks.

A step-by-step guide for DEI implementation in AI involves a structured approach to embedding DEI principles in AI design and development. Proactive measures such as monitoring and validating AI results for discrimination are essential. Building trust and accountability through transparent AI decision-making is key to promoting diversity and inclusivity in AI systems (European Commission, 2020). Incorporating DEI practices into AI development requires a systematic approach that aligns with established principles and guidelines. Drawing from recognized authorities in DEI and AI development, the following guidelines are recommended:

Guideline 1. Evaluate the organization's current stance on DEI and its alignment with AI development goals. Engage leadership to demonstrate commitment to DEI principles in AI initiatives. (Government of Canada, 2019)

Guideline 2. Define specific DEI goals related to AI development, such as promoting fairness, inclusivity, and non-discrimination. Set measurable objectives to track progress towards achieving DEI outcomes in AI projects (AI for Social Good Canada, 2020).

Guideline 3. Highlight the necessity of implementing comprehensive DEI training tailored for AI designers, developers, and stakeholders. This training should encompass modules on HR practices, AI ethics, and DEI principles relevant to the Canadian context. Educating teams on these aspects not only deepens their understanding but also equips them to effectively address biases and promote inclusivity in AI development. (Canadian Centre for Diversity and Inclusion, 2021)

Guideline 4. Embed DEI considerations early in AI development to pre-emptively tackle bias. Incorporate diverse perspectives into AI design teams to ensure inclusivity and equity from project initiation. (Canadian Institute for Advanced Research, 2022)

Guideline 5. Monitor and validate AI results to identify and mitigate biases or discriminatory outcomes. Utilize diverse and representative datasets to prevent societal prejudices from influencing AI systems. (University of Toronto, 2021)

Guideline 6. Promote transparency in AI decision-making processes to build trust and uphold ethical practices. Document decision-making criteria to enhance accountability and scrutiny for potential biases. (Government of Ontario, 2020)

Guideline 7. Regularly evaluate DEI implementation in AI projects to measure effectiveness and refine strategies based on feedback and data analysis. Adopt a culture of continuous learning and adaptation to sustain DEI as a central focus in AI development efforts. (Canadian AI Innovation, 2021)

THE ROLE OF AI IN ENHANCING DEI AND MITIGATE BIASES IN HR PROCESSES

In recent years, the importance of DEI has increased significantly and to create and sustain the momentum, innovative technologies play a key role. In this section, we will focus on AI, which is becoming part of the moment to create more inclusive environments through DEI. Currently, DEI initiatives are human driven but one of the major downfalls here can be human bias. Here, AI comes as a savior for us in mitigating those biases and taking better decisions which creates a more inclusive environment. This capability is particularly important in HRM where crucial decisions are being made around recruitment and training. Let us look at some of the case studies from around the world where AI is being used in enhancing DEI.

With the increase in technology, data breaches are becoming super common. To prevent organizations from data breaches, spreading knowledge and giving training to the employees is the only solution. Straits Interactive, one of the leading data governance solutions recognized the need and incorporated AI in training employees on this.

Straits Interactive employees were facing problems in understanding complex legal texts regarding data privacy and protection information in different parts of the world due to their cultural and language difference. The texts were so complex that they needed to have trained legal experts to translate these texts into simpler, commonly used language for the employees (Rackspace Technology, 2023).

The company collaborated with an AI company Rackspace to develop an AI driven solution and incorporated a tool called AI data protection officer assistant. A tool which can translate, convert the text in any language and can make the texts simpler to understand allowing employees to access the data protection information effortlessly. Earlier, the organization had to bear huge costs in training employees on these policies and having trained professionals to translate. But now, AI has made the process of accessing this information so easy by creating a 24/7 availability of chatbots to explain complex texts.

In a recent study done by US National Bureau of Economic Research, they found out that people who have "white people sounding names such as Emily and Greg are more likely to get recruited than people named as Jamal (Makoff-Clark, 2019). To overcome such human biases, AI is our best bet to create DEI in organizations.

Mastercard, a well-known company in finance sector leveraged AI to revolutionize the talent acquisition process by using an intelligent Talent experience platform powered by AI. Mastercard was facing many problems in their Talent Experience Platform. Firstly, there was no real-time connection to the CRM database on the existing career site, hindering the ability to edit content quickly. Secondly, Due to significant hiring volume, the team faced administrative burdens with a manual interview scheduling process, which resulted in delays and lose candidates to the competitive job market. Thirdly, Inconsistent candidate experiences with over 100 regional career sites that don't connect to their talent CRM: After identifying these shortcomings in their tools and technologies, Mastercard's talent acquisition team realized they needed a comprehensive solution to align recruitment marketing with talent sourcing with their overall people and business strategies, which led them to partner with Phenom to solve these problems.

- In partnership with Phenom, Mastercard improved the candidate, employee, recruiter, HR, manager, and HRIS experiences by leveraging their Intelligent Talent Experience platform, ultimately putting people at the center of its talent acquisition efforts.
- By leveraging Phenom's recruitment marketing, talent sourcing, and automated interview scheduling tools, Mastercard hoped to attract, engage, and convert more talent.
- Mastercard focused on improving candidate experience by reducing interview scheduling time, providing valuable insights into the candidate journey, and engaging with candidates more efficiently.

Reduced time to schedule interviews by over 85%, improving candidate experience and streamlining internal processes. Utilized Phenom Talent Analytics to quantify the impact of new strategies and processes, providing valuable insights into the candidate journey and improving engagement with candidates. Contributed to over 2,000 influenced hires in 2023 through recruitment marketing and talent sourcing campaigns, showcasing the effectiveness of the new strategies. Enhanced candidate, employee, recruiter, HR, manager, and HRIS experiences through the Phenom Intelligent Talent Experience platform, leading to improved efficiencies and a best-in-class candidate experience" (Phenom, 2023). Finally, through this partnership, Mastercard was able to update processes, reduce administrative burdens, and create a seamless experience for candidates, recruiters, and hiring managers with the use of AI.

Examples of discrimination cases involving AI systems have been reported in various contexts, underscoring the urgent need to address bias and ensure equitable outcomes. One notable case involves the use of biased algorithms in hiring processes, where AI systems have been found to favor certain demographics over others, leading to discriminatory outcomes. Another example is the deployment of predictive policing algorithms, which have been criticized for perpetuating racial profiling and unfairly targeting minority communities. Additionally, AI-powered facial recognition systems have exhibited racial bias, resulting in misidentifications and wrongful arrests of individuals from marginalized groups. These examples highlight the critical importance of addressing bias and discrimination in AI systems to ensure fair and equitable outcomes for all individuals.

Scholars and researchers play an important role in promoting diversity and equity in AI through various avenues. Firstly, conducting research to identify biases and discrimination in AI systems, developing algorithms that mitigate bias, and proposing solutions to promote fairness and inclusivity are essential steps. Collaboration with diverse teams and stakeholders is also vital, as it brings different perspectives to the table and ensures that AI technologies are developed with inclusivity in mind. Additionally, scholars can educate the AI community about the importance of DEI in AI systems, raise awareness about potential biases, and advocate for ethical guidelines that prioritize fairness and inclusivity. Engaging in policy discussions and advocating for regulations that promote diversity and equity in AI development and deployment are also critical actions. Lastly, contributing to the development of ethical guidelines for AI that incorporate principles of justice, fairness, and equity can help guide practitioners towards more inclusive practices. By actively engaging in these efforts, scholars and researchers can contribute to creating AI systems that are fair, transparent, and inclusive for all individuals.

Organizations aiming to implement inclusive AI practices should consider several key aspects to ensure fairness and equity in their systems. Firstly, building diverse teams with varied backgrounds and perspectives is key, as it helps in identifying and addressing biases in AI systems. Additionally, providing training on DEI to AI designers, developers, and stakeholders can raise awareness about potential biases and risks, ensuring that these issues are actively managed. Adhering to ethical guidelines that prioritize fairness, justice, and nondiscrimination is also essential for promoting inclusive AI practices. Furthermore, establishing inclusive governance structures that involve multiple stakeholders in the design, testing, and improvement of AI systems ensures that diverse perspectives are considered throughout the development process. Setting clear objectives and incentives, such as financial rewards for compliance with diversity and equity principles, can motivate organizations to prioritize inclusivity in their AI practices. Lastly, creating mechanisms to protect whistleblowers who raise concerns about diversity and equity issues promotes a culture of accountability and transparency, ensuring that organizations remain committed to these values. By addressing these aspects, organizations can develop and deploy AI systems that are both ethical and inclusive.

FUTURE INNOVATIONS IN DEI POLICIES

The landscape of DEI in Human Resource Management (HRM) is undergoing a transformation with the emergence of forward-thinking strategies and innovations aimed at cultivating inclusive and equitable work environments. One key area of advancement is the integration of technology, such as AI and data analytics, to enhance DEI initiatives by implementing bias detection tools in recruitment processes and utilizing virtual reality simulations for diversity training (Smith & Johnson, 2023). These technological advancements, specifically bias detection and removal tools in recruitment processes, and virtual reality simulations for diversity training, are designed to mitigate unconscious biases and promote empathy, understanding, and cultural competence among employees (Smith & Johnson, 2023).

Moreover, organizations are increasingly recognizing the importance of intersectionality and inclusivity in DEI policies (Brown & Lee, 2022). This concept of intersectionality was introduced by Kimberlé Crenshaw in 1989, highlights the interconnected nature of social categorizations such as race, gender, class, and sexuality. It recognizes that individuals can experience discrimination and privilege based on the intersection of these identities. For organizations, embracing intersectionality means understanding that employees and stakeholders may have multiple marginalized identities that intersect and influence their experiences and opportunities within the workplace. By acknowledging intersectionality, organizations can tailor their DEI strategies to address these unique intersections, ensuring inclusivity and equity for all. By embracing intersectionality, which acknowledges the overlapping dimensions of diversity, organizations can tailor their strategies to accommodate individuals with multiple marginalized identities, fostering a culture of respect and appreciation for diverse perspectives and experiences.

Globalization has also influenced the evolution of DEI policies, prompting organizations to adapt to the increasing diversity in workforces (Chen et al., 2021). Cultural competence training is becoming essential to navigate cross-cultural interactions effectively and promote diversity awareness. By incorporating diverse cultural practices and traditions into organizational policies, companies can create a more inclusive and welcoming environment that values the richness of diverse backgrounds.

Furthermore, holistic well-being and mental health support are gaining prominence in DEI initiatives. Integrating mental health services into DEI efforts prioritizes the well-being of all employees and creates a supportive workplace culture (Garcia & Martinez, 2020). Establishing inclusive spaces that destigmatize seeking help for mental health issues and offering resources tailored to diverse mental health needs are fundamental steps towards creating an integrated approach to well-being within organizations.

Collaborative partnerships and community engagement are also shaping the future of DEI policies (Jones & Nguyen, 2023). By forming alliances with community organizations and advocacy groups, organizations can enhance their DEI efforts and drive social impact both within and outside the workplace. Engaging in collaborative initiatives that promote social justice and equity contributes to broader societal change, while industry-wide collaborations address systemic DEI challenges collectively, driving meaningful progress towards diversity and inclusion.

In embracing these future innovations in DEI policies, organizations can create a workplace culture that values the unique contributions and experiences of all employees. By proactively advancing DEI initiatives, organizations can create a culture of respect, belonging, and empowerment, driving positive change in the evolving landscape of workplace diversity.

CHAPTER SUMMARY

This chapter probes deeply into the critical intersection of DEI with AI within the context of Human Resource Management (HRM). It highlights the essential need for organizations to strategically embed DEI principles into their HR practices, particularly as AI technologies continue to revolutionize workplace dynamics. Throughout its exploration, the chapter emphasizes the fundamental role of leadership commitment, comprehensive training initiatives, and ongoing assessment mechanisms in successfully integrating DEI and AI. It draws on diverse case studies and global perspectives to illustrate regional nuances and challenges, highlighting the importance of adaptable strategies that resonate with both organizational values and societal expectations.

The core argument of the chapter lies in advocating for a balanced approach: leveraging AI technologies to complement human capabilities in promoting fairness, transparency, and inclusivity across all facets of HRM. By highlighting real-world examples and emerging practices, the chapter underscores the transformative potential of AI in advancing DEI goals while navigating complex ethical considerations. In conclusion, the chapter calls upon organizations to embrace responsible innovation, ensuring that AI-driven advancements not only optimize talent management processes but also ensure environments where diversity is celebrated, equity is upheld, and inclusion is embedded in every aspect of organizational culture. It posits that by aligning AI capabilities with DEI imperatives, organizations can pave the way for more inclusive workplaces that thrive in the digital era.

REFERENCES

Adams, G., & White, M. (2023). Conflict resolution in crisis: Strategies for managing workplace conflicts. *The Journal of Applied Psychology*, 108(3), 401–415.

Aerodei. (2024, February 28). Unqork case study. *Aerodei*. https://www.aerodei.com/post/unqork-case-study

AI for Social Good Canada. (2020). *Sustainable AI: Building a future for ethical and environmentally friendly artificial intelligence.*https://aiforsocialgood.ca/

AI Now Institute. (2021). *Algorithmic Accountability Policy Toolkit*. https://ainowinstitute.org/policytoolkit.html

Bezrukova, K., Spell, C. S., Perry, J. L., & Jehn, K. A. (2016). A meta-analytical integration of over 40 years of research on diversity training evaluation. *Psychological Bulletin*, 142(11), 1227–1274. DOI: 10.1037/bul0000067 PMID: 27618543

Binns, R. (2018). Fairness in machine learning: Lessons from political philosophy. *Proceedings of the 2018 Conference on Fairness, Accountability, and Transparency*, 149-159. https://doi.org/DOI: 10.1145/3287560.3287589

Bogen, M., & Rieke, A. (2018). Help wanted: An examination of hiring algorithms, equity, and bias. *Upturn*. https://www.upturn.org/reports/2018/hiring-algorithms/

Bourne, B. (2023, May 19). *Top 5 Trends in DEI for 2023*. Purdue Global. https://www.purdueglobal.edu/blog/business/diversity-equity-inclusion-trends/

Brown, A., & Lee, C. (2022). Intersectionality and diversity: Strategies for inclusive workplaces. *The Journal of Applied Psychology*, 107(3), 389–402. DOI: 10.1037/apl0000987 PMID: 33983782

Caliskan, A., Bryson, J. J., & Narayanan, A. (2017). Semantics derived automatically from language corpora contain human-like biases. *Science*, 356(6334), 183–186. DOI: 10.1126/science.aal4230 PMID: 28408601

Canadian, A. I. Innovation. (2021). *AI for Everyone: Diversity & Inclusion in AI*. https://www.canadianai.ca/publications/diversity-inclusion-ai

Canadian Centre for Diversity and Inclusion. (2021). *Training Programs*. CCDI. https://ccdi.ca/training/

Canadian Institute for Advanced Research. (2022). *AI & Society Program*. Cifar. https://www.cifar.ca/programs/ai-society

Chen, J., Smith, T., & Williams, R. (2021). Globalization and diversity management: Challenges and opportunities. *International Journal of Human Resource Management*, 32(6), 1200–1221. DOI: 10.1080/09585192.2020.1843703

Clark, E. (2021). The benefits of a four-day workweek on employee productivity. *Harvard Business Review*. https://hbr.org

Cowgill, B., Dell'Acqua, F., Deng, S., & Deng, S. (2020). *Biased programmers? Or biased data? A field experiment in operationalizing AI ethics*. (Columbia Business School Research Paper). https://doi.org/DOI: 10.2139/ssrn.3685457

Cox, T. H., & Blake, S. (2017). Managing cultural diversity: Implications for organizational competitiveness. *The Academy of Management Perspectives*, 5(3), 45–56. DOI: 10.5465/ame.1991.4274465

Cox, T. H. (2017). *Cultural Diversity in Organizations: Theory, Research, and Practice*. Berrett-Koehler Publishers.

Davenport, T. H., & Ronanki, R. (2018). Artificial intelligence for the real world. *Harvard Business Review*. https://hbr.org

European Commission. (2020). *Ethics Guidelines for Trustworthy AI*. https://ec.europa.eu/digital-single-market/en/news/ethics-guidelines-trustworthy-ai

Ferdman, B. M., & Deane, B. R. (Eds.). (2014). *Diversity at Work: The Practice of Inclusion*. John Wiley & Sons.

Fujimoto, Y., & Hartel, C. E. J. (2017). Organizational diversity learning framework: Going beyond diversity training programs. *Personnel Review*, 46(6), 1120–1141. DOI: 10.1108/PR-09-2015-0254

Government of Canada. (2023). *Annual Report on First Nations Employment in the Federal Public Service*. https://www.canada.ca

Government of Canada. (2019). *Directive on Automated Decision-Making*. https://www.canada.ca/en/treasury-board-secretariat/services/information-technology/directive-automated-decision-making.html

Government of Ontario. (2020). *AI and Data Analytics Ethics Guidelines*. https://www.ontario.ca/page/ai-and-data-analytics-ethics-guidelines

Harrison, R., Patel, K., & Nguyen, T. (2023). Navigating risks in AI experimentation: Strategies for quality control and oversight. *Journal of AI Research*, 45(2), 123–135.

Indigenous Works. (2023). *Inclusion Continuum: A roadmap for organizational engagement with Indigenous communities*. https://www.indigenousworks.ca

Jones, A., & Brown, L. (2023). Adapting to AI: Opportunities and challenges for organizational adaptation. *Organizational Dynamics*, 52(4), 212–228.

Jones, K., & Nguyen, H. (2023). Community engagement and social impact: Enhancing diversity initiatives. *Journal of Business Ethics*, 155(4), 789–803. DOI: 10.1007/s10551-021-04877-9

Kalev, A., Dobbin, F., & Kelly, E. (2006). Best practices or best guesses? Assessing the efficacy of corporate affirmative action and diversity policies. *American Sociological Review*, 71(4), 589–617. DOI: 10.1177/000312240607100404

Kaplan, S. E., Wiley, J. W., & Maertz, C. P. (2018). The role of ERGs in fostering inclusivity: An empirical examination of ERG functions and their impact. *Human Resource Management*, 57(5), 1111–1123.

Kim, P. T. (2022). Data-driven discrimination at work. *William and Mary Law Review*, 58(3), 857–936. https://scholarship.law.wm.edu/wmlr/vol58/iss3/5

Kossek, E. E., & Ollier-Malaterre, A. (2020). Desperately seeking sustainable flexibility: Identifying the core components of work-life policies. *Human Resource Management Review*, 30(4), 100–127.

Lindsey, A. P., King, E. B., Membere, A., & Cheung, H. K. (2017). Two steps forward, one step back: The intricacies of promoting diversity through leader messaging. *Journal of Business Ethics*, 142(3), 499–513.

Lee, K. (2018). *AI superpowers: China, Silicon Valley, and the new world order.* Houghton Mifflin Harcourt.

Makoff-Clark, A. (2019, January 23). *Is blind recruitment the secret to the perfect hire?*https://www.peoplemanagement.co.uk/article/1742220/blind-recruitment-secret-perfect-hire

Manyika, J., Chui, M., Bughin, J., Dobbs, R., Bisson, P., & Marrs, A. (2017). *Artificial intelligence: The next digital frontier?* McKinsey Global Institute. https://www.mckinsey.com

McRae, E. R. (2024, January 25). *9 Trends that will shape work in 2024 and beyond.* Harvard Business Review. https://hbr.org/2024/01/9-trends-that-will-shape-work-in-2024-and-beyond

McRae, S. (2024). The future of work: Global trends and organizational strategies. *Journal of Management*, 30(1), 45–61.

Mor Barak, M. E. (2016). *Managing Diversity: Toward a Globally Inclusive Workplace.* Sage Publications.

Nishii, L. H. (2013). The benefits of climate for inclusion for gender-diverse groups. *Academy of Management Journal*, 56(6), 1754–1774. DOI: 10.5465/amj.2009.0823

Paluck, E. L., & Green, D. P. (2009). Prejudice reduction: What works? A review and assessment of research and practice. *Annual Review of Psychology*, 60(1), 339–367. DOI: 10.1146/annurev.psych.60.110707.163607 PMID: 18851685

Phenom. (2023, July 5). *Transforming Mastercard's talent acquisition | Case study*. Phenom. https://www.phenom.com/resource/transforming-mastercard-talent-acquisition?utm_source=vktr.com

Roberson, Q. M., Ryan, A. M., & Ragins, B. R. (2017). The evolution and future of diversity at work. *The Journal of Applied Psychology*, 102(3), 711–716. DOI: 10.1037/apl0000161 PMID: 28125255

Raghavan, M., Barocas, S., Kleinberg, J., & Levy, K. (2020). Mitigating bias in algorithmic hiring: Evaluating claims and practices. In *Proceedings of the 2020 Conference on Fairness, Accountability, and Transparency* (pp. 469-481). https://doi.org/DOI: 10.1145/3351095.3372828

Raji, I. D., & Buolamwini, J. (2019). Actionable auditing: Investigating the impact of publicly naming biased performance results of commercial AI products. *Proceedings of the 2019 AAAI/ACM Conference on AI, Ethics, and Society*, 429-435. https://doi.org/DOI: 10.1145/3306618.3314244

Randel, A. E., Dean, M. A., Ehrhart, K. H., Chung, B. G., Shore, L. M., & Singh, G. (2018). Leader inclusiveness, psychological diversity climate, and helping behaviors. *The Journal of Applied Psychology*, 103(7), 793–806.

Rivera, M. (2022, March 30). For leaders who mess up on DEI: A case study the startup - medium. *Medium*. https://medium.com/swlh/for-leaders-who-mess-up-on-dei-a-case-study-efaf856aaa61

Roberson, Q. M. (2006). Disentangling the meanings of diversity and inclusion in organizations. *Group & Organization Management*, 31(2), 212–236. DOI: 10.1177/1059601104273064

Roberson, Q. M., King, E. B., & Hebl, M. R. (2020). Designing more effective practices for reducing workplace inequality. *Social Issues and Policy Review*, 14(1), 226–257. DOI: 10.1111/sipr.12065

Russell, S., & Norvig, P. (2020). *Artificial Intelligence: A Modern Approach* (4th ed.). Pearson.

Sabat, I. E., Lindsey, A. P., King, E. B., & Ahmad, A. (2020). The good, the bad, and the ugly: Impact of diversity training on attitudes and practices towards LGBTQ employees. *Group & Organization Management*, 45(1), 15–38. DOI: 10.1177/1059601119827229

Sabat, I. E., Lindsey, A. P., & King, E. B. (2020). The future of diversity at work: Inclusion and equity. *Industrial and Organizational Psychology: Perspectives on Science and Practice*, 13(4), 473–491.

Schwab, K. (2017). *The fourth industrial revolution*. Crown Business.

Smith, J., & Johnson, M. (2022). Addressing the rising costs of work: Strategies for organizational sustainability. *Journal of Business Economics*, 78(3), 211–225.

Smith, R., & Lee, K. (2023). Advancing diversity and inclusion: Strategies for enhancing workplace cohesion. *The Journal of Applied Behavioral Science*, 59(2), 176–190.

Smith, E., & Johnson, M. (2023). Advancements in AI and diversity: Implications for HRM. *Human Resource Management Review*, 33(2), 264–278. DOI: 10.1016/j.hrmr.2022.100885

Straits Interactive & Rackspace Technology. (2023). *Rackspace Technology*. https://www.rackspace.com/en-ca/case-studies/straits-interactive

Statistics Canada. (2023). *Age distribution in the Canadian workforce*. https://www.statcan.gc.ca

Suresh, H., & Guttag, J. V. (2021). A framework for understanding unintended consequences of machine learning. *Communications of the ACM*, 64(8), 62–71. DOI: 10.1145/3463492

Thomas, K. M., Plaut, V. C., & Tran, N. M. (2019). Diversity ideologies in organizations. *APA Handbook of Industrial and Organizational Psychology, 2*, 405-437.

Thomas, D. A., & Ely, R. J. (2019). Making sense of belonging: A key to diversity and inclusion. *MIT Sloan Management Review*, 60(2), 39–45.

University of Toronto. (2021). *Fairness and Bias in Machine Learning*. https://www.cs.toronto.edu/~mvolkovs/fairness.html

KEY TERMS AND DEFINITIONS

Artificial Intelligence (AI): Technology that enables machines to simulate human intelligence and perform tasks typically requiring human cognition.

Bias Detection Tools: AI-driven solutions to identify and mitigate unconscious biases in various processes.

Bias Mitigation: Efforts to reduce and eliminate biases, particularly in decision-making processes.

Community Engagement: Collaborative efforts with external organizations to drive social impact and enhance diversity initiatives.

Cultural Competence: Ability to effectively interact with people from different cultural backgrounds.

DEI Initiatives: Programs and policies aimed at promoting Diversity, Equity, and Inclusion within organizations.

Diversity: Variety and differences among individuals in terms of race, ethnicity, gender, age, sexual orientation, etc.

Equity: Fairness and impartiality, ensuring everyone has access to opportunities and resources needed to succeed.

Ethical Considerations: Moral principles and guidelines that govern behavior and decision-making.

Ethical Guidelines: Principles guiding fair and transparent AI development, emphasizing justice and equity.

Fairness: Treating all individuals equitably and justly.

Global Perspectives: Insights and viewpoints that consider diverse cultural, economic, and social contexts worldwide.

Globalization: Influence on workplace diversity, prompting adaptation to diverse global workforces.

Inclusion: Creating environments where all individuals feel respected, valued, and able to fully participate.

Inclusive Governance Structures: Frameworks involving diverse stakeholders in AI development and policymaking.

Inclusive Spaces: Environments that support diverse mental health needs and allows open dialogue.

Innovation.: Introduction of new ideas, methods, or technologies to improve processes or products.

Intersectionality: Recognition of overlapping social identities (e.g., race, gender, class) and their combined impacts on individuals.

Leadership Commitment: The dedication and support shown by organizational leaders towards specific goals or initiatives.

Organizational Culture: The shared values, beliefs, and behaviors that characterize an organization.

Policy Advocacy: Efforts to influence regulations that prioritize diversity and equity in AI deployment.

Social Impact: Effects on broader society through inclusive organizational practices and community partnerships.

Strategic Integration: Purposeful alignment of different elements or strategies to achieve overarching goals.

Training Programs: Educational sessions designed to enhance skills, knowledge, and understanding among employees.

Virtual Reality Simulations: Technology used for immersive diversity training and enhancing empathy among employees.

Chapter 7
HR Agility:
Embracing Change in Human Resource Practices

P. Bhanumathi
https://orcid.org/0000-0001-8670-8250
M.S. Ramaiah Institute of Management, India

P. Hemavathi
St. Joseph University, India

Vinodh T. S.
Vivekananda Institute of Management, India

ABSTRACT

In today's competitive business world, HR agility has emerged as a critical success factor for organizations that must embrace agility in their HR strategies to remain relevant and practical. Agility brings constant change, fosters organizational resilience, drives innovation, and maintains a competitive edge. Further, agility entails the HR department responding to the organization's evolving business needs, trends, and dynamics. It is a proactive change and encompasses various dimensions, namely talent acquisition, recruitment strategies, performance management, strategies for building and managing teams, challenges and overcoming resistance to change, leadership, and future trends in HR. Agile HR practices enable HR departments to align strategies with the objectives to achieve their goals and stay competitive. It will help identify skill gaps and attract, develop, and retain the best talent to meet the organization's needs. HR agility augments employee experience by enabling everyone to respond promptly to concerns and expectations.

DOI: 10.4018/979-8-3693-6402-4.ch007

INTRODUCTION

In today's competitive business world, HR agility has emerged as a critical success factor for organizations that must embrace agility in their HR strategies to remain relevant and practical. Agility brings constant change, fosters organizational resilience, drives innovation, and maintains a competitive edge. Further, agility entails the HR department responding to the organization's evolving business needs, trends, and dynamics. It is a proactive change and encompasses various dimensions, namely, talent acquisition, recruitment strategies, performance management, Strategies for building and managing teams, challenges and overcoming resistance to change, leadership, and future trends in HR.

Agile HR practices enable HR departments to align strategies with the objectives to achieve their goals and stay competitive. It will help identify skill gaps and attract, develop, and retain the best talent to meet the organization's needs. HR agility augments employee experience by enabling everyone to respond promptly to concerns and expectations. These agile practices allow change processes by providing resources, communicating effectively, and supporting employees and leaders at transition times. Further, it streamlines processes, optimizes resources, and reduces costs. Agile HR fosters employee innovation and creativity by encouraging experimentation, continuous improvement, and learning. It also helps integrate technologies to enhance HR processes, namely, performance management, training, and overall employee development. Globalization has provided many opportunities for organizations to grow and operate at all levels. HR agility is essential to managing such diverse employees, supporting them in overcoming cross-cultural differences and conforming with international labor laws and regulations.

1. INTRODUCTION TO HR AGILITY

In the present modern scenario, HR agility is the organization's human resources capability to implement changes and respond effectively to the challenges emerging in the business environment. Due to the fast development process in the business, it is necessary to accept the changes quickly and frame the policies and procedures. To survive in the present continuous advancement, organizations must face changes, which might be technical or changes in the market or the workforce. To meet these changes, organizations must adopt agile work practices throughout their functions. (Doz et al., 2008) study says agility has been recognized as an effective paradigmatic method for creating integrative strategies.

Importance of HR Agility

In today's fast-changing environment, HR agility has become essential for developing and facing challenges. HR agility is vital to create a flexible work environment. HR agility makes the employee feel happy and valued, which will help engage the employee and retain the talented employee. Agility has been recognized as an effective paradigmatic method for creating integrative strategies. (Nargis, et al., 2024) Study says that HR practices influence employee performance and engagement; flexible HR strategies help engage the workforce and increase performance.

HR agility will help solve the issues rapidly and provide resolutions. HR agility is essential to face competitive advantages; it enables necessary support for employees to overcome the changes. HR agility is vital for responsiveness and continuous development in a dynamic environment. (Alamro et al., 2019) study reveals organizations that follow HR agility tend to overcome challenges and changes with the help of strategies and staff.

Need for HR Agility

Figure 1. Need for HR Agility

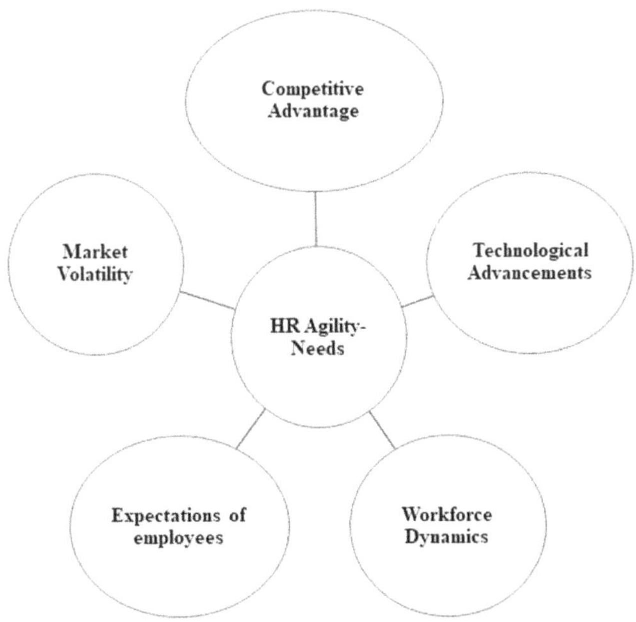

The need for HR agility from the fig .1 can be explained as follows:

- HR agility will help to manage the change in the workforce dynamics and the diverse workforce with different work styles (Nijssen et al., 2012). The study explains that with the HR agility strategy, the organization can measure the workforce knowledge and institutional practices and its potential to address the environmental consequences.
- HR agility will help the organization adapt to rapid technological advancement and utilize the tools and techniques for organizational development.
- The Present market is unstable due to economic fluctuation, competition, and changes in customer needs. HR agility will help to tackle all the market volatility. (Moloto et al.,2020) study shows that if agile is appropriately applied in the organization, it positively impacts the completion and success of the project and provides customer satisfaction, which will help the organization tackle the fluctuation in the economy.
- HR agility boosts a flexible culture and supportive environment, creating higher employee satisfaction and continuous learning.
- Maintaining a competitive edge through attracting and retaining talented employees and fostering innovation.

To achieve and sustain HR agility, organizations must focus on several key areas that are essential for fostering HR agility. The various trends and challenges are as follows:

The conventional HR functions focused more on administrative tasks and adherence to compliance and have shifted towards an agile approach. This transition requires a strategic shift to drive creativity, innovation, quick responses, and organizational agility to achieve success. To embrace agility, the organization has to anticipate future trends, fostering a culture of innovation, resilience, and continuous improvement within the workforce. The HR agility needs are as follows:

Flexible Work: Remote and flexible work is predominant post-COVID, driven by technologies and meeting employee expectations. The HR department must develop policies that support these arrangements by considering productivity and active employee engagement. Tools and technologies for virtual collaboration and communication are to be implemented; this trend necessitates agile HR strategies to ensure employees' effectiveness regardless of proximity.

Agile Talent Acquisition: The HR department is leveraging technology, data analytics, and sourcing techniques to quickly attract and retain the best talent. Conventional recruitment is replaced by agile talent acquisition strategies prioritizing flexibility, speed, and candidate experience (Kavitha et al., 2019). The agile methodology emphasizes continuous feedback, speedy modifications based on the hiring needs, and offering personalized candidate engagement in the hiring process.

Learning and Development: Upskilling and reskilling, continuous learning, and employee development are crucial in today's business to maintain employee effectiveness and competitiveness. Agile methodologies ensure employees' training, upskilling, and reskilling to meet the industry and organizational needs through e-learning platforms, micro-learning modules, and personalized development (Balsvik et al., 2022).

Performance Management: Conventional performance reviews are replaced by agile performance management approaches prioritizing regular feedback and goal alignment. HR agility in performance management includes setting clear, measurable goals aligned with organizational objectives by steering regular check-ins and real-time feedback systems (Gunn et al., 2021). This trend leads to continuous improvement, enhances the active engagement of employee engagement, and further raises a culture of accountability and transparency.

Employee Well-being: Employee well-being is an important aspect that has gained thrust, driven by awareness of mental health conditions or issues and the impact of work-life balance on organizational productivity. The Agile HR strategies integrate initiatives prioritizing employee wellness with mental health programs, flexible benefits packages, and policies promoting work-life integration.

Decision Making: HR departments increasingly adopt data-driven approaches to decisions across various organizational functions. Agile HR leverages data and people analytics, AI tools, and predictive models to provide more profound insights into workforce trends, performance metrics, and employee engagement. Through this analysis, HR can decide on recruitment, training effectiveness, succession planning, and organizational design, optimizing HR strategies that contribute to the overall business outcomes.

Diverse and Inclusive Workforce: The organization emphasizes diversity, equity, and inclusion (DEI) to enhance creativity, teamwork, problem-solving, employee morale and productivity, better decision-making, and higher profits.HR agility tries to ensure benefits can be leveraged quickly and effectively. HR needs to formulate strategies to encourage DEI to create an inclusive culture.

The Challenges in HR Agility

Implementing agile principles and practices within the HR function can be more challenging in achieving and sustaining HR agility. The various challenges, reasons, and possible solutions are in Table 1. (Nijssen et al., 2012):

Table 1. Challenges in HR Agility

Challenges	Reasons	Techniques to overcome the challenges
Resistance to change	Fear of the unknown and habituated to the conventional methods or processes.	Educating, training, and supporting the employees during the transition phase.
Lack of Agile Skills and Knowledge	Lack of specific skills to implement and sustain agile methodologies	• Provide comprehensive training on agile methods tailor-made to the HR process, such as Scrum, Kanban, and Lean. • Coaching and mentorship by external expertise
Inadequate tools and technology	Inherited HR tools don't support Agile principles.	• Upgrading the technology, such as HRIS and people analytics platforms, is also necessary. • Tools like Microsoft Teams, Slack, etc.,
Data privacy and security issues	Increased use of vast amounts of data in agile methodology	• Following the data privacy regulations and protecting employee data. • Use of data protection features.
Performance appraisal	Lack of fairness and equity in the evaluation process	• Identifying the criteria to evaluate • Continuous reviews • Implementing a 360-degree feedback system.
Managing remote and hybrid teams	Implementing agile principles and practices is challenging	• Virtual collaborative tools and regular virtual check-ins. • Training remote and hybrid employees to contribute more to the organization.

Organizations can successfully implement and sustain agile HR practices by addressing the challenges mentioned above through proper planning, rigorous training, technology investment, and an emphasis on equality and transparency; in turn, this enables HR to respond more effectively to organizational needs, augment active employee engagement, and drive its organizational performance (McMackin et al., 2021).

2. AGILE PRINCIPLES AND METHODOLOGIES

Agile principles are combined with HR practices to develop an organization's reactive and employee-oriented culture. Adapting HR agility is to develop a dynamic environment that can adapt to quick changes and fulfill the workforce's expectations. Agile principles act as a basis for creating a flexible and cooperative environment. Some of the agile methodologies are

The KANBAN method helps to track recruitment, training, placement, permanence analysis, and management. Its visual workflow method helps employees plan for the work, reduces work-in-process time, and helps them utilize resources effectively. The KANBAN implementation process can begin with mapping out the task and the set parameters to avoid overload and monitor the workflow to improve work efficiency. It is crucial to have a regular review process and feedback on KANBAN.

By implementing KANBAN, the HR team can develop and detect the bottlenecks and focus on work, leading to better management.

The lean method in HR helps to eradicate waste and maximize value, and the lean method helps to streamline the recruitment process, training, placement, and development. In the lean method, the non-value activities will be uninvolved, and the vital concept that encourages continuous improvement is planned.

Scrum is a framework that helps improve HR activities like talent and performance management. Scrum organizes the work in an order and sets goals for achievement. Some critical roles in scrum are HR managers, staff, and facilitators. Continuous review, follow-up, and transparency will help with development.

The HR team should analyze, review, and decide on the best agile methodology for the organization. Through the pilot study, the team can determine the type of agile methodology that will match the organization, and the organization can also integrate the agile methods, enabling the organization to respond. (Edison et al.,2021) The study says that the organization needs to identify the best method that fits the needs, and the success factor is how the methods have been helpful as per the plan.

The selection process to identify the suitable method and its implementation are as follows.

Identifying a suitable agile method and its implementation involves several steps, from understanding organizational needs to continuous evaluation and improvement(-Fig .1). Here's a comprehensive guide to the selection and implementation process:

Identifying a suitable agile method and its implementation are discussed as follows

1. Assessing the organizational needs and goals.
2. Agile methods understanding
3. Analyzing all agile frameworks and selecting the best fit for the organization
4. Decisions are taken based on the feedback received
5. Conducting pilot testing to check the feasibility.

Frameworks to meet organizational Needs / Implementation of agile methodology

After selecting a suitable agile method, organizations must implement it to improve their adaptability to the project and its outcomes and to achieve higher strategic goals(Holbeche, 2019).

- Develop a detailed implementation plan covering HR roles, responsibilities, timelines, and milestones with the organizational goals and objectives.

- Form cross-functional teams with the essential skills and know-how for effective implementation.
- Offer appropriate training and accessibility to agile tools.
- Follow Agile Practices to track the progress and identify bottlenecks, if any.
- Develop a change mechanism to foster an agile mindset.
- Develop KPIs (Key performance indicators) and measure the effectiveness of agile practices.
- Scale up the agile practices as required by supporting and encouraging continuous learning.

3. LEVERAGING TECHNOLOGY FOR AGILE TALENT ACQUISITION

Agile Talent acquisition identifies, attracts, recruits, and hires individuals with specific skills, experiences, and qualities desired to contribute to an agile organization. This agile process highlights adaptability, flexibility, speed, and the ability to adapt to market dynamics(Jooss et al.,2024).

- Adaptability and Flexibility: Agile environments emphasize adaptability, where the organization recruits employees who quickly adapt to the changes and upskill and reskill for any organizational role. Flexibility in talent acquisition guarantees the organization's response to changing business needs.
- Speed: The speed with which it delivers value through agile methodologies minimizes delays, if any. Streamline the hiring processes to reduce time-to-hire.
- Skills: Acquisition in an agile environment emphasizes recognizing candidates with extensive skills and abilities to work collaboratively across various functions, further enhancing the team's ability to be more creative, innovative, problem-solving, and bring high-quality outcomes.
- Cultural Fit: Talent acquisition plans are made by focusing on the organization's agile culture and values. Candidates who embrace agile principles foster cohesive team dynamics and promote a positive and conducive workspace.
- Learning and Continuous Improvement: Talent acquisition prioritizes candidates with a proper growth mindset and a willingness to learn continuously and contribute to the overall organizational growth.
- Retention and Engagement: Candidates well-suited to the agile environment can work and contribute, increasing job satisfaction and reducing turnover. Employees who contribute positively to agile initiatives can drive continuous organizational improvement.

Challenges Faced by Traditional Talent Acquisition

The various challenges faced in the traditional talent acquisition process are as follows(Safa et al., 2018):

- Traditional methods usually have screening, interviews, and approval processes, leading to lengthy hiring times. Lengthy processes could result in a negative experience among candidates, which reduces the likelihood of top talent accepting the job offer.
- The traditional method is usually rigid and follows stringent protocols
- Decisions are typically based on intuition rather than data-driven, leading to biases and wrong choices.
- Traditional methods rely on job postings, limiting potential candidates' diversity.
- Traditional methods often fail to evaluate candidates' cultural fit and adaptability to the organization's values and workspace.

(Bashynska et al.,2023) The study explains that using AI-driven human capital helps optimize agile workforce planning and talent acquisition and helps to face the uncertain business environment.

Leveraging technology enables the HR department to be responsive to environmental change, retain talented employees, and adequately streamline. The data-driven decision technologies to develop an agile talent acquisition are as follows:

- *Applicant Tracking System*: The automatic recruitment process enhances the HR department from announcing job vacancies to shortlisting candidates and placing new employees. ATS Support to screen many applications and ensure a quick and effective recruitment process.
- *Artificial Intelligence and Machine Learning:* AI tools can help screen candidate applications, analyze past data, and forecast future and present recruitment.
- *Social media recruiting*: Social media supports the HR team in reaching a wider audience through platforms like Twitter, Facebook, and LinkedIn, and it also provides vacancy information to candidates open to work.
- *Video Interviewing tools*: Regardless of geographical location, video interviewing tools like Zoom and Skype enable remote interviews and connect with the candidates, making the interview process fast and flexible.
- *Data Analytics*: The HR team can use data analytics in the recruitment process; it is easy to identify the issues in the hiring process and makes the

process easy and fast. It also helps determine future human resources requirements and adequately allocate the workforce.

- *Mobile Recruiting*: Developments in smartphones, digital recruitment processes, and apps have made it easy to get applications and facilitate faster communication and modernization of the recruitment process.
- *Employee Referral Programs:* Modern technology platforms help refer different updated technology to employees, and they also help track employee performance and progress.
- *Virtual Reality (VR) and Augmented Reality (AR)*: Virtual reality helps to provide office tours and helps the candidates understand the work culture and environment
- *Automated Communication Tools*: The automated communication tool provides regular communication and updates to the candidate about the application status and further procedures. It's a computerized tool that uses automated email and messages, and the information reaches the candidate in time.
- *Cloud-Based HR Solutions*: This technology benefits those who use remote work policies; it helps them access data and reports from anywhere.

4. AGILE RECRUITMENT STRATEGIES AND PROCESS

The agile recruitment strategies mainly focus on continuous improvement in the hiring process.

Some of the agile recruitment strategies are:

- Iterative and Incremental Approach (Scrum): This approach breaks down the hiring process into smaller ones, manages each stage regularly, and progresses each step.
- Cross-functional teams: To have diverse perspectives and effective decision-making, a cross-functional team includes different collaborative stakeholders like the HR manager and departmental manager in the hiring process.
- Data-driven Decision: Use the data and analytics to support the hiring process and measure the various recruitment strategies.
- The organization must be flexible and adapt recruitment strategies based on the changes and requirements. (Chowdhury, 2024) the result found that HR Practices encourage employee engagement and performance by implementing flexible HR practices
- The organization must create employer branding to retain talented employees and be unique to differentiate itself from its competitors. (Revutska et al., 2021), The study found that factors like flexibility and continuous learning

will have the significance of agile principles to create a smooth work environment for the modern generation.

Figure 2. Agile Recruitment Process

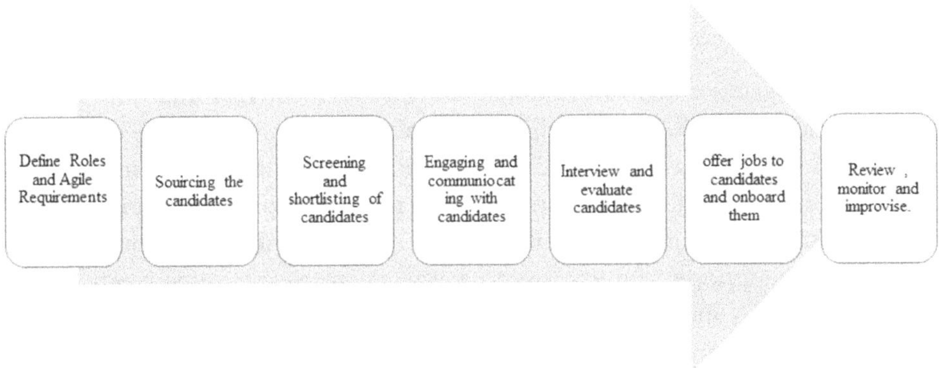

The recruitment process is explained as follows (Figure 2).

- The roles & responsibilities, and skills must be analyzed to ensure the stakeholders are informed regarding the job description.
- Different sources like social media, employee references, and AI tools can be used to streamline the source of candidates.
- Through emails and messages, regular communication can be made with the candidate during the process to inform and engage the candidates.
- A collaborative hiring method can be used, where all the members are involved in the process, and a structured interview is designed along with the technical and behavioral assessment. After selecting the right candidate, plan a competitive compensation structure to ensure a changeover for the new hire.
- After every sequence of the recruitment process, collect feedback from the stakeholders and candidates, and based on the input received, find out the areas that need improvement.

Scrum, Kanban, and Lean in the Recruitment

Scrum in Recruitment: It is an iterative, incremental framework for managing recruitment. The framework emphasizes setting specific recruitment goals, i.e., the number of candidates to interview based on the roles to be filled immediately in discussion with the recruitment team. It will help identify any roadblocks and take further steps to address any recruitment-related issues. Finally, by retrospection, determine what worked well and what didn't, and implement the changes to optimize the recruitment process iteratively.

Kanban in Recruitment: It is a visual workflow method used to envision the recruitment process in stages such as sourcing, screening, interviewing, and hiring. Each candidate or job role is represented by a card that passes across the board if there is any progress. This monitors time-to-fill, time-to-hire, and candidate drop-off rates to identify and address recruitment bottlenecks. Make real-time adjustments as per the flow of candidates and changing requirements.

Lean in Recruitment: This focuses on minimizing waste and maximizing value, significantly streamlining the process. This method helps identify and map the value-added to reduce the waste of unnecessary delays and eliminate redundancies, unnecessary interviews, and excessive paperwork in the recruitment process. It also ensures timely interaction with candidates and hiring persons by streamlining communication channels.

Agile recruitment planning, sourcing, resume screening, interview process, selection, acceptance, onboarding (Gregory et al., 2022)

Agile Recruitment Planning: The Agile framework helps in setting the objectives for the recruitment process based on the quality of hire needs to be done, time-to-fill, and the candidate experience. It Identifies critical performance indicators (KPIs) to quantify the success in terms of time-to-hire, offer acceptance rate, and candidate satisfaction. An agile recruitment team encompasses HR professionals, hiring managers, and other HR members, and their roles and responsibilities are defined to ensure better accountability and clarity. Also, emphasize and work on open positions and arrange them based on need.

Agile Sourcing: Agile sourcing helps identify potential candidates by posting job openings on related job portals, boards, social media platforms, and other websites. Also, it helps create and maintain a talent pool of earlier interested or passive candidates for various organizational roles. Continuously monitor and build a pipeline of potential candidates, even when no immediate openings exist, by attending various industry and network events and job fairs to connect with potential candidates.

Agile Resume Screening: Agile resume screening uses AI-driven tools to screen various resumes with relevant skill sets, experience, and qualifications for a specific job. The tool looks for keywords to match quickly and meet the job requirements. The hiring managers and their team are involved in the resume screening process for diverse viewpoints. They conduct review meetings regularly to deliberate on the qualified candidates and make decisions collaboratively.

Agile Interview Process: The agile interview follows a structured framework with standardized questions to confirm uniformity and fairness. The questions covered are behavioral and technical for a specific role. Panel interviews are conducted to assess candidates from multiple perspectives for the best fit and offer feedback to the management through collaborative tools.

Agile Selection: The agile selection process analyses the data from various assessments and interviews to make decisions. The scorecards are used to evaluate candidates based on job criteria, selecting and offering jobs to the preferred candidates to minimize the risk of losing them to competitors. The offer covers various details like salary and benefits. The salary package is negotiable to attract the best candidates for the organization.

Agile Onboarding: Agile onboarding involves sending the necessary information and resources to the selected candidates before they start. Ensure all the required setup and equipment are ready to use and conduct a comprehensive orientation for the new hires to introduce them to the company, culture, department, and team. Design and develop training with clear milestones and performance indicators and regular check-ins of the new hire to address any issues. Allot a mentor or buddy employee to support the selected candidates during their initial working days and enhance their experience and effectiveness (Gregory et al., 2022)

5. AGILE PERFORMANCE MANAGEMENT

It is a modern approach to managing employee performance that emphasizes flexibility, continuous feedback, and iterative upgrading. The differences between traditional and agile performance management are in Table 2.

Table 2. Difference between Traditional and Agile Performance Management

Criteria's	**Traditional Performance Management**	**Agile Performance Management**
Frequency of assessment	Annual, twice a year	Continuous, regular check-ins
Performance Goals	Rigid goals are set annually	Dynamic Goals and updated regularly
Approach	Top-down	Bottom-up (Peer, collaborative and self inputs)
Focus	Focused on the present	Future-oriented
Manager's role	Act as Assessor or evaluator	Acts as mentor or coach

Implementing agile performance management practices in an organization creates a responsive, engaging, and development-focused environment, leading to higher satisfaction, improved employee performance, and alignment with organizational goals.

Agile performance goals, agile reviews, coaching, recognition, and rewards in Agile environments

Agile performance goals must be flexible and easily adaptable to changes in the environment. (Subramanian et al., 2022), The study explains that performance analysis provides information and suggestions for improvements and also provides a framework for evaluating using agile techniques.

Some of the principles for preparing performance goals are:

- Align with Organizational Objectives: The individual goal and organizational goals should align together with the objective of the organization, and they should be communicated to employees.
- Use OKRs (Objectives and Key Results): The organization's objective should be achievable, and the key results should be precise.
- Plan for short-term goals: The larger goals are fragmented into smaller goals, and regular assessments must be designed.
- Collaborative Goal Setting: Involve: Collaborative goal setting involves team members and develops discussions between team members regarding organizational goals.
- Focus on Outcomes, Not Just Activities: The desired outcome needs to be concentrated rather than the task (Fagerholm et al., 2015)

Agile Performance Reviews

- Continuous Feedback and Adjustment: The continuous review progress helps to get feedback and try to modify the goals based on the feedback
- SMART Criteria: The goals need to meet the criteria that must be specific, measurable, achievable, and relevant.
- Focus on Team and Individual Development: The goals need to be established to focus on individual and growth development, and the goals should also match the career objectives.
- Transparency and Accountability: Goals must be transparent to the employees, and techniques must be used to track the progress of the goals (Fagerholm et al., 2015).

Agile Coaching

- Managers must be coaches rather than just being and evaluators in supporting and guiding employees to achieve their individual and organizational goals.

- Managers must establish ongoing dialogues with employees about their career aspirations, challenges, and overall personal development. Further, develop personalized plans based on employees' abilities, strengths, and weaknesses.
- Training programs, workshops, and courses offer continuous support, resources, and employee learning and development opportunities.
- Pair employees with mentors for guidance and support, empowering them to take ownership of their performance (Fagerholm et al., 2015).

Agile Recognition

Agile Recognition: Recognizing and rewarding employee achievements leads to reinforcing positive behavior. Regularly verbally acknowledge the best work and use emails, newsletters, or broadcast or intranet messages to highlight employee achievements. Organizations offer frequent awards or tokens of appreciation to encourage employees to recognize each other's contributions through platforms like Kudos, enabling peer recognition (Fagerholm et al., 2015).

Agile Rewards: The reward for the best performer in organizations will be training opportunities, conferences, or team outings. Offer regular rewards to motivate specific behaviors, achievements, career advancement, and personal growth. Organizations apply tools, namely 15Five Culture Amp, to track feedback on performance goals, and they also utilize tools like Slack and Microsoft Teams for continual communication with employees (Fagerholm et al., 2015).

6. STRATEGIES FOR BUILDING AND MANAGING AGILE TEAMS

Agile teams are classically small and cross-functional clusters of people who work collaboratively to offer value to customers in a dynamic yet competitive business scenario. The Agile teams have complete autonomy and are self-organized to achieve the goals within the project boundaries and values incrementally and iteratively. Agile teams are part of agile methodology, namely, Scrum, Kanban, and Extreme Programming (XP), which highlights continuous improvement, flexibility, and customer satisfaction.

Agile methodologies have found significant applications across various domains, including Human Resources (HR). Implementing Agile practices in HR can bring a considerable transformation in how HR teams operate, bringing many benefits (McMackin et al.2021).

Characteristics of Agile Teams

Cross-functional -Members of the agile teams have diverse skill sets and expertise to complete any task or project, having various roles as developers, testers, etc.

Self-Organizing- Teams have complete autonomy to manage any work that comes in the way of the organization's functioning and how best they achieve their set goals and objectives, further enhancing creativity and innovation, and they will be accountable for the work.

Collaborative – the collaborative approach of agile teams ensures an environment where team members actively communicate, share responsibilities, and work together towards common goals and objectives, further enhancing productivity and product quality (Santos et al.,2015).

Iterative and Incremental- Work will be divided into short sprints (typically 1-4 weeks) where the team assesses, reassesses, and brings improvements based on the feedback.

Continuous Improvement- Agile teams believe in self-reflection, which helps identify areas for improvement and implement changes to enhance efficiency and effectiveness (Saruchera et al., 2022).

Benefits of Agile Teams

1. **Flexibility and Responsiveness** -Teams quickly respond to organizational changes, market conditions, or regulatory requirements. Team flexibility ensures that HR practices remain more relevant and practical.HR teams can continuously assess and polish their strategies and processes to bring more dynamic and responsiveness to their work.
2. **Employee engagement** -Agile practice empowers team members to make decisions and be accountable for the work; this autonomy leads to higher job satisfaction and better engagement levels (Malik et al.2021). Also, the team implements a consistent feedback system, which helps identify the various concerns and issues and address them on a timely basis to create a positive work environment.
3. **Efficiency and productivity**-Agile teams prioritize the value-creation activities and tasks that improve overall efficiency. The iterative and continuous improvement processes streamline the HR workflows, reduce unwanted steps, and increase productivity (Trzeciak et al., 2022).
4. **Talent management** -Agile teams can adapt speedily to changing business scenarios and respond well to attract and retain the best talent. Also, teams design, develop and implement training programs to meet the employees' needs and achieve the organizational goals (Martinez et al., 2023).

5. **Continuous Improvement**-Self-reflection makes the HR teams reflect on their various process and outcomes, which helps identify areas for improvement and implement changes. This culture of continuous improvement leads to more effective and innovative HR practices (Ajayi et al., 2024).
6. **Transparency and Trust** -Agile teams aim at a transparent approach across the organization and emphasize an open communication system that ensures trust among all stakeholders, further building employee and management confidence.
7. **Collaboration and communication** -Agile teams include members from various HR functions, namely recruitment, training, performance appraisal, and payroll, who work together. This cross-functional approach further enhances collaboration and ensures that different perspectives are considered and analyzed. Regular meetings and an open communication system ensure team members are aligned with team and organizational goals and informed about enduring activities and priorities.
8. **Alignment with business goals** - Teams work meticulously with other business units to align HR strategies and initiatives with overall business goals. The ability to quickly adapt to changing business requirements ensures that HR functions support and drive organizational success (Javed et al., 2023).

Agile HR Team Composition

The composition of Agile teams in HR reflects the principles of cross-functionality tailored to fit the unique needs of HR functions (Moh'd et al., 2023).

- HR Manager

The manager outlines the vision for HR initiatives, prioritizes tasks, and manages and ensures alignment with organizational goals. They act as liaisons between stakeholders and the HR Agile team.

- Scrum Master / Agile Coach

A coach facilitates agile practices within the team, which removes obstacles and ensures adherence to improve processes and productivity.

- HR Specialists (Cross-Functional HR Team Members)

Team members possess HR skills and expertise and work cohesively and collaboratively to deliver solutions. The specialists include recruitment specialists, learning and development experts, compensation and benefits analysts, employee relations officers, HR generalists, etc. (Lingras et al., 2021).

- HR Data Analyst

Analyzes HR data to provide insights that inform decision-making and strategy. They work closely with the team to ensure data-driven approaches to HR initiatives. Change Manager

- Change Manager

They focus on managing change initiatives and ensuring that HR projects are executed smoothly and effectively.

- Learning and Development Specialist

L&D specialists design and implement training and development programs to promote employee growth and meet organizational needs. They coordinate and collaborate well with the team members to ensure continuous learning and development.

DEI (Diversity, Equity, and Inclusion) Teams and Its Composition

DEI initiatives across organizations are vital to creating an inclusive and equitable workplace. Integrating Agile methodologies into DEI within Human Resources (HR) enhances effectiveness and adaptability (Oswal et al., 2023) (Lingras et al., 2021).

Composition of DEI agile teams:

- DEI lead or Manager
- Agile coach
- DEI specialist
- HR data analyst
- Change manager
- L & D Specialist.

Strategies to Empower Agile Teams

Agile teams must be empowered to drive and innovate high-quality outcomes for organizational success. The following are the strategies adopted to empower the agile teams.

1. **Autonomy and Ownership -**Organizations must allow agile teams to decide their level, encouraging a sense of belongingness, ownership, and accountability. Encourage teams to organize their work and define their workflows. This enhances their ability to respond quickly to changes and improves productivity (Laussen et al., 2021).
2. **Enhance Collaboration and Communication -** Establish tools and practices that promote open, transparent communication between the team and stakeholders. Confirm teams have diverse skills, enabling them to manage different aspects of the project independently and collaboratively(Engelsberger et al., 2023).
3. **Support Continuous Learning and Development -** Provide ongoing training and access to learning resources to keep team members updated on Agile practices and technologies. Implement mentoring programs for agile practitioners' guides and support team members.
4. **Clarify Goals and Vision -** Communicate the project goals, vision, and success criteria clearly to ensure the team understands the direction and purpose. Conducting review sessions to provide constructive feedback and ensure alignment with the project's goals.
5. **Adopt a Supportive Leadership Style -** Leaders should act as facilitators, providing the necessary support and removing impediments rather than directing every action (Amy et al.2008). Understand and address team members' needs and challenges, offering emotional and professional support.
6. **Implement Effective Agile Practices -** Conduct stand-up meetings to ensure alignment and promptly address any obstacles. Break projects into manageable iterations or sprints, allowing for regular assessment and adaptation.
7. **Encourage Innovation and Experimentation -** Create a culture where experimentation is encouraged, and failures are viewed as learning opportunities. Allocating time for team members to work on innovative ideas or side projects that could benefit the project.
8. **Recognize and Reward Contributions -**Acknowledge and celebrate individual and team achievements to boost morale and motivation. Offer tangible rewards for exceptional contributions, aligning incentives with team goals.

9. **Provide the Right Tools and Resources** -Equip teams with tools that support Agile methodologies, such as project management software, collaboration platforms, and automated testing tools. Ensure teams can access the necessary resources, including time, budget, and information.
10. **Facilitate Continuous Improvement** - Conduct regular retrospectives to reflect on what's working well and what can be improved, fostering a culture of continuous improvement. Use insights from retrospectives to make iterative changes to processes and practices(Kerth, 2013).

By implementing these strategies, you can empower Agile teams to be more effective, innovative, and productive, leading to better project outcomes and higher team satisfaction.

Benefits of Empowering Agile Teams

Empowerment includes giving teams and their members the authority, resources, and support to make decisions and take ownership of carried work. Empowered agile teams are crucial for many reasons, such as enhancing creativity, effectiveness in work, innovation, and productivity, and they will also adapt well to changing scenarios, resulting in better performance (Chukwurah et al., 2024).

Decision-Making: Teams are empowered to make decisions speedily without waiting for any formal higher-up's approval, reducing further delays and allowing the team to perform quickly to the changing needs and challenges.

Team Motivation and Management: Team members who are valued and trusted get motivated and engage well in their work. Empowerment fosters a sense of ownership and accountability, leading to higher job satisfaction and commitment.

Problem-Solving and Innovation: Teams are empowered to make decisions for any issues and concerns related to the business, making them more innovative. Through this empowerment, team members can adopt various approaches to identify the most efficient and practical approach to achieve organizational goals and objectives.

Collaboration and Communication: Agile methodology emphasizes coordination and cooperation among team members. Empowered teams communicate openly and work collaboratively, which further helps them to share their ideas freely and give feedback for continuous improvement.

Quick Adaptation to Change: Agile methodologies make employees adapt quickly to business scenarios.

Quality Outcome: Empowered teams have the authority to make decisions about the work and process what they follow, which will help them give quality outcomes. They identify and address any issues and concerns that come their way.

Lessen Bottlenecks: Empowered teams streamline the workflows by eliminating unnecessary approvals and bureaucracy, further reducing bottlenecks and improving the development process's overall efficiency.

Scalability: Empowered teams operate independently, and upscaling becomes easier. Every team manages its workload and contributes better to achieve the goals and business objectives.

Resilience and Sustainability: Empowered teams will be more resilient during setbacks. They will have complete autonomy to find solutions and overcome failures, contributing to long-term business sustainability (Podger, 2023).

Customer Satisfaction: Empowered agile teams focus on delivering high value to customers speedily and effectively (Grass et al., 2020). Based on customer feedback, the end product outcomes are achieved by continuously iterating.

Measuring Agile Team Performance

Team assessment is based on various quantitative and qualitative measurements to confirm that the team members are working efficiently and effectively and delivering value while focusing on continuous improvement.

Quantitative and quantitative metrics are as follows:

Velocity: The amount of teamwork completion for a specified tenure helps to understand the team's capacity and plan for future work.

Burn-up & Burn-down Charts: The chart helps identify the progress and completion of the project. It will be the graphical or visual representation by which team deviations are identified.

Cycle Time: cycle time gives the time taken to complete any task, measures the efficiency of the workflow flow, and identifies the team bottlenecks.

Lead Time: Lead time talks about the number of tasks completed, which is the total time from when a task is created to when it is finished. It reflects and measures the overall team efficiency and helps optimize the workflow.

Throughput: It measures the team's productivity and helps in capacity planning based on the number of tasks completed in a given period.

Defects: The number of deficiencies identified per unit of work and the output quality, which helps to focus on improvements and further measures the team's efficiency and effectiveness.

Customer Satisfaction: Based on the survey feedback and Net Promoter Score (NPS), customer satisfaction with the delivered product will be assessed and, in turn, on the team.

Team Satisfaction and Morale: A one-on-one meeting, surveys, and self-reflection process gauges the team's well-being and helps identify areas for improvement.

Collaboration and Communication: Observation and feedback enable the management to ensure that the team works well together and maintains effective communication channels.

Value Delivered: Value creation and delivery to the customer could be measured through revenue outcomes, KPIs, and user engagement levels.

Innovation Rate: Measurement is based on the innovative idea the team applies while focusing on continuous improvement.

Retrospectives: Meet regularly to know what went well and what didn't and how to foster a culture emphasizing continuous improvement.

Root Cause Analysis: Techniques like the "5 Whys" or Fishbone Diagram identify underlying performance issues and find solutions.

Learning and Development: Measurement based on the learning ability and continuously upgrading their skill sets for the betterment of the organization.

The performance of agile teams can measured to identify their efficiency and whether they deliver high-quality products that meet customer needs (Almeida et al., 2023).

Scaling Agile Teams

Scaling up agile teams means applying agile practices and principles from smaller to larger organizations. The main aim of this scaling is to get the benefits of agile practices in terms of flexibility in handling complex issues or concerns based on regular feedback.

Frameworks for Scaling Agile:

SAFe (Scaled Agile Framework): It provides detailed direction on roles, responsibilities, and practices and emphasizes collaboration, alignment, and work delivery across various Agile teams.

LeSS (Large-Scale Scrum): This framework is predominantly for larger groups and emphasizes simplicity and maximizing the learning process across teams by using minimal additional roles and artifacts.

DA (Disciplined Agile): Combines Scrum, Kanban, and other methods. It adopts the best approach depending on the context.

Spotify Model: The model focuses on autonomous squads, tribes, chapters, and guilds and prioritizes the culture and autonomy of the team over rigid structures (Verwijs et al., 2024).

Challenges in Scaling Agile

The various challenges of scaling agile are as follows

- Cultural resistance occurs as a result of a shift from a traditional team to an agile one, and this can be resolved by having a strong leader and their support, as well as by continuous improvement and education.
- Communication becomes more challenging once the agile teams scale up, and this problem can be resolved using appropriate tools (Like Scrum).
- Agile scaling presents a more structured setup, which reduces flexibility. Ensuring autonomy and encouraging continuous improvement practices can help to retain agility among teams (Putta et al., 2018).

Tools for Agile Scaling

Based on the organization's needs, the right tools and frameworks to be adopted for the desired outcomes. Implementing tools and frameworks ensures that Agile practices are effectively scaled up to meet the expectations of complex projects, fostering collaboration, transparency, and continuous improvement across the organization.

The various tools for agile scaling are as follows:

Enterprise-level Agile Management Tools: Jira, Rally, and VersionOne, which help manage backlogs, track progress, and facilitate collaboration.

Collaborative Tools: Slack, Microsoft Teams, and Confluence, which ensures effective communication across teams and helps in documentation.

DevOps Tools: Jenkins, Docker, and Kubernetes aid in Continuous Integration (CI) and Continuous Delivery (CD) to shorten the development life cycle

Organizations can achieve greater efficiency, collaboration, and adaptability by understanding and implementing appropriate frameworks, practices, and tools (Block, 2023).

Agile Teams' Resilience

The various strategies adopted for agile team resilience are as follows:

1. **Encourage the team's Psychological Safety** -Create a conducive workspace where members can freely express their views, ideas, concerns, and mistakes. The team treats failures as learning opportunities and does blameless post-mortems to know what went wrong and how to resolve it.
2. **Team Growth Mindset -**Encourage team members for Continuous education and learning through various training, workshops, and conferences. The team believes in recognizing and celebrating small achievements, which leads to confidence and morale.

3. **Team Cohesion** -Organizing several activities builds trust and develops diverse skills that promote collaboration and knowledge sharing. Team cohesion is essential for Agile teams to perform effectively and efficiently and deliver high-quality results, strengthening the relationships and unity among team members.
4. **Adaptability and Flexibility**-Encouraging teams to be more flexible and open to change, aligning with Agile principles.
5. **Supportive Leadership** -Empowering teams to make decisions and take ownership of the work.
6. **Health and Well-Being** -Promoting a healthy work-life balance prevents stress and burnout and maintains high energy levels among team members.
7. **Effective Communication** -Ensure that information flows freely between the members of the team and across the organization.
8. **Foster Innovation** -Allow team members to work on innovative ideas for better outcomes. Create a culture that ensures creative-solving abilities.
9. **Resilient Processes** -Developing and standardizing the various processes that help respond to the organization's different issues and challenges.
12. **Team Culture** -Recognizing and rewarding team members' positive behaviors and contributions.

Building resilience among Agile teams is an enduring effort that involves creating a conducive working space, creating open communication, encouraging and promoting continuous learning, and reassuring adaptability. By applying these strategies, teams can better handle challenges, adapt to the expected changes, and achieve higher performance (Marder et al., 2021).

7. CHALLENGES AND OVERCOMING RESISTANCE TO CHANGE

Change management is a systematic approach to transforming an organization's goals, processes, or technologies. The main aim is to ensure that change occurs smoothly and successfully and to achieve long-lasting benefits.

Types of Change

- Strategic Change: Changes occur on a large scale that affect the overall way of the organization.
- Operational Change: Day-to-day changes that affect the business.
- Technological Change: Technical changes to improve the overall organizational process.

- Cultural Change: Changes in the organization's culture, values, beliefs, and behaviors.

Phases of Change Management

The different phases of change management are explained in Figure 3.

Figure 3. Phases of Change Management

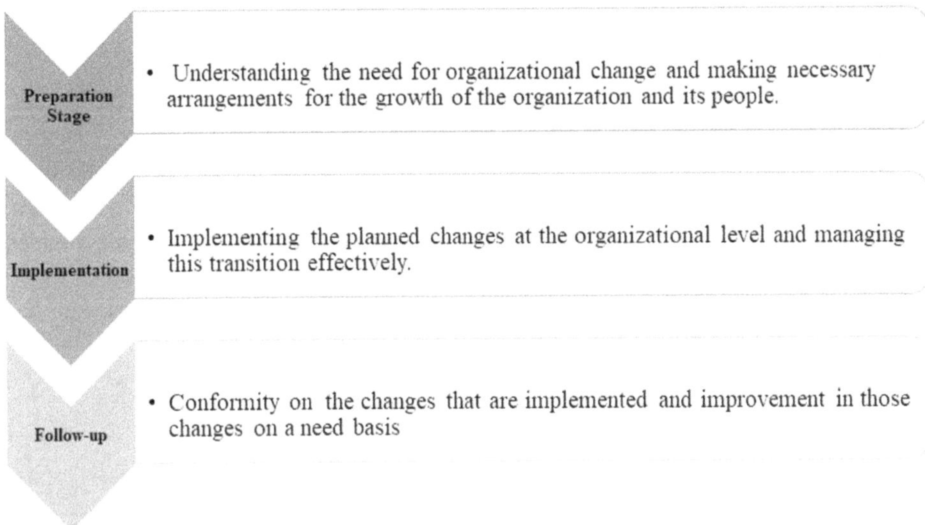

Steps in Change Management

- **Define the Change**: Identify the changes to be made for the overall growth, stay competitive in the market, and assess its scope and impact on the organization.
- **Create a Plan**: A detailed plan to be developed covering timelines, resources to be Develop a detailed change plan that comprises timelines, resources, and important milestones to be achieved in due course and also assessing the risk associated with it and how to mitigate the same for the betterment of the organization.
- **Communicate** A communication plan to be prepared to update on the organizational change to its stakeholders to ensure transparency.
- **Engage Stakeholders**: Address the key stakeholders to get feedback on the resistance to change and educate and support them to overcome it.

- **Implement the Change**: Implement the planned change, monitor the progress, and make necessary modifications accordingly.
- **Support and Training**: Training programs are to be designed and conducted to help employees adapt to the expected changes and provide the necessary support system for a smooth transformation.
- **Monitor and Evaluate**: Continuously monitor the implemented change, evaluate the results against the set objectives, and make necessary modifications.
- **Sustain the Change**: Reinforce the change to make it part of the organizational culture. Recognize and reward efforts to sustain the change (Mızrak, 2024).

Challenges/Resistance to Change Management

- Employees resist the change because of fear of failure, fear of the unknown, and fear of being unable to compete and complete the work in the new setup, and they may also feel that they may not have control over the process based on the past change.
- Constant changes in any organizational setup led to employee fatigue and decreased morale.
- Employees may lack the perceived benefits.
- Poor communication about the changes leads to confusion and a lack of stakeholders' buy-in.
- Changes disturb employees' routines and comfort zones, which causes total discomfort and resistance.
- Employees may fear the change will lead to job insecurity.
- Employees may resist because of a lack of trust in the leadership.
- Without training, employees may struggle to adapt to new procedures, processes, or technologies (Laidoune et al., 2022).

Change Models

- Lewin's Change Management Model: Involves three stages—Unfreeze, Change, and Refreeze. Lewin's model is a structured approach to overcoming employee resistance to change initiatives in an organizational space. In the first unfreezing stage, the employee may not accept the changes due to the unknown, feeling they might lose control over the job and power. The management must create awareness and communicate about the changes to be made and the benefits they will get over time. This transparent approach builds confidence and trust among employees so that they start thinking about the change and work towards it by undergoing training and getting support from leaders. In the second stage of change, during the transition, employees might resist because of habituation and lack of efficacy toward the new process and procedure. For this, leaders must offer detailed training to upskill and reskill employees, empowering them and continuous programs to build employee confidence and reduce any organizational uncertainties. In the third refreezing stage, the employees who were part of the change are to be rewarded and acknowledged to retain the change and move forward in the same direction. The leaders must reinforce the expected behaviors by institutionalizing these changes as organizational policies and procedures.

- ADKAR Model: The change management framework focuses on individual change and involves Awareness, Desire, Knowledge, Ability, and Reinforcement (Laidoune et al., 2022). This model tries to address the employee resistance to organizational changes by emphasizing every employee and the way employees are involved in the entire change process. This is possible by communicating and creating awareness, the desire for change, updated knowledge to bring changes, and improved ability and capabilities for better transition.

The organization's various strategies to overcome employee resistance are as follows.

- Organizations must focus on better planning to create awareness of the change and ensure firm support and commitment from employees and management.
- Organizations must establish a clear vision and objectives for the planned change.
- Organizations must involve employees in the change process so that all know the importance and benefits. The leaders must listen to employee concerns and address them openly. Provide reassurance and clarity on how the change will impact them.
- The change process in any setup involves open communication across the organization and addressing employees' concerns and fears towards the change process.
- Regular feedback and assessment of the changed process are to be made to know the impact at the organizational level.
- Offer training and resources to help employees develop the required skills to adapt to the planned change.
- Leaders must build and maintain trust among employees by being transparent, consistent in their work, honest, and committed throughout the change process.

- o A positive culture is to be created wherein employees view change as an opportunity rather than a threat.
- o Recognize and reward employees who actively participate in the change process. Incentives would motivate employees to embrace the planned change (Zuperkienė et al., 2023).

Some of the Successful Initiatives Taken by Companies Are as Follows

- Maruthi Suzuki: During the automation of its manufacturing plant, Maruti Suzuki negotiated with members and took care of their concerns, further reducing the resistance and easing the transition.
- Larsen & Toubro(L&T): The company initiated reward and incentive schemes for its employees for their efforts towards digitalization. This reinforcement positively impacted employees to mitigate resistance.
- JSW Steel: During its digitalization drive, the company supported, appraised, and addressed job-related concerns by providing multiple opportunities. They also offered detailed training programs for employees transitioning to new-fangled roles.
- Tata Steel: The company designed a program called 'Aspire,' emphasizing change management initiatives to introduce newer technology to their manufacturing processes. The employees were involved in the change management plan and decision stages, which helped ease concerns and create a sense of belongingness and ownership.

Building Resilience to Change

Every individual and organization needs to thrive in an ever-evolving changing environment. Change resilience is adapting effectively to new conditions, improving from setbacks, and remaining positive despite disruptions.

Components of Change Resilience

- Growth Mindset: Every employee must believe that skills and abilities can be developed through dedication and hard work, which fosters a love of learning and resilience, which are essential for accomplishment.
- Optimistic: Employees must be confident that planned change might reduce stress and tension and motivate them to achieve positively.
- Self-Regulation: Manage emotions healthily, stay calm under pressure, and control impulsive reactions towards organizational change.

- Empathy: Recognize and understand others' emotions, support everyone, and build strong relationships during change.
- Flexibility: Employees must have a flexible mindset and adapt to organizational challenges.
- Problem-Solving Skills: Develop employees' ability to think creatively and logically to drive solutions in the transition phase.
- Social Support: Building solid relationships with family, friends, colleagues, and mentors provides strong emotional support and practical advice at times of difficulty.
- Professional Networks: Encourage professional groups and communities to express their views and share their experiences and strategies for managing the planned change.
- Empathy and Support: Leaders should demonstrate empathy and support team members in participating actively in the change process (He et al., 2023).

Strategies for Building Change Resilience

Various strategies are to be adopted to build resilience for change.
At the Individual Level: Strategies for the individual are as follows:

1. Focus on continuous Learning: Individuals must engage in constant learning, i.e., life learning, as learning is never a never-ending process. Learning will enable skill updates and make them stay up-to-date and adaptable. Also, individuals must attend industry-related seminars and workshops to gain deeper insights and knowledge.
2. Emotional Intelligence-Individuals must practice mindfulness to know their emotions and reactions to others. Also, understand others' views and feelings emphatically and develop strong relationships.
3. Nurture a Growth Mindset-Individuals must think from the growth perspective and view the challenges as opportunities for growth and learning. Accept feedback to improve and develop the necessary skill sets.
4. Strengthen the Network

Individuals must establish a strong connection with colleagues, mentors, and peer groups to create a support system. This support system helps share their experiences, views, and strategies to manage the planned change in an organizational space.

5. Stress Management Practices- Individuals must practice meditation and yoga daily to manage stress and regular exercise to maintain physical fitness and health.
6. Realistic Goals: Individuals must set realistic goals that are practically achievable. The goals must be flexible enough to alter as per the circumstances.
7. Self-Care -Individuals must follow a healthy lifestyle and have a proper state of mind to take up any activity. Self-care is possible by maintaining a balanced diet, getting adequate sleep, being hydrated, and engaging in activities that promote mental wellness.

At the organizational Level- Strategies for the individual are as follows.

1. Effective Communication: Organizations must develop an open and transparent communication channel to deal with the planned change and its impact, including adequate feedback support.
2. Leadership -Organizations must train leaders to be more empathetic and supportive during times of change.
3. Employee empowerment- Providing autonomy to employees to make decisions about their activity and take initiatives for organizational growth.
4. Training and Development -Offer training and development programs focusing on skills and techniques required for the change and its management.
5. Organizational Culture- Develop a culture that supports innovation and continuous improvement and recognizes and rewards those employees who exhibit resilience and adaptability.
6. Support Systems- Counseling, mental wellness, and employee assistance programs to build change Resilience
7. Scenario Planning – Organizations must do a risk assessment to identify the various challenges and to develop a contingent plan to execute the change.
    9. Encouraging innovative ideas - Organizations must provide a platform to share employee views, ideas, and creative practices for the betterment of the work.
    10. Measure success - Define and track change resilience based on the milestones achieved that boost employee morale and reinforce positive change (Su et al., 2023).

8. AGILE LEADERSHIP IN HR

Agile leadership plays a predominant role in today's fast-paced business space. Agile leaders focus on vision, adaptability, collaboration, continuous learning, emotional intelligence, and customer focus, offering an agile culture, delivering high value and tremendous success. Agile leaders are pivotal in driving and sustaining agile methodologies within organizations, promoting a culture of continuous improvement, and effectively responding to change.

Agile Human Resources (HR) leadership involves applying agile principles and practices to the various HR functions to make a collaborative, adaptive, and responsive department. This approach helps HR team members achieve goals, quickly respond to changes, and add value to employees and stakeholders. The characteristics of agile leadership are explained in Table 3.

Table 3. Characteristics of Agile Leaders

Characteristics	Agile Leaders
Adaptable nature	Able to quickly adjust to any strategies and approaches for the planned change. The change will be considered an opportunity rather than a threat.
Customer Centric	Agile leaders always emphasize adding value to the customer to meet their expectations. Leaders' efforts aligned with customers' needs and feedback to reach out to customer expectations.
Transparency	Agile leaders exercise transparency and open communication policies to inform their team members about goals, challenges, and changes, which helps build trust and aligns with the organization's overall growth.
Decisiveness nature	Agile leaders make appropriate decisions when needed to take projects forward.
Collaboration	Agile leaders emphasize a collaborative environment and empower team members to share views and ideas. Agile leaders will not encourage silos and encourage cross-functional work across teams.
Continuous Improvement	Agile leaders are loyal and committed to continuous learning and encourage team members to self-reflect to enhance efficiency and effectiveness.
Resilience	Agile leaders establish resilience for any challenges and setbacks in the organization. They are always future and solution-oriented, offering stability and guidance to their teams.
Courage	Agile leaders dare to take organizational risks and adopt innovative approaches to maintain the status quo and further organizational growth.
Emotional Intelligence	Agile leaders have high emotional intelligence, which allows them to effectively manage their own emotions and influence the feelings of others. This EI helps to build solid relationships and create a robust and positive culture.
Outcome orientation	Agile leaders always work towards achieving the desired result as expected and focus on value-addition (Tabassum et al.,2024).

Roles and Responsibilities of an Agile Leader

They play a prominent role in any organizational workspace and promote better collaboration, a flexible workspace, and continuous improvement. The roles are discussed below.

Facilitator: Agile leaders act as facilitators to ensure the team members follow and adhere to the agile practices and identify and eliminate any obstacles that stop the team's progress.

Empower Teams: Agile leaders empower their team members to make decisions and provide opportunities to grow and work on enhancing their skill sets.

Drive Continuous Improvement: Agile leaders believe that team members' self-reflection drives continuous improvement in various organizational processes and enhances productivity.

Support Collaboration and Communication: Agile leaders support open communication and transparency within and across the team, enabling trust and solid relationships for better collaborative work.

Aligning vision and business goals: Agile leaders focus on aligning teamwork with vision, customer needs, and expectations. They facilitate adaptive planning to meet market and project expectations. Agile leaders provide a clear vision, ensuring better contributions to organizational goals.

Servant Leadership: This approach focuses on their team members' growth and well-being and enables them to perform at their best.

Empowerment: Agile leaders empower team members to make decisions about their work and are accountable for their work, fostering a sense of belongingness.

Learning: Agile leaders always emphasize learning and encourage a learning mindset among team members, promoting experiential learning and knowledge sharing (Tabassum et al., 2024).

9. FUTURE TRENDS IN AGILE HR

Agile methodologies increasingly influence human resources (HR), leading to the development of Agile HR practices. This trend focuses on making HR processes flexible and people-centric. Future trends in Agile HR are discussed below:

1. Continuous Performance Management: Agile HR replaces traditional performance reviews with continuous performance reviews where data is collected in real-time. This approach adopts check-ins and coaching sessions, promoting team member's development. The Agile goal setting for the team members,

namely OKRs, i.e., Objective and Key Results, is formulated based on the work requirements.

Implications: It offers adaptability and real-time feedback. Alignment of dynamic business goals, better employee engagement, and improves productivity in a dynamic business environment.

2. Employee Experience and Engagement: Agile HR focuses on personalized employee experience in an organization, from onboarding to career progression. Agile methodology adopts pulse surveys to gauge employee engagement and satisfaction levels and respond to such concerns and issues.

Implications: provides a responsive, cooperative culture that drives motivation in a dynamic workspace.

3. Learning and Development: Agile HR emphasizes a culture of continuous learning through e-platforms, microlearning, and on-the-job training. It develops and nurtures the learning path, allowing employees to acquire the required skill sets for the changing business scenario.
4. Flexi-work Arrangements: Agile HR embraces the remote and hybrid work models to support employees in work-life balance and achieving higher productivity. They adapt digital tools and policies to collaborate well and accomplish the work per the organizational requirements. Also, an adaptive workspace can be created by reconfiguring it according to the changing needs of the team and the projects.
5. Data-Driven HR: Agile HR leverages advanced analytics and tools to gain insights into workforce trends, performance, and employee engagement. The digital tools forecast employee attrition and help identify the gaps between the current and desired employee competencies, skills, and behaviors.
6. Talent Acquisition and Management: Agile recruitment streamlines the process to be flexible and iterative, allowing for quicker hiring cycles and better alignment with business needs, which quickly respond to organizational hiring needs.
7. Diversity, Equity, and Inclusion (DEI): Agile HR techniques ensure diversity, equity, and inclusivity in the recruitment and selection processes. Regularly assess and iterate on DEI initiatives to promote an inclusive workplace culture.

Implications: Supports the creation of a dynamic, inclusive space where diverse perspectives are valued, which drives innovation and is transparent.

8. Empowerment and Autonomy: Agile HR offers self-managed, cross-functional teams autonomy to make decisions and drive organizational projects. Agile policies empower employees to take ownership and look for career progression.
9. Employee wellness and well-being: Agile practice develops detailed wellness programs that support employees' physical, mental, and emotional well-being.
10. Agile Leadership and Culture: Train leaders in agile principles and practices to develop a culture of agility at the organizational level. It creates a culture emphasizing collaboration, adaptability, and continuous organizational improvement.
11. Technology and Automation: Agile HR technology solutions help automate routine tasks and augment the strategic decision-making process. Agile HR uses artificial intelligence and machine learning, from recruitment to employee performance evaluation.
12. Agile HR Frameworks and Practices: Agile HR uses Kanban boards to visualize and manage the various HR tasks and workflows, which promotes transparency and efficiency. Adopting Scrum to HR projects augments an organization's collaboration, flexibility, and value delivery (Moh et al., 2023).

Technology Integration in Agile HR

Technology integration in HR Agile practices enhances HR processes' efficiency, flexibility, and responsiveness. The various technologies adopted in Agile HR are as follows (Popoola et al., 2024) in the below Table 4:

Table 4. Technology Integration in Agile HR

Technological Tool/ Platform	**Application**
HRMS(Human Resource Management Systems and HRIS(Human Resource Information Systems)	• HRMS and HRIS platforms offer centralized data that is easily accessible for decision-making and streamlines administrative tasks. • Automates routine tasks like payroll, report generation, etc., and HR professionals can focus on the organization's strategic tasks or core areas. Example of HRIS/HRMS Key features: Supports employee database management, offers self-service to employees, facilitates documentation processes, and optimizes HR processes and operations. Manage employee life cycle.

continued on following page

Table 4. Continued

Technological Tool/ Platform	Application
Recruitment and Talent management	• ATS(Applicant Tracking Systems)to manage the recruitment process more effectively and efficiently, right from job ads to onboarding the candidates to the job. • Leverage artificial intelligence to screen candidates' resumes, ensure they match the job requirements, and reduce bias in the entire hiring process. • Agile technology helps analyze recruitment metrics to augment hiring strategies and predict future talent requirements. Example: BambooHR, Lever, Greenhouse Key features of these tools: It maintains a centralized employee database. Track the job post candidates and extract candidate's resumes for the review process. It onboards new hires to the company, sets goals for them as individuals and teams, monitors their progress, offers feedback, and engages employees.
Performance Management	Integrating technology platforms to facilitate performance check-ins and offer feedback for better employee contribution. Also, technology helps in tracking employee's performance and identifying their areas of improvement. 15Five, Lattice, and Betterworks are some of the tools available for performance management. Key features of these tools: These tools will help with one-on-one conversations with employees, the check-in process, talent management, goal setting, and tracking newly hired and existing employees.
Learning and Development	• LMS(Learning Management Systems) offers learning resources, tracks the learner's progress, and facilitates continuous learning. • E-Learning provides training modules based on organizational requirements and microlearning to support skill development. • VR(Virtual reality) and AR(Augmented reality) for immersive training experiences, particularly for complex work. Example: Udeamy, Coursera, LinkedIn Features of these platforms: Offers course catalogs for easy access and enrolling, curated courses, offers learners personalized recommendations, mobile-friendly access for learners, industry-partnered certified courses, etc.,
Employee Engagement and Well-being	• Technological tools to conduct surveys to measure employee engagement levels and job satisfaction. • Also, it integrates technological apps to track the employees' state of mind, emotional well-being throughout the process, and support offered as per the requirements. • Applying gamification techniques to intensify employee engagement in wellness and other HR programs in the workspace. Example: Peakon, TINYpulse Key features of these tools: Offers customized feedback based on a real-time, pre-built template, supports advanced data analytics to analyze trends and identify areas of improvement, and has an action plan for employees to manage and complete tasks on time. Pulse survey anonymize the feedback process. Poll to elicit employee opinions and generate reports.

continued on following page

Table 4. Continued

Technological Tool/ Platform	Application
Collaboration and Communication	• Leveraging technologies to increase collaboration and transparent communication for the organization's remote and hybrid workspace mode. • Implement tools, namely Jira Trello, to manage HR activities and workflows effectively and efficiently. • Create an internal social network for employees to share their views and opinions, discuss the technology and processes related to the projects, and build an influential community for various organizational purposes. Examples: Zoom, Slack, Microsoft Teams, Social Media. Key features of these tools: Offers virtual setup, breakout rooms for teams, screen sharing, annotation of the content displayed, recording, generating transcription of the meeting, chatting, an option of collaborative editing, mobile friendly, high-quality audio-video options.
Predictive Analytics	• Analyze data to identify workforce trends, employee turnover, planning, and performance metrics. Example: Visier, Workday analytics Key features: Offers data-driven decisions, optimizes workforce deployment, measures DEI, financial analytics, workforce management, and real-time report generation.
Artificial Intelligence (AI) and Machine Learning (ML)	• AI Chatbots will answer and manage employee inquiries, offer support, and streamline the onboarding processes. • Machine learning identifies employees' behavioral patterns and performance, which enables HR to adopt personalized interventions.
Agile Project Management Tools	Kanban and Scrum tools help visualize HR tasks, track the work progress, and facilitate sprints and backlogs. Example: Trello, Jira Asana Key features: Offers customized scrum and kanban boards, generates reports, visualization of workflows, automates the repetitive task
Cloud-Based Solutions	Leverage cloud-based HR solutions for scalability with the organization's needs and can be accessed from anywhere, supporting remote and hybrid workspace. Example: IBM Cloud, Microsoft Azure Key features: Cater to networking, storage, security, and data analytics.

10. CONCLUSION

Agility in human resource practices is more critical in today's dynamic business space. By following agile principles and frameworks, HR departments can respond more quickly to changing needs and fostering a continuous improvement culture further augments overall employee engagement and satisfaction levels.

As we move forward, the role of HR will continue to evolve, necessitating a mindset that embraces change, leverages technology, and prioritizes the well-being and development of employees. Integrating technology in Agile HR is pivotal for enhancing HR functions' agility, efficiency, and responsiveness. By leveraging advanced tools and systems, HR departments can streamline processes, foster continuous improvement, and create a more engaging and supportive environment for employees. This technological integration is vital to meeting the evolving needs of modern workplaces and maintaining a competitive edge in talent management.

In conclusion, HR agility is not merely a trend but an essential shift in human resource management, and embracing this change will equip organizations with the tools to thrive in uncertainty, ensuring they remain competitive and capable of meeting future challenges.

REFERENCES

Ajayi, F. A., & Udeh, C. A. (2024). Agile work cultures in IT: A Conceptual analysis of HR's role in fostering innovation supply chain. *International Journal of Management & Entrepreneurship Research*, 6(4), 1138–1156. DOI: 10.51594/ijmer.v6i4.1004

Alamro, M. Q., Hosseini, S. B., & Farooq, A. (2019). Organizational Agility and HRM Practices: Theoretical Framework and Perspective. *Restaurant Business*, 118, 12.

Almeida, F., & Carneiro, P. (2023). Perceived Importance of Metrics for Agile Scrum Environments. *Information (Basel)*, 14(6), 327. DOI: 10.3390/info14060327

Amy, A. H. (2008). Leaders as facilitators of individual and organizational learning. *Leadership and Organization Development Journal*, 29(3), 212–234. DOI: 10.1108/01437730810861281

Balsvik, E., & Rønnevik, M. (2022). Employees as self-regulated learners: a case study of employees' upskilling through internal microlearning platforms (Master's thesis, Handelshøyskolen BI).

Bashynska, I., Prokopenko, O., & Sala, D. (2023). Managing Human Capital with AI: Synergy of Talent and Technology. *Zeszyty Naukowe Wyższej Szkoły Finansów i Prawa w Bielsku-Białej*, 27(3), 39–45.

Block, S. (2023). How to Adapt and Implement a Large-Scale Agile Framework in Your Organization. In *Large-Scale Agile Frameworks: Agile Frameworks, Agile Infrastructure and Pragmatic Solutions for Digital Transformation* (pp. 65–168). Springer Berlin Heidelberg. DOI: 10.1007/978-3-662-67782-7_4

Chowdhury, M. (2024). Navigating the VUCA Terrain: Unveiling HR Strategies for Modern Organizational Agility. *SEISENSE Journal of Management*, 7(1), 67–82. DOI: 10.33215/wbm33665

Chukwurah, E. G., & Aderemi, S. (2024). Elevating team performance with scrum: Insights from successful US technology companies. *Engineering Science & Technology Journal*, 5(4), 1357–1371. DOI: 10.51594/estj.v5i4.1038

Doz, Y., & Kosonen, M. (2008). The dynamics of strategic agility: Nokia's roller caster experience. *California Management Review*, 50(3), 95–118. DOI: 10.2307/41166447

Edison, H., Wang, X., & Conboy, K. (2021). Comparing methods for large-scale agile software development: A systematic literature review. *IEEE Transactions on Software Engineering*, 48(8), 2709–2731. DOI: 10.1109/TSE.2021.3069039

Engelsberger, A., Cavanagh, J., Bartram, T., & Halvorsen, B. (2023). Maximizing team development for open innovation in digital product development: The role of collaborative HRM and relational leadership. *Personnel Review*.

Fagerholm, F., Ikonen, M., Kettunen, P., Münch, J., Roto, V., & Abrahamsson, P. (2015). Performance Alignment Work: How software developers experience the continuous adaptation of team performance in Lean and Agile environments. *Information and Software Technology*, 64, 132–147. DOI: 10.1016/j.infsof.2015.01.010

Grass, A., Backmann, J., & Hoegl, M. (2020). From empowerment dynamics to team adaptability: Exploring and conceptualizing the continuous agile team innovation process. *Journal of Product Innovation Management*, 37(4), 324–351. DOI: 10.1111/jpim.12525

Gregory, P., Strode, D. E., Sharp, H., & Barroca, L. (2022). An onboarding model for integrating newcomers into agile project teams. *Information and Software Technology*, 143, 106792. DOI: 10.1016/j.infsof.2021.106792

Gunn, J., Zwickert, K., & Hilyard, K. (2021). Reinventing performance management in the public sector. In *Handbook on performance management in the public sector* (pp. 1–18). Edward Elgar Publishing. DOI: 10.4337/9781789901207.00006

He, Z., Huang, H., Choi, H., & Bilgihan, A. (2023). Building organizational resilience with digital transformation. *Journal of Service Management*, 34(1), 147–171. DOI: 10.1108/JOSM-06-2021-0216

Holbeche, L. (2019). Designing sustainably agile and resilient organizations. *Systems Research and Behavioral Science*, 36(5), 668–677. DOI: 10.1002/sres.2624

Javed, H. A., Nawaz, S., & Javed, H. A. (2023). Synthesis of Success: Crafting Sustainable Performance through E-HRM Innovation, Organizational Agility, and Cultural Harmony in SMEs. *Pakistan Journal of Humanities and Social Sciences*, 11(3), 3379–3395. DOI: 10.52131/pjhss.2023.1103.0621

Jooss, S., Collings, D. G., McMackin, J., & Dickmann, M. (2024). A skills-matching perspective on talent management: Developing strategic agility. *Human Resource Management*, 63(1), 141–157. DOI: 10.1002/hrm.22192

Kavitha, R., & Suresh, M. (2019, December). Agile practices in human resource management. In International Conference on Advances in Materials Research (pp. 713-721). Singapore: Springer Nature Singapore.

Kerth, N. L. (2013). *Project retrospectives: a handbook for team reviews*. Addison-Wesley.

Laidoune, A., Zid, C., & Sahraoui, N. (2022). Innovate and overcome resistance to change to improve the resilience of systems and organizations. *Journal of the Knowledge Economy*, 13(4), 1–16. DOI: 10.1007/s13132-021-00840-8

Laussen, J., & Sutanovac, A. (2021). Evaluation of Agile Team Performance.

Lingras, K. A., Alexander, M. E., & Vrieze, D. M. (2021). Diversity, equity, and inclusion efforts at a departmental level: Building a committee as a vehicle for advancing progress. *Journal of Clinical Psychology in Medical Settings*, 1–24. PMID: 34529234

Malik, M., Sarwar, S., & Orr, S. (2021). Agile practices and performance: Examining the role of psychological empowerment. *International Journal of Project Management*, 39(1), 10–20. DOI: 10.1016/j.ijproman.2020.09.002

Marder, B., Ferguson, P., Marchant, C., Brennan, M., Hedler, C., Rossi, M., Black, S., & Doig, R. (2021). 'Going agile': Exploring the use of project management tools in fostering psychological safety in group work within management discipline courses. *International Journal of Management Education*, 19(3), 100519. DOI: 10.1016/j.ijme.2021.100519

Martinez-Sanchez, A., & Vicente-Oliva, S. (2023). Supporting agile innovation and knowledge by managing human resource flexibility. *International Journal of Innovation Science*, 15(3), 558–578. DOI: 10.1108/IJIS-11-2021-0200

McMackin, J., & Heffernan, M. (2021). Agile for HR: Fine in practice, but will it work in theory? *Human Resource Management Review*, 31(4), 100791. DOI: 10.1016/j.hrmr.2020.100791

Mızrak, F. (2024). Effective change management strategies: Exploring dynamic models for organizational transformation. In *Perspectives on artificial intelligence in times of turbulence: Theoretical background to applications* (pp. 135–162). IGI Global.

Moh'd, S., Gregory, P., Barroca, L., & Sharp, H. (2023). Agile human resource management: A systematic mapping study. German Journal of Human Resource Management.

Moloto, M., Harmse, A., & Zuva, T. (2020). Impact of agile methodology use on project success in organizations systematic literature review. *Proceedings of the Computational Methods in Systems and Software*, 267-280. DOI: 10.1007/978-3-030-63322-6_21

Nargis, L., Brastoro, B., & Fuad, M. (2024). Agile HR: Adapting Human Resource Practices to Rapid Business Changes. *Journal of Economic, Business, and Accounting*, 7(4), 7396–7401. DOI: 10.31539/costing.v7i4.10330

Nijssen, M., & Paauwe, J. (2012). HRM in turbulent times: How to achieve organizational agility? *International Journal of Human Resource Management*, 23(16), 3315–3335. DOI: 10.1080/09585192.2012.689160

Oswal, N., Siddiqui, S., & Sharma, M. S. (2023). Diversity, equity, and inclusion in the workplace: Assessing the impact on organizational performance. *Boletin de Literatura Oral-The Literary Journal*, 10(1), 2931–2941.

Podger, O. M. (2023). Unleashing Community Empowerment through A New Regional Autonomy Concept in the 2024 Elections. *Journal of Interdisciplinary Socio-Economic and Community Study*, 3(1), 1–11. DOI: 10.21776/jiscos.03.1.01

Popoola, O. A., Adama, H. E., Okeke, C. D., & Akinoso, A. E. (2024). Conceptualizing agile development in digital transformations: Theoretical foundations and practical applications. *Engineering Science & Technology Journal*, 5(4), 1524–1541. DOI: 10.51594/estj.v5i4.1080

Putta, A., Paasivaara, M., & Lassenius, C. (2018). Benefits and challenges of adopting the scaled agile framework (SAFe): preliminary results from a multivocal literature review. *Product-Focused Software Process Improvement: 19th International Conference, PROFES 2018, Wolfsburg, Germany, November 28–30, 2018Proceedings*, 19, 334–351.

Revutska, O., & Maršíková, K. (2021). Agile approach in human resource management: Focus on Generation Y.

Safa, M., Weeks, K., Stromberg, R., & Azam, A. A. (2018). Strategic port human resource talent acquisition and training: challenges and opportunities. In Advances in Human Factors, Business Management, and Leadership: Proceedings of the AHFE 2017 International Conferences on Human Factors in Management and Leadership, and Business Management and Society, July 17– 21, 2017, The Westin Bonaventure Hotel, Los Angeles, California, USA 8 (pp. 205-215). Springer International Publishing. DOI: 10.1007/978-3-319-60372-8_20

Santos, V., Goldman, A., & De Souza, C. R. (2015). Fostering effective inter-team knowledge sharing in agile software development. *Empirical Software Engineering*, 20(4), 1006–1051. DOI: 10.1007/s10664-014-9307-y

Saruchera, F. (2022). Effective agile project leadership through competency-based self-reflection. In *Contemporary Challenges for Agile Project Management* (pp. 89–110). IGI Global. DOI: 10.4018/978-1-7998-7872-8.ch006

Su, W., & Junge, S. (2023). Unlocking the recipe for organizational resilience: A review and future research directions. *European Management Journal*, 41(6), 1086–1105. DOI: 10.1016/j.emj.2023.03.002

Subramanian, N., & Suresh, M. (2022). Assessment framework for agile HRM practices. Global Journal of Flexible Systems Management, 23(1), 135-149.

Tabassum, M., Raziq, M. M., Allen, M., Sarwar, N., & Golra, O. A. (2024). Exploring emergent leadership in agile teams: Network dynamics, roles and skills at the individual level. *Business Process Management Journal*, 30(5), 1615–1637. DOI: 10.1108/BPMJ-02-2024-0110

Trzeciak, M., & Banasik, P. (2022). Motivators influencing the efficiency and commitment of employees of agile teams. *Journal of Open Innovation*, 8(4), 176. DOI: 10.3390/joitmc8040176

Verwijs, C., & Russo, D. (2024). Do Agile scaling approaches make a difference? An empirical comparison of team effectiveness across popular scaling approaches. *Empirical Software Engineering*, 29(4), 1–57. DOI: 10.1007/s10664-024-10481-5

Župerkienė, E., Šimanskienė, L., Fiore, M., & Paulikas, J. (2023). Management of Employee Resistance Caused by Technological Change for Organisational Sustainability. In Technology, Business and Sustainable Development (pp. 67-84). Routledge.

Chapter 8
Future of Work: Generations and Retaining Talent Focus

K. Anitha
https://orcid.org/0000-0002-1940-2101
Meenakshi Academy of Higher Education and Research, India

Narkees Beevi S.
Meenakshi Academy of Higher Education and Research, India

J. Amala
https://orcid.org/0009-0002-9448-7106
DDGD Vaishnav College, India

ABSTRACT

The landscape of work is continuously evolving, driven by technological advancements, demographic shifts, and changing societal expectations. This research study delves into the future of work, focusing specifically on generational dynamics and talent retention strategies. The introduction highlights the imperative for workplace transformation, spurred by globalization, automation, and the increasing prevalence of remote work. In examining the future of work, this study explores several key advancements, including the rise of digital platforms, the integration of artificial intelligence, and the adoption of flexible work arrangements. These developments present both opportunities and challenges for organizations and workers. The study explores innovative methods adopted by organizations to address these challenges and retain talent effectively.

DOI: 10.4018/979-8-3693-6402-4.ch008

1. INTRODUCTION

The workplace is evolving. This change will be as profound as earlier generations of industries and agriculture's mechanization thanks to artificial intelligence and automation. Owing to changing cultural expectations, changing demographics, and technology breakthroughs, the nature of employment is about to undergo a radical transformation. This paradigm change is altering the dynamics of the workplace and calling for a review of current procedures and structures. The many sides of the future of work will be explored in this research study, including the effects of automation, the growth of flexible and remote work schedules, the significance of upgrading and upskilling, and the implications for corporate culture.

The widespread response to the COVID-19 pandemic has pushed the adoption of remote work as a pillar of the workplace of the future. Globally, businesses have adopted flexible work schedules, upending the idea of the office-centric work paradigm (T. Cockburn, 2020). Organizational structures, employee satisfaction, and work-life balance are all significantly affected by this change. It needs reevaluating leadership strategies and creating technological advancements that enable smooth distant collaboration.

The future job will also require continual education and skill development, which is another crucial aspect. Like how technology is evolving, the job market is also rapidly changing the skills that individuals must own. Organizations and people alike must prioritize upskilling and reskilling initiatives if they are to remain competitive in the ever-evolving market. As lifelong learning is increasingly recognized as a requirement for career success, there is a need for a shift in educational and professional development approaches.

Organizational cultures are evolving to accommodate the evolving nature of work in the future. It takes deliberate effort to foster a strong and inclusive business culture as remote and flexible work arrangements proliferate. Regardless of physical closeness, businesses need to rethink their values, communication plans, and employee engagement programs to foster a sense of community and shared purpose.

2. RELATED WORK

The concept of the Future of Work is not novel, yet following the global upheaval caused by the COVID-19 pandemic, it has surged to the forefront of discourse across all facets of life and has emerged as a pivotal focus of governmental policies worldwide. A cursory examination of existing literature reveals that discussions on the Future of Work encompass various dimensions, including the nature of activities (what), the methodologies of work (how), the individuals involved (who), and the physical environments of work (where), or any combination thereof. Moreover, the Future of Work can be analyzed from diverse perspectives, ranging from macro to micro levels, encompassing societal, industrial, or individual viewpoints.

Scholars increasingly assert that a comprehensive understanding of the Future of Work remains elusive. Gartner (2022) defines it as the forthcoming alterations in work methodologies over the next decade, influenced by technological advancements, generational shifts, and societal changes. Similarly, the Society for Human Resource Management (SHRM) describes it as a forecast of the evolution of work, workers, and workplaces in the coming years (SHRM, 2022). Deloitte characterizes the Future of Work as encompassing changes in work processes, the composition of the workforce, and the physical work environments (Schwartz et al., 2019).

Some researchers, such as Paul Deane (2021), emphasize the tendency to overemphasize the role of technology while overlooking its social context in shaping the future of work. Various studies categorize the Future of Work based on distinct characteristics or narratives. For instance, Balliester and Elsheikhi (2018) delineate it across five dimensions influenced by megatrends like technology, climate change, globalization, and demography, impacting job prospects, job quality, income distribution, social protection systems, and industrial relations. Others, like Mitchell et al. (2022), classify influential research such as workplace relations, workplace change, diversity, and personal skills.

While acknowledging the potential for significant disruptions in the workforce and skills due to technological advancements, Willcocks (2020) argues against exaggerated claims of net job loss. He contends that existing studies overlook factors such as increased work demands, aging populations, productivity gaps, and skill shortages. This perspective has gained traction among leading academics like Bessen et al. (2020) and Malone et al. (2020).

In recent years, new technologies have reshaped employment dynamics by enabling work fragmentation and facilitating complex employment relationships through digital platforms (Donnelly and Johns, 2021). Digitization supports flexible work arrangements, individualized employment relationships, and smaller, more isolated work units. However, it also necessitates greater oversight, impacting work design and potentially requiring organizations to adapt their core structures. These structural changes, though not immediately apparent, may become more evident as governments integrate digitization into their policies (Baptista et al., 2020)

3. REASONS FOR CHANGE IN THE WORKPLACE

The reasons for the change in the workplace have been illustrated in Figure 1.

Technological Advancements

The quick and unstoppable advancement of technology is one of the main drivers of the future of employment. Industries are changing, mundane jobs are becoming automated, and human talents are being enhanced by automation, artificial intelligence (AI), and machine learning. Combining these technologies not only changes the demands of jobs but also opens whole new career paths. As we enter the era of Industry 4.0, which redefines manufacturing and services through smart systems and connectivity, it is critical to understand how modern technologies affect the workforce (Griep, Y. et.al; 2021).

Figure 1. Reasons for Change in the Workplace

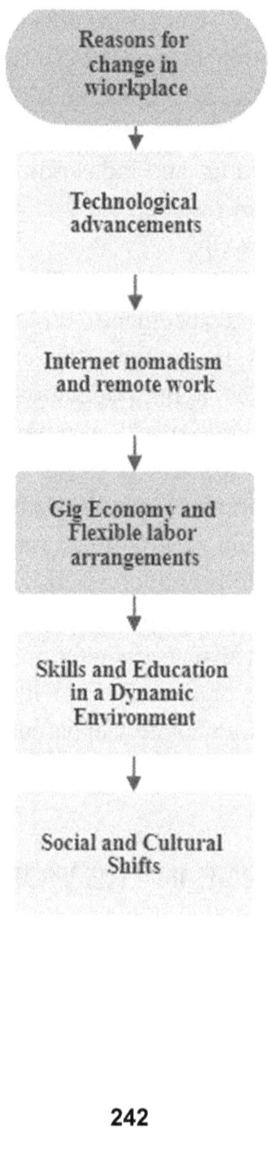

Internet Nomadism and Remote Work

The rise of internet connectivity has destroyed preconceived ideas about the workplace. Global events like the COVID-19 pandemic have hastened the trend of remote work, which has become widespread and revolutionary. The flexibility to work from any location significantly impacts organizational architecture, talent distribution across regions, and work-life balance (Hermann, I., Paris, C.M, 2020). Conventional notions of commuting and office-bound routines are further challenged by digital nomadism, which is made possible by ubiquitous internet connection.

Gig Economy and Flexible Labor Arrangements

The gig economy has brought about a notable change in the way individuals view work and labor arrangements. Project-based, flexible, and short-term jobs are getting more prevalent; they give people freedom and a variety of revenue sources. The gig economy bids flexibility and supplemental income but increases anxieties about job insecurity and benefits (Hibrida, A. R., & Sunarni. (2023). Research studies infer that the gig economy proposes prospects for income diversification (S. Palhad et.al., 2023). There are concerns over job security, benefits, and the conventional employer-employee relationship with this shift towards flex labor arrangements. Firms, employees, and legislators all must understand the ramifications of this development.

Skills and Education in a Dynamic Environment

Ability and Education in a Changing Work Environment: The dynamic character of the workforce needs a constant emphasis on the advancement of skills and education. Since the skills needed for different jobs become outdated quickly, lifelong learning is becoming increasingly a necessity rather than a luxury. Institutions of higher learning and training must change to give people the flexibility they need to deal with a labor market that is undergoing constant change. Soft skills, critical thinking, and flexibility play an ever-more-important role in getting people ready for the workplace of the future.

Social and Cultural Shifts

The future of labor is closely related to broader societal and cultural shifts. Diversity, fairness, and inclusion are increasingly seen as essential components of an innovative and successful workforce. Workplace cultures must be reevaluated considering the merging of work and home life, encouraging environments that prioritize diversity, inclusivity, and well-being.

Furthermore, broader cultural factors like diversity, equity, and inclusion are entwined with the future of employment. An opportunity to redress past inequities and build more inclusive workplaces is presented by the shift towards a more flexible and technologically driven work environment. Businesses that put a high priority on diversity and equity programs will be better equipped to manage the opportunities and problems brought about by the changing nature of the workplace.

The future of work is a multifaceted dynamic, and complex tapestry that is being formed by changes in society's expectations, work norms, and technology. Each of these facets will be addressed comprehensively in this research paper, giving readers a thorough grasp of the dynamics driving the transformation of labor. We hope to provide readers with insights into navigating the difficulties of the future of work by looking at the effects of automation, the growth of remote work, the significance of continuous learning, and the development of corporate culture.

4. ADVANCEMENTS IN THE FUTURE OF WORK

The advancements in the Future of work have been illustrated in Figure 2.

Flexibility and Work-Life Balance

People can better balance their personal and professional lives because of the enhanced flexibility that the future of work will provide. Flexible scheduling, remote work, and other work arrangements all improve employee happiness and well-being (Parajuli, S. K., 2023). Due to Technological advancement, the future of work will not only create an attractive work environment for employees but also prioritize minimizing workforce support costs.

Access to a Global Talent Pool

As remote employment becomes more common, geographic restrictions become less significant. Companies can draw from a broad and international talent pool to develop a team with a range of abilities and viewpoints. Increased creativity and critical thinking skills result from this. Diverse Applications like big data, Artificial intelligence, and machine learning facilitate identifying talent anywhere in the world. Because of this advancement has made digital talent management even more crucial nowadays (Stander, Rothmann, Popov, & Sun, 2022).

Figure 2. Advancements on the Future of Work

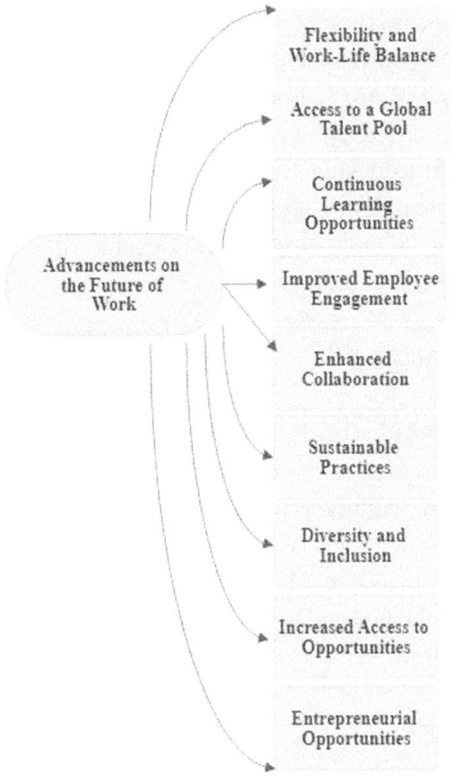

Continuous Learning Opportunities

The evolving job market needs a culture of lifelong learning. The future of work encourages continuous upskilling and reskilling opportunities, ensuring that individuals can adapt to changing skill requirements and stay competitive in their careers. Every organization will foster the growth and development of employees by provide continue training opportunities. These learning is not only contributing to the development of employees but also creates a favorable effect on the organization (Acar, S., & SARNIÇ, A. 2024).

Improved Employee Engagement

Employee engagement is crucial because it creates a positive impact on employees and also supports the company financially and organisationally (Sukoco et al, 2020). Employee with low level of engagement towards work will not have commitment towards the work which affect the growth of the organisation (Solihin & Sagala, 2020). So it is important to design Human-centric and a focus on employee well-being contributes to increased engagement. Organizations that prioritize a positive workplace culture, mental health support, and meaningful work experiences foster a motivated and committed workforce.

Enhanced Collaboration

Collaborative tools and platforms ease seamless communication and teamwork, even in dispersed work environments. The future of work emphasizes the importance of effective collaboration, leading to improved innovation, knowledge sharing, and project outcomes. A hybrid work setting offers flexibility while still supporting collaboration. For instance, companies are implementing an environment with the integration of technology which includes Generative AI collaboration and productivity tools (Singh 2024)

Diversity and Inclusion

Future work models encourage diversity and inclusion initiatives. Organizations that embrace diverse talent and foster an inclusive environment benefit from a broader range of perspectives, creativity, and adaptability. A diverse workforce from different backgrounds and ideologies can fosters creativity and problem-solving (Herring, 2009). In Addition, Inclusive workplace encourage employee engagement, employee retention and job satisfaction (Nishii, 2013).

Sustainable Practices

The future of work aligns with sustainability goals, promoting environmentally responsible business practices. Organizations committed to reducing their ecological footprint contribute to a more sustainable future and appeal to an environmentally conscious workforce. Innovation that is driven by sustainability can stimulate creativity, and drive the invention of goods and services, which will improve a company's competitiveness and sustainability over a longer period (Coker et al., 2023)

Entrepreneurial Opportunities

Flexible work arrangements, gig economies, and remote work create opportunities for individuals to pursue entrepreneurial endeavors. The future of work allows for the exploration of various projects and income streams, fostering a spirit of innovation and self-directed work. Digital technologies shape entrepreneurs by identifying and utilizing core competencies (Reis et al., 2021)

Increased Access to Opportunities

Technology enables greater access to job opportunities, particularly for individuals in remote or underprivileged areas. The future of work, eased by digital connectivity, ensures a more inclusive job market. Artificial intelligence and digital technologies will change the nature of work and profoundly affect people's work lives by increasing access to a wide range of job opportunities (Naqshbandi et al., 2024).

5. CHALLENGES TO THE FUTURE OF WORK

Job Insecurity and Technological Overload

As automation and artificial intelligence grow, worries about job displacement may arise. People in jobs that could be automated could experience job instability and must learn new skills to pursue other career options. Job insecurity has become a more protruding problem for officials, psychologists, and business executives alike (Wilson JM et al., 2020). Stress and burnout can result from a constant state of connectedness and dependence on technology. The study conducted by (An H et al., 2023) delivers experimental support for the claim that employees with pervasive job stress will likely develop anxiety symptoms which are a major challenge. In the workplace of the future, it will be difficult to strike a balance between utilizing technology to increase productivity and preventing technological overload. Also, within the next few years, learning high-tech developments like AI is expected to become a key skill for many employees (Cetindamar D et al., 2022 & Jarrahi MH et al., 2022). Another research deliberates AI as an additional for certain tasks that will lead to job displacement (Georgieff & Hyee, 2022)

Absence of Face-to-Face Engagement and Skill Shortage

Although helpful, remote work and virtual collaboration may lead to a lack of face-to-face engagement. In a virtual workplace, setting up and preserving relationships, encouraging team spirit, and guaranteeing efficient communication becomes difficult. The employment market is changing quickly, which could result in skill shortages that need constant upskilling. The changing skill demands may make it difficult for educational institutions to keep up, which presents problems for both individuals and companies. Education policymakers focus more on enhancing fundamental STEM skills through the education system to bridge the gap in skill shortage (Mickinsey et al., 2017).

Possibility of Worsening Inequality and Opposition to Change

The future of work presents chances to access talent worldwide, but it also carries the risk of making inequality worse. Unequal access to technology, learning materials, and distant employment prospects may exacerbate already-existing socioeconomic divides. Out of a fear of change, organizations and individuals may be reluctant to adopt modern technologies and work styles. One of the challenges in preparing for the future of work is overcoming resistance and cultivating an adaptive culture. Urban areas are home to technology hubs and online work centres while ignoring the needs of rural areas are neglected which possibility of worsening inequality (Bandi et al., 2020).

Security, Privacy Concerns, and Legal and Regulatory Challenges

Cybersecurity and privacy issues are brought up by people's growing reliance on digital tools and their remote jobs. Strong security measures are necessary for organizations to safeguard confidential information and guarantee the privacy of workers who use it remotely. Given the perception of recent development in labour market due to technology advancement, the viability of social protection systems is being questionable (Codagnone, et,al., 2016). Modifications to legal and regulatory frameworks may be necessary in light of the evolving work paradigms. For both enterprises and governments, there are obstacles in understanding cross-border employment legislation, resolving concerns like remote worker rights, and adapting to new policies.

Difficulty in Maintaining Organizational Culture

When workers are scattered, it can be difficult to set up and preserve an integrated corporate culture. Implementation of digital work is a long-term process and time consuming (Dittes, et, al.,2019). For an organization to succeed, it is essential to develop strategies that promote a feeling of community and shared values in a virtual setting. While giving people some degree of autonomy at work is important, it also needs to be tempered with accountability. Effective performance management and communication are essential to guaranteeing that remote workers stay productive and in line with company aims. The future of work has many advantages, but it also brings with it several difficult problems that need careful thought through. A successful transition to the future of work requires finding a balance between welcoming technology breakthroughs, promoting diversity, and tackling issues of inequality and employment instability.

6. METHODS ADOPTED TO FACE THE CHANGE

The methods employed to navigate the future of work are as diverse as the challenges and opportunities it presents. This comprehensive exploration delves into a myriad of strategies, policies, and frameworks that individuals, organizations, and policymakers can adopt to harness the transformative forces shaping the world of work and is illustrated in Figure 3.

Agile Work Practices, Telecommuting, and Remote Work

Adopting agile approaches changes how teams manage tasks and projects in ways that go beyond software development. Agile work methods highly value adaptability, teamwork, and iterative development. This approach helps firms quickly adjust to changing conditions, which is an essential skill in the ever-changing world of work (Ford et al., 2021). The rise in remote work needs clear guidelines and infrastructure. Crucial elements of effective remote work strategies include setting up policies for working from home, making technological investments that enable remote collaboration, and encouraging a healthy work-life balance (Kniffin et al., 2021. These regulations guarantee that remote work is an essential part of the company culture and not just a transient solution. Golden, T. & Eddleston, K (2020), also found that telecommuting improves insights of autonomy, which leads to enhanced performance.

Figure 3. Methods

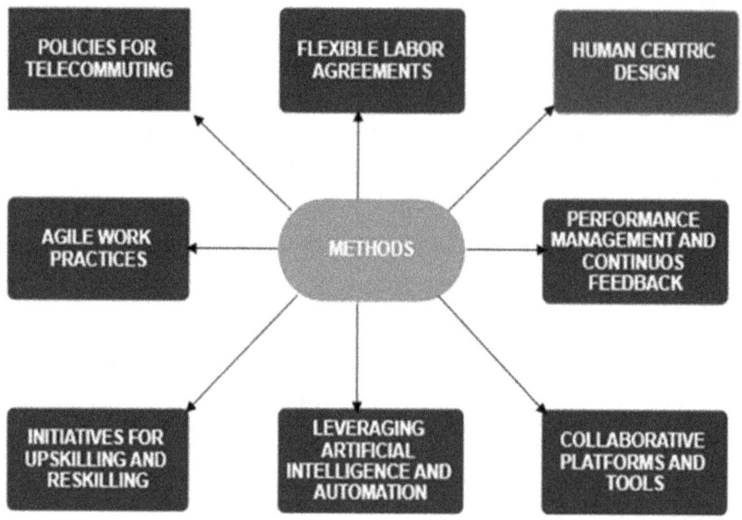

Initiatives for Upskilling and Reskilling and Flexible Labor Agreements

Organizations need to help workforces recognize the skills required for AI implementation, improve current skills, and develop new skills (Morandini, S. et.al., 2023). Because reskilling and skilling are so important to maximize the impact of new technologies, they may be challenging in certain nations with low levels of education and skill development, where vulnerable workers are excluded from the formal economy, businesses are reluctant to invest in training, and informal skilling is the only option (Hammer & Karmakar, 2021; Ramaswamy, 2018). I Upskilling and reskilling programs are necessary for organizations and educational institutions to provide workers with the changing skills that employers need. Through these approaches, people may remain competitive and relevant in a workforce that is changing quickly. The influence of AI on human skills will perhaps be contingent on the precise errands and skills being robotic (Chuang, 2022). Initiatives such as hackathons (Medina Angarita, & Nolte, 2020), hands-on learning models (Oliveira et al., 2022), and quality circles (Ellingrud et al., 2020) should be implemented to enhance reskilling & upskilling among the workforce.

Organizations can implement flexible labor agreements in recognition of the gig economy and the predominance of gig work. Accepting project-based, freelancing, and part-time job arrangements is necessary for this. Flexibility like this helps employees and companies alike. Employees receive help from autonomy and a variety of work experiences, while employers get access to a wide talent pool.

Human-Centric Design, Performance Management, and Continuous Feedback

The first and foremost step of developing Human-centric design is to identify and analysis the current known about workers (Gomide, et.al., 2024). Human Centric design is the Making employee happiness and well-being a top priority is essential to the transition from profit-driven to human-centric design methodologies. This approach considers factors such as the company culture, mental health resources, and opportunities for career and personal growth. Human-centric design results in a more engaged and productive workforce. Conventional performance reviews are giving way to tools for continual feedback. Employees can quickly adjust to shifting expectations because of agile performance management techniques, real-time feedback, and regular check-ins. This strategy aids in coordinating personal aims with corporate goals and promotes a culture of continual improvement.

Leveraging Artificial Intelligence and Automation

Organizations can intentionally use artificial intelligence to supplement human capabilities, even while automation may replace some tasks. This entails figuring out how AI may increase productivity in certain areas so that workers can concentrate on difficult, creative, and valuable jobs that machines cannot do. The implications of the risk related to adopting AI-enabled devices or systems in the workplace must be considered before implementation (Howard J., 2019). In a distributed and ever-changing work environment, promoting collaboration is essential. Businesses can spend money on communication and collaboration systems that allow team members to work together seamlessly no matter where they are in the world. These resources foster creativity, cooperation, and knowledge exchange.

Strategies for managing the nature of employment in the future are interrelated and need a comprehensive strategy. A resilient and adaptable workforce is a result of a variety of factors, including agile practices, regulations about remote work, upskilling programs, human-centric design, diversity initiatives, sustainability initiatives, constant feedback systems, and the smart use of technology. Adopting these strategies enables people and businesses to prosper in the rapidly changing future of work, as we stand on the cusp of unprecedented transformation.

7. CONCLUSION

In conclusion, the future of work presents both daunting challenges and exciting opportunities for organizations globally. The energetic interplay of technological innovation, shifting demographics, and developing workplace prospects imposes a proactive approach to talent management and organizational adaptation. As highlighted throughout this research study, understanding, and addressing generational differences is vital for nurturing a cohesive and productive workforce. Moreover, embracing technological advancements and flexible work arrangements can enhance efficiency and employee satisfaction, while also posing challenges related to skill development and work-life balance.

To prosper in the future of work, organizations must promote a culture of continuous learning, agility, and inclusivity. By devoting themselves to employee development programs, fostering collaboration across generations, and leveraging technology to streamline processes, organizations can position themselves for success in a progressively competitive scene. Additionally, prioritizing diversity, equity, and inclusion initiatives is essential for attracting and retaining top talent from diverse backgrounds.

Ultimately, the future of work is not prearranged but shaped by the decisions and actions of individuals, organizations, and policymakers. By staying informed, adaptable, and committed to fostering a supportive and inclusive work environment, organizations can navigate the complexities of the future of work and emerge stronger and more resilient than ever before.

REFERENCES

Acar, S., & Sarniç, A. (2024). A qualitative study on talent management in enterprises within the Industry 4.0 process. *SEISENSE Journal of Management*, 7(1), 101–116. DOI: 10.33215/t02k1p32

An, H., Gu, X., Obrenovic, B., & Godinic, D. (2023, August 18). The Role of Job Insecurity, Social Media Exposure, and Job Stress in Predicting Anxiety Among White-Collar Employees. *Psychology Research and Behavior Management*, 16, 3303–3318. DOI: 10.2147/PRBM.S416100 PMID: 37614323

Balliester, T., & Elsheikhi, A. (2018). The future of work: A literature review. ILO Research Department Working Paper, 29, 1–54.

Bandi, R. K., Klein, S., Madon, S., Monteiro, E., & Ranjini, C. R. (2020). The future of digital work: The challenge of inequality. In *The Future of Digital Work: The Challenge of Inequality: IFIP WG 8.2, 9.1, 9.4 Joint Working Conference, IFIPJWC 2020, Hyderabad, India, December 10–11, 2020, Proceedings* (pp. 3-10). Springer International Publishing.

Baptista, J., Stein, M., Klein, S., Watson-Manheim, M. B., & Lee, J. (2020). Digital work and organizational transformation: Emergent digital/human work configurations in modern organizations. *The Journal of Strategic Information Systems*, 29(2), 101618. DOI: 10.1016/j.jsis.2020.101618

Bessen, J., Goos, M., Salomons, A., & van den Berge, W. (2020). *Automation: A guide for policymakers*. Economic Studies at Brookings Institution.

Cetindamar, D., Kitto, K., Wu, M., Zhang, Y., Abedin, B., & Knight, S. (2022). Explicating AI literacy of employees at digital workplaces. *IEEE Transactions on Engineering Management*, •••, 1–14. DOI: 10.1109/TEM.2021.3138503

Chuang, S. (2022). Indispensable skills for human employees in the age of robots and AI. *European Journal of Training and Development*. Advance online publication. DOI: 10.1108/EJTD-06-2022-0062

Cockburn, T. (2020). Emerging Impacts of Socio digital Technology in the' New Normal' of the Post-COVID19 Resilience, Regrowth and Renewal Period 2020-2021 and Beyond (Presentation Slides). *Regrowth and Renewal Period*, 2021, 2020.

Codagnone, C. (2016). *The Future of Work in the 'Sharing Economy'. Market Efficiency and Equitable Opportunities or Unfair Precarisation? EU Science Hub.* European Commission.

Coker, J. O., Uzougbo, N. S., Oguejiofor, B. B., & Akagha, O. V. (2023). The Role of Legal Practitioners in Mitigating Corporate Risks In Nigeria: A Comprehensive Review Of Existing Literature On The Strategies And Approaches Adopted By Legal Practitioners In Nigeria To Mitigate Corporate Risks. *Finance & Accounting Research Journal*, 5(10), 309–332. DOI: 10.51594/farj.v5i10.579

Croatti, A., & Ricci, A. (2020). *From virtual worlds to mirror worlds: A model and platform for building agent-based extended realities. In multi-agent systems and agreement technologies*. Springer.

Deane, P. (2021). Just why is it so hard to predict the future? RTE Brainstorm. https://www.rte.ie/brainstorm/2019/0715/1062197-just-why-is-it-sohard-to-predict-the-future/

Dittes, S., Richter, S., Richter, A., & Smolnik, S. (2019). Toward the workplace of the future: How organizations can facilitate digital work. *Business Horizons*, 62(5), 649–661. DOI: 10.1016/j.bushor.2019.05.004

Donnelly, R., & Johns, J. (2021). Recontextualising remote working and its HRM in the digital economy: An integrated framework for theory and practice. *International Journal of Human Resource Management*, 32(1), 84–105. DOI: 10.1080/09585192.2020.1737834

Ellingrud, K., Gupta, R., & Salguero, J. (2020). Building the vital skills for the future of work in operations. McKinsey & Company. https://www.mckinsey.com/capabilities/operations/our-insights/building-the-vital-skills-forthe-future-of-work-in-operations

Ford, R. C., Piccolo, R. F., & Ford, L. R. (2021). Strategies for retaining employees in the post-COVID-19 workplace: The role of management and workplace flexibility. *Journal of Management*, 47(7), 1682–1700. DOI: 10.1177/01492063211013737

Gartner. (2022). Future of Work. Gartner Human Resource Glossary. https:// www.gartner.com/en/human-resources/glossary/future-of-work

Georgieff, A., & Hyee, R. (2022). Artificial intelligence and employment: New cross-country evidence. *Frontiers in Artificial Intelligence*, 5, 832736. DOI: 10.3389/frai.2022.832736 PMID: 35620279

Golden, T., & Eddleston, K. (2020). 'Is there a price telecommuters pay? Examining the relationship between telecommuting and objective career success. *Journal of Vocational Behavior*, 116, 1–13. DOI: 10.1016/j.jvb.2019.103348

Gomide, P., Patricio, R., & Gancho, S. (2024). Human-Centered Design Approaches to Industry 4.0 Challenges: Directions for Future Research. *The International Journal of Design Management and Professional Practice*, 19(1), 1–34. DOI: 10.18848/2325-162X/CGP/v19i01/1-34

Griep, Y., Vranjes, I., van Hooff, M. M. L., Beckers, D. G. J., & Geurts, S. A. E. (2021). Technology in the Workplace: Opportunities and Challenges. In Korunka, C. (Ed.), *Flexible Working Practices and Approaches*. Springer. DOI: 10.1007/978-3-030-74128-0_6

Hammer, A., & Karmakar, S. (2021). Automation, AI and the future of work in India. *Employee Relations*, 43(6), 1327–1341. DOI: 10.1108/ER-12-2019-0452

Hermann, I., & Paris, C. M. (2020). Digital Nomadism: The nexus of remote working and travel mobility. *Information Technology & Tourism*, 22(3), 329–334. DOI: 10.1007/s40558-020-00188-w

Herring, C. (2009). Does diversity pay? Race, gender, and the business case for diversity. *American Sociological Review*, 74(2), 208–224. DOI: 10.1177/000312240907400203

Hibrida, A. R., & Sunarni, . (2023). The Future of Work: Navigating the Challenges and Opportunities of Automation, Gig Economy, and Skills Evolution in a Post-Pandemic World. *West Science Interdisciplinary Studies*, 1(08), 657–666. DOI: 10.58812/wsis.v1i08.186

Hoendervanger, J. G., De Been, I., Van Yperen, N. W., Mobach, M. P., & Albers, C. J. (2016). Flexibility in use: Switching behavior and satisfaction in activity-based work environments. *Journal of Corporate Real Estate*, 18(1), 48–62. DOI: 10.1108/JCRE-10-2015-0033

Howard, J. (2019). Artificial intelligence: Implications for the future of work. *American Journal of Industrial Medicine*, 62(11), 917–926. DOI: 10.1002/ajim.23037 PMID: 31436850

Jarrahi, M. H., Kenyon, S., Brown, A., Donahue, C., & Wicher, C. (2022). Artificial intelligence: A strategy to harness its power through organizational learning. *The Journal of Business Strategy*, 3, 456.

Kniffin, K. M., Narayanan, J., Anseel, F., Antonakis, J., Ashford, S. P., Bakker, A. B., Bamberger, P., Bapuji, H., Bhave, D. P., Choi, V. K., Creary, S. J., Demerouti, E., Flynn, F. J., Gelfand, M. J., Greer, L. L., Johns, G., Kesebir, S., Klein, P. G., Lee, S. Y., & Vugt, M. (2021). COVID-19 and the workplace: Implications, issues, and insights for future research and action. *The American Psychologist*, 76(1), 63–77. DOI: 10.1037/amp0000716 PMID: 32772537

Kolade, O., & Owoseni, A. (2022). Employment 5.0: The work of the future and the Future of Work. *Technology in Society*, 71, 102086. DOI: 10.1016/j.techsoc.2022.102086

Lynn, T. (Ed.). (2023). *The Future of Work*. Palgrave Studies in Digital Business & Enabling Technologies. DOI: 10.1007/978-3-031-31494-0

Lynn, T., Rosati, P., Conway, E., Curran, D., Fox, G., & O'Gorman, C. (2022). *Digital towns: Accelerating and measuring the digital transformation of rural societies and economies*. Springer Nature. DOI: 10.1007/978-3-030-91247-5

Malone, T. W., Rus, D., & Laubacher, R. (2020). Artificial intelligence and the future of work. A report prepared by MIT Task Force on the work of the future. *Research Brief*, 17, 1–39.

Manyika, J. (2017). Technology, jobs, and the future of work. McKinsey Insights.

Medina Angarita, M. A., & Nolte, A. (2020). What do we know about hackathon outcomes and how to support them? A systematic literature review. In *International Conference on Collaboration Technologies and Social Computing* (pp. 50-64). Springer. DOI: 10.1007/978-3-030-58157-2_4

Morandini, S., Fraboni, F., De Angelis, M., Puzzo, G., Giusino, D., & Pietrantoni, L. (2023). The impact of artificial intelligence on workers' skills: Upskilling and reskilling in organizations. Informing Science. *The International Journal of an Emerging Transdiscipline*, 26, 39–68. DOI: 10.28945/5078

Naqshbandi, M. M., Kabir, I., Ishak, N. A., & Islam, M. Z. (2024). The future of work: Work engagement and job performance in the hybrid workplace. *The Learning Organization*, 31(1), 5–26. DOI: 10.1108/TLO-08-2022-0097

Nishii, L. H. (2013). The benefits of climate for inclusion for gender-diverse groups. *Academy of Management Journal*, 56(6), 1754–1774. DOI: 10.5465/amj.2009.0823

Oliveira, A., Assumpcao, H., Queiroz, J., Piardi, L., Parra, J., & Leitao, P. (2022). Hands-on learning modules for upskilling in industry 4.0 technologies. Paper presented at the 2022 IEEE 5th International Conference on Industrial Cyber-Physical Systems, ICPS 2022. DOI: 10.1109/ICPS51978.2022.9816909

Palhad, Onwubu, Singh, Thakur, Thakur, & Mkhize. (2023). The Benefits and Challenges of the Gig Economy: Perspective of Gig Workers and Small Medium and Micro Enterprises (SMMEs) in South Africa. African Journal of Inter/Multidisciplinary Studies, 5(1), 1–12.

Parajuli, S. K. (2023). Remote and Flexible work: A Systematic Review. *Nepal Journal of Multidisciplinary Research*, 6(2), 131–144. DOI: 10.3126/njmr.v6i2.57656

Ramaswamy, K. V. (2018). Technological change, automation and employment: A short review of theory and evidence. *International Review of Business and Economics*, 2(2), 1–27. DOI: 10.56902/IRBE.2018.2.2.1

Reis, D. A., Fleury, A. L., & Carvalho, M. M. (2021). Consolidating core entrepreneurial competencies: Toward a meta-competence framework. *International Journal of Entrepreneurial Behaviour & Research*, 27(1), 179–204. DOI: 10.1108/IJEBR-02-2020-0079

Santana, M., & Cobo, M. J. (2020). What is the future of work? A science mapping analysis. *European Management Journal*, 38(6), 846–862. DOI: 10.1016/j.emj.2020.04.010

Schwartz, J., Hatfeld, S., Jones, R., & Anderson, S. (2019). *What is the future of work? Redefining work, workforces, and workplaces*. Deloitte.

Singh, A., Jha, S., Srivastava, D. K., & Somarajan, A. (2022). Future of work: A systematic literature review and evolution of themes. *Foresight*, 24(1), 99–125. DOI: 10.1108/FS-09-2020-0093

Singh, S. (2024). The Future of Work: Exploring the Future of Work in Canada and How Human Connections Are Made Through Workplace Design.

Society for Human Resource Management (SHRM). (2022). What is meant by "the future of work"? https://www.shrm.org/resourcesandtools/tools-andsamples/hr-qa/pages/what-is-meant-by-the-future-of-work.aspx

Solihin, M. B., & Sagala, E. J. (2020). Pengaruh Work Engagement Dan Komitmen Organisasi Terhadap Tingkat Turnover Intention Karyawan Di Pt Telkom Akses Balikpapan. *EProceedings of Management*, 7(2), 5635–5643.

Stander, F., Rothmann, S., Popov, V., & Sun, L. (2022). A framework for digital talent assessment: Guidelines and applications. *Journal of Psychology in Africa*, 32(5), 1–6. DOI: 10.1080/14330237.2022.2075543

Stoepfgeshoff, S. (2018). The Future of Work: Work for the future. ISM Journal of International Business, 2(2).

Sukoco, I., Fuadah, N., & Muttaqin, Z. (2020). Work engagement of millennial generation employees pada PT. X Bandung. *Jurnal Pemikiran Dan Penelitian Administrasi Bisnis Dan Kewirausahaan*, 5(3), 263–281.

Willcocks, L. (2020). Robo-Apocalypse cancelled? Reframing the automation and future of work debate. *Journal of Information Technology*, 35(4), 286–302. DOI: 10.1177/0268396220925830

Wilson, J. M., Lee, J., Fitzgerald, H. N., Oosterhoff, B., Sevi, B., & Shook, N. J. (2020). Job insecurity and financial concern during the COVID-19 pandemic are associated with worse mental health. *Journal of Occupational and Environmental Medicine*, 62(9), 686–691. DOI: 10.1097/JOM.0000000000001962 PMID: 32890205

Chapter 9
Optimizing Talent Acquisition:
The Synergy of AI and Human Expertise in Creating Enhanced Candidate Experience

Tanusree Chakraborty
Administrative Staff College of India, India

Sharada V. S.
https://orcid.org/0009-0006-7378-2949
Administrative Staff College of India, India

ABSTRACT

This study examines the revolutionary effects of artificial intelligence (AI) on hiring in organizations. AI maximizes efficiency by automating processes like resume review, candidate matching, and engagement through chatbots. AI-driven predictive analytics support diversity and inclusion by predicting recruiting needs and reducing biases in job advertisements and candidate selection. The study finds that AI and human collaboration enhances analytical decision-making and the creative capacities of the talent acquisition process. It highlights the shift towards data-driven hiring and the significance of AI-driven insights in talent analytics and decision-making. However, the study asserts the necessity of human touch and emotional intelligence, even with EI tools, to create a positive candidate experience. Candidate experience is pivotal in talent acquisition, requiring harmonious collaboration between AI and human expertise. AI streamlines processes and enhances efficiency, while the human touch adds empathy and personalized engagement.

DOI: 10.4018/979-8-3693-6402-4.ch009

1. INTRODUCTION

In the dynamic landscape of modern talent acquisition, the fusion of artificial intelligence (AI) and human collaboration has emerged as a pivotal strategy in talent acquisition (Fayoumi and Loucopoulos, 2023). It is a fact that, AI has significantly impacted recruitment processes (Ferry, 2018), with 63% of talent acquisition professionals and 34% of recruiters stating it will significantly shape future hiring practices (Spara et al., 2018). This kind of synergistic approach harnesses the unparalleled speed and unwavering consistency of AI algorithms while seamlessly integrating the typical element of human judgment and intuition. At the heart of this convergence lies the deep aim of not only automating processes but elevating the crux of hiring itself. It is a realm where algorithms explain through resumes with precision, yet it is human discernment that deciphers the elaborate blend of soft skills and cultural alignment. The present trend enfolds that AI and human collaborations works hand in hand. Together, they take a path toward a strong, inclusive, and equitable recruitment landscape. This makes us curious to take a journey to unknot the complicated dimensions of this collaboration, exploring its capacity to not only enhance the quality of hiring decisions but also to champion the principles of diversity and fairness. Of late, it has been realized that, artificial intelligence is increasingly important in talent acquisition and recruitment, automating and enlightening various functions in the process. On one hand, the AI recruitment tools modernize processes, on the other hand human skills are indispensable for better decision-making and competitiveness. When we look at the recent trends and strategies in talent acquisitions to feel the convergence of AI's potential to supply companies with accurate data, clear objectives, and a balanced strategy, we are also left with the puzzle whether human contribution in the process can completely be done away with in near future.

Probing into the matter deeply, we find that AI systems are assisting humans in broadening their capabilities through three primary avenues. Those are, a) they have the capacity to improve our cognitive aptitudes, serving as *cognitive amplifiers*; b) they engage with both applicants and the HR department, freeing us from mechanical and routine tasks and c) they have human-like skills, thus extending our physical capacities and capabilities.

AI technology is not meant to displace human efforts but augment their capabilities and simplify laborious manual processes. Through task automation, AI empowers recruitment teams to allocate additional time and energy to other strategic endeavors. When seamlessly integrated, AI becomes a valuable asset in the recruitment toolkit.

Scholars in this area have tried to delve into the problems of AI-applicable areas in the R&S Process, with chatbots, screening software, and task automation (Albert, 2019), assistances of eHRM in terms of AI in talent acquisition (Black and van Esch, 2021; Johnson, Stone, &Lukaszewski, 2021), role of ethics in AI and talent acquisition (Chamorro-Premuzic, 2019), AI technology adoption dynamics for talent acquisition (Pillai and Sivathanu, 2020). It has also looked into the areas of AI evolution in talent, role of AI in removing recruitment biases (Chen, 2023). Role of customized AI in recruitment (Veglianti et al., 2023). Role of HR leaders in AI adoption in talent identifications (França et al., 2023), comparative studies between AI and human recruiters (Will et al., 2023). Studies raise concerns about using AI in recruitment but do not cover all concerns for each AI-based recruitment strategy (Albassam,2023). While Albassam (2023) highlights concerns, the papers mentioned do not comprehensively address all these concerns for each AI-based recruitment strategy. Earlier scholars in this area have dealt with various aspects of AI in recruitment, but there appears a research gap in the form of concerns and challenges associated with using AI in recruitment and how AI and human collaboration can be complimentary to each other. There appears a wide gap in research as to how AI and human collaboration has the potential to transform various aspects of work and everyday life. By recognizing the strengths and limitations of both AI and humans and fostering ethical, user-centric design, we can harness the power of AI to enhance productivity, decision-making, creativity, and overall human well-being.

After reviewing the available literature, it was discovered that while human and artificial intelligence (AI) collaboration in talent acquisition and other talent management processes had been studied, one of the most crucial aspects of the recruitment process—the relationship between the emotional intelligence of the recruiters and the efficiency of the talent acquisition process—had not gotten much attention.

In the present study we attempt to explore the role of AI and human collaboration in talent acquisition process. We try to posit that candidate experience is crucial in the hiring process, and it is essential that technology, especially AI, and human expertise work in harmony. The human touch adds empathy and personalized interaction, while AI streamlines procedures and increases productivity. Together, they design an effective and emotionally engaging recruitment process, using data to inform their choices and cultivating an impressionable prospect pool. The novelty and contribution of the study lie in its investigation of the relatively unexplored intersection of AI and human collaboration and talent acquisition processes. While AI's role in recruitment has been widely discussed, the specific focus on emotional AI, which encompasses technologies capable of recognizing and responding to human emotions, represents a novel approach. By delving into how AI and human collaboration can influence and enhance talent acquisition, the study contributes to the emerging field of AI-driven HR practices. It offers insights into how AI and human collaboration can be leveraged to improve candidate interactions, assess emotional intelligence in job seekers, and potentially optimize the hiring process for better cultural fit within organizations. This study can shed light on innovative practices that bridge the gap between technology and human emotion in talent acquisition, thereby offering valuable contributions to HR professionals and researchers alike.

2. LITERATURE REVIEW

2.1 Strategic Approaches to Talent Acquisition With AI

In order to increase efficiency and quality, artificial intelligence is used throughout the hiring process as part of strategic approaches to talent acquisition (Hmoud and Laszlo, 2019). The identification of top talent is accelerated by employing AI-powered candidate sourcing and screening technologies, which engage candidates and streamline initial contacts. (Mehrotra ans Khanna, 2022). Artificial intelligence (AI) systems that automatically handle the most time-consuming applicant sourcing, screening, and communication duties. Trending AI applications in talent acquisition include chatbots, intelligent search engines, intelligent applicant tracking systems (ATS), and candidate relationship management (CRM) (Bilal and Várallyai, 2021). To promote inclusion and diversity, AI systems decrease bias and proactively locate applicants with different backgrounds. In addition, AI supports customized onboarding and training, identifies skill shortages, and assures adherence to data protection laws. The unbiased hunting and screening of candidates are leveraged through various top AI recruiting software. Hiretual Review, XOR, Paradox review, Humanly, Textio, Pymetrics, LOXO, Eightfold, Allyo, seekout, Talkpush, Myintervew are some tools to seek out the right applicant (Lakshmi et al., 2020). By integrating AI in sourcing platforms like Applicant Tracking System (ATS) and candidate relationship management, it helps in broadening the search results and increases the accuracy, thus enabling the recruiters to get the right candidates for the organization (Mallick, 2019). The role of AI has become essential in candidate sourcing when there is a bulk-hiring (Dijkkamp, 2019) in the organization. Thus, AI augments the hiring managers to be better decision-makers which adds value to the business. Continuous feedback, collaboration between humans and AI, and cautious vendor selection all contribute to the implementation of AI in talent acquisition being as successful and equitable as possible. Providing real-time answers to the candidates' questions, offering quick feedback, and suggesting the steps for further proceedings develop a good rapport between the organization and candidate. Also, it builds a brand image for the organization ((Lakshmi et al., 2020)

The above literature review tells us that the transformative impact of Artificial Intelligence (AI) in various Human Resource Management (HRM) functions, with a primary emphasis on recruitment and talent management is immense. However, several research gaps warrant further exploration. These include the need for robust ethical AI practices, strategies for mitigating biases in AI-driven recruitment, a deeper understanding of human-AI collaboration dynamics in HRM, comprehensive data privacy and security considerations, strategies to overcome cost and adoption barriers, and a more in-depth analysis of the effectiveness of AI-powered candidate sourcing. Additionally, there is a call for research to quantify the impact of AI on the candidate experience, delve into precise skill gap analysis methods, and provide guidelines for prudent AI vendor selection. Continued investigation in these areas can enhance our understanding and application of AI in HRM, addressing both opportunities and challenges.

2.2 AI in Talent Management and Acquisition

Artificial Intelligence (AI) has profoundly impacted various facets of Human Resource Management (HRM). It plays a pivotal role in recruitment, selection, training, development, performance appraisal, employee engagement, and grievance handling (McGovern et al., 2018). AI's influence is especially pronounced in recruitment, encompassing job postings, resume screening, candidate assessments, and onboarding (Budhwar et al., 2022; Ore and Sposato, 2021). Traditional HR processes, burdened with administrative tasks such as advertising vacancies, sourcing, screening, and scheduling interviews, benefit greatly from AI automation (Talwalkar, 2019). Globally, AI has significantly reshaped the hiring landscape (Geeta and Bhanu, 2018). AI distinguishes itself by offering more accurate predictions of candidates' work-related behaviors and potential compared to traditional methods (Chamorro-Premuzic, 2019). Also studiers have concentrated on AI's potential in talent management, and asserted that the focus should shift from developing ethical HR systems to ensuring ethical AI practices (Mishra et al., 2020). AI assistants with AI and NLP capabilities engage candidates via web, mobile, and social media, streamlining communication and scheduling (Upadhyay and Khandelwal, 2018). AI enhances the efficiency of attracting, retaining, and motivating talent (Raviprolu, 2017), replacing repetitive tasks formerly handled by human recruiters (Upadhyay and Khandelwal, 2018). However, concerns persist about its potential dehumanization of the recruitment process (Amritaa and Achwani, 2018).

2.3 Process Ease in Using AI in Talent Acquisition

AI has revolutionised talent acquisition by streamlining and improving the hiring process in a variety of ways. It boosts productivity by automating time-consuming operations like resume screening and candidate sourcing, lowering the time it takes to fill job vacancies. A considerable number of literatures recognize benefits with the implementation of AI in recruiting. For instance, AI enable the use of an automated recruiting and screening system which results to cost savings and improved hiring process efficiency. Another AI use case is when AI is used to perform interviews in response to costly face-to-face interview (Suen et al., 2019). Jhonson et al. (2021) identified a number of benefits of using e-selection and AI-enabled hiring decisions including simplifying job analysis, facilitating employment testing, enabling remote video interviewing and supporting overall selection decisions. AI eliminates bias in decision-making while encouraging diversity and inclusiveness in employment. AI-driven continuous improvement and scalability make it a critical tool for organisations with different hiring needs, assisting them in remaining competitive in an ever-changing job market while adhering to regulatory rules. HR leaders have positive approach in terms of efficiency, quality and cost for the function of talent acquisition. In this case it is observed that innovation characteristics have high probability for the AI adoption in talent acquisition (Tiwari et al., 2022). While AI provides tremendous benefits in talent acquisition, it also introduces new problems that organizations must face. One significant concern is the possibility of bias in AI algorithms, which might perpetuate existing prejudices in previous data, leading to unfair hiring practices. There's also the issue of data privacy, as AI algorithms frequently require access to sensitive candidate data, necessitating stringent data security safeguards. Dealing with people is different from dealing with data or variables. Artificial intelligence (AI) tools can be expensive to implement at times, especially for smaller organizations, which may be a barrier to adoption. It is crucial for organizations to identify patterns in their data that may help them make more educated decisions about the development and retaining of talent pools, in addition to automating routine chores using AI apps, such as advertising openings and screening applicants' resumes (Faqihi and Miah, 2023).

2.4 Human-AI Collaboration in Talent Management

The importance of AI in enhancing workplace processes has been the subject of a great number of studies (Pereira et al., 2023). The promise and reality of AI in workforce management are worlds apart when it comes to acquiring, managing, and retaining people, particularly in scenarios involving complexity, data set limits, and fairness (Tambe et al., 2019). New opportunities and problems have emerged as a result of technology advancement (Armstrong and Taylor, 2017).To rapidly improve talent management and take advantage of the potential of diverse data sets through the use of AI technologies, it is essential to develop information systems- solutions that allow organisations to establishing more ethical HR systems and at the same achieve greater efficiencies (Chamorro-Premuzic et al., 2019). Additionally, by minimising unconscious biases, AI helps to create recruiting practises that are more equitable and inclusive. AI is a strategically that helps with employee attrition prediction, skill gap analysis, and personalising learning and development initiatives. While artificial intelligence (AI) improves objectivity and data-driven decision-making, it also collaborates with human oversight and judgement to guarantee moral and responsible talent management practises. In this dynamic environment, human-AI talent management collaboration holds the promise of empowering organisations in their efforts to recruit, develop, and maximise their staff. It also improves the process by utilising personalised interactions and automated feedback, all while lowering recruitment costs (Dixit et al., 2022). One ongoing challenge since the application of AI in TA has been the programming of technology to replicate human decision-making, which can result in the perpetuation of implicit bias (Cohen, 2019) The use of AI in the recruitment process may result in a lack of human touch, potentially discouraging candidates who value personal engagement. So, much data is required to understand people's psychology and mindset is always complicated (Raviprolu, A. 2017). The cost implications and lack of understanding of business benefits and value currently act as barriers for the extensive usage of AI in TA(Oracle, 2019). Studies highlight ethical and legal concerns related to AI in recruitment, including potential bias (Yam and Skorburg, 2021), discrimination, privacy violations, and the need for transparency and accountability (Hunkenschroer and Luetge, 2022).

Research Questions

a) How does AI-human collaboration in talent acquisition influence human touch and candidate experience?
b) Does AI and human collaboration enhance analytical decision-making in talent acquisition?
c) Can AI and human collaboration foster creative capacities in the talent acquisition process?
d) Does AI and human collaboration contribute to a satisfactory candidate experience in the talent acquisition process?

3. METHOD

We adopted a systematic approach to investigate the influence of AI utilization within the talent acquisition process. Our methodology consisted of a comprehensive literature review aimed at gaining insights into established theories and concepts related to candidate experiences and satisfaction in talent acquisition. In addition, we conducted expert interviews to gather valuable perspectives on the intricate relationship between these variables. Drawing upon these insights, we developed a robust conceptual framework. The qualitative analysis of the data unearthed valuable insights into how AI and human collaboration contribute to analytical decision-making and creative capacities in talent acquisition. Furthermore, our study examined whether emotional experiences and the human touch in candidate interactions are effectively integrated and nurtured within this evolving process.

4. RESULTS

4.1 AI and Analytical Decision-Making

A crucial topic of research that has significance for contemporary recruiting practises is the study of how AI-human collaboration in talent acquisition affects hiring quality. The first research question is how introducing AI with human side of talent acquisition enhances decision making in talent acquisition. This study attempts to comprehend the complex dynamics and results of this synergy by focusing on the seamless integration of artificial intelligence tools and human expertise throughout the recruitment process. AI has indeed demonstrated its capacity to enhance analytical decision-making in talent acquisition. As highlighted by Budhwar et al. (2022), AI-powered tools can efficiently process and analyze vast volumes of data, including resumes, job descriptions, and candidate profiles. Effective AI usage can enhance recruitment tactics (Ore and Sposato, 2022). This data-driven analysis uncovers valuable patterns and insights that may elude human recruiters, contributing to more informed hiring decisions in much lesser span of time. Furthermore, the predictive analytics capabilities of AI have been acknowledged (Ore and Sposato, 2022), enabling organizations to forecast candidate success and job fit by leveraging historical hiring data and candidate profiles. Many commonplace recruitment and selection procedures can be automated through the integration of these technologies, increasing productivity. This predictive power empowers recruiters to select candidates who are likely to excel in specific roles, increasing the likelihood of successful hires. AI's efficiency gains have been underscored by its ability to automate repetitive tasks like resume screening (Talwalkar, 2019), allowing recruiters to redirect their efforts toward strategic aspects of talent acquisition. This efficiency not only accelerates the hiring process but also reduces time-to-fill job vacancies (Johnson et al., 2021). Moreover, AI's role in reducing unconscious biases in hiring decisions has been emphasized (Cohen, 2019), ensuring a more objective and equitable evaluation of candidates. While AI's contributions to analytical decision-making are undeniable, it's essential to maintain a collaborative approach where AI complements rather than replaces the nuanced judgment and interpersonal skills of human recruiters, as noted by Tambe et al. (2019). In this synergy between technology and human expertise, organizations can harness the full potential of AI to make well-informed and inclusive talent acquisition decisions. AI, which is collectively referred to as a "engine," may support operations throughout the firm, improving supply chain management, customer relations, product creation and delivery, and business planning, to mention a few. Currently, AI is gaining ground in HR procedures and staff management, notably in the areas of sourcing, hiring, onboarding, training, and employee lifecycle management. Another way how AI use enhances analytical decision making is Deep learning, which typically refers to the use of enormous neural networks, such those employed by Eightfold.ai, which uses over 1 million unique talents, billions of profiles, and global data points to deliver data-driven insights on skills. Eightfold.ai assists businesses in determining the prevalence of capabilities on a worldwide level so they may uncover talent in specific places with the aim of understanding an applicant's potential (Jones, 2022).

Researchers explore whether this collaboration enhances or diminishes candidates' perceptions of the hiring process and whether it fosters greater transparency and communication, ultimately yielding favorable candidate feedback. Understanding how recruiters adapt to this collaborative paradigm is another key facet of this research, unraveling the requisite skills and training for recruiters to effectively partner with AI and shedding light on the transformation of recruiters' roles and responsibilities. Lastly, ethical considerations surrounding bias and fairness must be addressed. Researchers investigate whether AI-human collaboration mitigates bias in hiring decisions or introduces new ethical challenges, and they explore mechanisms to ensure fairness and accountability in this evolving context. By addressing these multifaceted aspects, research endeavors to provide comprehensive insights into the impact of AI-human collaboration on hiring quality and to offer actionable guidance on optimizing this partnership within talent acquisition, empowering organizations to make more informed, equitable, and successful hiring decisions in today's rapidly evolving recruitment landscape.

4.2 AI and Creative Capacities in Talent Management

The capacity for creativity within organisations is transformed by the incorporation of AI in talent acquisition. HR professionals may free up critical time and mental resources by using AI to streamline and automate mundane operations like resume screening and first evaluations. They can now concentrate on more strategic and innovative parts of talent acquisition thanks to their increased efficiency. AI can help HR teams make more intelligent and creative judgements by assisting in the identification of patterns and trends in candidate data. For instance, AI-driven analytics can provide information about talent pools, skill shortages, and new trends in hiring. With this knowledge, HR professionals may come up with innovative tactics to draw in and keep top people, adjust to shifting market conditions, and maintain a competitive edge in the talent acquisition process. AI can also improve the personalisation of candidate engagement and interactions. AI can personalise communication and recruitment methods to each candidate by analysing their data and interests, resulting in a more innovative and interesting candidate experience. In conclusion, AI's contribution to talent acquisition goes beyond automation; by enabling more personalised interactions, data-driven insights, and recruiting process innovation, AI enables HR professionals to better utilise their creative capacities.

4.3 Missing Role of Emotional Intelligence in AI-Enabled Talent Acquisition Process

A significant hole in the talent acquisition landscape is created by the absence of emotional intelligence in AI-enabled talent acquisition procedures. To manage relationships and resolve conflicts, recruiters need to have strong emotional intelligence levels. When discussions start, headhunting can quickly go poorly, but an effective negotiator must be able to perceive both the position on the table and a strategy to create trust. The ultimate goal is for both parties to leave content; this indicates a successful placement. At this time, it's crucial to set emotions aside, know when to pause, consider things through before acting or speaking, and manage disagreements. While AI is excellent at automating certain aspects of hiring, it frequently lacks the ability to understand and react to the complex emotional cues displayed by candidates. The capacity to effectively recognise, comprehend, and control emotions is a component of emotional intelligence. HR positions involving applicant contacts require this ability in particular. A number of problems can arise when AI lacks emotional intelligence. First of all, it could lead to encounters with candidates lacking in empathy and customization, which might make candidates feel unappreciated or misunderstood. A company's reputation and the relationships between candidates and the organization may suffer as a result of this emotional connection deficit. Research continuously emphasizes how important emotional intelligence is during the hiring process. According to studies, emotionally intelligent recruiters are better able to evaluate the fitness of candidates, determine cultural fit, and make more precise hiring judgements. Additionally, by displaying empathy and understanding, they improve the candidate experience and make it more interesting. Organisations should think about how to include emotional intelligence into their AI-driven talent acquisition procedures in order to close this gap. This might entail teaching AI systems to detect and react to emotional indicators in candidate conversation or combining AI with emotionally astute human recruiters. Organisations can improve recruiting outcomes, improve candidate experiences, and develop more sympathetic and emotionally engaging recruitment practises by doing this. AI intensive processes

4.4 Need of Human Engagement in Creating Candidate Experience

Human engagement is vital to the talent acquisition process, especially when it comes to giving applicants the critical feedback and direction they require (Grossman and Schoolderman, 2022). While AI algorithms may effectively perform duties like resume screening and preliminary evaluations, human recruiters are essential for providing individualised comments, encouraging open communication, and determining whether a candidate will fit in with the company's culture. They are skilled in conducting interviews, assessing behavioural responses, and assisting candidates throughout the hiring process to make it a pleasant and enjoyable process. Additionally, human recruiters can help candidates understand the complexities of the recruiting process and offer insights into potential career routes inside the company while establishing rapport and trust with them. The human touch is still a crucial part of hiring, complementing AI's effectiveness and improving the overall candidate experience. The study of candidate responses to computer-based testing, which delivers tests using personal computers or internal computer systems rather than the Internet, has long been a focus in the field of selection (Alkhadher et al., 1994; Bartram, 1994). According to Straus, Miles, and Levesque (2001), several studies have examined how applicants react to various techniques of conducting job interviews. But a careful examination of the enormous body of data in this area reveals a number of results that might be described as varied and complex. Human recruiters mostly handle the critical role of communicating clearly and setting expectations in the talent acquisition process. Human recruiters are exceptional at creating channels of communication with candidates that are honest and thorough in conveying job descriptions, corporate values, and role requirements. They are essential in answering questions from applicants, going through duties, and dispelling any ambiguities so that there is mutual understanding between the candidate and the company. This human-driven method helps create a pleasant candidate experience by fostering the trust and rapport that are essential for effective talent acquisition efforts. It also ensures that candidates have a realistic understanding of the role. On the one hand, a number of studies have shown that applicants perform better on computer-based tests than on conventional paper-and-pencil tests (Drauden and Martin, 1990; Schmitt et al., 1993). However, a number of studies either failed to find any results (Wiechmann and Ryan, 2003) or discovered proof of the applicants' adverse responses. Meier and Lambert (1991); Martin and Nagao (1989). Leaders with high EQ have the capacity to demonstrate empathy, consider multiple points of view, and give importance to the long-term interests of all stakeholders. They can also promote moral behaviour among their staff and guarantee that AI is used ethically (Cardenas, 2023). It is particularly significant that the study by Wiechmann and Ryan (2003) underlines the importance of adopting carefully designed experimental adjustments of test-taking conditions. The study claim that straightforward post-test reaction designs might overlook significant moderator factors like applicant mood, prior experience with computer-based tests, computer anxiety, and more. Candidates' opinions of the computer-based testing session were influenced by the test's design as well as moderator variables such the test administration procedure, how candidates were handled generally during the selection process, and the availability of feedback on test performance. This is therefore the most plausible reason for these conflicting results. Automation and personalization can complement one other to improve the candidate experience and boost response rates. Automation involves using tools or platforms to automate and schedule your messages while personalization entails adapting them to each candidate's profile, hobbies, and demands. the pivotal tasks of clear information sharing, setting expectations, and adopting a candidate-centric approach that prioritizes candidate needs are expertly managed by human recruiters. These skilled professionals excel in establishing effective communication channels, ensuring that job descriptions, company values, and role expectations are conveyed transparently and comprehensively. Simultaneously, they tailor the recruitment process to suit individual candidate preferences and goals, offering personalized interactions, empathetic support, and guidance throughout the hiring journey. This human-driven approach not only fosters a mutual understanding between the candidate and the organization but also ensures that candidates feel valued and respected, ultimately contributing to enhanced candidate satisfaction and stronger candidate-organization relationships. It is through these efforts that human recruiters play a pivotal role in making the candidate experience truly satisfactory in the talent acquisition process.

4.5 AI Drives Efficiency and Objectivity

Recruiters consistently grapple with the task of achieving more with constrained resources. This is precisely where the utility of AI recruitment tools becomes evident, presenting an efficient solution to address the tasks that consume considerable time. Artificial Intelligence (AI) is integral to various facets of talent acquisition, streamlining processes and augmenting decision-making. AI is instrumental in automating resume screening, efficiently matching candidates to job roles, and enhancing candidate engagement through chatbots and virtual assistants. It facilitates the evaluation of candidates' skills, personalities, and cultural fit, ensuring a more objective assessment. Additionally, AI-driven predictive analytics aids in forecasting future hiring needs and optimizing workforce planning. AI also plays a role in identifying potential biases in job postings and candidate selection, contributing to diversity and inclusion efforts. With AI's assistance, interview scheduling becomes more efficient, and onboarding processes are streamlined, ensuring a smoother transition for new hires. Furthermore, AI supports candidate relationship management and talent analytics, offering valuable insights into trends and performance. Altogether, AI transforms talent acquisition into a data-driven, efficient, and objective process while improving the overall candidate experience. AI can be a valuable asset by furnishing employees with personalized information and counsel, aiding them in making improved decisions. This is particularly advantageous for frontline workers, as their decisions often wield substantial influence on the overall financial outcomes.

5. HUMAN AI COLLABORATION IN TALENT ACQUISITION: WAY FORWARD

To navigate the challenges of AI and human collaboration in talent acquisition effectively, several strategic steps must be taken. First and foremost, HR professionals should prioritize continuous learning and upskilling to stay informed about AI advancements and maximize their utility in the hiring process. Ethical AI usage is paramount, requiring organizations to establish clear guidelines for algorithmic decision-making and transparent communication with candidates about AI's role in the process. Rather than replacing human expertise, AI should be seen as a decision support tool for HR, helping interpret insights and enhancing the final hiring decisions with a human touch. Personalization and enhanced candidate engagement through AI-driven interactions can improve the overall candidate experience, strengthening the organization's brand. Lastly, leveraging AI for advanced skill assessments ensures a more accurate evaluation of candidates, aligning them with the right job roles efficiently and objectively. By adopting these strategies, organizations can harness the collaborative potential of AI and human resources in talent acquisition, overcoming challenges and capitalizing on the advantages it brings.

6. THEORETICAL AND MANAGERIAL IMPLICATIONS

This study provides useful theoretical insights into the changing talent acquisition landscape, highlighting the crucial role of AI in modernising conventional HR practises. By emphasising the shift towards data-driven recruiting, where AI-driven analytics and prediction technologies play a crucial role in decision-making, it improves talent acquisition theory. The article also advances diversity and inclusion ideas by highlighting AI's ability to detect and reduce prejudices during the hiring process, encouraging a more inclusive strategy. From a managerial standpoint, the paper offers HR managers practical advice on how to increase recruiting effectiveness, enhance the candidate experience, and take advantage of data-driven decision-making. It emphasises how important it is to use AI technologies to improve several parts of hiring, from resume screening to onboarding, ultimately resulting in a more effective and diverse hiring environment.

7. CONCLUSION

In conclusion, the evolution of talent acquisition, driven by the dynamic partnership between human expertise and artificial intelligence, stands as a testament to the transformative potential of modern technology. As organizations navigate the complexities of today's competitive job market, the fusion of AI's computational prowess with human intuition and empathy emerges as an indispensable asset. Our exploration into the realm of human-AI collaboration in talent acquisition has illuminated not only its profound advantages but also the challenges that necessitate vigilance and innovation. The journey forward beckons us to embrace a commitment to ethical AI practices, continuous learning, and personalization, ensuring that the candidate experience remains at the forefront of our endeavors. As we forge ahead, the promise of this collaboration lies not merely in automating tasks but in elevating the essence of hiring itself. It is a commitment to inclusivity, fairness, and adaptability that empowers organizations to attract, engage, and retain top talent effectively. In the years to come, the landscape of talent acquisition will undoubtedly continue to evolve, marked by AI's ever-expanding capabilities and our unwavering commitment to human values. It is within this delicate balance, where technology meets humanity, that we discover the blueprint for a brighter, more efficient, and more equitable future in talent acquisition. Together, we move forward, driven by the belief that the fusion of human and AI capabilities will shape the next era of talent acquisition excellence.

REFERENCES

Albert, E. T. (2019). AI in talent acquisition: A review of AI-applications used in recruitment and selection. *Strategic HR Review*, 18(5), 215–221. DOI: 10.1108/SHR-04-2019-0024

Alkhadher, O., Anderson, N., & Clarke, D. (1994). Computer-based testing: A review of recent developments in research and practice. *European Work and Organizational Psychologist*, 4(2), 169–187. DOI: 10.1080/13594329408410482

Amritaa, K. S., & Achwani, S. (2018). A study on use of artificial intelligence in human resource management. *Gavesana Journal of Management*, 10(2), 45–56.

Bartram, D. (1994). Computer-based assessment. In Cooper, C. L., & Robertson, I. T. (Eds.), *International Review of Industrial and Organizational Psychology* (pp. 31–69). John Wiley & Sons Ltd.

Bilal, H., & Várallyai, L. (2021). Artificial intelligence in talent acquisition, do we trust it? *Journal of Agricultural Informatics/Agrárinformatika Folyóirat, 12*(1).

Black, J. S., & van Esch, P. (2021). AI-enabled recruiting in the war for talent. *Business Horizons*, 64(4), 513–524. DOI: 10.1016/j.bushor.2021.02.015

Budhwar, P., Malik, A., De Silva, M. T. T., & Thevisuthan, P. (2022). Artificial intelligence–challenges and opportunities for international HRM: A review and research agenda. *International Journal of Human Resource Management*, 33(6), 1065–1097. DOI: 10.1080/09585192.2022.2035161

Cardenas, J. (2023, August 28). Why EQ is important in the age of Artificial Intelligence. HRDQ. https://hrdqu.com/emotional-intelligence-assessment/why-eq-is-important-artificial-intelligence/#:~:text=EQ%20is%20Key%20for%20Social%20Responsibility%20and%20Ethics%3A&text=Leaders%20with%20high%20EQ%20can%20exercise%20empathy%2C%20consider%20different%20perspectives,the%20ethical%20use%20of%20AI

Chamorro-Premuzic, T., Polli, F., & Dattner, B. (2019). Building ethical AI for talent management. *Harvard Business Review*, 21, 1–15.

Chen, Z. (2023). Collaboration among recruiters and artificial intelligence: Removing human prejudices in employment. *Cognition Technology and Work*, 25(1), 135–149. DOI: 10.1007/s10111-022-00716-0 PMID: 36187287

Cohen, T. (2019). How to leverage artificial intelligence to meet your diversity goals. *Strategic HR Review*, 18(2), 62–65. DOI: 10.1108/SHR-12-2018-0105

Dijkkamp, J. (2019). *The recruiter of the future, a qualitative study in AI supported recruitment process* [Unpublished Master's thesis]. University of Twente.

Dixit, S., Sharma, N., Maurya, M., & Dharwal, M. (2022). AI power: Making recruitment smarter. In *Evolution of digitized societies through advanced technologies* (pp. 165–180). Springer Nature Singapore. DOI: 10.1007/978-981-19-2984-7_14

Fayoumi, A., & Loucopoulos, P. (2023). Bridging the strategy execution gap of designing intelligent talent acquisition systems using enterprise modelling and simulation. *Enterprise Information Systems*, 17(6), 2005149. DOI: 10.1080/17517575.2021.2005149

Ferry, K. (2018, January 18). Korn Ferry Global Survey: Artificial intelligence (AI) reshaping the role of the recruiter. https://www.kornferry.com/about-us/press/korn-ferry-global-survey-artificial-intelligence-reshaping-the-role-of-the-recruiter

França, T. J. F., São Mamede, H., Barroso, J. M. P., & Dos Santos, V. M. P. D. (2023). Artificial intelligence applied to potential assessment and talent identification in an organisational context. *Heliyon*, 9(4). PMID: 37035361

Geetha, R., & Bhanu, S. R. D. (2018). Recruitment through artificial intelligence: A conceptual study. *International Journal of Mechanical Engineering and Technology*, 9(7), 63–70.

Grossman, K. W., & Schoolderman, A. (2022). *Candidate experience: How to improve talent acquisition to drive business performance*. Kogan Page Publishers.

Hmoud, B., & Laszlo, V. (2019). Will artificial intelligence take over human resources recruitment and selection. *Network Intelligence Studies*, 7(13), 21–30.

Hunkenschroer, A. L., & Luetge, C. (2022). Ethics of AI-enabled recruiting and selection: A review and research agenda. *Journal of Business Ethics*, 178(4), 977–1007. DOI: 10.1007/s10551-022-05049-6

Johnson, R. D., Stone, D. L., & Lukaszewski, K. M. (2021). The benefits of eHRM and AI for talent acquisition. *Journal of Tourism Futures*, 7(1), 40–52. DOI: 10.1108/JTF-02-2020-0013

Jones, K. (2022, August 16). How ai is transforming the Talent Acquisition Process: TechTarget. HR software. https://www.techtarget.com/searchhrsoftware/tip/6-ways-AI-can-improve-the-talent-acquisition-process

Lakshmi, R. S., Sowdamini, T., & Biswas, A. K. (2020). The rise of artificial intelligence in talent acquisition. *Workforce, 3.*

Martin, C. L., & Nagao, D. H. (1989). Some effects of computerized interviewing on applicant response. *The Journal of Applied Psychology*, 74(1), 72–80. DOI: 10.1037/0021-9010.74.1.72

McGovern, S. L., Aldrich, T., Myers, C., Desai, C., & Gera, M. (2018). The new age: artificial intelligence for human resource opportunities and functions. Retrieved from https://www.ey.com/Publication/vwLUAssets/EY-the-new- age-artificialintelligence-for-human-resource-opportunities- and -functions/$FILE/EY-the-new-ageartificial-intelligence-for-human-resource-opportunities- and -functions.pdf

Mehrotra, S., & Khanna, A. (2022). Recruitment through AI in selected Indian companies. *Metamorphosis*, 21(1), 31–39. DOI: 10.1177/09726225211066220

Meier, S. T., & Lambert, M. E. (1991). Psychometric properties and correlates of three computer aversion scales. *Behavior Research Methods, Instruments, & Computers*, 231(1), 9–15. DOI: 10.3758/BF03203329

Mishra, R., Rodriguez, R., & Portillo, V. (2020). An ai based talent acquisition and benchmarking for job. *arXiv preprint arXiv:2009.09088.*

Ore, O., & Sposato, M. (2022). Opportunities and risks of artificial intelligence in recruitment and selection. *The International Journal of Organizational Analysis*, 30(6), 1771–1782. DOI: 10.1108/IJOA-07-2020-2291

Pereira, V., Hadjielias, E., Christofi, M., & Vrontis, D. (2023). A systematic literature review on the impact of artificial intelligence on workplace outcomes: A multi-process perspective. *Human Resource Management Review*, 33(1), 100857. DOI: 10.1016/j.hrmr.2021.100857

Pillai, R., & Sivathanu, B. (2020). Adoption of artificial intelligence (AI) for talent acquisition in IT/ITeS organizations. *Benchmarking*, 27(9), 2599–2629. DOI: 10.1108/BIJ-04-2020-0186

Raviprolu, A. (2017). Role of artificial intelligence in recruitment [International journal] of Engineering Technology. *Management and Applied Sciences, 5*(4).

Schmitt, N., Gilliland, S. W., Landis, R. S., & Devine, D. (1993). Computer-based testing applied to selection of secretarial applicants. *Personnel Psychology*, 46(1), 149–165. DOI: 10.1111/j.1744-6570.1993.tb00871.x

Spar, B., Pletenyuk, I., Reilly, K., & Ignatova, M. (2018). Global recruiting trends. *LinkedIn website, 2018* [Rep.]. https://news.linkedin.com/2018/1/global-recruiting -trends-2018

Straus, S. G., Miles, J. A., & Levesque, L. L. (2001). The effects of videoconference, telephone, and face-to-face media on interviewer and applicant judgments in employment interviews. *Journal of Management*, 27(3), 363–381. DOI: 10.1177/014920630102700308

Suen, H.-Y., Chen, M. Y.-C., & Lu, S.-H. (2019). Does the use of synchrony and artificial intelligence in video interviews affect interview ratings and applicant attitudes? *Computers in Human Behavior*, 98, 93–101. DOI: 10.1016/j.chb.2019.04.012

Talwalkar, P., Deshmukh, V., & Bhole, M. (2019). Prevalence of hypothyroidism in patients with type 2 diabetes mellitus and hypertension in India: A cross-sectional observational study. *Diabetes, Metabolic Syndrome and Obesity*, 12, 369–376. DOI: 10.2147/DMSO.S181470 PMID: 30936734

Tambe, P., Cappelli, P., & Yakubovich, V. (2019). Artificial intelligence in human resources management: Challenges and a path forward. *California Management Review*, 61(4), 15–42. DOI: 10.1177/0008125619867910

Tiwari, P., Rajput, N., & Garg, V. (2022, April). Artificial Intelligence and Talent Acquisition-Role of HR leaders in Adoption. In *3rd International Conference on Intelligent Engineering and Management (ICIEM)* (pp. 313–317). IEEE Publications. DOI: 10.1109/ICIEM54221.2022.9853104

Upadhyay, A. K., & Khandelwal, K. (2018). Applying artificial intelligence: Implications for recruitment. *Strategic HR Review*, 17(5), 255–258. DOI: 10.1108/SHR-07-2018-0051

Veglianti, E., Trombin, M., Pinna, R., & De Marco, M. (2023). Customized artificial intelligence for talent recruiting: A bias-free tool? In *Smart technologies for organizations: Managing a sustainable and inclusive digital transformation* (pp. 245–261). Springer International Publishing., DOI: 10.1007/978-3-031-24775-0_15

Wiechmann, D., & Ryan, A. M. (2003). Reactions to computerized testing in selection contexts. *International Journal of Selection and Assessment*, 11(2–3), 215–229. DOI: 10.1111/1468-2389.00245

Will, P., Krpan, D., & Lordan, G. (2023). People versus machines: Introducing the HIRE framework. *Artificial Intelligence Review*, 56(2), 1071–1100. DOI: 10.1007/s10462-022-10193-6

Yam, J., & Skorburg, J. A. (2021). From human resources to human rights: Impact assessments for hiring algorithms. *Ethics and Information Technology*, 23(4), 611–623. DOI: 10.1007/s10676-021-09599-7

Compilation of References

Ababneh, O. M. A. (2021). How do green HRM practices affect employees' green behaviors? The role of employee engagement and personality attributes. *Journal of Environmental Planning and Management*, 64(7), 1204–1226.

Abdalla, A. A. (2024g). Understanding the impact of top management green commitment and green human resource management practices on employee green behaviors and green creativity: Evidence from the UAE higher education sector. In M. Y. Yusliza & D. Renwick, D. (eds.), *Green Human Resource Management: A View from Global South Countries* (pp. 347-366). Singapore: Springer Nature Singapore. https://doi.org/DOI: 10.1007/978-981-99-7104-6_20

Abdalla, A. A. (2024a). *Managing for Sustainability: The Impact of Green Human Resource Management Practices on Employee Green Behavior and Green Innovation, Reference Module in Social Sciences*. Elsevier. DOI: 10.1016/B978-0-443-13701-3.00423-0

Aboramadan, M., Kundi, Y. M., & Becker, A. (2022). Green human resource management in nonprofit organizations: Effects on employee green behavior and the role of perceived green organizational support. *Personnel Review*, 51(7), 1788–1806. DOI: 10.1108/PR-02-2021-0078

Acar, S., & Sarniç, A. (2024). A qualitative study on talent management in enterprises within the Industry 4.0 process. *SEISENSE Journal of Management*, 7(1), 101–116. DOI: 10.33215/t02k1p32

Adams, G., & White, M. (2023). Conflict resolution in crisis: Strategies for managing workplace conflicts. *The Journal of Applied Psychology*, 108(3), 401–415.

Adams, J. S. (1963). Towards an understanding of inequity. *Journal of Abnormal and Social Psychology*, 67(5), 422–436. DOI: 10.1037/h0040968 PMID: 14081885

Adriana, L. T. D., Fahira, K. T., Nailissa'adah, M., & El Maula, H. (2020). A review the important of green human resource management practices toward employee green behaviour in organization. *Journal of international conference proceedings, 3*(1), 124-135.

Aerodei. (2024, February 28). Unqork case study. *Aerodei.* https://www.aerodei.com/post/unqork-case-study

Afandi, A. R., & Kurnia, H. (2023). Revolusi Teknologi: Masa Depan Kecerdasan Buatan (AI) dan Dampaknya Terhadap Masyarakat. *Academy of Social Science and Global Citizenship Journal*, 3(1), 9–13. DOI: 10.47200/aossagcj.v3i1.1837

Afsar, B., Badir, Y. F., & Khan, M. M. (2020). Impact of Green HRM on employees' green behavior and innovative performance: An empirical study. *International Journal of Environmental Research and Public Health*, 17(18), 6638. DOI: 10.3390/ijerph17186638 PMID: 32932983

Agarwal, N., & Jain, S. (2021). Green Human Resource Management and sustainable organizational performance: The mediating role of employee green behavior. *Sustainability*, 13(4), 1742. DOI: 10.3390/su13041742

Agarwal, U. A. (2003). The impact of human resource practices on employee productivity: A critical review. *International Journal of Human Resource Management*, 14(3), 299–320. DOI: 10.1080/0958519032000058530

Aguilera, A., Lethiais, V., Rallet, A., & Proulhac, L. (2016). Home-based telework in France: Characteristics, barriers and perspectives. *Transportation Research Part A, Policy and Practice*, 92, 1–11. DOI: 10.1016/j.tra.2016.06.021

Aguinis, H. (2009). *Performance management*. Pearson Prentice Hall.

Ahmed, U. Z., Fiaz, M., & Taous, M. (2023). Improving hotel environmental performance via green training, green performance management, and green employee involvement: A systematic study. *Open Access Organization and Management Review*, 2(1), 14–25. DOI: 10.59644/oagmr.2(1).44

AI for Social Good Canada. (2020). *Sustainable AI: Building a future for ethical and environmentally friendly artificial intelligence.* https://aiforsocialgood.ca/

AI Now Institute. (2021). *Algorithmic Accountability Policy Toolkit.* https://ainowinstitute.org/policytoolkit.html

Ajayi, F. A., & Udeh, C. A. (2024). Agile work cultures in IT: A Conceptual analysis of HR's role in fostering innovation supply chain. *International Journal of Management & Entrepreneurship Research*, 6(4), 1138–1156. DOI: 10.51594/ijmer.v6i4.1004

Ajzen, I. (1991). The theory of planned behavior. *Organizational Behavior and Human Decision Processes*, 50(2), 179–211. DOI: 10.1016/0749-5978(91)90020-T

Akter, S., Michael, K., Uddin, M. R., McCarthy, G., & Rahman, M. (2022). Transforming business using digital innovations: The application of AI, blockchain, cloud and data analytics. *Annals of Operations Research*, 308(1-2), 7–39. DOI: 10.1007/s10479-020-03620-w

Alamro, M. Q., Hosseini, S. B., & Farooq, A. (2019). Organizational Agility and HRM Practices: Theoretical Framework and Perspective. *Restaurant Business*, 118, 12.

Albert, E. T. (2019). AI in talent acquisition: A review of AI-applications used in recruitment and selection. *Strategic HR Review*, 18(5), 215–221. DOI: 10.1108/SHR-04-2019-0024

Alexandria. (2022, December 27). *Remote Work Is Here for Good*. HRNews. https://www.proquest.com/abicomplete/docview/2758589240/E33E90B228874210PQ/1?accountid=177838&sourcetype=Trade%20Journals#center

Alexandria. (2023, September 14). *Coworking Spaces Can Help Prevent Employee Loneliness, Isolation*. HRNews. https://www.proquest.com/abicomplete/docview/2864920195/945F018B129C4C98PQ/2?accountid=177838&sourcetype=Trade%20Journals

Alkhadher, O., Anderson, N., & Clarke, D. (1994). Computer-based testing: A review of recent developments in research and practice. *European Work and Organizational Psychologist*, 4(2), 169–187. DOI: 10.1080/13594329408410482

Allen, N. J., & Meyer, J. P. (1996). Affective, Continuance, and Normative Commitment to the Organization: An Examination of Construct Validity. *Journal of Vocational Behavior*, 49(3), 252–276. https://sci-hub.se/10.1006/jvbe.1996.0043. DOI: 10.1006/jvbe.1996.0043 PMID: 8980084

Almeida, N. G. (2016). A importância da metodologia científica através do projeto de pesquisa para a construção da monografia. *Revista de Biblioteconomia e Ciência Da Informação*, 57–66. https://periodicos.ufca.edu.br/ojs/index.php/folhaderosto/article/view/92/67

Almeida, F., & Carneiro, P. (2023). Perceived Importance of Metrics for Agile Scrum Environments. *Information (Basel)*, 14(6), 327. DOI: 10.3390/info14060327

Amjad, F., Abbas, W., Zia-Ur-Rehman, M., Baig, S. A., Hashim, M., Khan, A., & Rehman, H. U. (2021). Effect of green human resource management practices on organizational sustainability: The mediating role of environmental and employee performance. *Environmental Science and Pollution Research International*, 28, 28191–28206. PMID: 33527245

Amritaa, K. S., & Achwani, S. (2018). A study on use of artificial intelligence in human resource management. *Gavesana Journal of Management*, 10(2), 45–56.

Amrutha, V. N., & Geetha, S. N. (2020). A systematic review on green human resource management: Implications for social sustainability. *Journal of Cleaner Production*, 247, 119131. DOI: 10.1016/j.jclepro.2019.119131

Amy, A. H. (2008). Leaders as facilitators of individual and organizational learning. *Leadership and Organization Development Journal*, 29(3), 212–234. DOI: 10.1108/01437730810861281

Anand, A. A., & Acharya, S. N. (2021). Employee Engagement in A Remote Working Scenario. *International Research Journal of Business Studies, 14*(2). https://pdfs.semanticscholar.org/3845/990aadc017a468cfbd7838000f9dd5468cd0.pdf

Andersson, S., & Eriksson, T. (2023). High-performance work practices and organizational performance: Evidence from the IT sector. *Journal of Organizational Behavior*, 44(1), 58–76. DOI: 10.1002/job.2487

An, H., Gu, X., Obrenovic, B., & Godinic, D. (2023, August 18). The Role of Job Insecurity, Social Media Exposure, and Job Stress in Predicting Anxiety Among White-Collar Employees. *Psychology Research and Behavior Management*, 16, 3303–3318. DOI: 10.2147/PRBM.S416100 PMID: 37614323

Antony, D. A. J., Arulandu, S., & Parayitam, S. (2024). Gender and experience as moderators between talent management and turnover intention among faculty members in higher educational institutions in India. *The Learning Organization*, 31(4), 526–546. DOI: 10.1108/TLO-04-2023-0051

Appelbaum, E., Bailey, T., Berg, P., & Kalleberg, A. L. (2000). *Manufacturing competitiveness: A study of high-performance work practices*. ILR Press.

Appelbaum, S. H., & Fewster, B. M. (2003). Global aviation human resource management: Contemporary employee and labor relations practices. *Management Research News*, 26(10/11), 56–69. DOI: 10.1108/01409170310784069

Armstrong, D. J., Brooks, N. G., & Riemenschneider, C. K. (2015). Exhaustion from information system career experience. *Management Information Systems Quarterly*, 39(3), 713–728. DOI: 10.25300/MISQ/2015/39.3.10

Artigo 165º, de 28 de abril de 2023. *Código do Trabalho.* Autoridade para as condições do Trabalho.

Ashton, D. (2005). High-performance work systems and organizational performance: A review. *International Journal of Human Resource Management*, 16(3), 331–356. DOI: 10.1080/09585190500083037

Ayyagari, R., Grover, V., & Purvis, R. (2011). Technostress: Technological antecedents and implications. *Management Information Systems Quarterly*, 35(4), 831–858. DOI: 10.2307/41409963

Azpíroz-Dorronsoro, C., Fernández-Muñiz, B., Montes-Peón, J. M., & Vázquez-Ordás, C. J. (2023). Technostress and work-family conflict in ICT-user employees during the COVID-19 pandemic: The role of social support and mindfulness. *Behaviour & Information Technology*, 43(8), 1531–1553. DOI: 10.1080/0144929X.2023.2220051

Bakker, A. B., & Leiter, M. P. (2010). *Work Engagement: A Handbook of Essential Theory and Research.* Psychology Press. DOI: 10.4324/9780203853047

Balliester, T., & Elsheikhi, A. (2018). The future of work: A literature review. ILO Research Department Working Paper, 29, 1–54.

Balsvik, E., & Rønnevik, M. (2022). Employees as self-regulated learners: a case study of employees' upskilling through internal microlearning platforms (Master's thesis, Handelshøyskolen BI).

Bamford, K. L., & Xystouri, T. (2017). A systematic literature review of employee engagement in the maritime industry. *WMU Journal of Maritime Affairs*, 16(2), 123–140. DOI: 10.1007/s13437-016-0119-3

Bandi, R. K., Klein, S., Madon, S., Monteiro, E., & Ranjini, C. R. (2020). The future of digital work: The challenge of inequality. In *The Future of Digital Work: The Challenge of Inequality: IFIP WG 8.2, 9.1, 9.4 Joint Working Conference, IFIPJWC 2020, Hyderabad, India, December 10–11, 2020, Proceedings* (pp. 3-10). Springer International Publishing.

Baptista, J., Stein, M., Klein, S., Watson-Manheim, M. B., & Lee, J. (2020). Digital work and organizational transformation: Emergent digital/human work configurations in modern organizations. *The Journal of Strategic Information Systems*, 29(2), 101618. DOI: 10.1016/j.jsis.2020.101618

Barardo, R. de O. (2021). *A afirmação do Teletrabalho no setor terciário: Desafios e Oportunidades* [Master Dissertation, ISCAL - Instituto Superior de Contabilidade e Administração de Lisboa]. https://repositorio.ipl.pt/bitstream/10400.21/15238/1/Tese%20Ricardo%20Barardo%20-%20Imprimir.pdf

Barney, J. (1991). Firm resources and sustained competitive advantage. *Journal of Management*, 17(1), 99–120. DOI: 10.1177/014920639101700108

Barney, J., & Wright, P. M. (1998). On becoming a strategic partner: The role of human resources in gaining competitive advantage. *Human Resource Management*, 37(1), 31–46. DOI: 10.1002/(SICI)1099-050X(199821)37:1<31::AID-HRM4>3.0.CO;2-W

Baron, J. N., & Kreps, D. M. (1999). *Strategic human resources: Frameworks for general managers*. Wiley.

Bartlett, C. A., & Ghoshal, S. (1989). *Managing across borders: The transnational solution*. Harvard Business School Press.

Bartram, D. (1994). Computer-based assessment. In Cooper, C. L., & Robertson, I. T. (Eds.), *International Review of Industrial and Organizational Psychology* (pp. 31–69). John Wiley & Sons Ltd.

Bashynska, I., Prokopenko, O., & Sala, D. (2023). Managing Human Capital with AI: Synergy of Talent and Technology. *Zeszyty Naukowe Wyższej Szkoły Finansów i Prawa w Bielsku-Białej*, 27(3), 39–45.

Beckel, J. L. O., & Fisher, G. G. (2022). Telework and Worker Health and Well-Being: A Review and Recommendations for Research and Practice. *International Journal of Environmental Research and Public Health*, 19(7), 3879. DOI: 10.3390/ijerph19073879 PMID: 35409563

Becker, B. E., & Huselid, M. A. (2006). Strategic human resources management: Where do we go from here? *Journal of Management*, 32(6), 898–925. DOI: 10.1177/0149206306293668

Bekhit, K. E., El Leithy, W., & Mahmoud, A. (2023). The impact of green human resource management practices on employee retention and environmental sustainability: A conceptual model. *Ymer*, 22(01), 1004–1034.

Benevene, P., & Buonomo, I. (2020). Green human resource management: An evidence-based systematic literature review. *Sustainability*, 12(15), 5974.

Bessen, J., Goos, M., Salomons, A., & van den Berge, W. (2020). *Automation: A guide for policymakers*. Economic Studies at Brookings Institution.

Bezrukova, K., Spell, C. S., Perry, J. L., & Jehn, K. A. (2016). A meta-analytical integration of over 40 years of research on diversity training evaluation. *Psychological Bulletin*, 142(11), 1227–1274. DOI: 10.1037/bul0000067 PMID: 27618543

Bhalla, A. (2011). Innovation and HR practices: A study of high-performance work practices in the IT sector. *Human Resource Management Review*, 21(2), 115–129. DOI: 10.1016/j.hrmr.2010.03.002

Bilal, H., & Várallyai, L. (2021). Artificial intelligence in talent acquisition, do we trust it? *Journal of Agricultural Informatics/Agrárinformatika Folyóirat, 12*(1).

Binns, R. (2018). Fairness in machine learning: Lessons from political philosophy. *Proceedings of the 2018 Conference on Fairness, Accountability, and Transparency*, 149-159. https://doi.org/DOI: 10.1145/3287560.3287589

Bissing-Olson, M. J., Iyer, A., Fielding, K. S., & Zacher, H. (2013). Relationships between daily affect and pro-environmental behavior at work: The moderating role of pro-environmental attitude. *Journal of Organizational Behavior*, 34(2), 156–175. DOI: 10.1002/job.1788

Black, J. S., & van Esch, P. (2021). AI-enabled recruiting in the war for talent. *Business Horizons*, 64(4), 513–524. DOI: 10.1016/j.bushor.2021.02.015

Block, S. (2023). How to Adapt and Implement a Large-Scale Agile Framework in Your Organization. In *Large-Scale Agile Frameworks: Agile Frameworks, Agile Infrastructure and Pragmatic Solutions for Digital Transformation* (pp. 65–168). Springer Berlin Heidelberg. DOI: 10.1007/978-3-662-67782-7_4

Bloom, N., Han, R., & Liang, J. (2022). *How Hybrid Working From Home Works Out*.

Boccoli, G., Gastaldi, L., & Corso, M. (2023). The evolution of employee engagement: Towards a social and contextual construct for balancing individual performance and wellbeing dynamically. *International Journal of Management Reviews*, 25(1), 75–98. DOI: 10.1111/ijmr.12304

Bogen, M., & Rieke, A. (2018). Help wanted: An examination of hiring algorithms, equity, and bias. *Upturn*. https://www.upturn.org/reports/2018/hiring-algorithms/

Bombiak, E., & Marciniuk-Kluska, A. (2018). Green human resource management as a tool for the sustainable development of enterprises: Polish young company experience. *Sustainability*, 10(6), 1739. DOI: 10.3390/su10061739

Bourlakis, M., Nisar, T. M., & Prabhakar, G. (2023). How technostress may affect employee performance in educational work environments. *Technological Forecasting and Social Change*, 193, 122674. DOI: 10.1016/j.techfore.2023.122674

Bourne, B. (2023, May 19). *Top 5 Trends in DEI for 2023*. Purdue Global. https://www.purdueglobal.edu/blog/business/diversity-equity-inclusion-trends/

Bowen, D. E., & Ostroff, C. (2004). Understanding HRM-firm performance linkages: The role of the "strength" of the HRM system. *Academy of Management Review*, 29(2), 203–221. DOI: 10.5465/amr.2004.12736076

Brewster, C., Chung, C., & Sparrow, P. (2016). *Globalizing human resource management.* Routledge.

Brewster, C., Mayrhofer, W., & Smale, A. (2016). Crossing the streams: HRM in multinational enterprises and comparative HRM. *Human Resource Management Review*, 26(4), 285–297. DOI: 10.1016/j.hrmr.2016.04.002

Brod, C. (1984). *Technostress: The Human Cost of the Computer Revolution.* Addison-Wesley.

Brown, A., & Lee, C. (2022). Intersectionality and diversity: Strategies for inclusive workplaces. *The Journal of Applied Psychology*, 107(3), 389–402. DOI: 10.1037/apl0000987 PMID: 33983782

Budhwar, P., Malik, A., De Silva, M. T. T., & Thevisuthan, P. (2022). Artificial intelligence–challenges and opportunities for international HRM: A review and research agenda. *International Journal of Human Resource Management*, 33(6), 1065–1097. DOI: 10.1080/09585192.2022.2035161

Califf, C. B., & Brooks, S. (2020). An empirical study of techno-stressors, literacy facilitation, burnout, and turnover intention as experienced by K-12 teachers. *Computers & Education*, 157, 103971. DOI: 10.1016/j.compedu.2020.103971

Califf, C. B., Sarker, S., & Sarker, S. (2020). The Bright and Dark Sides of Technostress: A Mixed-Methods Study Involving Healthcare IT. *Management Information Systems Quarterly*, 44(2), 809–856. DOI: 10.25300/MISQ/2020/14818

Caliskan, A., Bryson, J. J., & Narayanan, A. (2017). Semantics derived automatically from language corpora contain human-like biases. *Science*, 356(6334), 183–186. DOI: 10.1126/science.aal4230 PMID: 28408601

Calisto, M. D. L., Umbelino, J., Gonçalves, A., & Viegas, C. (2021). Environmental sustainability strategies for smaller companies in the hotel industry: Doing the right thing or doing things right? *Sustainability*, 13(18), 10380.

Canadian Centre for Diversity and Inclusion. (2021). *Training Programs.* CCDI. https://ccdi.ca/training/

Canadian Institute for Advanced Research. (2022). *AI & Society Program.* Cifar. https://www.cifar.ca/programs/ai-society

Canadian, A. I. Innovation. (2021). *AI for Everyone: Diversity & Inclusion in AI.* https://www.canadianai.ca/publications/diversity-inclusion-ai

Cao, X., Guo, X., Vogel, D., & Zhang, X. (2016). Exploring the influence of social media on employee work performance. *Internet Research*, 26(2), 529–545. DOI: 10.1108/IntR-11-2014-0299

Cardenas, J. (2023, August 28). Why EQ is important in the age of Artificial Intelligence. HRDQ. https://hrdqu.com/emotional-intelligence-assessment/why-eq-is-important-artificial-intelligence/#:~:text=EQ%20is%20Key%20for%20Social%20Responsibility%20and%20Ethics%3A&text=Leaders%20with%20high%20EQ%20can%20exercise%20empathy%2C%20consider%20different%20perspectives,the%20ethical%20use%20of%20AI

Carrasco-Garrido, C., De-Pablos-Heredero, C., & Rodríguez-Sánchez, J.-L. (2023). Exploring hybrid telework: A bibliometric analysis. *Heliyon*, 9(12), 1–15. DOI: 10.1016/j.heliyon.2023.e22472 PMID: 38076145

Carter, S., & Davis, M. (2023). Employee empowerment and its impact on job performance: Evidence from the IT industry. *The Journal of Applied Psychology*, 108(4), 532–546. DOI: 10.1037/apl0000698

Cesário, F., Sabino, A., Moreira, A., & Azevedo, T. (2022). Green human resources practices and person-organization fit: The moderating role of the personal environmental commitment. *Emerging Science Journal*, 6(5), 938–951.

Cetindamar, D., Kitto, K., Wu, M., Zhang, Y., Abedin, B., & Knight, S. (2022). Explicating AI literacy of employees at digital workplaces. *IEEE Transactions on Engineering Management*, •••, 1–14. DOI: 10.1109/TEM.2021.3138503

Chafi, M. B., Hultberg, A., & Yams, N. B. (2022). Post-pandemic office work: Perceived challenges and opportunities for a sustainable work environment. *Sustainability (Basel)*, 14(1), 294. Advance online publication. DOI: 10.3390/su14010294

Chamorro-Premuzic, T., Polli, F., & Dattner, B. (2019). Building ethical AI for talent management. *Harvard Business Review*, 21, 1–15.

Chan, D. (2000). The story of Singapore Airlines and the Singapore Girl. *Journal of Management Development*, 19(6), 456–472. DOI: 10.1108/02621710010372873

Chang, C. H. (2011). The influence of corporate environmental ethics on competitive advantage: The mediation role of green innovation. *Journal of Business Ethics*, 104, 361–370. DOI: 10.1007/s10551-011-0914-x

Chang, P. C., Zhang, W., Cai, Q., & Guo, H. (2024). Does AI-Driven Technostress Promote or Hinder Employees' Artificial Intelligence Adoption Intention? A Moderated Mediation Model of Affective Reactions and Technical Self-Efficacy. *Psychology Research and Behavior Management*, 17, 413–427. DOI: 10.2147/PRBM.S441444 PMID: 38343429

Chaudhary, R. (2019). Green human resource management in Indian automobile industry. *Journal of Global Responsibility*, 10(2), 161–175. DOI: 10.1108/ JGR-12-2018-0084

Cheema, S., Afsar, B., & Javed, F. (2020). Employee green behavior as a linchpin for sustainable development: The moderating role of green HRM and ethical leadership. *International Journal of Environmental Research and Public Health*, 17(15), 5380. DOI: 10.3390/ijerph17155380 PMID: 32722624

Chen, C. F., & Chen, S. C. (2012). Burnout and work engagement among cabin crew: Antecedents and consequences. *The International Journal of Aviation Psychology*, 22(1), 41–58. DOI: 10.1080/10508414.2012.635125

Cheng, B., Lin, H., & Kong, Y. (2023). Challenge or hindrance? How and when organizational artificial intelligence adoption influences employee job crafting. *Journal of Business Research*, 164, 113987. DOI: 10.1016/j.jbusres.2023.113987

Chen, H., & Zheng, X. (2024). The influence of Green HRM on employees' green behavior and organizational performance: The mediating role of environmental commitment. *Journal of Environmental Management*, 340, 118252. DOI: 10.1016/j.jenvman.2024.118252

Chen, J., Smith, T., & Williams, R. (2021). Globalization and diversity management: Challenges and opportunities. *International Journal of Human Resource Management*, 32(6), 1200–1221. DOI: 10.1080/09585192.2020.1843703

Chen, L., Zhao, Y., & Wang, Q. (2024). Tailoring HR practices to enhance productivity in the IT industry: An empirical study. *Journal of Business Research*, 147, 356–365. DOI: 10.1016/j.jbusres.2022.03.001

Chen, M. F., Lin, C. P., & Lien, G. Y. (2011). Modelling job stress as a mediating role in predicting turnover intention. *Service Industries Journal*, 31(8), 1327–1345. DOI: 10.1080/02642060903437543

Chen, Z. (2023). Collaboration among recruiters and artificial intelligence: Removing human prejudices in employment. *Cognition Technology and Work*, 25(1), 135–149. DOI: 10.1007/s10111-022-00716-0 PMID: 36187287

Chiguvi, D., & Keneilwe Bakani, . (2023). Exploring the effects of remote work on employee productivity in Botswana amidst the COVID-19 Pandemic. *International Journal of Research in Business and Social Science*, 12(6), 101–117. DOI: 10.20525/ijrbs.v12i6.2505

Choi, S. (2018). Managing flexible work arrangements in government: Testing the effects of institutional and managerial support. *Public Personnel Management*, 47(1), 26–50. DOI: 10.1177/0091026017738540

Choudhury, P. (2020, November). Our Work-from-Anywhere Future. *Harvard Business Review*, 23(SPEC. ISS.). Advance online publication. DOI: 10.1002/job.145

Chowdhury, M. (2024). Navigating the VUCA Terrain: Unveiling HR Strategies for Modern Organizational Agility. *SEISENSE Journal of Management*, 7(1), 67–82. DOI: 10.33215/wbm33665

Cho, Y. J., & Lewis, G. B. (2012). Turnover intention and turnover behavior: Implications for retaining federal employees. *Review of Public Personnel Administration*, 32(1), 4–23. DOI: 10.1177/0734371X11408701

Chuang, S. (2022). Indispensable skills for human employees in the age of robots and AI. *European Journal of Training and Development*. Advance online publication. DOI: 10.1108/EJTD-06-2022-0062

Chukwurah, E. G., & Aderemi, S. (2024). Elevating team performance with scrum: Insights from successful US technology companies. *Engineering Science & Technology Journal*, 5(4), 1357–1371. DOI: 10.51594/estj.v5i4.1038

Clark, E. (2021). The benefits of a four-day workweek on employee productivity. *Harvard Business Review*. https://hbr.org

Cockburn, T. (2020). Emerging Impacts of Socio digital Technology in the' New Normal' of the Post-COVID19 Resilience, Regrowth and Renewal Period 2020-2021 and Beyond (Presentation Slides). *Regrowth and Renewal Period*, 2021, 2020.

Codagnone, C. (2016). *The Future of Work in the 'Sharing Economy'. Market Efficiency and Equitable Opportunities or Unfair Precarisation? EU Science Hub*. European Commission.

Cohen, T. (2019). How to leverage artificial intelligence to meet your diversity goals. *Strategic HR Review*, 18(2), 62–65. DOI: 10.1108/SHR-12-2018-0105

Coker, J. O., Uzougbo, N. S., Oguejiofor, B. B., & Akagha, O. V. (2023). The Role of Legal Practitioners in Mitigating Corporate Risks In Nigeria: A Comprehensive Review Of Existing Literature On The Strategies And Approaches Adopted By Legal Practitioners In Nigeria To Mitigate Corporate Risks. *Finance & Accounting Research Journal*, 5(10), 309–332. DOI: 10.51594/farj.v5i10.579

Colquitt, J. A., Greenberg, J., & Zapata-Phelan, C. P. (2005). What is organizational justice? A historical overview. Handbook of organizational justice, 1, 3-56.

Colquitt, J. A. (2001). On the dimensionality of organizational justice: A construct validation of a measure. *The Journal of Applied Psychology*, 86(3), 386–400. DOI: 10.1037/0021-9010.86.3.386 PMID: 11419799

Cowgill, B., Dell'Acqua, F., Deng, S., & Deng, S. (2020). *Biased programmers? Or biased data? A field experiment in operationalizing AI ethics*. (Columbia Business School Research Paper). https://doi.org/DOI: 10.2139/ssrn.3685457

Cox, T. H. (2017). *Cultural Diversity in Organizations: Theory, Research, and Practice*. Berrett-Koehler Publishers.

Cox, T. H., & Blake, S. (2017). Managing cultural diversity: Implications for organizational competitiveness. *The Academy of Management Perspectives*, 5(3), 45–56. DOI: 10.5465/ame.1991.4274465

Cristina, A. C. (2021). *Bem Estar E Satisfação No Trabalho Remoto: Comparação Entre Trabalhadores Independenes E Trabalhadores Dependentes* [Master Dissertation, ISPA - Instituto Universitário Ciências Psicológicas, Sociais e da Vida]. https://repositorio.ispa.pt/bitstream/10400.12/8017/1/22463.pdf

Croatti, A., & Ricci, A. (2020). *From virtual worlds to mirror worlds: A model and platform for building agent-based extended realities. In multi-agent systems and agreement technologies*. Springer.

Cummings, T. G., & Worley, C. G. (2014). *Organization development and change*. Cengage Learning.

D'Arcy, J., Gupta, A., Tarafdar, M., & Turel, O. (2014). Reflecting on the "dark side" of information technology use. *Communications of the Association for Information Systems*, 35(1), 109–118. DOI: 10.17705/1CAIS.03505

Dangaiso, P., & Mukucha, P. (2024). Evaluating the impact of service encounter incivility on employee job stress, turnover intentions and labor attrition: A study on frontline employees in the fast food service industry. *Cogent Business & Management*, 11(1), 2355671. DOI: 10.1080/23311975.2024.2355671

Danirmala, L., & Prajogo, W. (2022). The mediating role of green training to the influence of green organizational culture to green organizational citizenship behavior and green employee involvement. *IJHCM*, 6(1), 66–75.

Datta, D. K., Guthrie, J. P., & Wright, P. M. (2005). HRM and firm performance: The role of employee involvement and organizational commitment. *Industrial Relations Research Association*, 37(4), 315–335. DOI: 10.1177/0019793905046004002

Davenport, T. H., & Ronanki, R. (2018). Artificial intelligence for the real world. *Harvard Business Review*. https://hbr.org

Deane, P. (2021). Just why is it so hard to predict the future? RTE Brainstorm. https://www.rte.ie/brainstorm/2019/0715/1062197-just-why-is-it-sohard-to-predict-the-future/

Delaney, J. T., & Huselid, M. A. (1996). The impact of human resource management practices on perceptions of organizational performance. *Academy of Management Journal*, 39(4), 949–969. DOI: 10.2307/256718

Dijkkamp, J. (2019). *The recruiter of the future, a qualitative study in AI supported recruitment process* [Unpublished Master's thesis]. University of Twente.

Dingel, J. I., & Neiman, B. (2020). How many jobs can be done at home? *Journal of Public Economics*, 189, 104235. DOI: 10.1016/j.jpubeco.2020.104235 PMID: 32834177

Dittes, S., Richter, S., Richter, A., & Smolnik, S. (2019). Toward the workplace of the future: How organizations can facilitate digital work. *Business Horizons*, 62(5), 649–661. DOI: 10.1016/j.bushor.2019.05.004

Dixit, S., Sharma, N., Maurya, M., & Dharwal, M. (2022). AI power: Making recruitment smarter. In *Evolution of digitized societies through advanced technologies* (pp. 165–180). Springer Nature Singapore. DOI: 10.1007/978-981-19-2984-7_14

Donnelly, R., & Johns, J. (2021). Recontextualising remote working and its HRM in the digital economy: An integrated framework for theory and practice. *International Journal of Human Resource Management*, 32(1), 84–105. DOI: 10.1080/09585192.2020.1737834

Doz, Y., & Kosonen, M. (2008). The dynamics of strategic agility: Nokia's roller caster experience. *California Management Review*, 50(3), 95–118. DOI: 10.2307/41166447

Duan, Y., Edwards, J. S., & Dwivedi, Y. K. (2019). Artificial intelligence for decision making in the era of Big Data–evolution, challenges and research agenda. *International Journal of Information Management*, 48, 63–71. DOI: 10.1016/j.ijinfomgt.2019.01.021

Duarte, T. (2009). *A possibilidade da investigação a 3: reflexões sobre triangulação (metodológica)* (e-WORKING PAPER N. º 60/2009).

Dumont, J., Shen, J., & Deng, X. (2017). Effects of green HRM practices on employee workplace green behavior: The role of psychological green climate and employee green values. *Human Resource Management*, 56(4), 613–627. DOI: 10.1002/hrm.21792

Earley, P. C. (1993). East meets West meets Mideast: Further explorations of collectivistic and individualistic work groups. *Academy of Management Journal*, 36(2), 319–348. DOI: 10.2307/256525

Edison, H., Wang, X., & Conboy, K. (2021). Comparing methods for large-scale agile software development: A systematic literature review. *IEEE Transactions on Software Engineering*, 48(8), 2709–2731. DOI: 10.1109/TSE.2021.3069039

Edwards, J. R. (1996). An examination of competing versions of the person-environment fit approach to stress. *Academy of Management Journal*, 39(2), 292–339. DOI: 10.2307/256782

Edwards, J. R., & Cooper, C. L. (1990). The person-environment fit approach to stress: Recurring problems and some suggested solutions. *Journal of Organizational Behavior*, 11(4), 293–307. DOI: 10.1002/job.4030110405

Ehnert, I., & Harry, W. (2024). Advancements in HR practices and their implications for performance: A focus on emerging economies. *Journal of Human Resource Management*, 41(2), 174–193. DOI: 10.1080/09585192.2024.2226765

Eisenberger, R., Armeli, S., Rexwinkel, B., Lynch, P. D., & Rhoades, L. (2001). Recipients' perception of organizational support: Contributions to perceived organizational support and employee outcomes. *The Journal of Applied Psychology*, 86(1), 42–51. DOI: 10.1037/0021-9010.86.1.42 PMID: 11302232

Ellingrud, K., Gupta, R., & Salguero, J. (2020). Building the vital skills for the future of work in operations. McKinsey & Company. https://www.mckinsey.com/capabilities/operations/our-insights/building-the-vital-skills-forthe-future-of-work-in-operations

Engelsberger, A., Cavanagh, J., Bartram, T., & Halvorsen, B. (2023). Maximizing team development for open innovation in digital product development: The role of collaborative HRM and relational leadership. *Personnel Review*.

Ennen, E., & Richter, A. (2010). The role of HRM in organizational innovation: A review and research agenda. *Human Resource Management Review*, 20(4), 445–458.

Erez, M. (2010). Culture and job design. *Journal of Organizational Behavior*, 31(2-3), 389–400. DOI: 10.1002/job.651

Ergun, G. S., Bozkurt, H. O., Arslan, E., Kendir, H., & Yayla, O. (2023). Psychological capital as a moderator in the relationship between job insecurity, job stress, and hotel employees' turnover intention during the Russia-Ukraine war. *International Journal of Hospitality Management*, 111, 103475. DOI: 10.1016/j.ijhm.2023.103475

Ericksen, J. (2007). High-performance work systems in small firms: Impact and implications. *Small Business Economics*, 29(3), 185–199. DOI: 10.1007/s11187-006-9033-x

Eriksson, L., & Santesson, H. (2021). *Organizational Culture in a Remote Setting - A Qualitative Study on Organizational Culture and the Effects of Remote Work* [Master Dissertation, Uppsala University]. https://www.diva-portal.org/smash/get/diva2:1579041/FULLTEXT01.pdf

European Commission. (2020). *Ethics Guidelines for Trustworthy AI.* https://ec.europa.eu/digital-single-market/en/news/ethics-guidelines-trustworthy-ai

Fagerholm, F., Ikonen, M., Kettunen, P., Münch, J., Roto, V., & Abrahamsson, P. (2015). Performance Alignment Work: How software developers experience the continuous adaptation of team performance in Lean and Agile environments. *Information and Software Technology*, 64, 132–147. DOI: 10.1016/j.infsof.2015.01.010

Farnham, D. (2008). *Managing employment relations.* Routledge.

Fasbender, U., Burmeister, A., & Wang, M. (2023). Managing the risks and side effects of workplace friendships: The moderating role of workplace friendship self-efficacy. *Journal of Vocational Behavior*, 143, 103875. DOI: 10.1016/j.jvb.2023.103875

Fasbender, U., Van der Heijden, B. I., & Grimshaw, S. (2019). Job satisfaction, job stress and nurses' turnover intentions: The moderating roles of on-the-job and off-the-job embeddedness. *Journal of Advanced Nursing*, 75(2), 327–337. DOI: 10.1111/jan.13842 PMID: 30187541

Fayoumi, A., & Loucopoulos, P. (2023). Bridging the strategy execution gap of designing intelligent talent acquisition systems using enterprise modelling and simulation. *Enterprise Information Systems*, 17(6), 2005149. DOI: 10.1080/17517575.2021.2005149

Felstead, A., & Henseke, G. (2017). Assessing the growth of remote working and its consequences for effort, well-being and work-life balance. *New Technology, Work and Employment*, 32(3), 195–212. DOI: 10.1111/ntwe.12097

Feng, W., Tu, R., Lu, T., & Zhou, Z. (2019). Understanding forced adoption of self-service technology: The impacts of users' psychological reactance. *Behaviour & Information Technology*, 38(8), 820–832. DOI: 10.1080/0144929X.2018.1557745

Ferdman, B. M., & Deane, B. R. (Eds.). (2014). *Diversity at Work: The Practice of Inclusion*. John Wiley & Sons.

Ferreira, A., & Oliveira, M. (2012). Human resource management practices and organizational performance: The mediating role of organizational learning. *International Journal of Human Resource Management*, 23(16), 3415–3439.

Ferry, K. (2018, January 18). Korn Ferry Global Survey: Artificial intelligence (AI) reshaping the role of the recruiter. https://www.kornferry.com/about-us/press/korn-ferry-global-survey-artificial-intelligence-reshaping-the-role-of-the-recruiter

Fitzer, M. M. (1997). *Managing from afar: Performance and rewards in a telecommuting environment - ProQuest*. 65–73. https://www.proquest.com/docview/213677152/fulltextPDF/D46E45301DD84791PQ/1?accountid=177838&sourcetype=Trade%20Journals

Fock, H., Hui, M. K., Au, K., & Bond, M. H. (2013). Moderation effects of power distance on the relationship between types of empowerment and employee satisfaction. *Journal of Cross-Cultural Psychology*, 44(2), 281–298. DOI: 10.1177/0022022112443415

Ford, R. C., Piccolo, R. F., & Ford, L. R. (2021). Strategies for retaining employees in the post-COVID-19 workplace: The role of management and workplace flexibility. *Journal of Management*, 47(7), 1682–1700. DOI: 10.1177/01492063211013737

Fornell, C., & Larcker, D. F. (1981). Evaluating structural equation models with unobservable variables and measurement error. *JMR, Journal of Marketing Research*, 18(1), 39–50. DOI: 10.1177/002224378101800104

França, T. J. F., São Mamede, H., Barroso, J. M. P., & Dos Santos, V. M. P. D. (2023). Artificial intelligence applied to potential assessment and talent identification in an organisational context. *Heliyon*, 9(4). PMID: 37035361

Fujimoto, Y., & Hartel, C. E. J. (2017). Organizational diversity learning framework: Going beyond diversity training programs. *Personnel Review*, 46(6), 1120–1141. DOI: 10.1108/PR-09-2015-0254

Galanti, T., Guidetti, G., Mazzei, E., Zappalà, S., & Toscano, F. (2021). Work From Home During the COVID-19 Outbreak: The Impact on Employees' Remote Work Productivity, Engagement, and Stress. *Journal of Occupational and Environmental Medicine*, 63(7), e426–e432. DOI: 10.1097/JOM.0000000000002236 PMID: 33883531

Garavand, A., Jalali, S., Talebi, A. H., & Sabahi, A. (2022). Advantages and disadvantages of teleworking in healthcare institutions during COVID-19: A systematic review. *Informatics in Medicine Unlocked*, 34, 101119. DOI: 10.1016/j.imu.2022.101119 PMID: 36373130

Garavan, T., Ullah, I., O'Brien, F., Darcy, C., Wisetsri, W., Afshan, G., & Mughal, Y. H. (2023). Employee perceptions of individual green HRM practices and voluntary green work behaviour: A signalling theory perspective. *Asia Pacific Journal of Human Resources*, 61(1), 32–56. DOI: 10.1111/1744-7941.12342

Garg, N., Mahipalan, M., & Sharma, N. (2023). Does workplace toxicity influence turnover intentions among Indian healthcare employees? Investigating the moderating role of gratitude. *Journal of Health Organization and Management*, 37(2), 250–272. DOI: 10.1108/JHOM-08-2022-0233 PMID: 36733231

Garg, R., & Rani, S. (2023). Green HRM and organizational sustainability: The role of employee eco-innovation and green behaviors. *Journal of Cleaner Production*, 401, 136267. DOI: 10.1016/j.jclepro.2023.136267

Gartner. (2022). Future of Work. Gartner Human Resource Glossary. https:// www.gartner.com/en/human-resources/glossary/future-of-work

Geetha, R., & Bhanu, S. R. D. (2018). Recruitment through artificial intelligence: A conceptual study. *International Journal of Mechanical Engineering and Technology*, 9(7), 63–70.

Geisser, S. (1974). A predictive approach to the random effect model. *Biometrika*, 61(1), 101–107. DOI: 10.1093/biomet/61.1.101

Gelfand, M. J., Erez, M., & Aycan, Z. (2007). Cross-cultural organizational behavior. *Annual Review of Psychology*, 58(1), 479–514. DOI: 10.1146/annurev.psych.58.110405.085559 PMID: 17044797

Georgieff, A., & Hyee, R. (2022). Artificial intelligence and employment: New cross-country evidence. *Frontiers in Artificial Intelligence*, 5, 832736. DOI: 10.3389/frai.2022.832736 PMID: 35620279

Gerhart, B., & Fang, M. (2015). Pay and performance in the context of high-performance work systems. *Journal of Management*, 41(2), 533–566. DOI: 10.1177/0149206314562271

Ghosh, B., Daugherty, P. R., Wilson, H. J., & Burden, A. (2019). Taking a systems approach to adopting AI. *Harvard Business Review*.

Gim, G. C., Ooi, S. K., Teoh, S. T., Lim, H. L., & Yeap, J. A. (2022). Green human resource management, leader-member exchange, core self-evaluations and work engagement: The mediating role of human resource management performance attributions. *International Journal of Manpower*, 43(3), 682–700. DOI: 10.1108/IJM-05-2020-0255

Gittell, J. H., Von Nordenflycht, A., & Kochan, T. A. (2004). Mutual gains or zero sum? Labor relations and firm performance in the airline industry. *Industrial & Labor Relations Review*, 57(2), 163–180. DOI: 10.1177/001979390405700201

Godard, J. (2004). A critical assessment of the high-performance work systems framework. *Industrial Relations Research Association*, 37(4), 401–423. DOI: 10.1177/0019793905046004005

Golden, T., & Eddleston, K. (2020). 'Is there a price telecommuters pay? Examining the relationship between telecommuting and objective career success. *Journal of Vocational Behavior*, 116, 1–13. DOI: 10.1016/j.jvb.2019.103348

Gomide, P., Patricio, R., & Gancho, S. (2024). Human-Centered Design Approaches to Industry 4.0 Challenges: Directions for Future Research. *The International Journal of Design Management and Professional Practice*, 19(1), 1–34. DOI: 10.18848/2325-162X/CGP/v19i01/1-34

Goretszko, D., Pham, T. T., & Buhner, M. (2019). Exploratory factor analysis: Current use, methodological developments, and recommendations for good practice. *Current Psychology (New Brunswick, N.J.)*, 38(3), 1003–1025. DOI: 10.1007/s12144-018-00303-4

Gosnell, K. (2020, July 17). Commitments Good Employees Make While Working Remotely. *Forbs*. https://www.forbes.com/sites/forbescoachescouncil/2020/07/17/commitments-good-employees-make-while-working-remotely/?sh=3c3e08873c51

Government of Canada. (2019). *Directive on Automated Decision-Making*. https://www.canada.ca/en/treasury-board-secretariat/services/information-technology/directive-automated-decision-making.html

Government of Canada. (2023). *Annual Report on First Nations Employment in the Federal Public Service*. https://www.canada.ca

Government of Ontario. (2020). *AI and Data Analytics Ethics Guidelines*. https://www.ontario.ca/page/ai-and-data-analytics-ethics-guidelines

Grass, A., Backmann, J., & Hoegl, M. (2020). From empowerment dynamics to team adaptability: Exploring and conceptualizing the continuous agile team innovation process. *Journal of Product Innovation Management*, 37(4), 324–351. DOI: 10.1111/jpim.12525

Green, A., & Wright, P. (2024). The role of performance enhancement programs in improving employee productivity. *Human Resource Management Journal*, 34(1), 85–101. DOI: 10.1111/1748-8583.12312

Greenberg, J., & Baron, R. A. (2003). *Behavior in organizations*. Prentice Hall.

Gregory, P., Strode, D. E., Sharp, H., & Barroca, L. (2022). An onboarding model for integrating newcomers into agile project teams. *Information and Software Technology*, 143, 106792. DOI: 10.1016/j.infsof.2021.106792

Griep, Y., Vranjes, I., van Hooff, M. M. L., Beckers, D. G. J., & Geurts, S. A. E. (2021). Technology in the Workplace: Opportunities and Challenges. In Korunka, C. (Ed.), *Flexible Working Practices and Approaches*. Springer. DOI: 10.1007/978-3-030-74128-0_6

Grossman, K. W., & Schoolderman, A. (2022). *Candidate experience: How to improve talent acquisition to drive business performance*. Kogan Page Publishers.

Grzegorczyk, M., Mariniello, M., Nurski, L., & Schraepen, T. (2021). *Blending the physical and virtual: A hybrid model for the future of work*. http://hdl.handle.net/10419/251067

Gunn, J., Zwickert, K., & Hilyard, K. (2021). Reinventing performance management in the public sector. In *Handbook on performance management in the public sector* (pp. 1–18). Edward Elgar Publishing. DOI: 10.4337/9781789901207.00006

Gupta, A., & Sharma, N. (2023). Modern HR practices and their impact on IT industry performance: An empirical analysis. *Journal of Business Research*, 155, 405–415. DOI: 10.1016/j.jbusres.2023.04.016

Gupta, M., & Gupta, A. (2023). Enhancing employee green behavior through Green HRM practices: A study in the Indian manufacturing sector. *Sustainability*, 15(2), 502. DOI: 10.3390/su150200502

Gupta, S. K., & Gupta, S. (2018). Pollution prevention' is the key to drive sustainability: Preliminary findings from a tannery unit in India. *Management of Environmental Quality*, 29(3), 416–426.

Guthrie, J. P. (2001). High-involvement work practices, turnover, and productivity: Evidence from New Zealand. *Academy of Management Journal*, 44(1), 180–190. DOI: 10.2307/3069345

Hackman, J. R., & Oldham, G. R. (1975). Development of the job diagnostic survey. *The Journal of Applied Psychology*, 60(2), 159–170. DOI: 10.1037/h0076546

Hackman, J. R., & Oldham, G. R. (1976). Motivation through the design of work: Test of a theory. *Organizational Behavior and Human Performance*, 16(2), 250–279. DOI: 10.1016/0030-5073(76)90016-7

Haenlein, M., & Kaplan, A. (2019). A brief history of artificial intelligence: On the past, present, and future of artificial intelligence. *California Management Review*, 61(4), 5–14. DOI: 10.1177/0008125619864925

Hair, J. F., Black, W. C., Anderson, R. E., & Babin, B. J. (2018). *Multivariate data analysis* (8th ed.). Cengage Learning EMEA.

Hair, J. F., Matthews, L. M., Matthews, R. L., & Sarstedt, M. (2017). PLS-SEM or CB-SEM: Updated guidelines on which method to use. *International Journal of Multivariate Data Analysis*, 1(2), 107–123. DOI: 10.1504/IJMDA.2017.087624

Hair, J. F., Risher, J. J., Sarstedt, M., & Ringle, C. M. (2019). When to use and how to report the results of PLS-SEM. *European Business Review*, 31(1), 2–24. DOI: 10.1108/EBR-11-2018-0203

Hakim, A. L., Sudarmiatin, U., & Sutrisno, U. (2018). The Effect of Work Stress on Turnover Intention with Work Satisfaction and Commitment as Intervening Variable (Study at PT Infomedia Solusi Humanika in Malang). *European Journal of Business and Management*, 10(12), 85–94.

Hall, E. T. (1976). *Beyond culture*. Anchor.

Hameed, Z., Khan, I. U., Islam, T., Sheikh, Z., & Naeem, R. M. (2020). Do green HRM practices influence employees' environmental performance? *International Journal of Manpower*, 41(7), 1061–1079. DOI: 10.1108/IJM-08-2019-0407

Hammer, A., & Karmakar, S. (2021). Automation, AI and the future of work in India. *Employee Relations*, 43(6), 1327–1341. DOI: 10.1108/ER-12-2019-0452

Harris, K. J., Harris, R. B., Valle, M., Carlson, J., Carlson, D. S., Zivnuska, S., & Wiley, B. (2022). Technostress and the entitled employee: Impacts on work and family. *Information Technology & People*, 35(3), 1073–1095. DOI: 10.1108/ITP-07-2019-0348

Harrison, R., Patel, K., & Nguyen, T. (2023). Navigating risks in AI experimentation: Strategies for quality control and oversight. *Journal of AI Research*, 45(2), 123–135.

Harter, J. K., Schmidt, F. L., & Hayes, T. L. (2002). Business-unit-level relationship between employee satisfaction, employee engagement, and business outcomes: A meta-analysis. *The Journal of Applied Psychology*, 87(2), 268–279. DOI: 10.1037/0021-9010.87.2.268 PMID: 12002955

Harvey, M. (2001). *The role of HRM in managing organizational performance*. Pearson Education.

Hausknecht, J. P., & Holwerda, J. A. (2013). When does employee turnover matter? Dynamic member configurations, productive capacity, and collective performance. *Organization Science*, 24(1), 210–225. DOI: 10.1287/orsc.1110.0720

Hebles, M., Trincado-Munoz, F., & Ortega, K. (2022). Stress and turnover intentions within healthcare teams: The mediating role of psychological safety, and the moderating effect of COVID-19 worry and supervisor support. *Frontiers in Psychology*, 12, 758438. DOI: 10.3389/fpsyg.2021.758438 PMID: 35173646

Henseler, J., Ringle, C. M., & Sarstedt, M. (2015). A new criterion for assessing discriminant validity in variance-based structural equation modeling. *Journal of the Academy of Marketing Science*, 43(1), 115–135. DOI: 10.1007/s11747-014-0403-8

Henseler, J., Ringle, C. M., & Sarstedt, M. (2016). Testing measurement invariance of composites using partial least squares. *International Marketing Review*, 33(3), 405–431. DOI: 10.1108/IMR-09-2014-0304

Hermann, I., & Paris, C. M. (2020). Digital Nomadism: The nexus of remote working and travel mobility. *Information Technology & Tourism*, 22(3), 329–334. DOI: 10.1007/s40558-020-00188-w

Herring, C. (2009). Does diversity pay? Race, gender, and the business case for diversity. *American Sociological Review*, 74(2), 208–224. DOI: 10.1177/000312240907400203

He, Z., Huang, H., Choi, H., & Bilgihan, A. (2023). Building organizational resilience with digital transformation. *Journal of Service Management*, 34(1), 147–171. DOI: 10.1108/JOSM-06-2021-0216

Hibrida, A. R., & Sunarni, . (2023). The Future of Work: Navigating the Challenges and Opportunities of Automation, Gig Economy, and Skills Evolution in a Post-Pandemic World. *West Science Interdisciplinary Studies*, 1(08), 657–666. DOI: 10.58812/wsis.v1i08.186

Hmoud, B., & Laszlo, V. (2019). Will artificial intelligence take over human resources recruitment and selection. *Network Intelligence Studies*, 7(13), 21–30.

Hobfoll, S. E. (2001). The influence of culture, community, and the nested-self in the stress process: Advancing conservation of resources theory. *Applied Psychology*, 50(3), 337–421. DOI: 10.1111/1464-0597.00062

Hoboubi, N., Choobineh, A., Ghanavati, F. K., Keshavarzi, S., & Hosseini, A. A. (2017). The impact of job stress and job satisfaction on workforce productivity in an Iranian petrochemical industry. *Safety and Health at Work*, 8(1), 67–71. DOI: 10.1016/j.shaw.2016.07.002 PMID: 28344843

Hoendervanger, J. G., De Been, I., Van Yperen, N. W., Mobach, M. P., & Albers, C. J. (2016). Flexibility in use: Switching behavior and satisfaction in activity-based work environments. *Journal of Corporate Real Estate*, 18(1), 48–62. DOI: 10.1108/JCRE-10-2015-0033

Hofstede, G. (2001). *Culture's consequences: Comparing values, behaviors, institutions, and organizations across nations*. Sage Publications.

Holbeche, L. (2019). Designing sustainably agile and resilient organizations. *Systems Research and Behavioral Science*, 36(5), 668–677. DOI: 10.1002/sres.2624

Hooi, L. W., Liu, M. S., & Lin, J. J. (2022). Green human resource management and green organizational citizenship behavior: Do green culture and green values matter? *International Journal of Manpower*, 43(3), 763–785. DOI: 10.1108/ IJM-05-2020-0247

Hossain, M. D., Miah, M. J., & Khatun, R. (2011). The effects of high-performance work practices on organizational performance. *Asian Business & Management*, 10(2), 197–211. DOI: 10.1057/abm.2010.12

Howard, J. (2019). Artificial intelligence: Implications for the future of work. *American Journal of Industrial Medicine*, 62(11), 917–926. DOI: 10.1002/ajim.23037 PMID: 31436850

Howard, M. C. (2016). A review of exploratory factor analysis reliability and validity. *Measurement & Evaluation in Counseling & Development*, 49(4), 249–268. DOI: 10.1177/0748175616658005

Hulland, J. (1999). Use of partial least squares (PLS) in strategic management research: A review of four recent studies. *Strategic Management Journal, 20*(2), 195-204. https://doi.org/3E3.0.CO;2-7DOI: 10.1002/(SICI)1097-0266(199902)20:2%3C195::AID-SMJ13%

Hunkenschroer, A. L., & Luetge, C. (2022). Ethics of AI-enabled recruiting and selection: A review and research agenda. *Journal of Business Ethics*, 178(4), 977–1007. DOI: 10.1007/s10551-022-05049-6

Huselid, M. A. (1995). The impact of human resource management practices on turnover, productivity, and corporate financial performance. *Academy of Management Journal*, 38(3), 635–672. DOI: 10.2307/256741

Huselid, M. A., & Rau, D. (1997). The impact of human resource management practices on corporate financial performance. *Academy of Management Journal*, 40(3), 671–688.

Indigenous Works. (2023). *Inclusion Continuum: A roadmap for organizational engagement with Indigenous communities*. https://www.indigenousworks.ca

Izquierdo, I., Olea, J., & Abad, F. J. (2014). Exploratory factor analysis in validation studies: A guide to best practice. *Turkish Psychological Articles*, 17(1), 68–81. DOI: 10.5080/u11409

Jamal, M. T., Anwar, I., Khan, N. A., & Ahmad, G. (2024). How do teleworkers escape burnout? A moderated-mediation model of the job demands and turnover intention. *International Journal of Manpower*, 45(1), 169–199. DOI: 10.1108/IJM-12-2022-0628

Jamil, S., Zaman, S. I., Kayikci, Y., & Khan, S. A. (2023). The role of green recruitment on organizational sustainability performance: A study within the context of green human resource management. *Sustainability*, 15(21), 15567.

Jarrahi, M. H., Kenyon, S., Brown, A., Donahue, C., & Wicher, C. (2022). Artificial intelligence: A strategy to harness its power through organizational learning. *The Journal of Business Strategy*, 3, 456.

Jasim, W. T., & Altaee, A. H. (2023). The Effect of Green Training and Development on Sustainable Performance: An Analytical Research in the Ministry of Environment. *Journal of Economics and Administrative Sciences*, 29(138), 1–21.

Javed, H. A., Nawaz, S., & Javed, H. A. (2023). Synthesis of Success: Crafting Sustainable Performance through E-HRM Innovation, Organizational Agility, and Cultural Harmony in SMEs. *Pakistan Journal of Humanities and Social Sciences*, 11(3), 3379–3395. DOI: 10.52131/pjhss.2023.1103.0621

Jena, R. K. (2015). Technostress in ICT enabled collaborative learning environment: An empirical study among Indian academician. *Computers in Human Behavior*, 51, 1116–1123. DOI: 10.1016/j.chb.2015.03.020

Jöhnk, J., Weißert, M., & Wyrtki, K. (2021). Ready or not, AI comes—An interview study of organizational AI readiness factors. *Business & Information Systems Engineering*, 63(1), 5–20. DOI: 10.1007/s12599-020-00676-7

Johnson, R. D., Stone, D. L., & Lukaszewski, K. M. (2021). The benefits of eHRM and AI for talent acquisition. *Journal of Tourism Futures*, 7(1), 40–52. DOI: 10.1108/JTF-02-2020-0013

Jones, K. (2022, August 16). How ai is transforming the Talent Acquisition Process: TechTarget. HR software. https://www.techtarget.com/searchhrsoftware/tip/6-ways-AI-can-improve-the-talent-acquisition-process

Jones, A., & Brown, L. (2023). Adapting to AI: Opportunities and challenges for organizational adaptation. *Organizational Dynamics*, 52(4), 212–228.

Jones, K., & Nguyen, H. (2023). Community engagement and social impact: Enhancing diversity initiatives. *Journal of Business Ethics*, 155(4), 789–803. DOI: 10.1007/s10551-021-04877-9

Joo, B. K., & Park, S. (2010). Career satisfaction, organizational commitment, and turnover intention: The effects of goal orientation, organizational learning culture and developmental feedback. *Leadership and Organization Development Journal*, 31(6), 482–500. DOI: 10.1108/01437731011069999

Jooss, S., Collings, D. G., McMackin, J., & Dickmann, M. (2024). A skills-matching perspective on talent management: Developing strategic agility. *Human Resource Management*, 63(1), 141–157. DOI: 10.1002/hrm.22192

Joshi, S., & Gupta, R. (2021). Artificial intelligence in HRM: Transforming employee productivity and decision-making. *International Journal of Human Resource Management*, 32(5), 980–1001. DOI: 10.1080/09585192.2021.1886864

Kakar, A. S., Misron, A., Meyer, N., & Durrani, D. K. (2023). Job insecurity as a mediator between fearing COVID-19 and turnover intention: Empirical evidence during the COVID-19 pandemic. *International Journal of Educational Management*, 37(4), 752–767. DOI: 10.1108/IJEM-12-2022-0511

Kalev, A., Dobbin, F., & Kelly, E. (2006). Best practices or best guesses? Assessing the efficacy of corporate affirmative action and diversity policies. *American Sociological Review*, 71(4), 589–617. DOI: 10.1177/000312240607100404

Kang, S. C., & Snell, S. A. (2009). Intellectual capital architectures and ambidextrous learning: A framework for HR managers. *Journal of Human Resource Management*, 48(3), 597–617. DOI: 10.1002/hrm.20299

Kaplan, S. E., Wiley, J. W., & Maertz, C. P. (2018). The role of ERGs in fostering inclusivity: An empirical examination of ERG functions and their impact. *Human Resource Management*, 57(5), 1111–1123.

Kapoor, S., & Singh, V. (2023). Retention strategies in the IT workforce: A contemporary analysis. *Journal of Information Technology*, 38(3), 215–228. DOI: 10.1057/jit.2023.1

Karatepe, O. M., & Vatankhah, S. (2015). High-performance work practices, career satisfaction, and service recovery performance: A study of flight attendants. *Tourism Review*, 70(1), 56–71. DOI: 10.1108/TR-01-2014-0004

Kavitha, R., & Suresh, M. (2019, December). Agile practices in human resource management. In International Conference on Advances in Materials Research (pp. 713-721). Singapore: Springer Nature Singapore.

Kawakami, A., Sivaraman, V., Cheng, H. F., Stapleton, L., Cheng, Y., Qing, D., & Holstein, K. (2022, April). Improving human-AI partnerships in child welfare: understanding worker practices, challenges, and desires for algorithmic decision support. In *Proceedings of the 2022 CHI Conference on Human Factors in Computing Systems* (pp. 1-18). DOI: 10.1145/3491102.3517439

Kerth, N. L. (2013). *Project retrospectives: a handbook for team reviews*. Addison-Wesley.

Khawaja, K. F., Sarfraz, M., Rashid, M., & Rashid, M. (2022). How is COVID-19 pandemic causing employee withdrawal behavior in the hospitality industry? An empirical investigation. *Journal of Hospitality and Tourism Insights*, 5(3), 687–706. DOI: 10.1108/JHTI-01-2021-0002

Kim, B. J., & Kim, M. J. (2024). The influence of work overload on cybersecurity behavior: A moderated mediation model of psychological contract breach, burnout, and self-efficacy in AI learning such as ChatGPT. *Technology in Society*, 77, 102543. DOI: 10.1016/j.techsoc.2024.102543

Kim, P. T. (2022). Data-driven discrimination at work. *William and Mary Law Review*, 58(3), 857–936. https://scholarship.law.wm.edu/wmlr/vol58/iss3/5

Kirkman, B. L., Chen, G., Farh, J. L., Chen, Z. X., & Lowe, K. B. (2009). Individual power distance orientation and follower reactions to transformational leaders: A cross-level, cross-cultural examination. *Academy of Management Journal*, 52(4), 744–764. DOI: 10.5465/amj.2009.43669971

Kirkman, B. L., Lowe, K. B., & Gibson, C. B. (2006). A quarter century of culture's consequences: A review of empirical research incorporating Hofstede's cultural values framework. *Journal of International Business Studies*, 37(3), 285–320. DOI: 10.1057/palgrave.jibs.8400202

Kniffin, K. M., Narayanan, J., Anseel, F., Antonakis, J., Ashford, S. P., Bakker, A. B., Bamberger, P., Bapuji, H., Bhave, D. P., Choi, V. K., Creary, S. J., Demerouti, E., Flynn, F. J., Gelfand, M. J., Greer, L. L., Johns, G., Kesebir, S., Klein, P. G., Lee, S. Y., & Vugt, M. (2021). COVID-19 and the workplace: Implications, issues, and insights for future research and action. *The American Psychologist*, 76(1), 63–77. DOI: 10.1037/amp0000716 PMID: 32772537

Kolade, O., & Owoseni, A. (2022). Employment 5.0: The work of the future and the Future of Work. *Technology in Society*, 71, 102086. DOI: 10.1016/j.techsoc.2022.102086

Kossek, E. E., & Ollier-Malaterre, A. (2020). Desperately seeking sustainable flexibility: Identifying the core components of work-life policies. *Human Resource Management Review*, 30(4), 100–127.

Kranc, J. (2023, July 20). Hybrid work models continue to grow, study finds. *Benefits PRO*. https://www.proquest.com/abicomplete/docview/2840035890/AFE0D5984D9C4A69PQ/3?accountid=177838&sourcetype=Trade%20Journals#center

Kristof-Brown, A. L., Zimmerman, R. D., & Johnson, E. C. (2005). Consequences of individuals' fit at work: A meta-analysis OF person–job, person–organization, person–group, and person–supervisor fit. *Personnel Psychology*, 58(2), 281–342. DOI: 10.1111/j.1744-6570.2005.00672.x

Kumar, A., Krishnamoorthy, B., & Bhattacharyya, S. S. (2024). Machine learning and artificial intelligence-induced technostress in organizations: A study on automation-augmentation paradox with socio-technical systems as coping mechanisms. *The International Journal of Organizational Analysis*, 32(4), 681–701. DOI: 10.1108/IJOA-01-2023-3581

Laidoune, A., Zid, C., & Sahraoui, N. (2022). Innovate and overcome resistance to change to improve the resilience of systems and organizations. *Journal of the Knowledge Economy*, 13(4), 1–16. DOI: 10.1007/s13132-021-00840-8

Lakshmi, R. S., Sowdamini, T., & Biswas, A. K. (2020). The rise of artificial intelligence in talent acquisition. *Workforce, 3*.

Laussen, J., & Sutanovac, A. (2021). Evaluation of Agile Team Performance.

Lee, K. (2018). *AI superpowers: China, Silicon Valley, and the new world order*. Houghton Mifflin Harcourt.

Lee, D. (2024). High-performance work systems in the digital era: A study of the IT sector. *Journal of Management*, 50(2), 327–348. DOI: 10.1177/0149206321998524

Lepak, D. P., & Snell, S. A. (1999). The human resource architecture: Toward a theory of human capital allocation and development. *Academy of Management Review*, 24(1), 31–48. DOI: 10.2307/259035

Leung, K. (2005). How generalizable are justice effects across cultures? In Greenberg, J., & Colquitt, J. A. (Eds.), *Handbook of organizational justice* (pp. 555–586). Lawrence Erlbaum Associates.

Liang, H. L., Kao, R. H., & Lin, C. C. (2020). Job crafting and work engagement: The mediating role of person-job fit. *International Journal of Environmental Research and Public Health*, 17(5), 1761. DOI: 10.3390/ijerph17051761 PMID: 32182731

Liao, C., & Wang, Y. (2021). Green human resource management and environmental performance: The roles of employee eco-friendly behavior and innovation. *Journal of Cleaner Production*, 294, 126362. DOI: 10.1016/j.jclepro.2021.126362

Li, L., & Wang, X. (2021). Technostress inhibitors and creators and their impacts on university teachers' work performance in higher education. *Cognition Technology and Work*, 23(2), 315–330. DOI: 10.1007/s10111-020-00625-0

Lindsey, A. P., King, E. B., Membere, A., & Cheung, H. K. (2017). Two steps forward, one step back: The intricacies of promoting diversity through leader messaging. *Journal of Business Ethics*, 142(3), 499–513.

Lingras, K. A., Alexander, M. E., & Vrieze, D. M. (2021). Diversity, equity, and inclusion efforts at a departmental level: Building a committee as a vehicle for advancing progress. *Journal of Clinical Psychology in Medical Settings*, 1–24. PMID: 34529234

Liu, C., Spector, P. E., & Shi, L. (2007). Cross-national job stress: A quantitative and qualitative study. *Journal of Organizational Behavior*, 28(2), 209–239. DOI: 10.1002/job.435

Liu, J., & Meyer, J. P. (2023). Commitment to the organization and well-being: The mediating role of psychological empowerment. *Journal of Organizational Behavior*, 44(3), 443–462. DOI: 10.1002/job.2587

Liu, J., Zhu, B., Wu, J., & Mao, Y. (2019). Job satisfaction, work stress, and turnover intentions among rural health workers: A cross-sectional study in 11 western provinces of China. *BMC Family Practice*, 20(1), 1–11. DOI: 10.1186/s12875-019-0904-0 PMID: 30642261

Longoni, A., & Cagliano, R. (2018). Sustainable innovativeness and the triple bottom line: The role of organizational time perspective. *Journal of Business Ethics*, 151(4), 1097–1120. DOI: 10.1007/s10551-016-3239-y

Lucjan, K., Szostek, D., Balcerzak, A. P., & Rogalska, E. (2023). Relationships Between Leadership Style And Organizational Commitment: The Moderating Role Of The System Of Work. *Economics & Sociology (Ternopil)*, 16(4), 11–39. DOI: 10.14254/2071-789X.2023/16-4/1

Lu, J., Guo, S., Qu, J., Lin, W., & Lev, B. (2023). "Stay" or "Leave": Influence of employee-oriented social responsibility on the turnover intention of new-generation employees. *Journal of Business Research*, 161, 113814. DOI: 10.1016/j.jbusres.2023.113814

Luo, Y., Wang, Y., & Zhong, B. (2012). Effect of organizational justice on work engagement of employees. [Social Sciences Edition]. *Journal of Beijing University of Aeronautics and Astronautics*, 25(2), 50–55.

Luo, Y., & Zhu, Y. (2022). Green HRM and employee innovative behavior: The mediating role of green work climate. *Business Strategy and the Environment*, 31(4), 1456–1470. DOI: 10.1002/bse.3016

Lynn, T. (Ed.). (2023). *The Future of Work*. Palgrave Studies in Digital Business & Enabling Technologies. DOI: 10.1007/978-3-031-31494-0

Lynn, T., Rosati, P., Conway, E., Curran, D., Fox, G., & O'Gorman, C. (2022). *Digital towns: Accelerating and measuring the digital transformation of rural societies and economies*. Springer Nature. DOI: 10.1007/978-3-030-91247-5

MacDuffie, J. P. (1995). Human resource bundles and manufacturing performance: Organizational logic and flexible production systems in the world auto industry. *Industrial & Labor Relations Review*, 48(2), 197–221. DOI: 10.1177/001979399504800201

Makoff-Clark, A. (2019, January 23). *Is blind recruitment the secret to the perfect hire?*https://www.peoplemanagement.co.uk/article/1742220/blind-recruitment-secret-perfect-hire

Malik, M., Sarwar, S., & Orr, S. (2021). Agile practices and performance: Examining the role of psychological empowerment. *International Journal of Project Management*, 39(1), 10–20. DOI: 10.1016/j.ijproman.2020.09.002

Malik, N., Tripathi, S. N., Kar, A. K., & Gupta, S. (2021). Impact of artificial intelligence on employees working in industry 4.0 led organizations. *International Journal of Manpower*, 43(2), 334–354. DOI: 10.1108/IJM-03-2021-0173

Malone, T. W., Rus, D., & Laubacher, R. (2020). Artificial intelligence and the future of work. A report prepared by MIT Task Force on the work of the future. *Research Brief*, 17, 1–39.

Manoppo, V. P. (2020). Transformational leadership as a factor that decreases turnover intention: A mediation of work stress and organizational citizenship behavior. *The TQM Journal*, 32(6), 1395–1412. DOI: 10.1108/TQM-05-2020-0097

Mantovani, C. M. C. A. (2011). *Narrativas Da Mobilidade: Comunicação, Cultura E Produção Em Espaços Informacionais* [Doctoral Dissertation]. Universidade Federal de Minas Gerais.

Manyika, J. (2017). Technology, jobs, and the future of work. McKinsey Insights.

Manyika, J., Chui, M., Bughin, J., Dobbs, R., Bisson, P., & Marrs, A. (2017). *Artificial intelligence: The next digital frontier?* McKinsey Global Institute. https://www.mckinsey.com

Marchiori, D. M., Mainardes, E. W., & Rodrigues, R. G. (2019). Do Individual Characteristics Influence the Types of Technostress Reported by Workers? *International Journal of Human-Computer Interaction*, 35(3), 218–230. DOI: 10.1080/10447318.2018.1449713

Marder, B., Ferguson, P., Marchant, C., Brennan, M., Hedler, C., Rossi, M., Black, S., & Doig, R. (2021). 'Going agile': Exploring the use of project management tools in fostering psychological safety in group work within management discipline courses. *International Journal of Management Education*, 19(3), 100519. DOI: 10.1016/j.ijme.2021.100519

Margherita, A., Elia, G., & Klein, M. (2021). Managing the COVID-19 emergency: A coordination framework to enhance response practices and actions. *Technological Forecasting and Social Change*, 166, 120656. DOI: 10.1016/j.techfore.2021.120656 PMID: 33551496

Markus, H. R., & Kitayama, S. (1991). Culture and the self: Implications for cognition, emotion, and motivation. *Psychological Review*, 98(2), 224–253. DOI: 10.1037/0033-295X.98.2.224

Martin, C. L., & Nagao, D. H. (1989). Some effects of computerized interviewing on applicant response. *The Journal of Applied Psychology*, 74(1), 72–80. DOI: 10.1037/0021-9010.74.1.72

Martínez-Martínez, A., Cegarra-Navarro, J. G., Cobo, M. J., & de Valon, T. (2023). Impacts and implications for advancing in environmental knowledge in hospitality industry in COVID Society: A bibliometric analysis. *Journal of the Knowledge Economy*, 14(2), 2026–2053. DOI: 10.1007/s13132-022-00910-5

Martinez-Sanchez, A., & Vicente-Oliva, S. (2023). Supporting agile innovation and knowledge by managing human resource flexibility. *International Journal of Innovation Science*, 15(3), 558–578. DOI: 10.1108/IJIS-11-2021-0200

Masri, H. A., & Jaaron, A. A. M. (2017). Assessing green human resources management practices in Palestinian manufacturing context: An empirical study. *Journal of Cleaner Production*, 143, 474–489. DOI: 10.1016/j.jclepro.2016.12.087

McGovern, S. L., Aldrich, T., Myers, C., Desai, C., & Gera, M. (2018). The new age: artificial intelligence for human resource opportunities and functions. Retrieved from https://www.ey.com/Publication/vwLUAssets/EY-the-new- age-artificialintelligence-for-human-resource-opportunities- and -functions/$FILE/EY-the-new-ageartificial-intelligence-for-human-resource-opportunities- and -functions.pdf

McMackin, J., & Heffernan, M. (2021). Agile for HR: Fine in practice, but will it work in theory? *Human Resource Management Review*, 31(4), 100791. DOI: 10.1016/j.hrmr.2020.100791

McRae, E. R. (2024, January 25). *9 Trends that will shape work in 2024 and beyond*. Harvard Business Review. https://hbr.org/2024/01/9-trends-that-will-shape-work-in-2024-and-beyond

McRae, S. (2024). The future of work: Global trends and organizational strategies. *Journal of Management*, 30(1), 45–61.

Medina Angarita, M. A., & Nolte, A. (2020). What do we know about hackathon outcomes and how to support them? A systematic literature review. In *International Conference on Collaboration Technologies and Social Computing* (pp. 50-64). Springer. DOI: 10.1007/978-3-030-58157-2_4

Mehrotra, S., & Khanna, A. (2022). Recruitment through AI in selected Indian companies. *Metamorphosis*, 21(1), 31–39. DOI: 10.1177/09726225211066220

Meier, S. T., & Lambert, M. E. (1991). Psychometric properties and correlates of three computer aversion scales. *Behavior Research Methods, Instruments, & Computers*, 231(1), 9–15. DOI: 10.3758/BF03203329

Messersmith, J. G., & Guthrie, J. P. (2010). High-performance work systems in emergent organizations: Implications for firm performance. *Human Resource Management Review*, 20(4), 279–294. DOI: 10.1016/j.hrmr.2010.04.001

Meyer, J. P., & Allen, N. J. (2004). *TCM Employee Commitment Survey Academic Users Guide 2004*. The University of Western Ontario.

Meyer, J. P., Allen, N. J., & Smith, C. A. (1993). Commitment to Organizations and Occupations: Extension and Test of a Three-Component Conceptualization. *The Journal of Applied Psychology*, 78(4), 538–551. DOI: 10.1037/0021-9010.78.4.538

Mishra, R., Rodriguez, R., & Portillo, V. (2020). An ai based talent acquisition and benchmarking for job. *arXiv preprint arXiv:2009.09088*.

Mızrak, F. (2024). Effective change management strategies: Exploring dynamic models for organizational transformation. In *Perspectives on artificial intelligence in times of turbulence: Theoretical background to applications* (pp. 135–162). IGI Global.

Mobley, W. H., Horner, S. O., & Hollingsworth, A. T. (1978). An evaluation of precursors of hospital employee turnover. *The Journal of Applied Psychology*, 63(4), 408–414. DOI: 10.1037/0021-9010.63.4.408 PMID: 701211

Moglia, M., Hopkins, J., & Bardoel, A. (2021). Telework, Hybrid Work and the United Nation's Sustainable Development Goals: Towards Policy Coherence. *Sustainability, 13*(16), 9222. DOI: 10.3390/su13169222

Moh'd, S., Gregory, P., Barroca, L., & Sharp, H. (2023). Agile human resource management: A systematic mapping study. German Journal of Human Resource Management.

Moloto, M., Harmse, A., & Zuva, T. (2020). Impact of agile methodology use on project success in organizations systematic literature review. *Proceedings of the Computational Methods in Systems and Software*, 267-280. DOI: 10.1007/978-3-030-63322-6_21

Mor Barak, M. E. (2016). *Managing Diversity: Toward a Globally Inclusive Workplace*. Sage Publications.

Moradeke, F. T., Ishola, G. K., & Okikiola, O. L. (2021). Green training and development practices on environmental sustainability: Evidence from WAMCO PLC. *Journal of Educational Management and Social Sciences*, 2(1), 1–19.

Morandini, S., Fraboni, F., De Angelis, M., Puzzo, G., Giusino, D., & Pietrantoni, L. (2023). The impact of artificial intelligence on workers' skills: Upskilling and reskilling in organizations. Informing Science. *The International Journal of an Emerging Transdiscipline*, 26, 39–68. DOI: 10.28945/5078

Mowday, R. T., Porter, L. W., & Steers, R. M. (2013). *Employee—organization linkages: The psychology of commitment, absenteeism, and turnover*. Academic Press.

Mtembu, V. S., & Mishi, S. (2022). Green HRM and employee environmental behaviors: The mediating role of organizational commitment and green human capital. *Sustainability*, 14(5), 2771. DOI: 10.3390/su14052771

Naqshbandi, M. M., Kabir, I., Ishak, N. A., & Islam, M. Z. (2024). The future of work: Work engagement and job performance in the hybrid workplace. *The Learning Organization*, 31(1), 5–26. DOI: 10.1108/TLO-08-2022-0097

Narahari, C. L., & Koneru, D. K. (2017). A study on the role of occupational stress in organizations. *International Journal of Engineering Technology. Management and Applied Sciences*, 5(1), 53–59.

Nargis, L., Brastoro, B., & Fuad, M. (2024). Agile HR: Adapting Human Resource Practices to Rapid Business Changes. *Journal of Economic, Business, and Accounting*, 7(4), 7396–7401. DOI: 10.31539/costing.v7i4.10330

Nascimento, L., Correia, M. F., & Califf, C. B. (2024). Towards a bright side of technostress in higher education teachers: Identifying several antecedents and outcomes of techno-eustress. *Technology in Society*, 76, 102428. DOI: 10.1016/j.techsoc.2023.102428

Nijssen, M., & Paauwe, J. (2012). HRM in turbulent times: How to achieve organizational agility? *International Journal of Human Resource Management*, 23(16), 3315–3335. DOI: 10.1080/09585192.2012.689160

Nishii, L. H. (2013). The benefits of climate for inclusion for gender-diverse groups. *Academy of Management Journal*, 56(6), 1754–1774. DOI: 10.5465/amj.2009.0823

Noblet, A., Rodwell, J., & Allisey, A. (2009). Job stress in the law enforcement sector: Comparing the linear, non-linear and interaction effects of working conditions. *Stress and Health*, 25(1), 111–120. DOI: 10.1002/smi.1227

Ofei, A. M. A., Poku, C. A., Paarima, Y., Barnes, T., & Kwashie, A. A. (2023). Toxic leadership behavior of nurse managers and turnover intentions: The mediating role of job satisfaction. *BMC Nursing*, 22(1), 374. DOI: 10.1186/s12912-023-01539-8 PMID: 37817145

Ojo, A. O., Tan, C. N. L., & Alias, M. (2022). Linking green HRM practices to environmental performance through pro-environment behaviour in the information technology sector. *Social Responsibility Journal*, 18(1), 1–18. DOI: 10.1108/SRJ-12-2019-0403

Oliveira, A., Assumpcao, H., Queiroz, J., Piardi, L., Parra, J., & Leitao, P. (2022). Hands-on learning modules for upskilling in industry 4.0 technologies. Paper presented at the 2022 IEEE 5th International Conference on Industrial Cyber-Physical Systems, ICPS 2022. DOI: 10.1109/ICPS51978.2022.9816909

Olson, M. H. (1983). Remote Office Work. *Changing Work Patterns In Space And Time.*, 26(3), 182–187.

Ore, O., & Sposato, M. (2022). Opportunities and risks of artificial intelligence in recruitment and selection. *The International Journal of Organizational Analysis*, 30(6), 1771–1782. DOI: 10.1108/IJOA-07-2020-2291

Osoian, C., & Petre, A. (2022). Employee Engagement and Job Burnout in the Context of Teleworking. *Studia Universitatis Babes-Bolyai Oeconomica*, 67(3), 14–26. DOI: 10.2478/subboec-2022-0012

Ostroff, C., & Bowen, D. E. (2000). Moving HR to a higher level: HR practices and organizational effectiveness. In Klein, K. J., & Kozlowski, S. W. (Eds.), *Multilevel theory, research, and methods in organizations: Foundations, extensions, and new directions* (pp. 211–266). Jossey-Bass.

Oswal, N., Siddiqui, S., & Sharma, M. S. (2023). Diversity, equity, and inclusion in the workplace: Assessing the impact on organizational performance. *Boletin de Literatura Oral-The Literary Journal*, 10(1), 2931–2941.

Paauwe, J., & Boselie, P. (2003). Challenging 'strategic HRM' and the relevance of the institutional setting. *Human Resource Management Journal*, 13(3), 56–70. DOI: 10.1111/j.1748-8583.2003.tb00098.x

Palhad, Onwubu, Singh, Thakur, Thakur, & Mkhize. (2023). The Benefits and Challenges of the Gig Economy: Perspective of Gig Workers and Small Medium and Micro Enterprises (SMMEs) in South Africa. African Journal of Inter/Multidisciplinary Studies, 5(1), 1–12.

Paluck, E. L., & Green, D. P. (2009). Prejudice reduction: What works? A review and assessment of research and practice. *Annual Review of Psychology*, 60(1), 339–367. DOI: 10.1146/annurev.psych.60.110707.163607 PMID: 18851685

Panda, D. K. (2023). The green identity and green strategy: An interplay. *Technology Analysis and Strategic Management*, 35(11), 1437–1452.

Parajuli, S. K. (2023). Remote and Flexible work: A Systematic Review. *Nepal Journal of Multidisciplinary Research*, 6(2), 131–144. DOI: 10.3126/njmr.v6i2.57656

Park, S., & Cho, Y. J. (2020). Does telework status affect the behavior and perception of supervisors? Examining task behavior and perception in the telework context. *The International Journal Of Human Resource Management*. https://sci-hub.se/10.1080/09585192.2020.1777183

Paschen, J., Wilson, M., & Ferreira, J. J. (2020). Collaborative intelligence: How human and artificial intelligence create value along the B2B sales funnel. *Business Horizons*, 63(3), 403–414. DOI: 10.1016/j.bushor.2020.01.003

Pass, S., & Ridgway, M. (2022). An informed discussion on the impact of COVID-19 and 'enforced' remote working on employee engagement. *Human Resource Development International*, 25(2), 254–270. DOI: 10.1080/13678868.2022.2048605

Pereira, V., Hadjielias, E., Christofi, M., & Vrontis, D. (2023). A systematic literature review on the impact of artificial intelligence on workplace outcomes: A multi-process perspective. *Human Resource Management Review*, 33(1), 100857. DOI: 10.1016/j.hrmr.2021.100857

Peters, P., Ligthart, P. E. M., Bardoel, A., & Poutsma, E. (2016). 'Fit' for telework'? Cross-cultural variance and task-control explanations in organizations' formal telework practices. *International Journal of Human Resource Management*, 27(21), 2582–2603. DOI: 10.1080/09585192.2016.1232294

Pfeffer, J. (1994). *Competitive advantage through people: Unleashing the power of the workforce*. Harvard Business Press. DOI: 10.2307/41165742

Pfeffer, J., & Veiga, J. F. (1999). Putting people first for organizational success. *The Academy of Management Perspectives*, 13(2), 37–48. DOI: 10.5465/ame.1999.1899547

Phenom. (2023, July 5). *Transforming Mastercard's talent acquisition | Case study*. Phenom. https://www.phenom.com/resource/transforming-mastercard-talent-acquisition?utm_source=vktr.com

Pillai, R., & Sivathanu, B. (2020). Adoption of artificial intelligence (AI) for talent acquisition in IT/ITeS organizations. *Benchmarking*, 27(9), 2599–2629. DOI: 10.1108/BIJ-04-2020-0186

Platts, K., Breckon, J., & Marshall, E. (2022). Enforced home-working under lockdown and its impact on employee wellbeing: A cross-sectional study. *BMC Public Health*, 22(1), 199. DOI: 10.1186/s12889-022-12630-1 PMID: 35093054

Poba-Nzaou, P., Galani, M., Uwizeyemungu, S., & Ceric, A. (2021). The impacts of artificial intelligence (AI) on jobs: An industry perspective. *Strategic HR Review*, 20(2), 60–65. DOI: 10.1108/SHR-01-2021-0003

Podger, O. M. (2023). Unleashing Community Empowerment through A New Regional Autonomy Concept in the 2024 Elections. *Journal of Interdisciplinary Socio-Economic and Community Study*, 3(1), 1–11. DOI: 10.21776/jiscos.03.1.01

Pohler, D., & Schmidt, J. A. (2016). Does pay-for-performance strain the employment relationship? The effect of manager bonus eligibility on nonmanagement employee turnover. *Personnel Psychology*, 69(2), 395–429. DOI: 10.1111/peps.12106

Popoola, O. A., Adama, H. E., Okeke, C. D., & Akinoso, A. E. (2024). Conceptualizing agile development in digital transformations: Theoretical foundations and practical applications. *Engineering Science & Technology Journal*, 5(4), 1524–1541. DOI: 10.51594/estj.v5i4.1080

Popovici, V., & Popovici, A.-L. (2020). Remote Work Revolution: Current Opportunities and Challenges for Organizations. *"Ovidius" University Annals, Economic Sciences Series, 20*(1).

Prasad, K., Rao Mangipudi, M., Muralidhar, B., & Vaidya, R. W. (2020). Organizational Climate, Opportunities, Challenges And Psychological Wellbeing Of The Remote Working Employees During Covid-19 Pandemic: A General Linear Model Approach With Reference To Information Technology Industry In Hyderabad. *International Journal of Advanced Research in Engineering and Technology*, 11(4), 372–389. http://www.iaeme.com/IJARET/index.asp372Availableonlineathttp://www.iaeme.com/IJARET/issues.asp?JType=IJARET&VType=11&IType=4http://www.iaeme.com/IJARET/index.asp373http://www.iaeme.com/IJARET/issues.asp?JType=IJARET&VType=11&IType=4

Price, J. L., & Mueller, C. W. (1986). *Handbook of organizational measurement*. Pitman Publishing Inc.

Purcell, J. (2004). *Strategy and human resource management*. Palgrave Macmillan.

Putta, A., Paasivaara, M., & Lassenius, C. (2018). Benefits and challenges of adopting the scaled agile framework (SAFe): preliminary results from a multivocal literature review. *Product-Focused Software Process Improvement: 19th International Conference, PROFES 2018, Wolfsburg, Germany, November 28–30, 2018Proceedings*, 19, 334–351.

Rademaker, M. E., Schuberth, F., & Dijkstra, T. K. (2019). Measurement error correlation within blocks of indicators in consistent partial least squares: Issues and remedies. *Internet Research*, 29(3), 448–463. DOI: 10.1108/IntR-12-2017-0525

Raghavan, M., Barocas, S., Kleinberg, J., & Levy, K. (2020). Mitigating bias in algorithmic hiring: Evaluating claims and practices. In *Proceedings of the 2020 Conference on Fairness, Accountability, and Transparency* (pp. 469-481). https://doi.org/DOI: 10.1145/3351095.3372828

Ragu-Nathan, T. S., Tarafdar, M., Ragu-Nathan, B. S., & Tu, Q. (2008). The consequences of technostress for end users in organizations: Conceptual development and empirical validation. *Information Systems Research*, 19(4), 417–433. DOI: 10.1287/isre.1070.0165

Raji, I. D., & Buolamwini, J. (2019). Actionable auditing: Investigating the impact of publicly naming biased performance results of commercial AI products. *Proceedings of the 2019 AAAI/ACM Conference on AI, Ethics, and Society*, 429-435. https://doi.org/DOI: 10.1145/3306618.3314244

Ramaswamy, K. V. (2018). Technological change, automation and employment: A short review of theory and evidence. *International Review of Business and Economics*, 2(2), 1–27. DOI: 10.56902/IRBE.2018.2.2.1

Ramsay, H., Scholarios, D., & Harley, B. (2000). Employees and high-performance work systems: Testing inside the black box. *British Journal of Industrial Relations*, 38(4), 501–531. DOI: 10.1111/1467-8543.00178

Randel, A. E., Dean, M. A., Ehrhart, K. H., Chung, B. G., Shore, L. M., & Singh, G. (2018). Leader inclusiveness, psychological diversity climate, and helping behaviors. *The Journal of Applied Psychology*, 103(7), 793–806.

Rangrez, S. N., Amin, F., & Dixit, S. (2022). Influence of role stressors and job insecurity on turnover intentions in start-ups: Mediating role of job stress. *Management and Labour Studies*, 47(2), 199–215. DOI: 10.1177/0258042X221074757

Rao, P. S., & Pradhan, N. (2021). An integrated model of airline employee motivation: A comparative study of full-service and low-cost carriers in India. *Journal of Air Transport Management*, 91, 101997. DOI: 10.1016/j.jairtraman.2020.101997

Raviprolu, A. (2017). Role of artificial intelligence in recruitment [International journal] of Engineering Technology. *Management and Applied Sciences, 5*(4).

Reis, D. A., Fleury, A. L., & Carvalho, M. M. (2021). Consolidating core entrepreneurial competencies: Toward a meta-competence framework. *International Journal of Entrepreneurial Behaviour & Research*, 27(1), 179–204. DOI: 10.1108/IJEBR-02-2020-0079

Ren, S., Tang, G., & Jackson, S. E. (2020). Effects of Green HRM and CEO ethical leadership on organizations' environmental performance. *International Journal of Manpower*, 42(6), 961–983. DOI: 10.1108/IJM-09-2019-0414

Ren, S., Zhang, L., & Weng, X. (2021). The impact of Green HRM on employees' pro-environmental behavior and innovation performance: A dual-process model. *Sustainability*, 13(22), 12345. DOI: 10.3390/su132212345

Revutska, O., & Maršíková, K. (2021). Agile approach in human resource management: Focus on Generation Y.

Rigdon, E. E. (2012). Rethinking partial least squares path modeling: In praise of simple methods. *Long Range Planning*, 45(5/6), 341–358. DOI: 10.1016/j.lrp.2012.09.010

Rindu, R., Lukman, S., Hardisman, H., Hafizurrachman, M., & Bachtiar, A. (2020). The relationship among transformational leadership, organizational commitment, work stress, and turnover intentions of nurse at private hospital in Indonesia. *Open Access Macedonian Journal of Medical Sciences, 8*(E), 551–557.

Ritchie, D. (2023, July 11). *Pros and Cons of Remote Work: Embracing a Flexible Future*. https://www.calendar.com/blog/pros-and-cons-of-remote-work-embracing-a-flexible-future/

Rivera, M. (2022, March 30). For leaders who mess up on DEI: A case study - the startup - medium. *Medium*. https://medium.com/swlh/for-leaders-who-mess-up-on-dei-a-case-study-efaf856aaa61

Roberson, Q. M. (2006). Disentangling the meanings of diversity and inclusion in organizations. *Group & Organization Management*, 31(2), 212–236. DOI: 10.1177/1059601104273064

Roberson, Q. M., King, E. B., & Hebl, M. R. (2020). Designing more effective practices for reducing workplace inequality. *Social Issues and Policy Review*, 14(1), 226–257. DOI: 10.1111/sipr.12065

Roberson, Q. M., Ryan, A. M., & Ragins, B. R. (2017). The evolution and future of diversity at work. *The Journal of Applied Psychology*, 102(3), 711–716. DOI: 10.1037/apl0000161 PMID: 28125255

Romeria, A. (2021). 79% dos profissionais afirma que o teletrabalho melhora a sua produtividade. *O Jornal Económico*. https://jornaleconomico.pt/noticias/79-dos-profissionais-afirma-que-o-teletrabalho-melhora-a-sua-produtividade-792574/

Russell, S., & Norvig, P. (2020). *Artificial Intelligence: A Modern Approach* (4th ed.). Pearson.

Sabat, I. E., Lindsey, A. P., & King, E. B. (2020). The future of diversity at work: Inclusion and equity. *Industrial and Organizational Psychology: Perspectives on Science and Practice*, 13(4), 473–491.

Sabat, I. E., Lindsey, A. P., King, E. B., & Ahmad, A. (2020). The good, the bad, and the ugly: Impact of diversity training on attitudes and practices towards LGBTQ employees. *Group & Organization Management*, 45(1), 15–38. DOI: 10.1177/1059601119827229

Saeed, B. B., Afsar, B., Hafeez, S., Khan, I., Tahir, M., & Afridi, M. A. (2019). Promoting employee's proenvironmental behavior through green human resource management practices. *Corporate Social Responsibility and Environmental Management*, 26(2), 424–438.

Safa, M., Weeks, K., Stromberg, R., & Azam, A. A. (2018). Strategic port human resource talent acquisition and training: challenges and opportunities. In Advances in Human Factors, Business Management, and Leadership: Proceedings of the AHFE 2017 International Conferences on Human Factors in Management and Leadership, and Business Management and Society, July 17– 21, 2017, The Westin Bonaventure Hotel, Los Angeles, California, USA 8 (pp. 205-215). Springer International Publishing. DOI: 10.1007/978-3-319-60372-8_20

Sahut, J. M., & Lissillour, R. (2023). The adoption of remote work platforms after the Covid-19 lockdown: New approach, new evidence. *Journal of Business Research*, 154, 113345. DOI: 10.1016/j.jbusres.2022.113345 PMID: 36193197

Sailer, M., & Homner, L. (2020). The gamification of learning: A meta-analysis. *Educational Psychology Review*, 32(1), 77–112. DOI: 10.1007/s10648-019-09498-w

Santana, M., & Cobo, M. J. (2020). What is the future of work? A science mapping analysis. *European Management Journal*, 38(6), 846–862. DOI: 10.1016/j.emj.2020.04.010

Santos, V., Goldman, A., & De Souza, C. R. (2015). Fostering effective inter-team knowledge sharing in agile software development. *Empirical Software Engineering*, 20(4), 1006–1051. DOI: 10.1007/s10664-014-9307-y

Saruchera, F. (2022). Effective agile project leadership through competency-based self-reflection. In *Contemporary Challenges for Agile Project Management* (pp. 89–110). IGI Global. DOI: 10.4018/978-1-7998-7872-8.ch006

Schaufeli, W. B., & Bakker, A. B. (2004). Job demands, job resources, and their relationship with burnout and engagement: A multi-sample study. *Journal of Organizational Behavior J. Organiz.Journal of Organizational Behavior*, 25(3), 293–315. DOI: 10.1002/job.248

Schaufeli, W. B., Bakker, A. B., & Salanova, M. (2006). The measurement of work engagement with a short questionnaire: A cross-national study. *Educational and Psychological Measurement*, 66(4), 701–716. DOI: 10.1177/0013164405282471

Schaufeli, W., & Bakker, A. (2004). *UWES Utrecht Work Engagement Scale Preliminary Manual*. Occupational Healt Psycology Unit Utrecht University.

Schmitt, N., Gilliland, S. W., Landis, R. S., & Devine, D. (1993). Computer-based testing applied to selection of secretarial applicants. *Personnel Psychology*, 46(1), 149–165. DOI: 10.1111/j.1744-6570.1993.tb00871.x

Schuler, R. S., & Jackson, S. E. (1987). Linking competitive strategies with human resource management practices. *The Academy of Management Executive*, 1(3), 207–219.

Schwab, K. (2017). *The fourth industrial revolution*. Crown Business.

Schwartz, J., Hatfeld, S., Jones, R., & Anderson, S. (2019). *What is the future of work? Redefining work, workforces, and workplaces*. Deloitte.

Shah, N., & Soomro, B. A. (2023). Effects of green human resource management practices on green innovation and behavior. *Management Decision*, 61(1), 290–312. DOI: 10.1108/MD-07-2021-0869

Shahzad, M. A., Jianguo, D., & Junaid, M. (2023). Impact of green HRM practices on sustainable performance: Mediating role of green innovation, green culture, and green employees' behavior. *Environmental Science and Pollution Research International*, 30(38), 88524–88547. DOI: 10.1007/s11356-023-28498-6 PMID: 37438507

Sharma, I., & Tiwari, V. (2023). Modeling the impact of techno-stress and burnout on employees' work-life balance and turnover intention: A job demands-resources theory perspective. *Global Business and Organizational Excellence*, 43(1), 121–134. DOI: 10.1002/joe.22206

Sharma, K., & Tiwari, R. (2021). Green HRM: Conceptualization and current research trends. *International Journal of Productivity and Performance Management*, 70(6), 1305–1327. DOI: 10.1108/IJPPM-12-2019-0603

Shukla, A., & Srivastava, R. (2016). Development of short questionnaire to measure an extended set of role expectation conflict, coworker support and work-life balance: The new job stress scale. *Cogent Business & Management, 3*(1), 1-19.

Siddiqi, K. O. (2024). Impact of technostress and work-family conflict on turnover intention among nurses in Bangladesh: A moderation effect of perceived supervisor support. *Journal of Computational Social Science*, 1–24. DOI: 10.1007/s42001-024-00296-1

Silva, B. R. R. (2021). *Implicações do trabalho remoto na função de RH: um estudo exploratório em empresas portuguesas* [Master Dissertation]. Instituto Superior de Contabilidade e Administração.

Singh, S. (2024). The Future of Work: Exploring the Future of Work in Canada and How Human Connections Are Made Through Workplace Design.

Singh, A., Jha, S., Srivastava, D. K., & Somarajan, A. (2022). Future of work: A systematic literature review and evolution of themes. *Foresight*, 24(1), 99–125. DOI: 10.1108/FS-09-2020-0093

Singh, S. K., Del Giudice, M., Chierici, R., & Graziano, D. (2020). Green innovation and environmental performance: The role of green transformational leadership and green human resource management. *Technological Forecasting and Social Change*, 150, 119762.

Singh, S. K., Gupta, S., Busso, D., & Kamboj, S. (2019). Top management knowledge value, knowledge sharing practices, open innovation, and organizational performance. *Journal of Business Research*, 128, 788–798. DOI: 10.1016/j.jbusres.2019.04.040

Singh, S., & Kumar, R. (2023). Green HRM and green innovation: Exploring the mediating role of employee green behavior. *International Journal of Environmental Research and Public Health*, 20(1), 12. DOI: 10.3390/ijerph20010012 PMID: 38276800

Smith, E., & Johnson, M. (2023). Advancements in AI and diversity: Implications for HRM. *Human Resource Management Review*, 33(2), 264–278. DOI: 10.1016/j.hrmr.2022.100885

Smith, J., & Johnson, M. (2022). Addressing the rising costs of work: Strategies for organizational sustainability. *Journal of Business Economics*, 78(3), 211–225.

Smith, R., & Lee, K. (2023). Advancing diversity and inclusion: Strategies for enhancing workplace cohesion. *The Journal of Applied Behavioral Science*, 59(2), 176–190.

Sobaih, A. E. E., Hasanein, A., & Elshaer, I. (2020). Influences of green human resources management on environmental performance in small lodging enterprises: The role of green innovation. *Sustainability*, 12(24), 10371.

Society for Human Resource Management (SHRM). (2022). What is meant by "the future of work"? https://www.shrm.org/resourcesandtools/tools-andsamples/hr-qa/pages/what-is-meant-by-the-future-of-work.aspx

Solihin, M. B., & Sagala, E. J. (2020). Pengaruh Work Engagement Dan Komitmen Organisasi Terhadap Tingkat Turnover Intention Karyawan Di Pt Telkom Akses Balikpapan. *EProceedings of Management*, 7(2), 5635–5643.

Somers, M. J. (2009). The combined influence of affective, continuance and normative commitment on employee withdrawal. *Journal of Vocational Behavior*, 74(1), 75–81. DOI: 10.1016/j.jvb.2008.10.006

Song, W., Yu, H., & Xu, H. (2021). Effects of green human resource management and managerial environmental concern on green innovation. *European Journal of Innovation Management*, 24(3), 951–967. DOI: 10.1108/EJIM-11-2019-0315

Sopiah, S., Wilujeng, I. P., Murdiono, A., & Sangadji, E. M. (2020, July). The Role of Perceived Teaching Quality as Mediator Variable That Affects Student Satisfaction. In *International Conference on Learning Innovation 2019 (ICLI 2019)* (pp. 37-48). Atlantis Press. DOI: 10.2991/assehr.k.200711.008

Souza, L. F. F., & Bittencourt-Kohn, C. (2018). Job redesign in the airline industry: A qualitative study. *Journal of Air Transport Management*, 72, 25–33.

Spar, B., Pletenyuk, I., Reilly, K., & Ignatova, M. (2018). Global recruiting trends. *LinkedIn website, 2018* [Rep.]. https://news.linkedin.com/2018/1/global-recruiting-trends-2018

Sparrow, P., & Cooper, C. (2022). *Managing employee performance and reward: Concepts, practices, strategies*. Routledge.

Srđana, T., & Jasmina, P. (2023). The Influence Of Cultural And Personal Properties On Job Performances And Organizational Commitment In Teleworkers. *South East European Journal of Economics and Business, 18*(2). DOI: 10.2478/jeb-2023-0015

Srivastava, S., Khan, M., Kumari, A., & Jain, A. K. (2024). A study of workplace bullying and coping strategies in hospitality sector: Role of moral injury and inclusive leadership. *Journal of Organizational Effectiveness: People and Performance*, 11(1), 18–34. DOI: 10.1108/JOEPP-03-2023-0069

Stahl, G. K., & Björkman, I. (2006). *International human resource management: A European perspective*. Routledge.

Stander, F., Rothmann, S., Popov, V., & Sun, L. (2022). A framework for digital talent assessment: Guidelines and applications. *Journal of Psychology in Africa*, 32(5), 1–6. DOI: 10.1080/14330237.2022.2075543

Statistics Canada. (2023). *Age distribution in the Canadian workforce*. https://www.statcan.gc.ca

Stoepfgeshoff, S. (2018). The Future of Work: Work for the future. ISM Journal of International Business, 2(2).

Stone, M. (1974). Cross-validatory choice and assessment of statistical predictions. *Journal of the Royal Statistical Society. Series B, Statistical Methodology*, 36(2), 111–133. DOI: 10.1111/j.2517-6161.1974.tb00994.x

Straits Interactive & Rackspace Technology. (2023). *Rackspace Technology*. https://www.rackspace.com/en-ca/case-studies/straits-interactive

Straus, S. G., Miles, J. A., & Levesque, L. L. (2001). The effects of videoconference, telephone, and face-to-face media on interviewer and applicant judgments in employment interviews. *Journal of Management*, 27(3), 363–381. DOI: 10.1177/014920630102700308

Subramanian, N., & Suresh, M. (2022). Assessment framework for agile HRM practices. Global Journal of Flexible Systems Management, 23(1), 135-149.

Suen, H.-Y., Chen, M. Y.-C., & Lu, S.-H. (2019). Does the use of synchrony and artificial intelligence in video interviews affect interview ratings and applicant attitudes? *Computers in Human Behavior*, 98, 93–101. DOI: 10.1016/j.chb.2019.04.012

Sukoco, I., Fuadah, N., & Muttaqin, Z. (2020). Work engagement of millennial generation employees pada PT. X Bandung. *Jurnal Pemikiran Dan Penelitian Administrasi Bisnis Dan Kewirausahaan*, 5(3), 263–281.

Suleman, A. R., Amponsah-Tawiah, K., Adu, I. N., & Boakye, K. O. (2022). The curious case of green human resource management practices in the Ghanaian manufacturing industry; A reality or a mirage? *Management of Environmental Quality*, 33(3), 739–755. DOI: 10.1108/MEQ-12-2021-0269

Sundar, S. S. (2020). Rise of machine agency: A framework for studying the psychology of human–AI interaction (HAII). *Journal of Computer-Mediated Communication*, 25(1), 74–88. DOI: 10.1093/jcmc/zmz026

Suresh, H., & Guttag, J. V. (2021). A framework for understanding unintended consequences of machine learning. *Communications of the ACM*, 64(8), 62–71. DOI: 10.1145/3463492

Su, W., & Junge, S. (2023). Unlocking the recipe for organizational resilience: A review and future research directions. *European Management Journal*, 41(6), 1086–1105. DOI: 10.1016/j.emj.2023.03.002

Syarifuddin, S., Rizqifajri, M. I., Fakhri, M., Gilang, A., & Pradana, M. (2021). The Influence of Work Stress Towards Turnover Intention at State-Owned Bank in Bandung Area. In *Proceedings of the International Conference on Industrial Engineering and Operations Management* (pp. 915-920). DOI: 10.46254/IN01.20210256

Tabassum, M., Raziq, M. M., Allen, M., Sarwar, N., & Golra, O. A. (2024). Exploring emergent leadership in agile teams: Network dynamics, roles and skills at the individual level. *Business Process Management Journal*, 30(5), 1615–1637. DOI: 10.1108/BPMJ-02-2024-0110

Talwalkar, P., Deshmukh, V., & Bhole, M. (2019). Prevalence of hypothyroidism in patients with type 2 diabetes mellitus and hypertension in India: A cross-sectional observational study. *Diabetes, Metabolic Syndrome and Obesity*, 12, 369–376. DOI: 10.2147/DMSO.S181470 PMID: 30936734

Tambe, P., Cappelli, P., & Yakubovich, V. (2019). Artificial intelligence in human resources management: Challenges and a path forward. *California Management Review*, 61(4), 15–42. DOI: 10.1177/0008125619867910

Tams, S., Thatcher, J. B., & Grover, V. (2018). Concentration, competence, confidence, and capture: An experimental study of age, interruption-based technostress, and task performance. *Journal of the Association for Information Systems*, 19(9), 857–908. DOI: 10.17705/1jais.00511

Tang, G., Chen, Y., Jiang, Y., Paillé, P., & Jia, J. (2018). Green human resource management practices: Scale development and validity. *Asia Pacific Journal of Human Resources*, 56(1), 31–55. DOI: 10.1111/1744-7941.12147

Tannenbaum, S. I., & Yukl, G. (1992). *Training and development in organizations*. Jossey-Bass.

Tarafdar, M., Cooper, C. L., & Stich, J. F. (2017). The technostress trifecta - techno eustress, techno distress and design: Theoretical directions and an agenda for research. *Information Systems Journal*, 29(1), 6–42. DOI: 10.1111/isj.12169

Tarafdar, M., Gupta, A., & Turel, O. (2013). The dark side of information technology use. *Information Systems Journal*, 23(3), 269–275. DOI: 10.1111/isj.12015

Tarafdar, M., Pullins, E. B., & Ragu-Nathan, T. S. (2015). Technostress: Negative effect on performance and possible mitigations. *Information Systems Journal*, 25(2), 103–132. DOI: 10.1111/isj.12042

Tarafdar, M., Tu, Q., Ragu-Nathan, B. S., & Ragu-Nathan, T. S. (2007). The impact of technostress on role stress and productivity. *Journal of Management Information Systems*, 24(1), 301–328. DOI: 10.2753/MIS0742-1222240109

Tarafdar, M., Tu, Q., & Ragu-Nathan, T. S. (2010). Impact of technostress on end-user satisfaction and performance. *Journal of Management Information Systems*, 27(3), 303–334. DOI: 10.2753/MIS0742-1222270311

Tarafdar, M., Tu, Q., Ragu-Nathan, T. S., & Ragu-Nathan, B. S. (2011). Crossing to the dark side: Examining creators, outcomes, and inhibitors of technostress. *Communications of the ACM*, 54(9), 113–120. DOI: 10.1145/1995376.1995403

Tavares, F., Santos, E., Diogo, A., & Ratten, V. (2020). Teleworking in Portuguese communities during the COVID-19 pandemic. *Journal of Enterprising Communities: People and Places in the Global Economy*. https://sci-hub.se/10.1108/jec-06-2020-0113

Tetteh, S., Wu, C., Opata, C. N., Asirifua Agyapong, G. N. Y., Amoako, R., & Osei-Kusi, F. (2020). Perceived organizational support, job stress, and turnover intention: The moderation of affective commitments. *Journal of Psychology in Africa*, 30(1), 9–16. DOI: 10.1080/14330237.2020.1722365

Thakur, P., & Arora, R. (2022). Exploring the Relationship Among Satisfaction and Intention to Stay Among Millennial Employees: The Moderating Role of Managerial Support. *International Journal of Human Capital and Information Technology Professionals*, 13(1), 1–17. DOI: 10.4018/IJHCITP.293229

Thomas, K. M., Plaut, V. C., & Tran, N. M. (2019). Diversity ideologies in organizations. *APA Handbook of Industrial and Organizational Psychology, 2*, 405-437.

Thomas, D. A., & Ely, R. J. (2019). Making sense of belonging: A key to diversity and inclusion. *MIT Sloan Management Review*, 60(2), 39–45.

Tiwari, P., Rajput, N., & Garg, V. (2022, April). Artificial Intelligence and Talent Acquisition-Role of HR leaders in Adoption. In *3rd International Conference on Intelligent Engineering and Management (ICIEM)* (pp. 313–317). IEEE Publications. DOI: 10.1109/ICIEM54221.2022.9853104

Tomer, G., Mishra, S. K., & Qureshi, I. (2022). Features of technology and its linkages with turnover intention and work exhaustion among IT professionals: A multi-study investigation. *International Journal of Information Management*, 66, 102518. DOI: 10.1016/j.ijinfomgt.2022.102518

Torrington, D., Hall, L., & Taylor, S. (2020). *Human resource management*. Pearson Education.

Tremblay, M. A., Blanchard, C. M., Taylor, S., Pelletier, L. G., & Villeneuve, M. (2009). Work Extrinsic and Intrinsic Motivation Scale: Its value for organizational psychology research. Canadian Journal of Behavioural Science/Revue canadienne des sciences du comportement, 41(4), 213-226. DOI: 10.1037/a0015167

Triandis, H. C. (1995). *Individualism & collectivism*. Westview Press.

Trzeciak, M., & Banasik, P. (2022). Motivators influencing the efficiency and commitment of employees of agile teams. *Journal of Open Innovation*, 8(4), 176. DOI: 10.3390/joitmc8040176

Tuten, T. L., & Neidermeyer, P. E. (2004). Performance, satisfaction and turnover in call centers: The effects of stress and optimism. *Journal of Business Research*, 57(1), 26–34. DOI: 10.1016/S0148-2963(02)00281-3

University of Toronto. (2021). *Fairness and Bias in Machine Learning*. https://www.cs.toronto.edu/~mvolkovs/fairness.html

Upadhyay, A. K., & Khandelwal, K. (2018). Applying artificial intelligence: Implications for recruitment. *Strategic HR Review*, 17(5), 255–258. DOI: 10.1108/SHR-07-2018-0051

Valta, M., Hildebrandt, Y., & Maier, C. (2024). Fostering the digital mindset to mitigate technostress: An empirical study of empowering individuals for using digital technologies. *Internet Research*. Advance online publication. DOI: 10.1108/INTR-09-2022-0766

van der Lippe, T., & Lippényi, Z. (2019). Co-workers working from home and individual and team performance. *New Technology, Work and Employment*, 35(1), 60–79. DOI: 10.1111/ntwe.12153 PMID: 32214593

Veglianti, E., Trombin, M., Pinna, R., & De Marco, M. (2023). Customized artificial intelligence for talent recruiting: A bias-free tool? In *Smart technologies for organizations: Managing a sustainable and inclusive digital transformation* (pp. 245–261). Springer International Publishing., DOI: 10.1007/978-3-031-24775-0_15

Verwijs, C., & Russo, D. (2024). Do Agile scaling approaches make a difference? An empirical comparison of team effectiveness across popular scaling approaches. *Empirical Software Engineering*, 29(4), 1–57. DOI: 10.1007/s10664-024-10481-5

Wang, H., Ding, H., & Kong, X. (2023). Understanding technostress and employee well-being in digital work: The roles of work exhaustion and workplace knowledge diversity. *International Journal of Manpower*, 44(2), 334–353. DOI: 10.1108/IJM-08-2021-0480

Wang, S., Liu, Y., Hu, Y., Zhang, J., Li, S., & Chen, Y. (2023). The honey-trap of workplace friendship: Developing and testing a three-way interaction model to understand when and why workplace friendship triggers employee withdrawal behavior. *International Journal of Psychology*, 58(5), 486–497. DOI: 10.1002/ijop.12925 PMID: 37332092

Wang, W., Wang, Y., Zhang, Y., & Ma, J. (2020). Spillover of workplace IT satisfaction onto job satisfaction: The roles of job fit and professional fit. *International Journal of Information Management*, 50, 341–352. DOI: 10.1016/j.ijinfomgt.2019.08.011

Weil, M. M., & Rosen, L. D. (1997). *Technostress: Coping with technology@ work@ home@ play* (Vol. 13). J. Wiley.

Wiechmann, D., & Ryan, A. M. (2003). Reactions to computerized testing in selection contexts. *International Journal of Selection and Assessment*, 11(2–3), 215–229. DOI: 10.1111/1468-2389.00245

Willcocks, L. (2020). Robo-Apocalypse cancelled? Reframing the automation and future of work debate. *Journal of Information Technology*, 35(4), 286–302. DOI: 10.1177/0268396220925830

Williamson, S., & Vijayakumar, K. (2021). Artificial intelligence techniques for industrial automation and smart systems. *Concurrent Engineering, Research and Applications*, 29(3), 291–292. DOI: 10.1177/1063293X211026275

Williams, P. (2019). Support for supervisors: HR enabling flexible work. *Employee Relations*, 41(5), 914–930. DOI: 10.1108/ER-03-2018-0077

Will, P., Krpan, D., & Lordan, G. (2023). People versus machines: Introducing the HIRE framework. *Artificial Intelligence Review*, 56(2), 1071–1100. DOI: 10.1007/s10462-022-10193-6

Wilson, J. M., Lee, J., Fitzgerald, H. N., Oosterhoff, B., Sevi, B., & Shook, N. J. (2020). Job insecurity and financial concern during the COVID-19 pandemic are associated with worse mental health. *Journal of Occupational and Environmental Medicine*, 62(9), 686–691. DOI: 10.1097/JOM.0000000000001962 PMID: 32890205

Wontorczyk, A., & Rożnowski, B. (2022). Remote, Hybrid, and On-Site Work during the SARS-CoV-2 Pandemic and the Consequences for Stress and Work Engagement. *International Journal of Environmental Research and Public Health*, 19(4), 2400. Advance online publication. DOI: 10.3390/ijerph19042400 PMID: 35206590

Wright, P. M., & McMahan, G. C. (2011). Exploring the human resource–firm performance relationship: A multi-level perspective. *Journal of Management*, 37(4), 1295–1317. DOI: 10.1177/0149206311407508

Yadav, R., & Pathak, R. D. (2022). Green HRM and its impact on organizational performance: Mediating role of employee green behavior. *Journal of Cleaner Production*, 343, 130891. DOI: 10.1016/j.jclepro.2022.130891

Yam, J., & Skorburg, J. A. (2021). From human resources to human rights: Impact assessments for hiring algorithms. *Ethics and Information Technology*, 23(4), 611–623. DOI: 10.1007/s10676-021-09599-7

Yilmaz, E., & Kiliç, Y. (2017). The impact of organizational commitment on trainee teachers' job satisfaction. *International Journal of Contemporary :Educational Research*, 4(1), 1–11. www.ijcer.net

Yong, J. Y., Yusliza, M. Y., Jabbour, C. J. C., & Ahmad, N. H. (2020). Exploratory cases on the interplay between green human resource management and advanced green manufacturing in light of the Ability-Motivation-Opportunity theory. *Journal of Management Development*, 39(1), 31–49. DOI: 10.1108/JMD-12-2018-0355

Yuan, D., Hu, M., Yao, N., Zhong, H., Xiao, Y., Zhou, X., Zhang, R., & Zhang, Y. (2024). Effects of perceived stress on turnover intention of female healthcare staff: A serial multiple mediation model. *BMC Public Health*, 24(1), 1198. DOI: 10.1186/s12889-024-18654-z PMID: 38685094

Yusliza, M. Y., Fawehinmi, O., & Mohamad, Z. F. (2020). Determinants of intention to stay and employee well-being: A case of Green HRM practices. *Global Business Review*, 21(3), 663–680. DOI: 10.1177/0972150918778910

Zapf, D., Seifert, C., Schmutte, B., Mertini, H., & Holz, M. (2008). Emotion work and job stressors and their effects on burnout. *Psychology & Health*, 16(5), 527–545. DOI: 10.1080/08870440108405525 PMID: 22804497

Zhang, S., Moeckel, R., Moreno, A. T., Shuai, B., & Gao, J. (2020). A work-life conflict perspective on telework. *Transportation Research Part A, Policy and Practice*, 141, 51–68. DOI: 10.1016/j.tra.2020.09.007 PMID: 32982087

Zhang, W., Li, J., & Wu, H. (2024). Green HRM practices, employee eco-friendly behaviors, and innovative performance: A cross-industry study. *Business Strategy and the Environment*, 33(1), 55–70. DOI: 10.1002/bse.3099

Zhao, J., Liu, H., & Sun, W. (2020). How proactive environmental strategy facilitates environmental reputation: Roles of green human resource management and discretionary slack. *Sustainability*, 12(3), 763.

Zhou, J., & George, J. M. (2001). When job dissatisfaction leads to creativity: Encouraging the expression of voice. *Academy of Management Journal*, 44(5), 1074–1083. DOI: 10.2307/3069410

Zhu, Q., & Geng, Y. (2020). Green HRM and environmental performance: Evidence from manufacturing firms in China. *Journal of Environmental Management*, 273, 111186. DOI: 10.1016/j.jenvman.2020.111186

Župerkienė, E., Šimanskienė, L., Fiore, M., & Paulikas, J. (2023). Management of Employee Resistance Caused by Technological Change for Organisational Sustainability. In Technology, Business and Sustainable Development (pp. 67-84). Routledge.

About the Contributors

Mitra Madanchian holds a Ph.D. in Business Management from Universiti Teknologi MARA (Malaysia), a Master of Administrative Science in Human Resources from Fairleigh Dickinson University, and a Master's and Bachelor's degrees in Applied Linguistics from University Putra Malaysia. With a strong passion for business management and research and development (R&D), Mitra has gained extensive industry experience working in both small and medium-sized enterprises (SMEs) and one of the Big Four firms, KPMG. With over 9 years of experience, she has become an esteemed industry expert in the fields of Business Management, Marketing, and Human Resource Management. Throughout her career, Mitra has held various roles, including Marketing Manager, Human Resource Manager, and Business Development Practitioner in international companies across different sectors, including IT, International Trade, Finance, and Education. In addition to her industry experience, Mitra has a keen interest in academic research, focusing on areas such as Business Management, Leadership, Human Resource Management, Marketing Management, FinTech, and IT Management. Her scholarly work has been published in reputable publishers, including Elsevier, IGI Global, and MDPI. She has authored over thirty scientific articles in peer-reviewed international journals and conference proceedings, as well as ten book chapters and one book on leadership. Currently, Mitra is an Assistant Professor- a full-time faculty member- at the University Canada West, teaching courses in Human Resource Management, Marketing Management, Digital Marketing, and Tourism & Hospitality. Simultaneously, she holds the position of HR Manager at OBS Tech Limited Company. She actively participates in professional organizations and is a member of CPHR British Columbia & Yukon.

* * *

Alaa Amin Abdalla is an Assistant Professor of Sustainable Development and Management (HRM) at Abu Dhabi University, UAE. She earned her Ph.D. in Sustainable Development and Management (HRM) from the University of Science Malaysia (USM), Malaysia. With a distinguished career spanning 15 years, Dr. Alaa has held academic and administrative roles across four countries and leadership positions in two. She is a certified SHRM-CP professional and has been honored with several academic awards. Her research contributions are notable, with publications in prestigious journals (Q1 top 1%, Q1, Q2). Dr. Alaa also serves as a section editor, an editorial board member, Scopus conference chair, and reviewer for several esteemed international journals.

P. Bhanumathi is an Associate Professor and Head Academics at M S Ramaiah Institute of Management, Bangalore. She completed her Ph.D. in Knowledge management from the University of Mysore. She has qualified in UGC NET and AMT certification from AIMA and has over 19+ years of teaching and eleven years of research experience. Ph.D. Guide ship @ Ramaiah University of Applied Sciences and the University of Mysore. Best Capstone Project Award 2023 on "Leadership Style Prediction Using Data Science & ML models from Boston -RVCE Centre of Excellence in AI research and Business solutions, RVCE, Bengaluru. She has four patent publications to her credit. Her thesis identified knowledge management enablers and processes for select SMEs in and around Bangalore and suggested a feasible model for improving organizational performance. She has published research papers in peer-reviewed journals, including UGC-listed and ABDC journals and a few reputed conferences. She handles courses in HR, Operations, Entrepreneurship, and General Management. She is a reviewer of the Journal of Human Resource Management, the University of Kelaniya, Sri Lanka, and many other top universities.

Sara Bordbar is a driven Master's student specializing in Industrial and Organizational Psychology. Her journey is marked by a passion for understanding human behavior in professional settings, complemented by joining the Industrial and Organizational Master program at Adler University. Research and coursework have armed her with insights to foster a conducive work environment and amplify HRM. Sara possesses a background in import/export operations and sales within the wood industry in her home country, Iran. Additionally, she has worked as a Customer Experience Manager at Nissan/Infiniti in Vancouver. Through these experiences, she has enhanced and deepened her understanding of global business intricacies. Sara is fascinated by DEI concepts and hopes to integrate her experience in import/export operations, sales, and customer experience management into the HRM field, focusing particularly on Industrial and Organizational Psychology. Through bridging business acumen with interpersonal skills, she strives to promote equity, diversity, and inclusion within organizations.

Tanusree Chakraborty is a Ph. D in Applied Psychology from Calcutta University, MA (Applied Psychology) with Specialization in Organizational Psychology, PGDHRM and MBA (HR), with 20 plus years of work experience. She has been associated with a number of B-Schools and Universities of repute in Kolkata, Madurai, Bangalore, and Chennai. Presently she is working with Administrative Staff College of India (ASCI), Hyderabad as a Faculty in the Centre for Management Studies. Having thoroughly good academic track record with university ranks, she is an Ex-research fellow of Indian Council of Medical Research. She has around 60 publications under her credit in reputed journals and books, among which Internet Research Journal, International Journal of Human Resource Management, International Journal of Productivity and Performance Management are great feathers in her cap. She has presented research papers in 80 plus international conferences of repute, where she has been awarded the Best Paper Award many times. She has conducted Management Development Programmes with the State Productivity Councils and National Productivity Councils. She has trained practicing managers of several Public and Private sector companies, in the areas of Behavioral Sciences and Human Resource Management. As a psychologist she has conducted Psychometric testing with 12,000 plus employees. As a trainer, she has trained 15,000 plus employees in her career. Companies where she has been a resource person include Indian Oil, BHEL, NHPC, NTPC, THDCIL, WBPDC, DVC, BPCL, DRDO, PFC, GAIL, ONGC, Exide Industries, NMDC, Power Grid Corp, Department of Science and Technology- GoI, National Institute of Communications Finance etc. Among the banks, she has associated herself as a trainer with State Bank of India, Canara Bank, Central Bank of India, Punjab National Bank, Axis Bank, etc. She has published books with the IGI Global Publishers, titled Appreciative Inquiry Approaches to Organizational Transformation, with Taylor and Francis, CRC Press, Human Resource Management in a Post-Epidemic Global Environment-Roles, Strategies, and Implementations, Agile Leadership for Industry 4.0 and Interdisciplinary Approaches in Management Education, Digitalization in Higher Education, Gender Equality in Modern Perspectives etc. A few more books are in the advanced stages of forthcoming publication. She has been a panel member in admission and recruitment processes, GDPIs conducted in academic institutes and corporate. Besides, she has also been a regular faculty for management institutes of repute including ASCI, teaching MBA and PGDM, where she has been a passionate teacher supporting students in academics and other institution building activities. She has been an active member in clubs and committees of the institutes she has worked for. She has been a reviewer and editor of reputed books and journals, and Editor-in Chief of the ASCI PGDM Chronicle- A Bi-annual Newsletter.

Bárbara de Sousa, 27 years old - Portugal, Oporto. PhD Student of the Doctoral Programme in Economics and Business at the International PhD School (EDIUS) of the University of Santiago de Compostela (USC). Master in Psychology, with specialization in Organizational, Social and Work Psychology at University of Porto. Coordinator of Consuelo Vieira da Costa Foundation (FCVC), Assistant Professor at ISAG - European Business School and Researcher at Researcher at the Research Center in Business Sciences and Tourism (CICET-FCVC).

Poonam Gahlot is working as an Assistant Professor in the Faculty of Finance and Commerce of Commerce, SRM University, Delhi-NCR, Sonipat. She has 10 year of Teaching Experience in reputed organizations. Her area of interest is in Marketing, Consumer Behaviour, Sustainable Development and Public Policy. She has published 9 Research articles in reputed journals like Francis and tailor and Scopus. She involved in various administrative works like Member of BoS, Coordinator of cultural activities, External research expert etc. She has the great ability to handle the behaviour of the students and boost their calibre with her effective teaching pedagogy. Her academic pursuits extend beyond publications, as evidenced by her active participation in over 25 conferences and 15 Faculty Development Programmes.

Anitha K. presently serves as the Head of the Department of Management Studies at Meenakshi Academy of Higher Education and Research (MAHER), located in India. In 2014, she earned her UGC NET Management & HRM qualification. Her research pursuits encompass AI applications in HRM, marketing, and sustainability. Dr. Anitha.K has authored numerous chapters in books published by Springer, Taylor & Francis CRC Press, and IGI Global, USA. She has 6 years of teaching experience and 4 years of industry experience and has actively participated in various conferences, consistently securing Best Paper awards for her contributions. Additionally, she has served as a resource person for faculty development programs. Within MAHER, she holds dual roles as Placement Officer and Assistant Director of Online Education. Notably, she has been honored with the Research Excellence Award consecutively since 2020 at MAHER.

Dhvani Malhotra is currently pursuing a Master's degree in I/O Psychology with the purpose of furthering her passion in understanding human behavior in organizational settings. She has co-authored a research paper titled "Understanding the relationship between values and self-conscious emotions: Implications for emotional well-being", demonstrating her keen interest in research. Dhvani gained practical experience in the HR industry by working with an Indian consulting firm. She facilitated training programs and workshops centering around DEI, conflict resolution productivity and many more. With a background in psychology and a passion for organizational behavior, she seeks to apply evidence-based strategies to enhance workplace culture, employee well-being, and organizational effectiveness.

Mrigeesha Mehta (she/her/hers) is currently a student at Adler University Vancouver Campus, studying the Master's of Industrial and Organizational Psychology (I/O Psychology) Program. Currently in her 5th semester of study, Mrigeesha is an international student from Dubai. She is the President of the I/O and Applied Psychology Student Society, and the Teaching Assistant for an HR Course, Personnel Selection and Assessments. Mrigeesha is passionate about utilizing the DEI lens to have a human-centered approach for framing organizational successes. In her efforts to progress in this, she continues to work closely with campus leaders in various departments including a student employee at the Centre for Diversity and Inclusion (CDI). She also serves as a member on the Anti-racism and Inclusion Committee for the Board of Trustees at Adler University.

Hawwa Shiuna Musthafa is an Assistant Professor at University Canada West as well as an Adjunct Professor at Adler University. With over 14 years of experience in the education sector, she's held roles including Assistant Professor, Senior Manager, Curriculum Developer, Principal, Lecturer and Course coordinator. She has also actively supervised student projects ranging from human resource management to social sciences genres. Her most recent experience includes being Chair to PhD committee and, being a member of the Research Ethics Board in Adler University where she also teaches Strategic Human Resource Management to their Industrial/Organizational students. Dr. Hawwa has a Doctoral degree in Curriculum Studies, Teaching, and Comparative Education from University of Cyprus. She holds a Master of Education in Leadership, Management, and Team Dynamics, along with a double Bachelor's degrees in Sociology, Psychology, English and a Bachelor's degree specializing in Teaching Social Sciences and English. She is also a presidential award winner in the Maldives for academic scholarship, achieved university's highest GPA in her Master's degree and is also the recipient of the merit-based PhD scholarship from the University of Cyprus. She has published papers, published reports in both management, and social sciences genres.

Ana Pinto Borges holds a PhD in Economics, Faculty of Economics, University of Porto, in 2009. Since 2010 is Coordinating Professor at ISAG - European Business School specializing on the areas of Economics, Management, and Finance, and since 2015 Coordinator of the Master's Degree in Business Management and President of the Pedagogical Council of ISAG. She is Scientific Coordinator of Research Centre in Business Sciences and Tourism (CICET – FCVC) since 2021 and coordinated the ISAG Research Centre (NIDISAG) between 2015 and 2021. Since 2018, she is researcher of the Centre for Research in Organizations, Markets and Industrial Management (COMEGI). She supervised 2 PhD theses and is now supervising other 2, in addition to having supervised more than 40 master's theses. She published more than 180 publications (around 120 indexed in Scopus/WoS databases) in journals/ book chapters/proceedings and 5 books (3 indexed in Scopus). She is associate editor at the Eurasian Business Review (indexed by Scopus/WoS – Q1) and editor and one of the founding members of the European Journal of Applied Business and Management (EJABM). She founded, integrated the organizer and scientific committees, and did the co-editor of the proceedings of International Conference in Applied Business and Management (ICABM – 5 eds since 2016), International Workshop in Tourism and Hospitality Management (IWTHM – 3 eds since 2017), and in Accounting and Taxation (IWAT – 3 eds since 2021). All these academic events have been indexed or are in evaluation by WoS and by EBSCO, among others. Furthermore, she is the coordinator and co-author of several applied projects financed by external entities (companies, municipalities, among others). She is Economist at the Portuguese Health Regulatory Authority since 2010 with the main function of carrying out sectoral studies and issuing opinions in the scope of access, quality and competition. Member of the Associação Portuguesa de Economia da Saúde (since 2005).

Radha Rani is an Assistant Professor and Programme Coordinator of B.Com. (Hons.) in Department of Commerce, SRM University, Delhi-NCR, Sonepat. She has been a Gold Medalist in M.Com. at Maharishi Dayanand University, Rohtak. She qualified N.E.T.(UGC) and received JRF from UGC for Ph.D. She holds a Ph.D. in Commerce from Maharshi Dayanand University, Rohtak. The topic of Ph.D. research was "Multilevel Marketing in India: Challenges and Prospects. She has more than 9 years of teaching experience. She is guiding Ph.D. scholars in the Department. She is continuously updating the knowledge by participating in Seminars, Conferences and FDPs. She has been doing research in the area of Marketing, Consumer Behaviour and published papers in National and International journals.

Charu Saxena is working as an Associate Professor, University School of Business, Chandigarh University, Mohali, Punjab, India.

Sushma Sharma is an Associate Professor and Programme Coordinator (BBA & Business Analytics) at SRM University, Delhi-NCR, Sonepat. She holds a PhD in Management from Maharshi Dayanand University, Rohtak and has 17 years of experience including corporate. Dr. Sharma has contributed significantly to academia with more than 25 research papers published in various prestigious international and national journals. Her academic pursuits extend beyond publications, as evidenced by her active participation in over 30 conferences and 20 Faculty Development Programmes. Noteworthy among her contributions is a book chapter titled "Innovation in the University 4.0 System based on Smart Technologies," published in Routledge, Taylor & Francis Group, USA and has published numerous research papers in journals of repute such as Psychology, Health & Medicine.

Neha Nazneen Siddiqui is an accomplished academic and researcher with over 10 years of teaching experience. She is currently working as an Associate Professor, having taught at institutes like Ashoka Institute of Technology & Management, Varanasi, and Ambalika Institute of Management & Technology in Lucknow, India. Dr. Siddiqui completed her Ph.D in Business Management from Integral University, Lucknow. Her doctoral thesis focused on "Empirical Study on Innovative Techniques of Motivation for Employee Retention: Comparative Study of Jet Airways and Indigo Flights to Lucknow". Prior to her Ph.D, she obtained her MBA in Human Resource & Marketing from Ambalika Institute of Management & Technology, Lucknow, securing 1st position with 70% marks. She completed her BBA from Lucknow University, again topping her class with 72% marks. As an Assistant Professor, Dr. Siddiqui has taught subjects like Research Methodology, Retail Management, Marketing Management, Human Resource Management, Industrial Management, Entrepreneurship Development, among others. Her key responsibilities have included working as a Class Coordinator, Project Guide for MBA students,and delivering lectures.

Pratibha Thakur is currently working as an Assistant Professor in Dr. Vishwanath Karad MIT World Peace University. With 3 years of teaching experience, she has published 11 research papers in national and international journals. She has also published 4 book chapters and has participated in several conferences.

Elvira Pacheco Vieira holds a PhD in Applied Economics at the University of Santiago de Compostela, in 2007. Since 2012, is Dean of ISAG - European Business School, where she is also Principal Coordinating Professor and Member of the Technical-Scientific Council. Invited Adjunct Professor at the Polytechnic Institute of Viana do Castelo - School of Business Sciences. Integrated Member at the Applied Management Research Unit (UNIAG) since 2010, and Collaborator Member at the Research Centre in Business Sciences and Tourism (CICET - FCVC), since 2021. Coordinated the ISAG Research Centre (NIDISAG) between 2009 and 2021. Author of more than 160 publications in scientific journals with peer reviewd, some indexed in the various international databases (WoS - Clarivate Analytics and Scopus). Published 12 book chapters and 3 books. Supervised 4 doctoral theses and 25 master's dissertations. Received 2 awards and/or honours. Has participated as a researcher in 30 projects and has been the lead researcher on 15. Works in the areas of Social Sciences with an emphasis on Economics, Management, Tourism, Regional and Cross-border Development, Innovation and Entrepreneurship, -Information and Communication Technologies and Corporate Governance.

Sharada V. S. is a dedicated researcher and management professional with a passion for organizational behavior and human resources. Currently pursuing a Post Graduate Diploma in Management at the Administrative Staff College of India, Hyderabad, she holds a Bachelor of Business Administration from Saint Mary's College, Hyderabad. Her academic journey reflects a commitment to excellence, demonstrated by her outstanding academic performance. With a strong foundation in research methodology and analytical skills, V.S. Sharada has actively contributed to the field of organizational behavior through her research and publications. She has explored various facets of employee engagement, leadership, and organizational dynamics, with a focus on understanding and improving the interaction between individuals and organizations. V.S. Sharada has presented her research findings at prestigious conferences, including the International HR Conference at the Indian Institute of Management Jammu, the Strategic Management Forum at the Indian Institute of Management Trichy, and the 3rd iMarC IIM International Marketing Conference at IIM Shillong. These presentations have enabled her to engage with scholars and practitioners, further enhancing her research insights. Driven by a desire to make meaningful contributions to the field of organizational behavior and human resources, V.S. Sharada is committed to continuous learning and growth. She seeks to leverage her skills, knowledge, and passion for research to address real-world challenges faced by organizations and individuals, ultimately striving to create positive and sustainable impacts in the realm of organizational dynamics.

Vaishnavi is an aspiring master's student in Industrial and Organizational Psychology with 4+ years of experience in Learning and Development in the Healthcare sector. Her work offers a unique blend of experience, skills and passion for creating an inclusive workplace culture through the power of Learning and Training. Vaishnavi strongly advocated DEI initiatives in her career as an HR generalist to make inclusive hiring practices and while taking the role of learning and development specialist, she initiated various diversity training that promotes equity. In the writing world, she was the chief editor for the book "Unlock your organizations Potential: A practical Approach to Learning and Development.

Jason Walker is an Associate Professor and Program Director for Industrial-Organizational and Applied Psychology Graduate Studies at Adler University in Vancouver, Canada. With over 20 years of expertise in mental health and organizational psychology, holding dual doctorates, he is renowned for research in workplace violence, bullying, sexual abuse and harassment. He has lived and worked in rural and remote Indigenous communities, providing essential mental health and social services for over a decade. Dr. Walker actively contributes as a reviewer for the Journal of Consulting Psychology and the Journal of Organizational Behaviour. He also holds a Clinical Adjunct position at the City University of Seattle Master of Counselling program. In acknowledgment of his contributions, Dr. Walker has received several accolades. These include an appointment to the Priory of Canada as a Serving Member of the Order of St John and the Canada Volunteer Award Medal of Honour from the Government of Canada.

Index

A

Agility 6, 74, 197, 198, 199, 200, 201, 202, 219, 230, 232, 233, 234, 235, 237, 252
AI 64, 67, 106, 107, 108, 122, 123, 125, 126, 127, 129, 131, 133, 145, 147, 148, 164, 173, 174, 175, 176, 179, 180, 182, 183, 184, 185, 186, 187, 188, 189, 190, 191, 192, 193, 194, 195, 196, 201, 205, 207, 208, 232, 234, 242, 246, 247, 250, 251, 253, 255, 259, 260, 261, 262, 263, 264, 265, 266, 267, 268, 269, 270, 271, 272, 273, 274, 275
Airlines 137, 138, 139, 140, 141, 142, 143, 144, 145, 146, 147, 148, 149, 150, 152, 153, 155, 156, 158, 159, 162, 163, 164, 165, 166, 167, 168
Automation 108, 130, 135, 145, 147, 224, 230, 239, 240, 242, 244, 247, 251, 253, 255, 257, 258, 260, 263, 268, 270

B

Bias Detection 187, 195

C

Candidate Experience 185, 186, 200, 208, 259, 261, 263, 265, 268, 269, 270, 271, 272, 274
Challenges 1, 4, 5, 6, 11, 18, 21, 27, 28, 29, 30, 31, 32, 33, 34, 36, 38, 39, 51, 52, 57, 58, 64, 65, 75, 77, 79, 80, 82, 93, 106, 110, 121, 122, 123, 127, 129, 138, 143, 145, 146, 162, 163, 174, 177, 178, 182, 188, 191, 192, 197, 198, 199, 200, 201, 202, 205, 211, 215, 216, 218, 220, 222, 225, 226, 227, 237, 238, 239, 247, 248, 249, 252, 255, 256, 261, 263, 267, 271, 272, 273, 276
Change Management 44, 162, 220, 221, 222, 223, 224, 236
Commitment 1, 2, 6, 8, 9, 10, 11, 12, 13, 14, 21, 22, 23, 25, 26, 27, 28, 29, 30, 31, 32, 33, 34, 35, 37, 38, 39, 40, 42, 43, 45, 52, 53, 54, 55, 69, 71, 74, 76, 78, 79, 92, 95, 97, 98, 99, 101, 109, 111, 112, 114, 122, 128, 129, 131, 132, 139, 140, 153, 159, 177, 183, 188, 195, 216, 223, 238, 246, 272
Community Engagement 188, 192, 195
Cultural Competence 187, 195

D

DEI Initiatives 174, 176, 177, 178, 180, 182, 184, 187, 188, 195, 214, 229
Diversity and Inclusion 182, 183, 188, 190, 193, 194, 246, 259, 271

E

Efficiency 7, 10, 19, 41, 51, 54, 106, 110, 113, 138, 141, 148, 149, 174, 179, 180, 202, 212, 217, 218, 219, 227, 230, 232, 238, 252, 253, 259, 261, 262, 263, 264, 266, 267, 270
Employee Motivation 55, 137, 138, 139, 140, 141, 142, 144, 145, 149, 150, 151, 152, 159, 163, 164, 165, 166, 167, 170
Engagement 1, 2, 5, 6, 7, 8, 11, 12, 13, 14, 15, 16, 17, 18, 19, 20, 21, 24, 29, 30, 31, 33, 34, 35, 36, 37, 38, 39, 40, 44, 48, 49, 51, 56, 64, 65, 67, 74, 79, 96, 97, 99, 111, 115, 122, 123, 131, 137, 138, 139, 140, 141, 143, 144, 145, 146, 147, 148, 149, 150, 151, 155, 156, 157, 158, 159, 162, 163, 164, 165, 166, 167, 168, 169, 170, 174, 176, 180, 182, 185, 188, 191, 192, 195, 199, 200, 201, 202, 204, 206, 212, 218, 229, 231, 232, 240, 246, 248, 256, 257, 259, 263, 265, 268, 269, 270, 271
Equity 54, 57, 137, 138, 139, 140, 141, 142, 143, 144, 145, 146, 149, 150, 151, 152, 153, 154, 162, 163, 164, 165, 166, 167, 173, 174, 177, 178,

184, 186, 187, 188, 189, 190, 194, 195, 196, 201, 202, 214, 229, 236, 237, 244, 252
Ethical Guidelines 186, 195

F

Fairness 138, 140, 142, 143, 150, 166, 167, 174, 182, 183, 186, 188, 190, 193, 194, 195, 202, 209, 243, 260, 264, 267, 272

G

Global Perspectives 174, 188, 195
Green Human Resources Management 100, 102
Green Innovation 73, 76, 79, 80, 81, 82, 83, 86, 87, 89, 91, 92, 93, 94, 97, 98, 101, 102

H

Hospitality Industry 73, 75, 76, 77, 83, 84, 85, 90, 92, 93, 100, 129
Human Collaboration 259, 260, 261, 265, 266, 267, 271
Hybrid Work 1, 3, 4, 5, 37, 38, 148, 229, 246

I

Inclusion 28, 92, 96, 115, 147, 156, 173, 174, 177, 178, 180, 182, 183, 188, 189, 190, 191, 193, 194, 195, 201, 214, 229, 236, 237, 243, 244, 246, 252, 256, 259, 262, 271
Innovation 10, 42, 43, 44, 45, 47, 48, 49, 62, 64, 65, 67, 68, 69, 73, 76, 79, 80, 81, 82, 83, 86, 87, 89, 90, 91, 92, 93, 94, 96, 97, 98, 99, 100, 101, 102, 106, 113, 123, 132, 170, 176, 184, 189, 190, 195, 197, 198, 200, 212, 215, 216, 218, 220, 226, 229, 234, 235, 236, 238, 246, 247, 252, 264, 268, 272
Intersectionality 175, 187, 190, 195
IT Sector 41, 44, 46, 47, 51, 56, 57, 64, 65, 66, 68, 71, 112, 119, 124

J

Job Redesign 139, 141, 142, 143, 144, 145, 146, 147, 148, 150, 158, 159, 162, 163, 164, 166, 167, 170

L

Leaders 30, 33, 44, 45, 47, 81, 147, 169, 178, 181, 193, 195, 198, 215, 223, 225, 226, 227, 228, 230, 234, 261, 264, 269, 273, 276
Leveraging Technology 64, 147, 200, 204, 205, 252

M

Methods Adopted 239, 249

P

Performance 3, 5, 7, 8, 9, 10, 11, 12, 19, 20, 36, 37, 40, 41, 42, 43, 44, 45, 47, 48, 50, 51, 52, 53, 54, 55, 56, 57, 58, 59, 60, 62, 63, 64, 65, 66, 67, 68, 69, 70, 71, 72, 73, 76, 77, 78, 81, 82, 85, 87, 89, 90, 91, 92, 93, 94, 95, 97, 98, 99, 100, 101, 102, 103, 106, 107, 110, 111, 112, 113, 114, 115, 119, 122, 125, 126, 128, 130, 132, 133, 134, 138, 140, 141, 142, 143, 144, 147, 152, 156, 158, 159, 162, 164, 166, 167, 169, 170, 174, 182, 193, 197, 198, 199, 201, 202, 203, 204, 206, 208, 209, 210, 211, 213, 216, 217, 218, 220, 228, 229, 230, 231, 232, 234, 235, 236, 237, 249, 251, 256, 263, 270, 271, 274
Predictive Analytics 123, 232, 259, 266, 270

R

Remote Work 1, 2, 3, 4, 6, 7, 10, 11, 12, 13, 14, 15, 18, 19, 20, 21, 25, 28, 29, 30, 31, 32, 33, 34, 35, 36, 37, 38, 39, 67, 108, 146, 148, 206, 239, 240, 243,

244, 247, 248, 249, 251

T

Task-Related Green Behaviors 73, 79, 80, 81, 82, 83, 87, 89, 91, 93
Technostress 105, 106, 107, 108, 110, 111, 112, 113, 115, 117, 118, 119, 120, 121, 122, 123, 124, 125, 126, 128, 129, 130, 131, 132, 133, 134
Turnover Intentions 105, 108, 111, 112, 113, 114, 115, 117, 118, 119, 120, 121, 122, 123, 124, 126, 127, 128, 130, 131, 132, 140

U

UAE 73, 76, 77, 84, 85, 90, 92, 93, 97

V

Voluntary Green Behaviors 73, 87, 89, 93

W

Work Stress 105, 108, 111, 113, 114, 115, 118, 119, 120, 123, 128, 130, 132, 133

www.ingramcontent.com/pod-product-compliance
Lightning Source LLC
LaVergne TN
LVHW081341300926
849161LV00008B/2042